Designing for Scalability
with Erlang/OTP

Francesco Cesarini and Steve Vinoski

Beijing · Boston · Farnham · Sebastopol · Tokyo

Designing for Scalability with Erlang/OTP

by Francesco Cesarini and Steve Vinoski

Printed in the United States of America.

Published by O'Reilly Media, Inc., 1005 Gravenstein Highway North, Sebastopol, CA 95472.

O'Reilly books may be purchased for educational, business, or sales promotional use. Online editions are also available for most titles (*http://safaribooksonline.com*). For more information, contact our corporate/institutional sales department: 800-998-9938 or *corporate@oreilly.com*.

Editor: Andy Oram
Production Editor: Nicholas Adams
Copyeditor: Christina Edwards
Proofreader: Rachel Head

Indexer: Lucie Haskins
Interior Designer: David Futato
Cover Designer: Karen Montgomery
Illustrator: Rebecca Demarest

May 2016:   First Edition

Revision History for the First Edition
2016-05-11:   First Release

See *http://oreilly.com/catalog/errata.csp?isbn=9781449320737* for release details.

978-1-449-32073-7

[LSI]

To Alison, Peter and baby Bump for being patient and supportive.
—Francesco

To Dooley and Ed, for teaching me how, and to Cindy, Ryan, Erin, Andrew, and Jake,
for being why.
—Steve

To Joe, Mike, Robert, for making that phone call.
—Francesco & Steve

Table of Contents

Preface

This book is what you get if you put together an Erlang enthusiast who worked on the R1 release of OTP in 1996 and a Distributed Systems specialist who discovered a decade later how Erlang/OTP allows you to focus on the real challenges of systems development while avoiding accidental difficulties.

By describing how OTP behaviors are built and why they are needed, we show you how to use them to architect standalone nodes. In our original proposal to O'Reilly, we stopped here. But when writing the book, we decided to push the bar further, documenting our practices, design decisions, and common pitfalls when architecting a distributed system. These patterns, through a set of design choices and tradeoffs we make, give us the scalability, reliability, and availability for which Erlang/OTP is well known. Contrary to popular belief, this does not happen magically or out of the box, but it sure is much easier to achieve than with any other programming language out there that does not emulate Erlang's semantics nor run on the BEAM virtual machine.

Francesco: Why This Book?

Someone once told me that writing books is a bit like having children. Once you've written one and are holding your paper copy, excitement takes over, you quickly forget the hard work and sacrifices, and you want to start writing another one. I've been intending to write the sequel to *Erlang Programming* (O'Reilly) since first holding the paper copy in June 2009. I had no children of my own when I started this project, but it ended up taking so long that my second one is now on its way. Whoever said that good things are not worth waiting for?

As with the first book, we based *Designing for Scalability with Erlang/OTP* on the examples in the Erlang Solution's OTP training material I developed. I used the examples and started explaining them, converting my lectures and approach to teaching into words. When done with a chapter, I went back and ensured the parts students struggled to understand were clear. Questions that were commonly asked by the best students ended up in sidebars, and long chapters were divided into smaller ones. It all went well until we reached Chapter 11 and 12, because there was no unified way of doing release handling or software upgrade. Rather, there were tools, many of them. Some were integrated in our client's build and release cycle, others worked out of the box. Some were unusable. The chapters are what we hope will become the ultimate guide to anyone wanting to understand how release handling and software upgrade of systems works behind the scenes. They also explain what you need to know should you have to troubleshoot existing tools or write your own.

But the real trouble started with Chapter 13. Not having examples or training material, I found myself formalizing what was in our heads and documenting the approaches we take when architecting Erlang/OTP systems, trying to align it with the theory of distributed computing. Chapter 13 turned into four chapters that took as long to write as the first ten. For those of you who bought the early access, I hope the wait was worth it. For those who wisely waited for us to finish before buying your copy, enjoy!

Steve: Why This Book?

I first discovered Erlang/OTP in 2006 while researching ways to develop enterprise integration software faster, cheaper, and better. No matter how I looked at it, Erlang/OTP was clearly superior to the C++ and Java languages my colleagues and I had long been using at that time. In 2007 I joined a new company and began using Erlang/OTP for a commercial product, and it turned out to be everything my earlier investigation promised it would be. I taught the language to some colleagues and before long, fewer than a handful of us were developing software that was more capable, more reliable, easier to evolve, and ready for production far faster than similar code being written by a significantly larger team of C++ programmers. To this day I remain wholly convinced of the impressive practical effectiveness of Erlang/OTP.

Over the years I've published quite a bit of technical material, and my intended audience for all of it has always been other practitioners like me. This book is no exception. In the first 12 chapters we provide the deep level of detail that practicing developers need in order to fully understand the fundamental design principles of OTP. With those details we mix a number of useful nuggets of practical knowledge— modules, functions, and approaches that will save you significant time and effort in your day-to-day design, development, and debugging efforts. In the final four chapters we shift gears, focusing more on the big picture of the tradeoffs involved in developing, deploying, and operating resilient, scalable distributed applications. Due to the staggering amount of knowledge, approaches, and tradeoffs involved in distributed systems, fault tolerance, and DevOps, writing these chapters concisely proved difficult, but I believe we hit just the right balance of providing plenty of great advice without getting lost in the weeds.

I hope this book helps you improve the quality and utility of the software and systems you develop.

Who Should Read This Book

This book's intended audience includes Erlang and Elixir developers and architects who have made their way through at least one of the introductory books and are ready to take their knowledge to the next level. It is not a book to start off with, but rather the book that picks up where all others leave you. Chapters 3–12 build on each other and should be read sequentially, as do Chapters 13–16. If you do not need an Erlang primer, feel free to skip Chapter 2.

How To Read This Book

We wrote this book to be compatible with Erlang Release 18.2. Most of the features we describe work with earlier releases; major features that don't are indicated in the book. Currently unknown incompatibilities with future releases will be detailed on our errata page and fixed in the book's github repository. You are encouraged to download the examples in the book from our github repository (*https://github.com/francescoc/scalabilitywitherlangotp*) and run them yourself to better understand them.

Acknowledgments

Writing this book has been a long journey. While undertaking it we've had a lot of great help from a lot of wonderful people. Our editor Andy Oram has been an endless source of ideas and suggestions, patiently guiding us, giving us feedback while providing ongoing encouragement. Thank you Andy, we couldn't have done it without you! Simon Thompson, coauthor of *Erlang Programming* helped with the book proposal and laid the foundation for the second chapter. Many thanks to Robert Virding for contributing some of the examples. We've had many readers, reviewers and contributors give us feedback as we drip-fed them the chapters. At the risk of forgetting someone, they are: are Richard Ben Aleya, Roberto Aloi, Jesper Louis Andersen, Bob Balance, Eva Bihari, Martin Bodocky, Natalia Chechina, Jean-François Cloutier, Richard Croucher, Viktória Fördős, Heinz Gies, Joacim Halén, Fred Hebert, Csaba Hoch, Torben Hoffmann, Bob Ippolito, Aman Kohli, Jan Willem Luiten, Jay Nelson, Robby Raschke, Andrzej Śliwa, David Smith, Sam Tavakoli, Premanand Thangamani, Jan Uhlig, John Warwick, David Welton, Ulf Wiger, and Alexander Yong. If we missed you, our sincere apologies! Drop us an email and you will be promptly added. A shout-out goes to the staff at Erlang Solutions for reading the chapters as they were being written and everyone else who submitted to the errata as part of the early release. A special thank you goes to all of you who cheered us on through social media channels, especially other authors. You know who you are! Last, but not least, thanks to the production, marketing, and conference teams at O'Reilly who kept on reminding us that it's not over until you are holding the paper copy. We really appreciate your support!

Conventions Used in This Book

The following typographical conventions are used in this book:

Italic

> Indicates new terms, applications, URLs, email addresses, filenames, directory names, and file extensions.

`Constant width`

> Used for program listings, as well as within paragraphs to refer to program elements such as variable or function names, databases, data types, environment variables, statements, and keywords. Also used for behaviors, commands, and command-line options.

`Constant width bold`

> Shows commands or other text that should be typed literally by the user.

`Constant width italic`

> Shows text that should be replaced with user-supplied values or by values determined by context.

 This icon signifies a tip or suggestion.

 This icon signifies a general note.

 This icon indicates a warning or caution.

Using Code Examples

Supplemental material (code examples, exercises, etc.) is available for download at: *https://github.com/francescoc/scalabilitywitherlangotp*

This book is here to help you get your job done. In general, you may use the code in this book in your programs and documentation. You do not need to contact us for permission unless you're reproducing a significant portion of the code. For example, writing a program that uses several chunks of code from this book does not require permission. Selling or distributing a CD-ROM of examples from O'Reilly books does require permission. Answering a question by citing this book and quoting example code does not require permission. Incorporating a significant amount of example code from this book into your product's documentation does require permission.

We appreciate, but do not require, attribution. An attribution usually includes the title, author, publisher, and ISBN. For example: "*Designing for Scalability with Erlang/OTP* by Francesco Cesarini and Steve Vinoski (O'Reilly). Copyright 2016 Francesco Cesarini and Stephen Vinoski, 978-1-449-32073-7."

If you feel your use of code examples falls outside fair use or the permission given above, feel free to contact us at *permissions@oreilly.com*.

Safari® Books Online

 Safari Books Online is an on-demand digital library that lets you easily search over 7,500 technology and creative reference books and videos to find the answers you need quickly.

With a subscription, you can read any page and watch any video from our library online. Read books on your cell phone and mobile devices. Access new titles before they are available for print, and get exclusive access to manuscripts in development and post feedback for the authors. Copy and paste code samples, organize your favorites, download chapters, bookmark key sections, create notes, print out pages, and benefit from tons of other time-saving features.

O'Reilly Media has uploaded this book to the Safari Books Online service. To have full digital access to this book and others on similar topics from O'Reilly and other publishers, sign up for free at *http://my.safaribooksonline.com*.

How to Contact Us

Please address comments and questions concerning this book to the publisher:

O'Reilly Media, Inc.
1005 Gravenstein Highway North
Sebastopol, CA 95472
800-998-9938 (in the United States or Canada)
707-829-0515 (international or local)
707-829-0104 (fax)

We have a web page for this book, where we list errata, examples, and any additional information. You can access this page at:

http://bit.ly/designing-for-scalability-with-erlangotp

To comment or ask technical questions about this book, send email to:

bookquestions@oreilly.com

For more information about our books, courses, conferences, and news, see our website at *http://www.oreilly.com*.

Find us on Facebook: *http://facebook.com/oreilly*

Follow us on Twitter: *http://twitter.com/oreillymedia*

Watch us on YouTube: *http://www.youtube.com/oreillymedia*

## CHAPTER 1

Introduction

You need to implement a fault-tolerant, scalable, soft real-time system with requirements for high availability. It has to be event-driven and react to external stimuli, load, and failure. It must always be responsive. You have heard, rightfully so, of many success stories telling you Erlang is the right tool for the job. And indeed it is—but while Erlang is a powerful programming language, it's not enough on its own to group these features all together and build complex reactive systems. To get the job done correctly, quickly, and efficiently, you also need middleware, reusable libraries, tools, design principles, and a programming model that tells you how to architect and distribute your system.

Our goal with this book is to explore multiple facets of availability and scalability, as well as related topics such as concurrency, distribution, and fault tolerance, in the context of the Erlang programming language and its OTP framework. Erlang/OTP was created when the team at the Ericsson Computer Science Laboratory (CS Lab) set out to investigate how they could efficiently develop the next generation of telecommunications systems in an industry where time to market was becoming critical. This was before the Web, before tablets and smartphones, massively multiuser online gaming, messaging, and the Internet of Things.

At that time, the only systems that required the levels of scalability and fault tolerance we take for granted today were boring phone switches. They had to handle massive traffic spikes on New Year's Eve, fulfill regulatory obligations for the availability of calls to emergency services, and avoid the painfully expensive contractual penalties forced on infrastructure suppliers whose equipment caused outages. In layman's terms, if you picked up the phone and did not hear the dial tone on the other end, you could be sure of two things: top-level management would get into serious trouble and the outage would make the front page news in the papers. No matter what, those switches were not allowed to fail. Even when components and infrastructure around them were failing, requests had to be handled. Today, regulators and fines have been replaced with impatient users with no loyalty who will not hesitate to switch suppliers, and front-page newspaper articles have been replaced by mass hysteria on social media. But the core problems of availability and scalability remain.

As a result, telecoms switches and modern systems alike have to react to failure as much as they have to react to load and internal events. So while the folks at the Ericsson Computer Science Lab did not set out to invent a programming language, the solution to the problem they were out to solve happened to be one. It's a great example of inventing a language and programming model that facilitates the task of solving a specific, well-defined problem.

Defining the Problem

As we show throughout this book, Erlang/OTP is unique among programming languages and frameworks in the breadth, depth, and consistency of the features it provides for scalable, fault-tolerant systems with requirements for high availability. Designing, implementing, operating, and maintaining these systems is challenging. Teams that succeed in building and running them do so by continuously iterating through those four phases, constantly using feedback from production metrics and monitoring to help find areas they can improve not only in their code, but also in their development and operating processes. Successful teams also learn how to improve scalability through other means, such as testing, experimentation, and benchmarking, and they keep up on research and development relevant to their system characteristics. Nontechnical issues such as organizational values and culture can also play a significant part in determining whether teams can meet or exceed their system requirements.

We used the terms *distributed*, *fault-tolerant*, *scalable*, *soft real-time*, and *highly available* to describe the systems we plan on building with OTP. But what do these words actually mean?

Scalable refers to how well a computing system can adapt to changes in load or available resources. Scalable websites, for example, are able to smoothly handle traffic spikes without dropping any client requests, even when hardware fails. A scalable chat system might be able to accommodate thousands of new users per day without disruption of the service it provides to its current users.

Distributed refers to how systems are clustered together and interact with each other. Clusters can be architected to scale horizontally by adding commodity (or regular) hardware, or on a single machine, where additional instances of standalone nodes are deployed to better utilize the available cores. Single machines can also be virtualized, so that instances of an operating system run on other operating systems or share the bare-metal resources. Adding more processing power to a database cluster could enable it to scale in terms of the amount of data it can store or how many requests per second it can handle. Scaling downward is often equally as important; for example, a web application built on cloud services might want to deploy extra capacity at peak times and release unused computing instances as soon as usage drops.

Systems that are *fault tolerant* continue to operate predictably when things in their environment are failing. Fault tolerance has to be designed into a system from the start; don't even consider adding it as an afterthought. What if there is a bug in your code or your state gets corrupted? Or what if you experience a network outage or hardware failure? If a user sending a message causes a process to crash, the user is notified of whether the message was delivered or not and can be assured that the notification received is correct.

By *soft real-time*, we mean the predictability of response and latency, handling a constant throughput, and guaranteeing a response within an acceptable time frame. This throughput has to remain constant regardless of traffic spikes and number of concurrent requests. No matter how many simultaneous requests are going through the system, throughput must not degrade under heavy loads. Response time, also known as latency, has to be relative to the number of simultaneous requests, avoiding large variances in requests caused by "stop the world" garbage collectors or other sequential bottlenecks. If your system throughput is a million messages per second and a million simultaneous requests happen to be processed, it should take 1 second to process and deliver a request to its recipient. But if during a spike, two million requests are sent, there should be no degradation in the throughput; not some, but all of the requests should be handled within 2 seconds.

High availability minimizes or completely eliminates downtime as a result of bugs, outages, upgrades, or other operational activities. What if a process crashes? What if the power supply to your data center is cut off? Do you have a redundant supply or battery backup that gives you enough time to migrate your cluster and cleanly shut down the affected servers? Or network and hardware redundancy? Have you dimensioned your system ensuring that, even after losing part of your cluster, the remaining hardware has enough CPU capacity to handle peak loads? It does not matter if you lose part of your infrastructure, if your cloud provider is experiencing an embarrassing outage, or if you are doing maintenance work; a user sending a chat message wants to be reassured that it reaches its intended recipient. The system's users expect it to just work. This is in contrast to *fault tolerance*, where the user is told it did not work, but the system itself is unaffected and continues to run. Erlang's ability to do software upgrades during runtime helps. But if you start thinking of what is involved when dealing with database schema changes, or upgrades to non–backward-compatible protocols in potentially distributed environments handling requests during the upgrade, simplicity fades very quickly. When doing your online banking on weekends or at night, you want to be sure you will not be met with an embarrassing "closed for routine maintenance" sign posted on the website.

Erlang indeed facilitates solving many of these problems. But at the end of the day, it is still just a programming language. For the complex systems you are going to implement, you need ready-built applications and libraries you can use out of the box. You also need design principles and patterns that inform the architecture of your system with an aim to create distributed, reliable clusters. You need guidelines on how to design your system, together with tools to implement, deploy, monitor, operate, and maintain it. In this book we cover libraries and tools that allow you to isolate failure on a node level, and create and distribute multiple nodes for scalability and availability.

You need to think hard about your requirements and properties, making certain you pick the right libraries and design patterns that ensure the final system behaves the way you want it to and does what you originally intended. In your quest, you will have to make tradeoffs that are mutually dependent—tradeoffs on time, resources, and features and tradeoffs on availability, scalability, and reliability. No ready-made library can help you if you do not know what you want to get out of your system. In this book, we guide you through the steps in understanding these requirements, and walk you through the steps involved in making design choices and the tradeoffs needed to achieve them.

OTP

OTP is a domain-independent set of frameworks, principles, and patterns that guide and support the structure, design, implementation, and deployment of Erlang systems. Using OTP in your projects will help you avoid accidental complexity: things that are difficult because you picked inadequate tools. But other problems remain difficult, irrespective of the programming tools and middleware you choose.

Ericsson realized this very early on. In 1993, alongside the development of the first Erlang product, Ericsson started a project to tackle tools, middleware, and design principles. The developers wanted to avoid accidental difficulties that had already been solved, and instead focus their energy on the hard problems. The result was BOS, the Basic Operating System. In 1995, BOS merged with the development of Erlang, bringing everything under one roof to form Erlang/OTP as we know it today. You might have heard the dream team that supports Erlang being referred to as the OTP team. This group was a spinoff of this merge, when Erlang was moved out of a research organization and a product group was formed to further develop and maintain it.

Spreading knowledge of OTP can promote Erlang adoption in more "tried and true" corporate IT environments. Just knowing there is a stable and mature platform available for application development helps technologists sell Erlang to management, a crucial step in making its industrial adoption more widespread. Startups, on the other hand, just get on with it, with Erlang/OTP allowing them to achieve speed to market and reduce their development and operations costs.

OTP is said to consist of three building blocks (Figure 1-1) that, when used together, provide a solid approach to designing and developing systems in the problem domain we've just described. They are Erlang itself, tools and libraries, and a set of design principles. We'll look at each in turn.

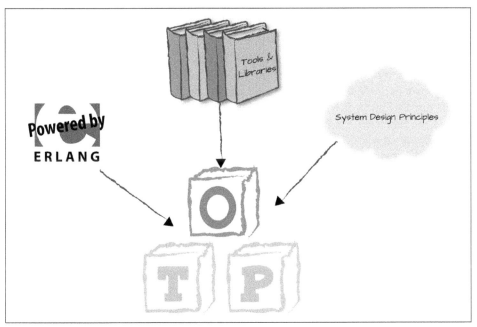

Figure 1-1. OTP components

What's in a Name?

What does OTP stand for? We'd rather not tell you. If you search for the "OTP song" you might be led to believe it means *One True Pair*. Or let your imagination go wild, and guess *Oh This is Perfect*, *On The Phone*, or *Open Transaction Platform*. Some might think OTP stands for *Online Transaction Processing*, but that's normally abbreviated as OLTP. More politically incorrect suggestions have also been made when hipsters were enlisted in an attempt to make Erlang more cool in the *Erlang the Movie* sequel. Alas, none of these are correct. OTP is short for Open Telecom Platform, a name coined by Bjarne Däcker, former head of the Computer Science Lab (the birthplace of Erlang) at Ericsson.

Open was a buzzword at Ericsson in the mid-90s. Everything had to be open: open systems, open hardware, open platforms. Ericsson's marketing department went as far as to print posters of open landscapes, hanging them in the corridors with the text

"Open Systems." No one really understood what was meant by Open Systems (or any of the other openness), but it was a buzzword, so why disappoint and not jump on an opportunity and (for once) be buzzword compliant? As a result, the Open in OTP became a no-brainer.

Today, we say that "open" stands for the openness of Erlang toward other programming languages, APIs, and protocols—a far cry from the openness of the days when it was first released. OTP R1 was in fact everything but open. Today, think of openness as being about JInterface, *ei* and *erl_interface*, HTTP, TCP/IP, UDP/IP, IDL, ASN.1, CORBA, SNMP, and other integration-oriented support provided by Erlang/OTP.

The word "telecom" was chosen when Erlang was used only internally within Ericsson for telecom products, long before open source would change the world. It might have made sense in the mid-90s, but no rebranding ever took place, so today we say that the telecom in the name refers to the distributed, fault-tolerant, scalable, soft real-time characteristics with requirements of high availability. These are characteristics present in telecom systems, but equally valid in a wide range of other verticals. The developers of OTP were solving a problem for telecom systems that became relevant to the rest of the software industry only when the Web was invented and everything had to be web scale. Erlang was web scale even before the Web itself!

The final word in OTP, "platform," while boring, is the only word truly describing the OTP middleware. It was chosen at a time when Ericsson's management was going over the top developing a variety of platforms. Everything software related had to be developed on a (preferably open) platform.

So indeed, Bjarne picked an acronym that made sense and would keep higher management happy, ensuring they kept on funding the project. They might not have understood what the CS Lab was working on and the trouble it was about to cause, but at least they were pleased and allowed it all to happen.

Since Erlang/OTP was released as open source in 1998, many discussions on rebranding have taken place, but none were conclusive. In the early days, developers outside of the telecoms sector mistakenly bypassed OTP, because—using their own words—they were "not developing telecom applications." The community and Ericsson have today settled for using OTP, toning down the telecom, but stressing its importance. This seems to be a fair compromise. In this book, this sidebar is the only place where telecom will be mentioned as being part of OTP.

Erlang

The first building block is Erlang itself, which includes the semantics of the language and its underlying virtual machine. Key language features such as lightweight processes, lack of shared memory, and asynchronous message passing will bring you a step closer to your goal. Just as important are links and monitors between processes, and dedicated channels for the propagation of the error signals. The monitors and error reporting allow you to build, with relative ease, complex supervision hierarchies with built-in fault recovery. Because message passing and error propagation are asynchronous, the semantics and logic of a system that was developed to run in a single Erlang node can be easily distributed without having to change any of the code base.

One significant difference between running on a single node and running in a distributed environment is the latency with which messages and errors are delivered. But in soft real-time systems, you have to consider latency regardless of whether the system is distributed or under heavy load. So if you have solved one facet of the problem, you have solved both.

Erlang lets you run all your code on top of a virtual machine highly optimized for concurrency, with a per-process garbage collector, yielding predictable and simple system behavior. Other programming environments do not have this luxury because they need an extra layer to emulate Erlang's concurrency model and error semantics. To quote Joe Armstrong, coinventor of Erlang, "You can emulate the logic of Erlang, but if it is not running on the Erlang virtual machine, you cannot emulate the semantics." The only languages that today get away with this are built on the BEAM emulator, the prevailing Erlang virtual machine. There is a whole ecosystem of them, with the Elixir and Lisp Flavored Erlang languages being the ones gaining most traction at the time of writing. What we write in this book about Erlang also applies to them.

Tools and Libraries

The second building block, which came about before open source became the widespread norm for software projects, includes applications that ship as part of the standard Erlang/OTP distribution. You can view each application as a way of packaging resources in OTP, where applications may have dependencies on other applications. The applications include tools, libraries, interfaces toward other languages and programming environments, databases and database drivers, standard components, and protocol stacks. The OTP documentation does a fine job of separating them into the following subsets:

- The basic applications include the following:
  - The Erlang runtime system (*erts*)
  - The *kernel*
  - The standard libraries (*stdlib*)
  - The system architecture support libraries (*sasl*)

  They provide the tools and basic building blocks needed to architect, create, start, and upgrade your system. We cover the basic applications in detail throughout this book. Together with the compiler, these are the minimal subset of applications necessary in any system written in Erlang/OTP to do anything meaningful.

- The database applications include *mnesia*, Erlang's distributed database, and *odbc*, an interface used to communicate with relational SQL databases. Mnesia is a popular choice because it is fast, runs and stores its data in the same memory space as your applications, and is easy to use, as it is accessed through an Erlang API.

- The operations and maintenance applications include *os_mon*, an application that allows you to monitor the underlying operating system; *snmp*, a Simple Network Management Protocol agent and client; and *otp_mibs*, management information bases that allow you to manage Erlang systems using SNMP.

- The collection of interface and communication applications provide protocol stacks and interfaces to work with other programming languages, including an ASN.1 (*asn1*) compiler and runtime support, direct hooks into C (*ei* and *erl_interface*) and Java (*jinterface*) programs, along with an XML parser (*xmerl*). There are security applications for SSL/TLS, SSH, cryptography, and public key infrastructure. Graphics packages include a port of wxWidgets (*wx*), together with an easy-to-use interface. The *eldap* application provides a client interface toward the Lightweight Directory Access Protocol (LDAP). And for telecom aficionados, there is a Diameter stack (as defined in RFC 6733), used for policy control and authorization, alongside authentication and accounting. Dig even deeper and you will find the Megaco stack. Megaco/H.248 is a protocol for controlling elements of a physically decomposed multimedia gateway, separating the media conversion from the call control. If you have ever used a smartphone, you have very likely indirectly taken the Erlang *diameter* and *megaco* applications for a spin.

- The collection of tools applications facilitate the development, deployment, and management of your Erlang system. We cover only the most relevant ones in this book, but outline them all here so you are aware of their existence:

  — The *debugger* is a graphical tool that allows you to step through your code while influencing the state of the functions.

  — The *observer* integrates the application monitor and the process manager, alongside basic tools to monitor your Erlang systems as they are being developed and in production.

  — The *dialyzer* is a static analysis tool that finds type discrepancies, dead code, and other issues.

  — The event tracer (*et*) uses ports to collect trace events in distributed environments, and *percept* allows you to locate bottlenecks in your system by tracing and visualizing concurrency-related activities.

  — Erlang Syntax Tools (*syntax_tools*) contains modules for handling Erlang syntax trees in a way that is compatible with other language-related tools. It also includes a module merger allowing you to merge Erlang modules, together with a renamer, solving the issue of clashes in a nonhierarchical module space.

— The *parsetools* application contains the parse generator (*yecc*) and a lexical analyzer generator for Erlang (*leex*).

— *Reltool* is a release management tool that provides a graphical front end together with back-end hooks that can be used by more generic build systems.

— *Runtime_tools* is a collection of utilities including DTrace and SystemTap probes, and *dbg*, a user-friendly wrapper around the trace built-in functions (BIFs).

— Finally, the *tools* application is a collection of profilers, code coverage tools, and module cross-reference analysis tools, as well as the Erlang mode for the emacs editor.

- The test applications provide tools for unit testing (*eunit*), system testing, and black-box testing. The Test Server (packaged in the *test_server* application) is a framework that can be used as the engine of a higher-level test tool application. Chances are that you will not be using it, because OTP provides one of these higher-level test tools in the form of *common_test*, an application suited for black-box testing. *Common_test* supports automated execution of Erlang-based test cases toward most target systems irrespective of programming language.

- We need to mention the Object Request Brokers (ORBs) and interface definition language (IDL) applications for nostalgic reasons, reminding one of the coauthors of his past sins. They include a broker called *orber*, an IDL compiler called *ic*, and a few other CORBA Common Object Services no longer used by anyone.

We cover and refer to some of these applications and tools in this book. Some of the tools we do not cover are described in *Erlang Programming* (O'Reilly), and those that aren't are covered by the set of reference manual pages and the user's guide that comes as part of the standard Erlang/OTP documentation.

These applications are not the full extent of tool support for Erlang; they are enhanced by thousands of other applications implemented and supported by the community and available as open source. We cover some of the prevailing applications in the latter half of the book, where we focus on distributed architectures, availability, scalability, and monitoring. They include the Riak Core (*https://github.com/basho/riak_core*) and Scalable Distributed (SD) Erlang (*http://www.dcs.gla.ac.uk/research/sd-erlang/*) frameworks; load regulation applications such as *jobs* and *safetyvalve*; and monitoring and logging applications such as *elarm*, *folsom*, *exometer*, and *lager*. Once you've read this book and before starting your project, review the standard and open source Erlang/OTP reference manuals and user's guides, because you never know when they will come in handy.

System Design Principles

The third building block of OTP consists of a set of abstract principles, design rules, and generic behaviors. The abstract principles describe the software architecture of an Erlang system, using processes in the form of generic behaviors as basic ingredients. Design rules keep the tools you use compatible with the system you are developing. Using this approach provides a standard way of solving problems, making code easier to understand and maintain, as well as providing a common language and vocabulary among the teams.

OTP generic behaviors can be seen as formalizations of concurrent design patterns. Behaviors are packaged into library modules containing generic code that solves a common problem. They have built-in support for debugging, software upgrade, generic error handling, and built-in functionality for upgrades.

Behaviors can be *worker processes*, which do all of the hard work, and *supervisor processes*, whose only tasks are to start, stop, and monitor workers or other supervisors. Because supervisors can monitor other supervisors, the functionality within an application can be chained so that it can be more easily developed in a modular fashion. The processes monitored by a supervisor are called its *children*.

OTP provides predefined libraries for workers and supervisors, allowing you to focus on the business logic of the system. We structure processes into hierarchical *supervision trees*, yielding fault-tolerant structures that isolate failure and facilitate recovery. OTP allows you to package a supervision tree into an application, as seen in Figure 1-2, where circles with double rings are supervisors and the other processes are workers.

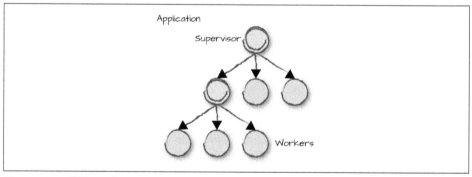

Figure 1-2. OTP application

Generic behaviors that come as part of the OTP middleware include:

- Generic servers, providing a client-server design pattern
- Generic finite state machines, allowing you to implement FSMs
- Event handlers and managers, allowing you to generically deal with event streams
- Supervisors, monitoring other worker and supervision processes
- Applications, allowing you to package resources, including supervision trees

We cover them all in detail in this book, as well as explaining how to implement your own. We use behaviors to create supervision trees, which are packaged into applications. We then group applications together to form a *release*. A release describes what runs in a node.

Erlang Nodes

An Erlang *node* consists of several loosely coupled applications, which might be comprised of some of the applications described in "Tools and Libraries" on page 7 combined with other third-party applications and applications you write specifically for the system you are trying to implement. These applications could be independent of each other or rely on the services and APIs of other applications. Figure 1-3 illustrates a typical release of an Erlang node with the virtual machine (VM) dependent on the hardware and operating system, and Erlang applications running on top of the VM interfacing with non-Erlang components that are OS and hardware dependent.

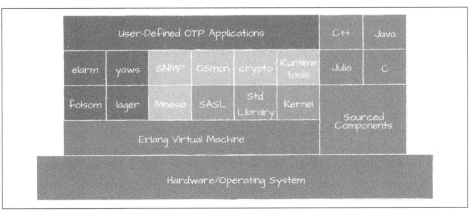

Figure 1-3. An Erlang node

Group together a cluster of Erlang nodes—potentially pairing them up with nodes written in other programming languages—and you have a distributed system. You can now scale your system by adding nodes until you hit certain physical limits.

These may be dictated by how you shared your data, by hardware or network constraints, or by external dependencies that act as bottlenecks.

Distribution, Infrastructure, and Multicore

Fault tolerance—one of Erlang's fundamental requirements from its telecom roots—has distribution as its mainspring. Without distribution, the reliability and availability of an application running on just a single host would depend heavily on the reliability of the hardware and software comprising that host. Any problems with the host's CPU, memory, persistent storage, peripherals, power supply, or backplane could easily take down the entire machine and the application along with it. Similarly, problems in the host's operating system or support libraries could bring down the application or otherwise render it unavailable. Achieving fault tolerance requires multiple computers with some degree of coordination between them, and distribution provides the avenue for that coordination.

For decades, the computing industry has explored how programming languages can support distribution. Designing general-purpose languages is difficult enough; designing them to support distribution significantly adds to that difficulty. Because of this, a common approach is to add distribution support to nondistributed programming languages through optional libraries. This approach has the benefit of allowing distribution support to evolve separately from the language itself, but it often suffers from an impedance mismatch with the language, feeling to developers as if it were "bolted on." Since most languages use function calls as the primary means of transferring control and data from one part of an application to another, add-on distribution libraries often model exchanges between distributed parts of an application as function calls as well. While convenient, this approach is fundamentally broken because the semantics of local and remote function calls, especially their failure modes, are markedly different.

In Erlang, processes communicate via asynchronous message passing. This works even if a process is on a remote node because the Erlang virtual machine supports passing messages from one node to another. When one node joins another, it also becomes aware of any nodes already known to the other. In this manner, all the nodes in a cluster form a mesh, enabling any process to send a message to another process on any other node in the cluster. Each node in the cluster also automatically tracks liveness of other nodes in order to become aware of nonresponsive nodes. The advantages of asynchronous message passing in systems running on a node is extended to systems running in clusters, as replies can be received alongside errors and timeouts.

Erlang's message passing and clustering primitives can serve as the basis for a wide variety of distributed system architectures. For example, service-oriented architecture (SOA), especially in its more modern variant, microservices, is a natural fit for Erlang given the ease of developing and deploying server-like processes. Clients treat such processes as services, communicating with them by exchanging messages. As another example, consider that Erlang clusters do not require master or leader nodes, which means that using them for peer-to-peer systems of replicas works well. Clients can send service request messages to any peer node in the cluster, and the peer can either handle the request itself or route it to another peer. The concept of standalone clusters, known as *groups* that communicate with each other through gateway nodes that can go up and down or lose connectivity exists in a framework called *SD Erlang*. Another popular distributed framework, inspired by the Amazon Dynamo paper (*http://bit.ly/riak-dynamo*) published in 2007, is *Riak Core*, offering consistent hashing to schedule jobs, recovery from partitioned networks and failed nodes through consistent hashing, eventual consistency, and virtual nodes dividing state and the data into small, manageable entities that can be replicated and moved across nodes.

With distributed systems, you can also achieve scalability. In fact, availability, consistency, and scalability go hand in hand, each affecting the others. It starts with the concurrency model and the concept of message passing within the node, which we extend across the network to use for clustering nodes. Erlang's virtual machine takes advantage of today's multicore systems by allowing processes to execute with true concurrency, running simultaneously on different cores. Because of the symmetric multiprocessing (SMP) capabilities of the Erlang virtual machine, Erlang is already prepared to help applications scale vertically as the number of cores per CPU continues to increase. And because adding new nodes to a cluster is easy—all it takes is to have that node contact just one other node to join the mesh—horizontal scaling is also well within easy reach. This, in turn, allows you to focus on the real challenge when dealing with distributed systems: namely, distributing your data and state across hosts and networks that are unreliable.

Summing Up

To make design, implementation, operation, and maintainability easier and more robust, your programming language and middleware have to be compact, their behavior in runtime predictable, and the resulting code base maintainable. We keep talking about fault-tolerant, scalable, soft real-time systems with requirements for high availability. The problems you have to solve do not have to be complicated in order to benefit from the advantages Erlang/OTP brings to the table. Advantages will be evident if you are developing solutions targeted for embedded hardware platforms such as the Parallela board, the BeagleBoard, or the Raspberry Pi. You will find Erlang/OTP ideal for the orchestration code in embedded devices, for server-side development where concurrency comes in naturally, and all the way up to scalable and distributed multicore architectures and supercomputers. It eases the development of the harder software problems while making simpler programs even easier to implement.

What You'll Learn in This Book

This book is divided into two sections. The first part, from Chapter 3 to Chapter 10, deals with the design and implementation of a single node. You should read these chapters sequentially, because their examples and explanations build on prior ones. The second half of the book, from Chapter 11 to Chapter 16, focuses on tools, techniques, and architectures used for deployment, monitoring, and operations, while explaining the theoretical approaches needed to tackle issues such as reliability, scalability, and high availability. The second half builds in part on the examples covered in the first half of the book, but can be read independently of it.

We begin with an overview of Erlang in Chapter 2, intended not to teach you the language but rather as a refresher course. If you do not yet know Erlang, we recommend that you first consult one or more of the excellent books designed to help you learn the language, such as Simon St. Laurent's *Introducing Erlang*, *Erlang Programming* by Francesco Cesarini and Simon Thompson, or any of the other books we mention in Chapter 2. Our overview touches on the major elements of the language, such as lists, functions, processes and messages, and the Erlang shell, as well as those features that make Erlang unique among languages, such as process linking and monitoring, live upgrades, and distribution.

Following the Erlang overview, Chapter 3 dives into process structures. Erlang processes can handle a wide variety of tasks, yet regardless of the particular tasks or their problem domains, similar code structures and process lifecycles surface, akin to the common design patterns that have been observed and documented for popular object-oriented languages like Java and C++. OTP captures and formalizes these common process-oriented structures and lifecycles into *behaviors*, which serve as the base elements of OTP's reusable frameworks.

In Chapter 4 we explore in detail our first worker process. It is the most popular and frequently used OTP behavior, the gen_server. As its name implies, it supports generic client-server structures, with the server governing particular computing resources—perhaps just a simple Erlang Term Storage (ETS) instance, or a pool of network connections to a remote non-Erlang server—and granting clients access to them. Clients communicate with generic servers synchronously in a call-response fashion, asynchronously via a one-way message called a *cast*, or via regular Erlang messaging primitives. Full consideration of these modes of communication requires us to scrutinize various aspects of the processes involved, such as what happens if the client or server dies in the middle of a message exchange, how timeouts apply, and what might happen if a server receives a message it does not understand. By addressing these and other common issues, the gen_server handles a lot of details independently of the problem domain, allowing developers to focus more of their time and energy on their applications. The gen_server behavior is so useful that it not only appears in most nontrivial Erlang applications but is used throughout OTP itself as well.

Prior to examining more OTP behaviors, we follow our discussion of gen_server with a look at some of the control and observation points the OTP behaviors provide (Chapter 5). These features reflect another aspect of Erlang/OTP that sets it apart from other languages and frameworks: built-in observability. If you want to know what your gen_server process is doing, you can simply enable debug tracing for that process, either at compile time or at runtime from an Erlang shell. Enabling traces causes it to emit information that indicates what messages it is receiving and what actions it is taking to handle them. Erlang/OTP also provides functions for peering into running processes to see their backtraces, process dictionaries, parent processes, linked processes, and other details. There are also OTP functions for examining status and internal state specifically for behaviors and other system processes. Because of these debug-oriented features, Erlang programmers often forego the use of traditional debuggers and instead rely on tracing to help them diagnose errant programs, as it is typically both faster to set up and more informative.

We then examine another OTP behavior, gen_fsm (Chapter 6), which supports a generic FSM pattern. As you may already know, an FSM is a system that has a finite number of states, and incoming messages can advance the system from one state to another, with side effects potentially occurring as part of the transitions. For example, you might consider your television set-top box as being an FSM where the current state represents the selected channel and whether any on-screen display is shown. Pressing buttons on your remote causes the set-top box to change state, perhaps selecting a different channel, or changing its on-screen display to show the channel guide or list any on-demand shows that might be available for purchase. FSMs are applicable to a wide variety of problem domains because they allow developers to more easily reason about and implement the potential states and state transitions of their applications. Knowing when and how to use gen_fsm can save you from trying to implement your own ad hoc state machines, which often quickly devolve into spaghetti code that is hard to maintain and extend.

Logging and monitoring are critical parts of any scalability success story, since they allow you to glean important information about your running systems that can help pinpoint bottlenecks and problematic areas that require further investigation. The Erlang/OTP gen_event behavior (Chapter 7) provides support for subsystems that emit and manage event streams reflecting changes in system state that can impact operational characteristics, such as sustained increases in CPU load, queues that appear to grow without bound, or the inability of one node in a distributed cluster to reach another. These streams do not have to stop with your system events. They could handle your application-specific events originating from user interaction, sensor networks, or third-party applications. In addition to exploring the gen_event behavior, we also take a look at the OTP system architecture support libraries (SASL) error-logging event handlers, which provide flexibility for managing supervisor reports, crash reports, and progress reports.

Event handlers and error handlers are staples of numerous programming languages, and they are incredibly useful in Erlang/OTP as well, but do not let their presence here fool you: dealing with errors in Erlang/OTP is strikingly different from the approaches to which most programmers are accustomed.

After gen_event, the next behavior we study is the supervisor (Chapter 8), which manages worker processes. In Erlang/OTP, supervisor processes start workers and then keep an eye on them while they carry out application tasks. Should one or more workers die unexpectedly, the supervisor can deal with the problem in one of several ways that we explain later in the book. This form of handling errors, known as "let it crash," differs significantly from the defensive programming tactics that most programmers employ. "Let it crash" and supervision, together a critical cornerstone of Erlang/OTP, are highly effective in practice.

We then look into the final fundamental OTP behavior, the application (Chapter 9), which serves as the primary point of integration between the Erlang/OTP runtime and your code. OTP applications have configuration files that specify their names, versions, modules, the applications upon which they depend, and other details. When started by the Erlang/OTP runtime, your application instance in turn starts a top-level supervisor that brings up the rest of the application. Structuring modules of code into applications also lets you perform code upgrades on live systems. A release of an Erlang/OTP package typically comprises a number of applications, some of which are part of the Erlang/OTP open source distribution and others that you provide.

Having examined the standard behaviors, we next turn our attention to explaining how to write your own behaviors and special processes (Chapter 10). Special processes are processes that follow certain design rules, allowing them to be added to OTP supervision trees. Knowing these design rules can not only help you understand implementation details of the standard behaviors, but also inform you of their trade-offs and allow you to better decide when to use them and when to write your own instead.

Chapter 11 describes how OTP applications in a single node are coupled together and started as a whole. You will have to create your own release files, referred to in the Erlang world as *rel* files. The rel file lists the versions of the applications and the runtime system that are used by the systools module to bundle up the software into a standalone release directory that includes the virtual machine. This release directory, once configured and packaged, is ready to be deployed and run on target hosts. We cover the community-contributed tools *rebar3* and *relx*, the best way to build your code and your releases.

The Erlang virtual machine has configurable system limits and settings you need to be aware of when deploying your systems. There are many, ranging from limits regulating the maximum number of ETS tables or processes to included code search paths and modes used for loading modules. Modules in Erlang can be loaded at startup, or when they are first called. In systems with strict revision control, you will have to run them in *embedded* mode, loading modules at startup and crashing if modules do not exist, or in *interactive* mode, where if a module is not available, an attempt to load it is made before terminating the process. An external monitoring *heart* process monitors the Erlang virtual machine by sending heartbeats and invoking a script that allows you to react when these heartbeats are not acknowledged. You implement the script yourself, allowing you to decide whether restarting the node is enough or whether—based on a history of previous restarts—you want to escalate the crash and terminate the virtual instance or reboot the whole machine.

Although Erlang's dynamic typing allows you to upgrade your module at runtime while retaining the process state, it does not coordinate dependencies among modules, changes in process state, or non–backward-compatible protocols. OTP has the tools to support system upgrades on a system level, including not only the applications, but also the runtime system. The principles and supporting libraries are presented in Chapter 12, from defining your own application-upgrade scripts to writing scripts that support release upgrades. Approaches and strategies for handling changes to your database schema are provided, as are guidelines for upgrades in distributed environments and non–backward-compatible protocols. For major upgrades in distributed environments where bugs are fixed, protocols improved, and database schema changed, runtime upgrades are not for the faint of heart. But they are incredibly powerful, allowing automated upgrades and nonstop operations. Finding your online banking is unavailable because of maintenance should now be a thing of the past. If it isn't, send a copy of this book to your bank's IT department.

Operating and maintaining any system requires visibility into what is going on. Scaling clusters require strategies for how you share your data and state. And fault tolerance requires an approach to how you replicate and persist it. In doing so, you have to deal with unreliable networks, failure, and recovery strategies. While each of these subjects merits a book of its own, the final chapters of this book will provide you with the theoretical background needed when distributing your systems and making them reliable and scalable. We provide this theory by describing the steps needed to design a scalable, highly available architecture in Erlang/OTP.

Chapter 13 will give you an overview of the approaches needed when designing your distributed architecture, breaking up your functionality into standalone nodes. In doing so, each standalone *node type* will be assigned a specific purpose, such as acting as a client gateway managing TCP/IP connection pools or providing a service such as authentication or payments. For each node type, we define an approach to specifying interfaces and defining the state and data each node needs. We conclude the chapter by describing the most common distributed architectural patterns and the different network protocols that can be used to connect them.

When you have your distributed architecture in place, you need to make design choices that will impact fault tolerance, resilience, reliability, and availability. You know what data and state you need in your node types, but how are you going to distribute it and keep it consistent? Are you going for the share-everything, share-something, or share-nothing approach, and what are the tradeoffs you need to make when choosing strong, causal, or eventual consistency? In Chapter 14, we describe the different approaches you can take, introducing the retry strategies you need to be aware of in case a request times out as the result of process, node, or network failure or the mere fact that the network or your servers are running over capacity.

It is easy to say that you are going to add hardware to make your system scale horizontally, but alas, the design choices introduced in Chapter 14 will have an impact on your system's scalability. In Chapter 15, we describe the impacts resulting from your data-sharing strategy, consistency model, and retry strategy. We cover capacity planning, including the load, peak, and stress tests you need to subject your system to to guarantee it behaves in a predictable way under heavy load even when the hardware, software, and infrastructure around it are failing.

Once you've designed your scalability and availability strategies, you need to tackle monitoring. If you want to achieve five-nines uptime, you need to not only know what is going on, but also be able to quickly determine what happened, and why. We conclude the book with Chapter 16, looking at how monitoring is used for preemptive support and postmortem debugging.

Monitoring focuses on metrics, alarms, and logs. This chapter discusses the importance of system and business metrics. Examples of system metrics include the amount of memory your node is using, process message queue length, and hard-disk utilization. Combining these with business metrics, such as the number of failed and successful login attempts, message throughput per second, and session duration, yields full visibility of how your business logic is affecting your system resources.

Complementing metrics is *alarming*, where you detect and report anomalies, allowing the system to take action to try to resolve them or to alert an operator when human intervention is required. Alarms could include a system running out of disk space (resulting in the automatic invocation of scripts for compressing or deleting logs) or a large number of failed message submissions (requiring human intervention to troubleshoot connectivity problems). Preemptive support at its best, detecting and resolving issues before they escalate, is a must when dealing with high availability. If you do not have a real-time view of what is going on, resolving issues before they escalate becomes extremely difficult and cumbersome.

And finally, *logging* of major events in the system helps you troubleshoot your system after a crash where you lost its state, so you can retrieve the call flow of a particular request among millions of others to handle a customer services query, or just provide data records for billing purposes.

With your monitoring in place, you will be ready to architect systems that are not only scalable, but also resilient and highly available. Happy reading! We hope you enjoy the book as much as we enjoyed writing it.

## CHAPTER 2

Introducing Erlang

This book assumes a basic knowledge of Erlang, which is best obtained through practice and by reading some of the many excellent introductory Erlang books out there (including two written for O'Reilly; see "Summing Up" on page 51). But for a quick refresher, this chapter gives you an overview of important Erlang concepts. We draw attention particularly to those aspects of Erlang you'll need to know when you come to learn OTP.

Recursion and Pattern Matching

Recursion is the way Erlang programmers get iterative or repetitive behavior in their programs. It is also what keeps processes alive in between bursts of activity. Our first example shows how to compute the factorial of a positive number:

```
-module(ex1).
-export([factorial/1]).

factorial(0) ->
    1;
factorial(N) when N > 0 ->
    N * factorial(N-1).
```

We call the function `factorial` and indicate that it takes a single argument (`factorial/1`). The trailing `/1` is the arity of a function, and simply refers to the number of arguments the function takes—in our example, 1.

If the argument we pass to the function is the integer `0`, we match the first clause, returning `1`. Any integer greater than `0` is bound to the variable `N`, returning the product of `N` and `factorial(N-1)`. The iteration will continue until we pattern match on the function clause that serves as the base case. The base case is the clause where recursing stops. If we call `factorial/1` with a negative integer, the call fails as no clauses match. But we don't bother dealing with the problems caused by a caller passing a noninteger argument; this is an Erlang principle we discuss later.

Erlang definitions are contained in modules, which are stored in files of the same name, but with a *.erl* extension. So, the filename of the preceding module would be *ex1.erl*. Erlang programs can be evaluated in the Erlang shell, invoked by the command `erl` in your Unix shell or by double-clicking on the Erlang icon. Make sure that you start your Erlang shell in the same directory as your source code. A typical session goes like this:

```
$ erl                   % Comments on interactions are given in this format.
Erlang/OTP 18 [erts-7.2] [smp:8:8] [async-threads:10] [kernel-poll:false]

Eshell V7.2  (abort with ^G)
1> c(ex1).
{ok,ex1}
2> ex1:factorial(3).
6
3> ex1:factorial(-3).
** exception error: no function clause matching
                    ex1:factorial(-3) (ex1.erl, line 4)
4> factorial(2).
** exception error: undefined shell command factorial/1
5> q().
ok
$
```

In shell command 1, we compile the Erlang file. We go on to do a fully qualified function call in command line 2, where by prefixing the module name to the function we are able to invoke it from outside the module itself. The call in shell command 3 fails with a function clause error because no clauses match for negative numbers. Before terminating the shell with the shell command q(), we call a local function, factorial(2), in shell command 4. It fails as it is not fully qualified with a module name.

Recursion is not just for computing simple values; we can write imperative programs using the same style. The following is a program to print every element of a list, separated by tabs. As with the previous example, the function is presented in two *clauses*, where each clause has a head and a body, separated by the arrow (->). In the head we see the function applied to a pattern, and when a function is applied to an argument, the first clause whose pattern matches the argument is used. In this example the [] matches an empty list, whereas [X|Xs] matches a nonempty list. The [X|Xs] syntax assigns the first element of the list, or head, to X and the remainder of the list, or tail, to Xs (if you have not yet noted it, Erlang variables such as X, Xs, and N all start with uppercase letters):

```
-module(ex2).
-export([print_all/1]).
```

```
print_all([]) ->
    io:format("~n");
print_all([X|Xs]) ->
    io:format("~p\t",[X]),
    print_all(Xs).
```

The effect is to print each item from the list, in the order that it appears in the list, with a tab (\t) after each item. Thanks to the base case, which runs when the list is empty (when it matches []), a newline (~n) is printed at the end. Unlike in the ex1:factorial/1 example shown earlier, the pattern of recursion in this example is *tail recursive*. It is used in Erlang programs to give looping behavior. A function is said to be tail recursive if the only recursive calls to the function occur as the last expression to be executed in the function clause. We can think of this final call as a "jump" back to the start of the function, now called with a different parameter. Tail-recursive functions allow last-call optimization, ensuring stack frames are not added in each iteration. This allows functions to execute in constant memory space and removes the risk of a stack overflow, which in Erlang manifests itself through the virtual machine running out of memory.

If you come from an imperative programming background, writing the function slightly differently to use a case expression rather than separate clauses may make tail recursion easier to understand:[1]

```
all_print(Ys) ->
    case Ys of
        [] ->
            io:format("~n");
        [X|Xs] ->
            io:format("~p\t",[X]),
            all_print(Xs)
    end.
```

When you test either of these print functions, note the ok printed out after the newline. Every Erlang function has to return a value. This value is whatever the last executed expression returns. In our case, the last executed expression is io:format("~n"). The newline appears as a side effect of the function, while the ok is the return value printed by the shell:

```
1> c(ex2).
{ok,ex2}
2> ex2:print_all([one,two,three]).
one     two     three
ok
3> Val = io:format("~n").
```

---

1 But uglier, as we are using a case expression instead of pattern matching in the function head.

```
ok
4> Val.
ok
```

The arguments in our example play the role of mutable variables, whose values change between calls. Erlang variables are single assignment, so once you've bound a value to a variable, you can no longer change that variable. In a recursive function variables of the same name, including function arguments, are considered fresh in every function iteration. We can see the behavior of single assignment of variables here:

```
1> A = 3.
3
2> A = 2+1.
3
3> A = 3+1.
** exception error: no match of right hand side value 4
```

In shell command 1, we successfully assign an unbound variable. In shell command 2, we pattern match an assigned variable to its value. Pattern matching fails in shell command 3, because the value on the right-hand side differs from the current value of A.

Erlang also allows pattern matching over binary data, where we match on a bit level. This is an incredibly powerful and efficient construct for decoding frames and dealing with network protocol stacks. How about decoding an IPv4 packet in a few lines of code?

```
-define(IP_VERSION, 4).
-define(IP_MIN_HDR_LEN, 5).

handle(Dgram) ->
   DgramSize = byte_size(Dgram),
   <<?IP_VERSION:4, HLen:4, SrvcType:8, TotLen:16, ID:16, ...,
     Flgs:3, FragOff:13, TTL:8, Proto:8,  HdrChkSum:16, ...,
     SrcIP:32, DestIP:32, Body/binary>> = Dgram,
   if
     (HLen >= 5) and (4*HLen =< DgramSize) ->
        OptsLen = 4*(HLen - ?IP_MIN_HDR_LEN),
        <<Opts:OptsLen/binary, Data/binary>> = Body,
        ...
   end.
```

We first determine the size (number of bytes) of Dgram, a variable holding an IPv4 packet as binary data previously received from a network socket. Next, we use pattern matching against Dgram to extract its fields; the left-hand side of the pattern matching assignment defines an Erlang binary, delimited by << and >> and containing a number of fields. The ellipses (...) within the binary are not legal Erlang code; they indicate fields we've left out to keep the example brief. The numbers following most of the fields specify the number of bits (or bytes for binaries) each field occupies. For example, `Flgs:3` defaults to an integer that matches 3 bits, the value of which it binds to the variable `Flgs`. At the point of the pattern match we don't yet know the size of the final field, `Body`, so we specify it as a binary of unknown length in bytes that we bind to the variable `Data`. If the pattern match succeeds, it extracts, in just a single statement, all the named fields from the `Dgram` packet. Finally, we check the value of the extracted `HLen` field in an `if` clause, and if it succeeds, we perform a pattern matching assignment against `Body` to extract `Opts` as a binary of `OptsLen` bytes and `Data` as a binary consisting of all the rest of the data in `Body`. Note how `OptsLen` is calculated dynamically. If you've ever written code using an imperative language such as Java or C to extract fields from a network packet, you can see how much easier pattern matching makes the task.

Functional Influence

Erlang was heavily influenced by other functional programming languages. One functional principle is to treat functions as first-class citizens; they can be assigned to variables, be part of complex data structures, be passed as function arguments, or be returned as the results of function calls. We refer to the functional data type as an *anonymous function*, or *fun* for short. Erlang also provides constructs that allow you to define lists by "generate and test," using the analogue of comprehensions in set theory. Let's first start with anonymous functions: functions that are not named and not defined in an Erlang module.

Fun with Anonymous Functions

Functions that take funs as arguments are called *higher-order functions*. An example of such a function is `filter`, where a predicate is represented by a fun that returns `true` or `false`, applied to the elements of a list. `filter` returns a list made up of those elements that have the required property; namely, those for which the fun returns `true`. We often use the term "predicate" to refer to a fun that, based on certain conditions defined in the function, returns the atoms `true` or `false`. Here is an example of how `filter/2` could be implemented:

```
-module(ex3).
-export([filter/2, is_even/1]).

filter(P,[]) -> [];
filter(P,[X|Xs]) ->
    case P(X) of
        true ->
            [X|filter(P,Xs)];
        _ ->
            filter(P,Xs)
    end.
```

```
is_even(X) ->
    X rem 2 == 0.
```

To use `filter`, you need to pass it a function and a list. One way to pass the function is to use a `fun` expression, which is a way of defining an anonymous function. In shell command 2, shown next, you can see an example of an anonymous function that tests for its argument being an even number:

```
2> ex3:filter(fun(X) -> X rem 2 == 0 end, [1,2,3,4]).
[2,4]
3> ex3:filter(fun ex3:is_even/1,[1,2,3,4]).
[2,4]
```

A `fun` does not have to be anonymous, and could instead refer to a local or global function definition. In shell command 3, we described the function by `fun ex3:is_even/1`; i.e., by giving its module, name, and arity. Anonymous functions can also be spawned as the body of a process and passed in messages between processes; we look at processes in general after the next topic.

If you're using Erlang/OTP 17.0 or newer, there's another way a fun does not have to be anonymous: it can be given a name. This feature is especially handy in the shell as it allows for easy definition of recursive anonymous functions. For example, we can implement the equivalent of `ex3:filter/2` in the shell like this:

```
4> F = fun Filter(_,[]) -> [];
4> Filter(P,[X|Xs]) -> case P(X) of true -> [X|Filter(P,Xs)];
4> false -> Filter(P,Xs) end end.
#Fun<erl_eval.36.90072148>
5> Filter(fun(X) -> X rem 2 == 0 end,[1,2,3,4]).
* 1: variable 'Filter' is unbound
6> F(fun(X) -> X rem 2 == 0 end,[1,2,3,4]).
[2,4]
```

We name our recursive function `Filter` by putting that name just after the `fun` keyword. Note that the name has to appear in both function clauses: the one on the first line, which handles the empty list case, and the one defined on the next two lines, which handles the case when the list isn't empty. You can see two places in the body of the second clause where we recursively call `Filter` to handle remaining elements in the list. But even though the function has the name `Filter`, we still assign it to shell variable F because the name `Filter` is local to the function itself, and thus can't be used outside the body to invoke it, as our attempt to call it on line 5 shows. On line 6, we invoke the named fun via F and it works as expected. And because shell variables and function names are in different scopes, we could have used the shell variable name `Filter` rather than F, thus naming the function the same way in both scopes.

List Comprehensions: Generate and Test

Many of the examples we have looked at so far deal with the manipulation of lists. We've used recursive functions on them, as well as higher-order functions. Another approach is to use *list comprehensions*, expressions that generate elements and apply tests (or filters) to them. The format is like this:

```
[Expression || Generators, Tests, Generators, Tests]
```

where each *Generator* has the format

```
X <- [2,3,5,7,11]
```

The effect of this is to successively bind the variable X to the values 2, 3, 5, 7, and 11. In other words, it *generates* the elements from the list: the symbol <- is meant to suggest the "element of" symbol for sets, ∈. In this example, X is called a *bound variable*. We've shown only one bound variable here, but a list comprehension can be built from multiple bound variables and generators; we show some examples later in this section.

The *Tests* are Boolean expressions, which are evaluated for each combination of values of the bound variables. If all the *Tests* in a group return true, then the *Expression* is generated from the current values of the bound variables. The use of *Tests* in a list comprehension is optional. The list comprehension construct as a whole generates a list of results, one for each combination of values of the bound variables that passes all the tests.

As a first example, we could rewrite the function filter/2 as a list comprehension:

```
filter(P,Xs) -> [ X || X<-Xs, P(X) ].
```

In this list comprehension, the first X is the expression, X<-Xs is the generator, and P(X) is the test. Each value from the generator is tested with the test, and the expression comprises only those values for which the test returns true. Values for which the test returns false are simply dropped. We can use list comprehensions directly in our programs, as in the previous filter/2 example, or in the Erlang shell:

```
1> [Element || Element <- [1,2,3,4], Element rem 2 == 0].
[2,4]
2> [Element || Element <- [1,2,3,4], ex3:is_even(Element)].
[2,4]
3> [Element || Element <- lists:seq(1,4), Element rem 2 == 0].
[2,4]
4> [io:format("~p~n",[Element]) || Element <- [one, two, three]].
one
two
three
[ok,ok,ok]
```

Note how, in shell command 4, we are using list comprehensions to create side effects. The expression still returns a list [ok,ok,ok] containing the return values of executing the io:format/2 expression on the elements.

The next set of examples show the effect of multiple generators and interleaved generators and tests. In the first, for each value of X, the values bound to Y run through 3, 4, and 5. In the second example, the values of Y depend on the value chosen for X (showing that the expression evaluates X before Y). The remaining two examples apply tests to both of the bound variables:

```
5> [ {X,Y} || X <- [1,2], Y <- [3,4,5] ].
[{1,3},{1,4},{1,5},{2,3},{2,4},{2,5}]
6> [ {X,Y} || X <- [1,2], Y <- [X+3,X+4,X+5] ].
[{1,4},{1,5},{1,6},{2,5},{2,6},{2,7}]
7> [ {X,Y} || X <- [1,2,3], X rem 2 /= 0, Y <- [X+3,X+4,X+5], (X+Y) rem 2 == 0 ].
[{1,5},{3,7}]
8> [ {X,Y} || X  <-[1,2,3], X rem 2 /= 0, Y <- [X+3,X+4,X+5], (X+Y) rem 2 /= 0 ].
[{1,4},{1,6},{3,6},{3,8}]
```

We'll leave you with one of our favorite list comprehensions, which we contemplated leaving as an exercise.[2] Given an 8 × 8 chessboard, how many ways can you place N queens on it so that they do not threaten each other? In our example, queens(N) returns choices of positions of queens in the bottom N rows of the chessboard, so that each of these is a list of column numbers (in the given rows) where the queens lie. To find out the number of different possible placements, we just count the permutations. Note the -- list difference operator. It complements ++, which appends lists together. We also use andalso instead of and, as it short-circuits the operation if an expression evaluates to false:

```
-module(queens).
-export([queens/1]).

queens(0) -> [[]];
queens(N) ->
    [[Row | Columns] || Columns <- queens(N-1),
        Row <- [1,2,3,4,5,6,7,8] -- Columns,    % -- returns the list difference
        safe(Row, Columns, 1)].

safe(_Row, [], _N) -> true;
safe(Row, [Column|Columns], N) ->
    (Row /= Column + N) andalso (Row /= Column - N) andalso
        safe(Row, Columns, (N+1)).
```

---

2 You should thank us for this example. When still a student, one of the authors spent two sleepless nights trying to figure this one out after Joe Armstrong told him it was possible to solve it with four lines of code.

Processes and Message Passing

Concurrency is at the heart of the Erlang programming model. Processes are light-weight, meaning that creating them involves negligible time and memory overhead. Processes do not share memory, and instead communicate with each other through message passing. Messages are copied from the stack of the sending process to the heap of the receiving one. As processes execute concurrently in separate memory spaces, these memory spaces can be garbage collected separately, giving Erlang programs very predictable soft real-time properties, even under sustained heavy loads. Millions of processes can run concurrently within the same VM, each handling a standalone task. Processes fail when exceptions occur, but because there is no shared memory, failure can often be isolated as the processes were working on standalone tasks. This allows other processes working on unrelated or unaffected tasks to continue executing and the program as a whole to recover on its own.

So, how does it all work? Processes are created via the spawn(Mod, Func, Args) BIF or one of its variants. The result of a spawn call is a process identifier, normally referred to as a *pid*. Pids are used for sending messages, and can themselves be part of the message, allowing other processes to communicate back. As we see in Figure 2-1, the process starts executing in the function Func, defined in the module Mod with arguments passed to the Args list.

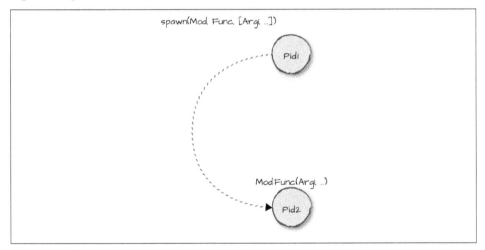

Figure 2-1. Spawning a process

The following example of an "echo" process shows these basics. The first action of the go/0 function is to spawn a process executing loop/0, after which it communicates with that process by sending and receiving messages. The loop/0 function receives messages and, depending on their format, either replies to them (and loops) or terminates. To get this looping behavior, the function is tail recursive, ensuring it executes in constant memory space.

We know the pid of the process executing loop/0 from the spawn, but when we send it a message, how can it communicate back to us? We'll have to send it our pid, which we find using the self() BIF:

```erlang
-module(echo).
-export([go/0, loop/0]).

go() ->
    Pid = spawn(echo, loop, []),
    Pid ! {self(), hello},
    receive
        {Pid, Msg} ->
        io:format("~w~n",[Msg])
    end,
    Pid ! stop.

loop() ->
    receive
        {From, Msg} ->
            From ! {self(), Msg},
            loop();
        stop ->
            ok
    end.
```

In this echo example, the go/0 function first spawns a new process executing the echo:loop/0 function, storing the resulting pid in the variable Pid. It then sends to the Pid process a message containing the pid of the sender, retrieved using the self() BIF, along with the atom hello. After that, go/0 waits to receive a message in the form of a pair whose first element matches the pid of the loop process; when such a message arrives, go/0 prints out the second element of the message, exits the receive expression, and finishes by sending the message stop to Pid.

The echo:loop/0 function first waits for a message. If it receives a pair containing a pid From and a message, it sends a message containing its own pid along with the received Msg back to the From process and then calls itself recursively. If it instead receives the atom stop, loop/0 returns ok. When loop/0 stops, the process that go/0 originally spawned to run loop/0 terminates as well, as there is no more code to execute.

Note how, when we run this program, the go/0 call returns stop. Every function returns a value, that of the last expression it evaluated. Here, the last expression is Pid ! go, which returns the message we just sent to Pid:

```erlang
1> c(echo).
{ok,echo}
```

```
2> echo:go().
hello
stop
```

Bound Variables in Patterns

Pattern matching is different in Erlang than in other languages with pattern matching because variables occurring in patterns can be *already bound*. In the go function in the echo example, the variable Pid is already bound to the pid of the process just spawned, so the receive expression will accept only those messages in which the first component is that particular pid; in the scenario here, it will be a message from that pid, in fact.

If a message is received with a different first component, then the pattern match in the receive will not be successful, and the receive will block until a message is received from process Pid.

Erlang message passing is asynchronous: the expression that sends a message to a process returns immediately and always appears to be successful, even when the receiving process doesn't exist. If the process exists, the messages are placed in the mailbox of the receiving process in the same order in which they are received. They are processed using the receive expression, which pattern matches on the messages in sequential order. Message reception is selective, meaning that messages are not necessarily processed in the order in which they arrive, but rather the order in which they are matched. Each receive clause selects the message it wants to read from the mailbox using pattern matching.

Suppose that the mailbox for the loop process has received the messages foo, stop, and {Pid, hello} in that order. The receive expression will try to match the first message (here, foo) against each of the patterns in turn; this fails, leaving the message in the mailbox. It then tries to do the same with the second message, stop; this doesn't match the first pattern but does match the second, with the result that the process terminates, as there is no more code to execute.

These semantics mean that *we can process messages in whatever order we choose*, irrespective of when they arrive. Code like this:

```
receive
    message1 -> ...
end
receive
    message2 -> ...
end
```

will process the atoms message1 and then message2. Without this feature, we'd have to anticipate all the different orders in which messages can arrive, and handle each of those, greatly increasing the complexity of our programs. With selective receive, all we do is leave them in the mailbox for later retrieval.

Multicore, Schedulers, and Reductions

The biggest challenges in scaling systems on multicore architectures are sequential code and the serialization of operations. These could be in your program, in libraries you use, in the underlying virtual machine, or all of the above. Memory lock contention is often the major bottleneck, caused when threads try to acquire a lock allowing them to access and manipulate shared memory. Erlang processes do not share memory, removing one of the major obstacles and making it the ideal language to fully utilize many-core computers. Program in Erlang as you would have done on a single-core architecture, ensuring you have a process for each truly concurrent activity, and your system will scale as you add more cores. You will be limited only by your sequential code and bottlenecks in the BEAM virtual machine—bottlenecks that release after release, are continually optimized or removed.

For every core, the BEAM virtual machine starts a thread that runs a scheduler. Each scheduler is responsible for a group of processes, and at any one time, a process from each scheduler executes in parallel on each core. Processes that are not suspended and are ready to execute are placed in the scheduler's run queue. The virtual machine also starts a separate thread pool used for drivers and file I/O that can operate without blocking any scheduler threads. At startup, you can limit the number of threads and schedulers, and specify whether you want schedulers to be bound to a core or be allowed to migrate from one core to another. Schedulers are not bound to cores by default because such binding can backfire, slowing down the system on certain architectures. However, it can result in speedups in other situations. Benchmark your system with both approaches. We cover how to set startup flags and parameters in "Arguments and Flags" on page 290 and benchmarking in Chapter 15.

If the system is running under full load, the schedulers try to guarantee soft real-time properties by retaining an even balance of CPU time across all processes. What the BEAM virtual machine tries to do is avoid cases where processes in a run queue with 10 processes get twice as much CPU time as those in a run queue with 20 processes. This is achieved by allowing processes to migrate between run queues, evening out their sizes across the schedulers. But if the system isn't fully loaded, the virtual machine migrates processes so they occupy fewer cores, and then pauses the unused scheduler threads. This allows cores to be shut down and put in energy saving mode, and later awakened when the load of the virtual machine increases.

Schedulers decide when to preempt processes based on an approximation of the workload they have executed. This approximation is called the *reduction count*. When a process is preempted, it stops running and is placed at the end of the run queue, allowing the process first in line to execute. Function calls and BIFs are assigned a value of one or more reductions, with the theory that expensive calls have a higher reduction count than cheaper ones. Each process is allowed to execute a predefined number of reductions before being preempted, allowing the process at the head of the run queue to execute. The number of reductions each process is allowed to execute before being suspended and the reduction count of each instruction are purposely not documented to discourage premature optimization, because the reduction count and the total number of reductions the scheduler allows a process to execute may change from one release and hardware architecture to another.

Scheduler balance, reductions, and the per-process garbage collector give the BEAM virtual machine predictable, soft real-time properties, even during times of peak and extended load, by maximizing fairness and ensuring there is no process starvation. Other programming languages and frameworks not running on BEAM don't provide preemptive multitasking. Application activities are not allowed to block, preventing the event loop from running frequently and dispatching events to their intended targets. If an application blocks, it blocks every part of the application, whereas in Erlang, the only way to block a scheduler (and all the processes in its run queue) is to drop into C code and either ignorantly or purposefully implement a misbehaving native implemented function (NIF) or driver. Lack of preemptive multitasking will therefore affect the soft real-time properties of a system, as it will either rely on the process to cooperatively preempt itself, or base preemption on specific operations instead of the number and cost of the operations themselves. Having said this, don't even get us started with "stop the world" garbage collectors in shared memory architectures, which force all threads to synchronize in order to determine which objects are still being used and which ones can be freed. No one named, no one shamed.

Fail Safe!

In "Recursion and Pattern Matching" on page 21 we saw the `factorial` example, and how passing a negative number to the function causes it to raise an exception. This also happens when `factorial` is applied to something that isn't a number, in this case the atom `zero`:

```
1> ex1:factorial(zero).
** exception error: bad argument in an arithmetic expression
in function  ex1:factorial/1
```

The alternative to this would be to program defensively, and explicitly identify the case of negative numbers, as well as arguments of any other type, by means of a *catch-all* clause:

```
factorial(0) ->
    1;
factorial(N) when N > 0, is_integer(N) ->
    N * factorial(N-1);
factorial(_) ->
    {error,bad_argument}.
```

The effect of this is would be to require every caller of the function to deal not only with proper results (like `120 = factorial(5)`) but also improper ones of the format `{error,bad_argument}`. If we do this, clients of any function need to understand its failure modes and provide ways of dealing with them, mixing correct computation and error-handling code. How do you handle errors or corrupt data when you do not know what these errors are or how the data got corrupted?

The Erlang design philosophy says "let it fail!" so that a function, process, or other running entity deals only with the correct case and leaves it to other parts of the system (specifically designed to do this) to deal with failure. One way of dealing with failure in sequential code is to use the mechanism for exception handling given by the `try-catch` construct. Using the definition:

```
factorial(0) ->
    1;
factorial(N) when N > 0, is_integer(N) ->
    N * factorial(N-1).
```

we can see the construct in action:

```
2> ex1:factorial(zero).
** exception error: no function clause matching ex1:factorial(zero)
3> try ex1:factorial(zero) catch Type:Error -> {Type, Error} end.
{error,function_clause}
4> try ex1:factorial(-2) catch Type:Error -> {Type, Error} end.
{error,function_clause}
5> try ex1:factorial(-2) catch error:Error2 -> {error, Error2} end.
{error,function_clause}
6> try ex1:factorial(-2) catch error:Error3 -> {error, Error3};
6>                            exit:Reason  -> {exit, Reason} end.
{error,function_clause}
```

The `try-catch` construct gives the user the opportunity to match on the different kinds of exceptions in the clauses, handling them individually. In this example, we match on an `error` exception caused by a pattern match failure. There are also `exit` and `throw` exceptions, the first being the result of a process calling the `exit` BIF and the latter the result of a user-generated exception using the `throw` expression.

Links and Monitors for Supervision

A typical Erlang system has lots of (possibly dependent) processes running at the same time. How do these dependencies work with the "let it fail" philosophy? Suppose process A interacts with processes B and C (Figure 2-2); these processes are dependent on each other, so if A fails, they can no longer function properly. A's failure needs to be detected, after which B and C need to be terminated before restarting them all. In this section we describe the mechanisms that support this approach, namely *process linking*, *exit signals*, and *monitoring*. These simple constructs enable us to build libraries with complex supervision strategies, allowing us to manage processes that may be subjected to failure at any time.

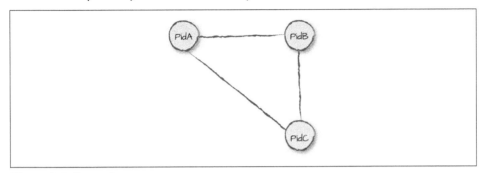

Figure 2-2. Dependent processes

Links

Calling link(Pid) in a process A creates a *bidirectional* link between processes A and Pid. Calling spawn_link/3 has the same effect as calling spawn/3 followed by link/1, except that it is executed atomically, eliminating the race condition where a process terminates between the spawn and the link. A link from the calling process to Pid is removed by calling unlink(Pid).

The key insight here is that the mechanism needs to be orthogonal to Erlang message passing, but effectuated with it. If two Erlang processes are linked, when either of them terminates, an exit signal is sent to the other, which will then itself terminate. The terminated process will in turn send the exit signal to all the processes in its linked set, propagating it through the system. This can be seen in Figure 2-3, where PidC terminates from whichever exit signal from PidA or PidB gets there first. The power of the mechanism comes from the ways that this default behavior can be modified, giving the designer fine control over the termination of the processes within a system. We now look at this in more detail.

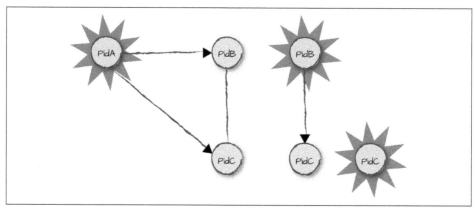

Figure 2-3. Exit signals propagating among linked processes

One pattern for using links is as follows: a server that controls access to resources links to a client while that client has access to a particular resource. If the client terminates, the server will be informed so it can reallocate the resource (or just terminate). If, on the other hand, the client hands back the resource, the server may unlink from the client.

Remember, though, that links are bidirectional, so if the server dies for some reason while client and server are linked, this will by default kill the client too, which you may not want to happen. If that's the case, use a monitor instead of a link, as we explain in "Monitors" on page 37.

Exit signals can be trapped by calling the process_flag(trap_exit, true) function. This converts exit signals into messages of the form {'EXIT', Pid, Reason}, where Pid is the process identifier of the process that has died and Reason is the reason it has terminated. These messages are stored in the recipient's mailbox and processed in the same way as all other messages. When a process is trapping exits, the exit signal is *not* propagated to any of the processes in its link set.

Why does a process exit? This can happen for two reasons. If a process has no more code to execute, it terminates *normally*. The Reason propagated will be the atom normal. *Abnormal termination* is initiated in case of a runtime error, receiving an exit signal when not trapping exits, or by calling the exit BIFs. Called with a single argument, exit(Reason) will terminate the calling process with reason Reason, which will be propagated in the exit signal to any other processes to which the exiting one is linked. When the exit BIF is called with two arguments, exit(Pid, Reason), it sends an exit signal with reason Reason to the process Pid. This will have the same effect as if the calling process had terminated with reason Reason.

As we said at the start of this section, users can control the way in which termination is propagated through a system. The options are summarized in Table 2-1 and vary depending on if the `trap_exit` process flag is set.

Table 2-1. Propagation semantics

Reason	Trapping exits	Not trapping exits
normal	Receives {'EXIT', Pid, normal}	Nothing happens
kill	Terminates with reason killed	Terminates with reason killed
Other	Receives {'EXIT', Pid, Other}	Terminates with reason Other

As the second column of the table shows, a process that is trapping exits will receive an 'EXIT' message when a linked process terminates, whether the termination is normal or abnormal. The kill reason allows one process to force another to exit along with it. This means that there's a mechanism for killing any process, even those that trap exits; note that its reason for termination is killed and not kill, ensuring that the unconditional termination does not itself propagate. If a process is not trapping exits, nothing happens if a process in its link set terminates normally. Abnormal termination, however, results in the process terminating.

Monitors

Monitors provide an alternative, unidirectional mechanism for processes to observe the termination of other processes. Monitors differ from links in the following ways:

- A monitor is set up when process A calls `erlang:monitor(process, B)`, where the atom `process` indicates we're monitoring a process and B is specified by a pid or registered name. This causes A to monitor B.

- Monitors have an identity given by an Erlang reference, which is a unique value returned by the call to `erlang:monitor/2`. Multiple monitors of B by A can be set up, each identified by a different reference.

- A monitor is *unidirectional* rather than bidirectional: if process A monitors process B, this does not mean that B monitors A.

- When a monitored process terminates, a message of the form {'DOWN', Refer ence, process, Pid, Reason} is sent to the monitoring process. This contains not only the Pid and Reason for the termination, but also the Reference of the monitor and the atom process, which tells us we were monitoring a process.

- A monitor is removed by the call `erlang:demonitor(Reference)`. Passing a second argument to the function in the format `erlang:demonitor(Reference, [flush])` ensures that any {'DOWN', Reference, process, Pid, Reason} messages from the Reference will be flushed from the mailbox of the monitoring process.

- Attempting to monitor a nonexistent process results in a {'DOWN', Reference, process, Pid, Reason} message with reason noproc; this contrasts with an attempt to link to a nonexistent process, which terminates the linking process.
- If a monitored process terminates, processes that are monitoring it and not trapping exits will not terminate.

 References in Erlang are used to guarantee the identity of messages, monitors, and other data types or requests. A reference can be generated indirectly by setting up a monitor, but also directly by calling the BIF make_ref/0. References are, for all intents and purposes, unique across a multinode Erlang system. References can be compared for equality and used within patterns, so that it's possible to ensure that a message comes from a particular process, or is a reply to a particular message within a communication protocol.

Taking monitor/2 and exit/2 for a trial run, we get the following self-explanatory results:

```
1> Pid = spawn(echo, loop, []).
<0.34.0>
2> erlang:monitor(process, Pid).
#Ref<0.0.0.34>
3> exit(Pid, kill).
true
4> flush().
Shell got {'DOWN',#Ref<0.0.0.34>,process,<0.34.0>,killed}
ok
```

Records

Erlang tuples provide a way of grouping related items, and unlike lists they provide convenient access to elements at arbitrary indexes via the element/2 BIF. In practice, though, they are most useful and manageable for groups of no more than about five or six items. Tuples larger than that can cause maintenance headaches by forcing you to keep track throughout your code of what field is in which position in the tuple, and using plain numbers to address fields through element/2 is error-prone. Pattern matching large tuples can be tedious due to having to ensure the correct number and placement of variables within the tuple. Worst of all, though, is that if you have to add or remove a field in a tuple, you have to find all the places your code uses it and make sure to change each occurrence to the correct new size.

Records address the shortcomings of tuples by providing a way to access fields of a tuple-like collection by name. Here's an example of a record used with the Erlang/OTP inet module, which provides access to TCP/IP information:

```
-record(hostent,
        {
            h_name                % offical name of host
            h_aliases = []        % alias list
            h_addrtype            % host address type
            h_length              % length of address
            h_addr_list = []      % list of addresses from name server
        }).
```

The -record directive is used to define a record, with the record name specified as the directive's first argument. The second argument, which resembles a tuple of atoms, defines the fields of the record. Fields can have specific default values, as shown here for the h_aliases and h_addr_list fields, both of which have the empty list as their defaults. Fields without specified defaults have the atom undefined as their default values.

Records can be used in assignments, in pattern matching, and as function arguments, similarly to tuples. But unlike tuples, record fields are accessed by name, and any fields not pertinent to a particular part of the code can be left out. For example, the type/1 function in this module requires access only to the h_addrtype field of a hostent record:

```
-module(addr).
-export([type/1]).

-include_lib("kernel/include/inet.hrl").

type(Addr) ->
    {ok, HostEnt} = inet:gethostbyaddr(Addr),
    HostEnt#hostent.h_addrtype.
```

First, note that to be able to use a record, we must have access to its definition. The -include_lib(...) directive here includes the *inet.hrl* file from the *kernel* application, where the hostent record is defined. In the final line of this example, we access the HostEnt variable as a hostent record by supplying the record name after the # symbol. After the record name, we access the required record field by name, h_addr type. This reads the value stored in that field and returns it as the return value of the type/1 function:

```
1> c(addr).
{ok,addr}
2> addr:type("127.0.0.1").
inet
3> addr:type("::1").
inet6
```

Another way to implement the type() function would be to pattern match the h_addrtype field against the return value of the inet:gethostbyaddr/1 function:

```
type(Addr) ->
    {ok, #hostent{h_addrtype=AddrType}} = inet:gethostbyaddr(Addr),
    AddrType.
```

Here, the AddrType variable within the pattern match captures the value of the h_addrtype field as part of the match. This form of pattern matching is quite common with records, and is especially useful within function heads to extract fields of interest into local variables. As you can see, this approach is also cleaner than the field access syntax used in the previous example.

To create a record instance, you set the fields as required:

```
hostent(Host, inet) ->
    #hostent{h_name=Host, h_addrtype=inet, h_length=4,
             h_addr_list=inet:getaddrs(Host, inet)}.
```

In this example, the hostent/2 function returns a hostent record instance with specific fields set. Any fields not explicitly set in the code retain their default values specified in the record definition.

Records are just syntactic sugar; under the covers, they are implemented as tuples. We can see this by calling the inet:gethostbyname/1 function in the Erlang shell:

```
1> inet:gethostbyname("oreilly.com").
{ok,{hostent,"oreilly.com",[],inet,4,
             [{208,201,239,101},{208,201,239,100}]}}
2> rr(inet).
[connect_opts,hostent,listen_opts,...]
3> inet:gethostbyname("oreilly.com").
{ok,#hostent{h_name = "oreilly.com",h_aliases = [],
             h_addrtype = inet,h_length = 4,
             h_addr_list = [{208,201,239,101},{208,201,239,100}]}}
```

In shell command 1, we call gethostbyname/1 to retrieve address information for the host *oreilly.com*. The second element of the result tuple is a hostent record, but the shell displays it as a plain tuple where the first element is the record name and the rest of the elements are the fields of the record in declaration order. Note that the names of the record fields are not part of the actual record instance. To have the record instance be displayed as a record instead of a tuple, we need to inform the shell of the record definition. We do that in shell command 2 using the rr shell command, which reads record definitions from its argument and returns a list of the definitions read (we abbreviated the returned list in this example by replacing most of it with an ellipsis). The argument passed to the rr command can either be a module name, the name of a source or include file, or a wildcarded name as specified for the filelib:wildcard/1,2 functions. In shell command 3, we again fetch address information for *oreilly.com*, but this time the shell prints the returned `hostent` value in record format, with field names included.

Correct Record Versions

You need to be extremely careful in dealing with all versions of records once you've changed their definition. You might forget to compile a module using the record (or compile it with the wrong version), load the wrong specification in the shell, or send it to a process running code that has not been upgraded. Doing so will in the best case throw an exception when trying to access or manipulate a field that does not exist, and in the worse case silently assign or return the value of a different field.

Maps

A map in Erlang is a key-value collection type that resembles the dictionary and hash types found in other programming languages. Maps differ from records in several ways: map is a built-in type, the number of its fields or key-value pairs is not fixed at compile time, and its keys can be any Erlang term rather than just atoms. While some have touted maps as a replacement for records, in practice they each fulfill different needs and both are useful. Records are fast, so use them when you have a fixed number of fields known at compile time, while maps should be used when you have a need to add fields at runtime.

Creating and manipulating a map is straightforward, as shown here:

```
1> EmptyMap = #{}.
#{}
2> erlang:map_size(EmptyMap).
0
3> RelDates = #{ "R15B03-1" => {2012, 11, 28}, "R16B03" => {2013, 12, 11} }.
#{"R15B03-1" => {2012,11,28},"R16B03" => {2013,12,11}}
4> RelDates2 = RelDates#{ "17.0" => {2014, 4, 2}}.
#{"17.0" => {2014,4,2},
  "R15B03-1" => {2012,11,28},
  "R16B03" => {2013,12,11}}
5> RelDates3 = RelDates2#{"17.0" := {2014, 4, 9}}.
#{"17.0" => {2014,4,9},
  "R15B03-1" => {2012,11,28},
  "R16B03" => {2013,12,11}}
6> #{ "R15B03-1" := Date } = RelDates3.
#{"17.0" => {2014,4,2},
  "R15B03-1" => {2012,11,28},
  "R16B03" => {2013,12,11}}
7> Date.
{2012,11,28}
```

In shell command 1, we bind the empty map #{} to the variable EmptyMap, and then we check its size in shell command 2 using the erlang:map_size/1 function. As expected, its size is 0 since it contains no key-value pairs. In shell command 3, we create a map with multiple entries, where each key is the name of an Erlang/OTP release paired with a value denoting its release date, using the => map association operator. Shell command 4 takes the existing RelDates map and adds a new key-value pair to create a new map, RelDates2. Unfortunately, the date we set in shell command 4 is off by one week and we need to change it; shell command 5 shows how we use the := map set-value operator to update the release date. Unlike the => operator, the := operator ensures that the key being updated already exists in the map, thereby preventing errors where the developer misspells the key and accidentally creates a new key-value pair instead of updating an existing key. Finally, shell command 6 shows how using a map in a pattern match allows us to capture the release date associated with the key "R15B03-1" into the variable Date, the value of which is accessed in shell command 7. Note that using the := set-value operator is required for map pattern matching.

Macros

Erlang has a macro facility, implemented by the Erlang preprocessor (*epp*), which is invoked prior to compilation of source code into BEAM code. Macros can be constants, as in:

```
-define(ANSWER,42).
-define(DOUBLE,2*).
```

or take parameters, as in:

```
-define(TWICE(F,X),F(F(X))).
```

As you can see from the definition of DOUBLE, it is conventional (but only conventional) to use uppercase names. The definition can be any legal sequence of Erlang tokens; it doesn't have to be a meaningful expression in its own right.

Macros are invoked by preceding them with a ? character, as in:

```
test() -> ?TWICE(?DOUBLE,?ANSWER)
```

It is possible to see the effect of macro definitions by compiling with the 'P' flag in the shell:

```
c(<filename>,['P']),
```

which creates a *filename.P* file in which the previous definition of test/0 becomes:

```
test() -> 2 * (2 * 42).
```

It is also possible for a macro call to record the text of its parameters. For example, if we define:

```
-define(Assign(Var,Exp), Var=Exp,
        io:format("~s = ~s -> ~p~n",[??Var,??Exp,Var]) ).
```

then `?Assign(Var,Exp)` has the effect of performing the assignment `Var = Exp`, but also, as a side effect, prints out a diagnostic message. For example:

```
test_assign() -> ?Assign(X, lists:sum([1,2,3])).
```

behaves like this:

```
1> macros:test_assign().
X = lists : sum ( [ 1 , 2 , 3 ] ) -> 6
ok
```

Using flags, you can define conditional macros, such as:

```
-ifdef(debug).
  -define(Assign(Var,Exp), Var=Exp,
          io:format("~s = ~s -> ~p~n",[??Var,??Exp,Var]) ).
-else.
  -define(Assign(Var,Exp), Var=Exp).
-endif.
```

Now, if you use the compiler flags `{d,debug}` to set the debug flag, `?Assign(Var,Exp)` will perform the assignment and print out the diagnostic code. Conversely, leaving the debug flag unset by default or clearing it through `{u,debug}` will cause the program to do the assignment without executing the io expression.

Upgrading Modules

One of the advantages of dynamic typing is the ability to upgrade your code during runtime, without the need to take down the system. One second, you are running a buggy version of a module, but you can load a fix without terminating the process and it starts running the fixed version, retaining its state and variables (Figure 2-4). This works not only for bugs, but also for upgrades and new features. This is a crucial property for a system that needs to guarantee "five-nines availability"—i.e., 99.999% uptime including upgrades and maintenance.

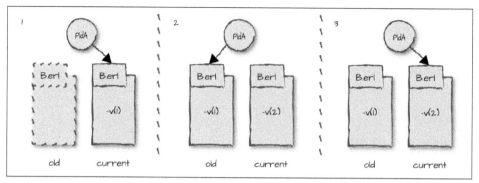

Figure 2-4. A software upgrade

At any one time, two versions of a module may exist in the virtual machine: the *old* and *current* versions. Frame 1 in Figure 2-4 shows PidA executing in the current version of module B. In Frame 2, new code for the module B is loaded, either by compiling the module in the shell or by explicitly loading it. After you load the module, PidA is still linked to the same version of B, which has now become the old version. But the next time PidA makes a fully qualified call to a function in module B, a check will be made to ensure that PidA is running the latest version of the code. (If you recall from earlier in this chapter, a fully qualified call is one where the module name is prefixed to the function name.) If the process is not running the latest version, the pointer to the code will be switched to the new current version, as shown in Frame 3. This applies to *all* functions in B, not just the function whose call triggered the switch. While this is the essence of a software upgrade, let's go through the fine print to make sure you understand all the details:

- Suppose that the code for the loop of a running process is itself upgraded. The effect depends on the form of the function call. If the function call is *fully qualified*—i.e., of the form B:loop()—the next call will use the upgraded code; otherwise (when the call is simply loop()), the process will continue to run the old code.

- The system holds only two versions of the code, so suppose that process p is still executing *v(1)* of module B, and another two new versions *v(2)* and *v(3)* are loaded: since only two versions may be present, the earliest version *v(1)* will be *purged,* and any process (such as p) looping in that version of the module will be unconditionally terminated.

- New code can be loaded in a number of ways. Compiling the module will cause code to be reloaded; this can be initiated in the shell by c(Module) or by calling the Erlang function compile:file(Module). Code can also be loaded explicitly in the shell by l(Module) or by a call to code:load_file(Module). In general, code is loaded by calling a function in a module that is not already loaded. This causes the compiled code, a *.beam* file, to be loaded, and for that to happen the code has to have been already compiled, perhaps using the *erlc* command-line tool. Note that recompiling a module with *erlc* does not cause it to be reloaded.

- While old code is purged when a new version is loaded, it is possible to call `code:purge(Module)` explicitly to purge an old version (without loading a new version). This has the effect of terminating all processes running the old code before removing the code. The call returns `true` if any processes were indeed terminated, and `false` if none were. Calling `code:soft_purge(Module)` will remove the code only if no processes were running it: the result is `true` in that case and `false` otherwise.

ETS: Erlang Term Storage

While lists are an important data type, they need to be linearly traversed and, as a result, will not scale. If you need a key-value store where the lookup time is constant, or the ability to traverse your keys in lexicographical order, Erlang Term Storage (ETS) tables come in handy. An ETS table is a collection of Erlang tuples, keyed on a particular position in the tuple.

ETS tables come in four different kinds:

Set
Each key-value tuple can occur only once.

Bag
Each key-value tuple combination can only occur once, but a key can appear multiple times.

Duplicate bag
Tuples can be duplicated.

Ordered set
These have the same restriction as sets, but the tuples can be visited in order by key.

Access time to a particular element is in constant time, except for ordered sets, where access time is proportional to the logarithm of the size of the table ($O(\log n)$ time).

Depending on the options passed in at table creation (`ets:new`), tables have one of the following traits:

`public`
Accessible to all processes.

private
    Accessible to the owning process only.

protected
    All processes can read the table, but only the owner can write to it.

Tables can also have their key position specified at creation time ({keypos,N}). This is mainly useful when storing records, as it allows the developer to specify a particular field of the record as the key. The default key position is 1.

Normally, programs access tables through the table ID returned by the call to new, but tables can also be named when created, which makes them accessible by name.

A table is linked to the process that creates it, and is deleted when that process terminates. ETS tables are in-memory only, but long-lived tables are provided by DETS tables, which are stored on disk (hence the "D").

Elementary table operations are shown in the following interaction:

```
1> TabId = ets:new(tab,[named_table]).
tab
2> ets:insert(tab,{haskell, lazy}).
true
3> ets:lookup(tab,haskell).
[{haskell,lazy}]
4> ets:insert(tab,{haskell, ghci}).
true
5> ets:lookup(tab,haskell).
[{haskell,ghci}]
6> ets:lookup(tab,racket).
[]
```

As can be seen, the default ETS table is a set, so that the insertion at line 4 overwrites the insertion at line 2, and the table is keyed at the first position. Note also that looking up a key returns a list of all the tuples matching the key.

Tables can be traversed, as seen here:

```
7> ets:insert(tab,{racket,strict}).
true
8> ets:insert(tab,{ocaml,strict}).
true
9> ets:first(tab).
racket
10> ets:next(tab,racket).
haskell
```

Since tab is a set ETS, the elements are not ordered by key; instead, their ordering is determined by a hash value internal to the table implementation. In the example here, the first key is racket and the next is haskell. However, using first and next on an ordered set will give traversal in order by key. It is also possible to extract bulk information using the match function:

```
11> ets:match(tab,{'$1','$0'}).
[[strict,ocaml],[ghci,haskell],[strict,racket]]
12> ets:match(tab,{'$1','_'}).
[[ocaml],[haskell],[racket]]
13> ets:match(tab,{'$1',strict}).
[[ocaml],[racket]]
```

The second argument, which is a symbolic tuple, is matched against the tuples in the ETS table. The result is a list of lists, with each list giving the values matched to the named variables '$0' etc., in ascending order; these variables match any value in the tuple. The wildcard value '_' also matches any value, but its argument is not reported in the result.

Let's implement code that uses an ETS table to associate phone numbers—or more accurately, mobile subscriber integrated services digital network (MSISDN) numbers —to pids in a module called hlr. We create the associations when phones attach themselves to the network and delete them when they detach. We then allow users to look up the pid associated with a particular phone number as well as the number associated with a pid. Read through this code, as we use it as part of a larger example in later chapters:

```
-module(hlr).
-export([new/0, attach/1, detach/0, lookup_id/1, lookup_ms/1]).

new() ->
    ets:new(msisdn2pid, [public, named_table]),
    ets:new(pid2msisdn, [public, named_table]),
    ok.

attach(Ms) ->
    ets:insert(msisdn2pid, {Ms, self()}),
    ets:insert(pid2msisdn, {self(), Ms}).

detach() ->
    case ets:lookup(pid2msisdn, self()) of
        [{Pid, Ms}] ->
            ets:delete(pid2msisdn, Pid),
            ets:delete(msisdn2pid, Ms);
        [] ->
            ok
    end.

lookup_id(Ms) ->
    case ets:lookup(msisdn2pid, Ms) of
        [] -> {error, invalid};
        [{Ms, Pid}] -> {ok, Pid}
    end.
```

```
lookup_ms(Pid) ->
    case ets:lookup(pid2msisdn, Pid) of
        [] -> {error, invalid};
        [{Pid, Ms}] -> {ok, Ms}
    end.
```

In our test run of the module, the shell process attaches itself to the network using the number 12345. We look up the mobile handset using both the number and the pid, after which we detach. When reading the code, note that we are using a named public table, meaning any process can read and write to it as long as they know the table name:

```
2> hlr:new().
ok
3> hlr:attach(12345).
true
4> hlr:lookup_ms(self()).
{ok,12345}
5> hlr:lookup_id(12345).
{ok,<0.32.0>}
6> hlr:detach().
true
7> hlr:lookup_id(12345).
{error,invalid}
```

Distributed Erlang

All of the examples we have looked at so far execute on a single virtual machine, also referred to as a node. Erlang has built-in semantics allowing programs to run across multiple nodes: processes can transparently spawn processes on other nodes and communicate with them using message passing. Distributed nodes can reside either on the same physical or virtual host or on different ones.

This programming model is designed to support scaling and fault tolerance on systems running behind firewalls over trusted networks. Out of the box, Erlang distribution is *not* designed to support systems operating across potentially hostile environments such as the Internet or shared cloud instances. Because different systems have different requirements on security, no one size fits all. Varying security requirements can easily (or not so easily) be addressed if you provide your own security layers and authentication mechanisms, or by modifying Erlang's networking and security libraries.

Naming and Communication

In order for an Erlang node to be part of a distributed Erlang system, it needs to be given a name. A short name is given by starting Erlang with `erl -sname node`, identifying the node on a local network using the hostname. On the other hand, starting a node with the -name flag means that it will be given a long name and identified by the fully qualified domain name or IP address. In a particular distributed system, all nodes must be of the same kind, i.e., all short or all long.

Processes on distributed nodes are identified in precisely the same way as local nodes, using their pids. This allows constructs such as Pid!Msg to send messages to a process running on any node in the cluster. On the other hand, registering a process with an alias is local to each host, so {bar,'foo@myhost'}!Msg is used to send the message Msg to the process named bar on the node 'foo@myhost'. Note the form of this node *identifier*: it is a combination of foo (the name of the node) and myhost (the short or local network name of the host on which the node foo is running).

You can spawn and link to processes on any node in the system, not just locally, using link(Pid), spawn(Node, Mod, Fun, Args), and spawn_link. If the call is successful, link will return the atom true, while spawn returns the pid of the process on the remote host.

 Code is not automatically deployed remotely for you! If you spawn a process remotely, it is your responsibility to ensure that the compiled code for the spawned process is already available on the remote host, and that it is placed in the search path for the node on that host.

Node Connections and Visibility

In order to communicate, Erlang nodes must share a secret cookie. By default, each node has a randomly generated cookie, unless there is already a value stored in the *.erlang.cookie* file in your home directory. If this file does not exist, it is created the first time you start a distributed Erlang node, and populated with a random sequence of characters. This behavior can be overridden by starting the node with the -setcookie Cookie flag, where *Cookie* is the cookie value. Cookie values can also be changed within a program by calling erlang:set_cookie(Node, Cookie).

In an Erlang distributed system, by default, all nodes know about and can interact with all others so long as they share a cookie. However, starting a node with the -hidden flag leaves it unconnected to anything initially, and any connections that it needs to make have to be set up by hand. The net_kernel module allows fine-grained control of this and other aspects of interconnections. Hidden nodes can have a variety of uses, including operations and maintenance, as well as serving as bridges between different node clusters.

Messages between two processes on different nodes are guaranteed to be delivered in order: the difference in a distributed system is that it is possible for a remote node to go down. A general mechanism for dealing with this is to monitor whether or not the remote node is alive. This is different from monitoring a local process, described in "Monitors" on page 37. Here's an example:

```
monitor_node(Node, true),
{serve, Node} ! {self(), Msg},
receive
    {ok, Resp} ->
        monitor_node(Node, false),
        <handle process response>;  % Pseudocode to handle the process response
    {nodedown, Node} ->
        <handle lack of response>   % Pseudocode to handle lack of response
end.
```

In this fragment, a message—such as a remote procedure call—is sent to the serve process on Node. Before sending the request, Node is monitored, so that if the node goes down, a {nodedown, Node} message will be received, and the lack of response can be handled. Once a response (Resp) is successfully received, the code switches off monitoring before processing the response. You can also use the monitor_node/2,3 BIFs to get notifications of the health of remote nodes.

To test distributed communications, start two distributed Erlang nodes using different names, but the same cookie:

```
erl -sname foo -setcookie abc
erl -sname bar -setcookie abc
```

In the following sequence, shell command 1 pings the remote node, creating a connection. Shell command 2 looks up all of the connected nodes using the nodes() BIF, binding the remote node to the variable Node. Shell command 4 spawns a process on the remote node, which sends the shell process on our local node its pid. We receive that pid in command 5 and inspect its node of origin in command 6 using the node/1 BIF. Shell command 7 spawns a process on a remote node, sending the node identifier back to the local node. Note how node names are atoms, and thus are defined within single quotes:

```
$ erl -sname bar -setcookie abc
Erlang/OTP 18 [erts-7.2] [smp:8:8] [async-threads:10] [kernel-poll:false]

Eshell V7.2  (abort with ^G)
(bar@macbook-pro-2)1> net_adm:ping('foo@macbook-pro-2').
pong
(bar@macbook-pro-2)2> [Node] = nodes().
['foo@macbook-pro-2']
(bar@macbook-pro-2)3> Shell = self().
<0.38.0>
(bar@macbook-pro-2)4> spawn(Node, fun() -> Shell ! self() end).
<5985.46.0>
(bar@macbook-pro-2)5> receive Pid -> Pid end.
<5985.46.0>
(bar@macbook-pro-2)6> node(Pid).
```

```
'foo@macbook-pro-2'
(bar@macbook-pro-2)7> spawn(Node, fun() -> Shell ! node() end).
<5985.47.0>
(bar@macbook-pro-2)8> flush().
Shell got 'foo@macbook-pro-2'
ok
```

Summing Up

In this chapter, we've given an overview of the basics of Erlang we believe are important for understanding the examples in the remainder of the book. The concurrency
model, error-handling semantics, and distributed processing not only make Erlang a
powerful tool, but are the foundation of OTP's design. Module upgrades during runtime is just the icing on the cake. Before you progress, be warned that the better you
understand the internals of Erlang, the more you are going to get out of the OTP
design principles and this book. We provide many more examples written in pure
Erlang, which for some might be enough to understand the OTP rationale. Try moving ahead, but if you find yourself struggling, we suggest reading *Erlang Programming*, published by O'Reilly and coauthored by one of the authors of this book. The
current book can be seen as a continuation of *Erlang Programming*, expanding many
of the original examples from that book. Other great titles that will also do the trick
include Simon St. Laurent's *Introducing Erlang*, also published by O'Reilly; Fred
Hébert's *Learn You Some Erlang for Great Good!* from No Starch Press (and also
available online free of charge); and *Programming Erlang*, written by Erlang coinventor Joe Armstrong and published by The Pragmatic Bookshelf.

What's Next?

In the upcoming chapters, we introduce process design patterns and OTP behaviors.
We start by providing an Erlang example of a client-server application, breaking it up
into generic and specific parts. The generic parts are those that can be reused from
one client-server application to another and are packaged in library modules. The
specific parts are those that are project-specific and have to be implemented for the
individual client-server applications. In Chapter 4, we migrate the code to an OTP-
based generic server behavior, introducing the first building block of Erlang-based
systems. As more behaviors are introduced in the subsequent chapters, it will become
clear how Erlang systems are architected and glued together.

## CHAPTER 3

Behaviors

As a prelude to learning how to structure our process supervision trees and architect our concurrency models, let's spend some time understanding the underlying principles behind behaviors. Instead of diving straight into the world of interface functions and callbacks, we explain what goes on behind the scenes, ensuring you use OTP behaviors efficiently and understand their benefits and advantages. So, what are they?

Erlang processes that solve radically different tasks follow similar design patterns. The most commonly used patterns have been abstracted and implemented in a set of generic library modules called the OTP behaviors. When reading about behaviors, you should see them as a formalization of process design patterns.

Although the strict concept of design patterns used in object-oriented programming hasn't been applied to Erlang, OTP provides a powerful, reusable solution for concurrent processes that hides and abstracts away all of the tricky aspects and borderline conditions. It ensures that projects do not have to reinvent the wheel, while maximizing reusability and maintainability through a solid, well-tested, generic, and reusable code base. These behaviors are, in "design pattern speak," implementation libraries of the concurrency models.

Process Skeletons

If you try to picture an Erlang process managing a key-value store and a process responsible for managing the window of a complex GUI system, they might at first glance appear very different in functionality and to have very little in common. That is often not the case, though, as both processes will share a common lifecycle. Both will:

- Be spawned and initialized
- Repeatedly receive messages, handle them, and send replies
- Be terminated (normally or abnormally)

Processes, irrespective of their purpose, have to be spawned. Once spawned, they will initialize their state. The state will be specific to what that particular process does. In the case of a window manager, it might draw the window and display its contents. In the case of a key-value store, it might create the empty table and fill it with data stored in backup files or populate it using other tables spread across a distributed cluster of nodes.

Once the process has been initialized, it is ready to receive events. These events could, in the case of the window manager, be keystrokes in the window entry boxes, button clicks, or menu item selections. They could also be dragging and dropping of widgets, effectively moving the window or objects within it. Events would be programmed as Erlang messages. Upon receiving a particular message, the process would handle the request accordingly, evaluating the content and updating its internal state. Keystrokes would be displayed and clicking buttons or choosing menu items would result in window updates, while dragging and dropping would result in objects being moved across the screen. A similar analogy could be given for the key-value store. Asynchronous messages could be sent to insert and delete elements in the tables, and synchronous messages—messages that wait for a reply from the receiver—could be used to look up elements and return their values to the client.

Finally, processes will terminate. A user might have picked the *Close* entry in the menus or clicked on the *Destroy* button. If that happens in the window manager, resources allocated to that window have to be released and the window hidden or shut down. Once the cleanup procedure is completed, there will be no more code for the process to execute, so it should terminate normally. In the case of the key-value store, a `stop` message might have been sent to the process, resulting in the table being backed up on another node or saved on a persistent medium.

Abnormal termination of the process might also occur, as a result of a trapped exception or an exit signal from one of the processes in the link set. Where possible, if caught through a `trap_exit` flag or a `try-catch` expression, the exception should prompt the process to call the same set of commands that would have been called as a result of a normal termination. We say "where possible," as the power cord of the computer might have been pulled out, the hard drive might have failed, the administrator might have tripped over the network cable, or the process might have been terminated unconditionally through an exit signal with the reason `kill`.

Figure 3-1 shows a typical process flow diagram outlining the lifecycle of a process.

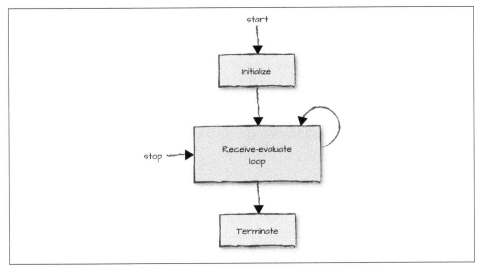

Figure 3-1. The process skeleton

As we've described, even if processes perform different tasks, they will perform these tasks in a similar way, following particular patterns. As a result of following these patterns, processes share a similar code base. A typical Erlang process loop, which has to be started, must handle events, and is finally terminated, might look like this:

```
start(Args) ->                      % Start the server.
    spawn(server, init, [Args]).

init(Args) ->                       % Initialize the internal process state.
    State = initialize_state(Args),
    loop(State).

loop(State) ->                      % Receive and handle messages.
    receive
        {handle, Msg} ->
            NewState = handle(Msg, State),
            loop(NewState);
        stop ->
            terminate(State)        % Stop the process.
    end.

terminate(State) ->                 % Clean up prior to termination.
    clean_up(State).
```

This pattern is typical of a client-server behavior. The server is started, then it receives requests in the handle/2 function, where necessary sends replies, changes the state, and loops ready to handle the next incoming message. Upon receiving a stop message, the process terminates after having cleaned up its resources.

Although we say that this is typical Erlang client-server behavior, it is in fact the pattern behind all patterns. It is so common that even code written without the OTP behavior libraries tends to use the same function names. This allows anyone reading the code to know that the process state is initialized in init/1, that messages are received in loop/1 and individually handled in the handle/2 call, and finally, that any cleaning up of resources is managed in the terminate/1 function. Someone trying to maintain the code later will understand the basic behavior without needing any knowledge of the communication protocol, underlying architecture, or process structure.

Design Patterns

Let's start drilling down into a more detailed example, focusing on client-server architectures implemented in Erlang. Clients and servers are represented as Erlang processes, with their requests and replies sent as messages. Have a look at Figure 3-2 and think of examples of client-server architectures that you have worked with or read about, preferably architectures with few similarities among them (as in our examples of a key-value store and a window manager). Focusing on Erlang constructs and patterns in the code of these applications, try to list the similarities and differences between the implementations. Ask yourself which parts of the code are generic and which parts are specific. What code is unique to that particular solution, and what code could be reused in other client-server applications?

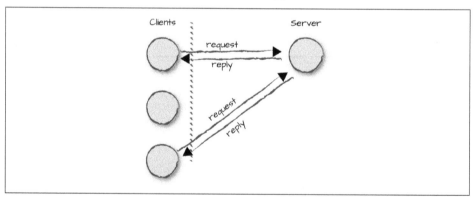

Figure 3-2. The client-server process architecture

Let's give you a hint in the right direction: sending a client request to a server will be generic. It can be done in a uniform manner across any client-server architecture, irrespective of what the server does. What will be specific, however, are the contents of that message.

We start off by spawning a server. Creating a process that calls the init/1 function is generic. What is specific are the arguments passed to the call and the expressions in the function that initialize the process state returning the loop data. The loop data plays the role of a variable that stores process data between calls.

Storing the loop data in between calls will be the same from one process to another, but the loop data itself will be specific. It changes not only according to the particular task the process might execute, but for each particular instance of the task.

Sending a request to the server will be generic, as is the client-server protocol used to manage replies. What is specific are the types and contents of the requests sent to the server, how they are handled, and the responses sent back to the client. While the response is specific, sending it back to the client process is handled generically.

It should be possible to stop servers. While sending a `stop` message or handling an exception or `EXIT` signal is generic, the functions called to clean up the state prior to termination will be specific.

Table 3-1 summarizes which parts of a client-server architecture are generic and which parts are specific.

Table 3-1. Client-server generic and specific code

Generic	Specific
• Spawning the server	• Initializing the server state
• Storing the loop data	• The loop data
• Sending requests to the server	• The client requests
• Sending replies to the client	• Handling client requests
• Receiving server replies	• Contents of server reply
• Stopping the server	• Cleaning up

Callback Modules

The idea behind OTP behaviors is to split up the code into two modules: one for the generic pattern, referred to as the *behavior module*, and one for specifics, referred to as the *callback module* (Figure 3-3). The generic behavior module can be seen as the driver. While it doesn't know anything about what the callback module does, it is aware of a set of exported callback functions it has to invoke and the format of their return values. The callback module isn't aware of what the generic module does either; it only complies with the format of the data it has to return when its callback functions are invoked.

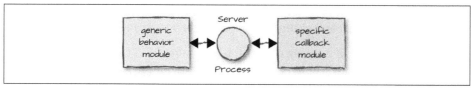

Figure 3-3. The callback module

Another way of explaining this is as a contract between the behavior and callback modules. They have to agree on a set of names and types for the functions in the callback API and respect the return values.

The behavior module contains all of the generic functionality reused from one implementation to another. Behaviors are provided by OTP as library modules. The callback module is implemented by the application developer. It contains all of the specific code for the implementation of that particular process.

OTP provides five behaviors that cover the majority of all cases. They are:

Generic server
> Used to model client-server behaviors

Generic finite state machine
> Used for FSM programming

Generic event handler/manager
> Used for writing event handlers

Supervisor
> Used for fault-tolerant supervision trees

Application
> Used to encapsulate resources and functionality

Generic servers are the most commonly used behavior. They are used to model processes using the client-server architecture, including the examples of the key-value store and the window manager we've already discussed.

Generic FSM behaviors provide all of the generic constructs needed when working with FSMs. Developers commonly use FSMs to implement automated control systems, protocol stacks, and decision-making systems. The code for the FSMs can be implemented manually or generated by another program.

Generic event handlers and managers are used for event-driven programming, where events are received as messages and one or more actions (called handlers) are applied to them. Typical examples of handler functionality include logging, metrics gathering, and alarming.

You can view handlers as a publish-subscribe communication layer, where publishers are processes sending events of a specific type and subscribers are consumers who do something with the events.

A supervisor is a behavior whose only tasks are to start, stop, and monitor its children, which can be workers as well as other supervisors. Allowing supervisors to monitor other supervisors results in process structures we call *supervision trees*. We cover supervision trees in the upcoming chapters. Supervisors restart children based on configuration parameters defined in the callback functions.

Supervision trees are packaged in a behavior we call an *application*. The application starts the top-level supervisor, encapsulating processes that depend on each other into the main building blocks of an Erlang node.

Generic servers, FSMs, and event handlers are examples of workers: processes that perform the bulk of the computations. They are held together by supervisors and application behaviors. If you need other behaviors not included as part of the standard library, you can implement them following a set of specific rules and directives explained in Chapter 10. We call them special processes.

Now you might be wondering: what is the point of adding a layer of complexity to our software? The reasons are many. Using behaviors, we are reducing the code base while creating a standardized programming style needed when developing software in the large. By encapsulating all of the generic design patterns in library modules, we reuse code while reducing the development effort. The behavior libraries we use consist of a solid, well-tested base that has been used in production systems since the mid-90s. They cover all the tricky aspects of concurrency, hiding them from the programmer. As a result, the final system will have fewer bugs[1] while being built on a fault-tolerant base. The behaviors have built-in functionality such as logs, tracing, and statistics, and are extensible in a generic way across all processes using that behavior.

Another important advantage of using behaviors is that they promote a common programming style. Anyone reading the code in a callback module will immediately know that the process state is initialized in the init function, and that terminate contains the cleanup code executed whenever the process is stopped. They will know how the communication protocol will work, how processes are restarted in case of failure, and how supervision trees are packaged. Especially when programming in the large, this approach allows anyone reading the code to focus on the project specifics while using their existing knowledge of the generics. This common programming

---

1 Bug-free systems exist only in the dreams of the bureaucrats. When using Erlang/OTP, equal focus should be placed on correctness and error recovery, as the bugs will manifest themselves in production systems whether you like it or not.

style also brings a component-based terminology to the table, giving potentially distributed teams a way to package their deliverables and use a standard vocabulary to communicate with each other. At the end of the day, much more time is spent reading and maintaining code than writing it. Making code easy to understand is imperative when dealing with complex systems that never fail.

So, with lots of advantages, what are the disadvantages? Learning to use behaviors properly and proficiently can be difficult. It takes time to learn how to properly create systems using OTP design principles, but as documentation has improved, training courses and books have become available, and tools have been written, this has become less of an issue. Just the fact that you are reading a book dedicated largely to OTP says it all.

Behaviors add a few layers to the call chain, and slightly more data will be sent with every message and reply. While this might affect performance and memory usage, in most cases the impact will be negligible, especially considering the improvement in quality and free functionality. What is the point of writing code that is fast but buggy? The small increase in memory usage and reduction in performance is a small price to pay for reliability and fault tolerance. The rule of thumb is to always start with behaviors, and optimize when bottlenecks occur. You will find that optimizations as a result of inefficient behavior code are rarely if ever needed.

Extracting Generic Behaviors

Having introduced behaviors, let's look at a familiar client-server example written in pure Erlang without using behaviors. We use the frequency server featured in the *Erlang Programming* book and implemented in the frequency module. No worries if you have not read the book and are not familiar with it; we explain what it does as we go along. The server is a frequency allocator for cell phones. When a phone connects a call, it needs to have a frequency allocated for it to use as a communication channel for that conversation. The client holds this frequency until the call is terminated, after which the frequency is deallocated, allowing other subscribers to reuse it (Figure 3-4).

As this is the first major Erlang example in the book, we step through it in more detail than usual. In the subsequent chapters, we speed up the pace, so if your Erlang is a bit rusty, take this opportunity to get up to speed. Here, we take the code from the frequency server example, find the generic parts embedded in the module, and extract them into a library module. The outcome will be two modules: one containing generic reusable code, the other containing specific code with the frequency server's business logic.

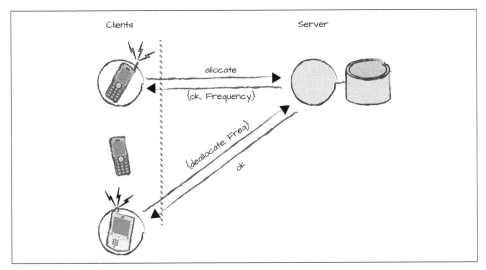

Figure 3-4. The frequency server

The clients and server are represented as Erlang processes, and the exchange of information between them occurs via message passing hidden behind a functional interface. The functional interface used by the clients contains the functions `allocate/0` and `deallocate/1`:

```
allocate() -> {ok, Frequency} | {error, no_frequency}
deallocate(Frequency) -> ok
```

The `allocate/0` function returns the result `{ok, Frequency}` if there is at least one available frequency. If all frequencies are in use, the tuple `{error, no_frequency}` is returned instead. When the client is done with a phone call, it can release the frequency it's using by making a function call to `deallocate/1`, passing the `Frequency` in use as an argument.

We start the server with the `start/0` call, later terminating it with `stop/0`:

```
start()-> true
stop() -> ok
```

The server is registered statically with the alias `frequency`, so no pids need to be saved and used for message passing.

A trial run of the `frequency` module from the shell might look like this. We start the server, allocate all six available frequencies, and fail to allocate a seventh one. Only by deallocating frequency 11 are we then able to allocate a new one. We terminate the trial run by stopping the server:

```
1> frequency:start().
true
2> frequency:allocate(), frequency:allocate(), frequency:allocate(),
```

```
      frequency:allocate(),frequency:allocate(), frequency:allocate().
{ok,15}
3> frequency:allocate().
{error,no_frequency}
4> frequency:deallocate(11).
ok
5> frequency:allocate().
{ok,11}
6> frequency:stop().
ok
```

If you need a deeper understanding of the code, feel free to download the module from the book's code repository and run the example. Next, we go through the code in detail, explain what it does, and separate out the generic and the specific parts.

Starting the Server

Let's begin with the functions used to create and initialize the server. The start/0 function spawns a process that calls the frequency:init/0 function, registering it with the frequency alias. The init function initializes the process state with a tuple containing the list of available frequencies, conveniently hardcoded in the get_frequencies/0 function, and the list of allocated frequencies, represented by the empty list. We bind the frequency tuple, referred to in the rest of the example as the *process state* or *loop data*, to the Frequencies variable. The process state variable changes with every iteration of the loop when available frequencies are moved between the lists of allocated and available ones.

Note how we export the init/0 function, because it is passed as an argument to the spawn BIF, and how we register the server process with the same name as the module. The latter, while not mandatory, is considered a good Erlang programming practice as it facilitates debugging and troubleshooting live systems:

```
-module(frequency).
-export([start/0, stop/0, allocate/0, deallocate/1]).
-export([init/0]).

start() -> register(frequency, spawn(frequency, init, [])).

init() ->
    Frequencies = {get_frequencies(), []},
    loop(Frequencies).

get_frequencies() -> [10,11,12,13,14,15].
```

Have a look at the preceding code and try to spot the generic expressions. Which expressions will not change from one client-server implementation to another?

Starting with the export directives, you always have to start and stop servers, irrespective of what they do. So, we consider these functions to be generic. Also generic are the spawning, registering, and calling of an initialization function containing the expressions used to initialize the process state. The process state will be bound to a variable and passed to the process loop. Note, however, that while the functions and BIFs might be considered generic, expressions in the functions and arguments passed to them aren't. They will differ between different client-server implementations. We've highlighted all the parts we consider generic in the following code example:

```erlang
-module(frequency).
-export([start/0, stop/0, allocate/0, deallocate/1]).
-export([init/0]).

start() ->
    register(frequency, spawn(frequency, init, [])).

init() ->
    Frequencies = {get_frequencies(), []},
    loop(Frequencies).

get_frequencies() -> [10,11,12,13,14,15].
```

From the generic, let's move on to the specific, which is the nonhighlighted code in the previous example. The first server-specific detail that stands out in the example is the module name `frequency`. Module names obviously differ from one server implementation to another. The client functions `allocate/0` and `deallocate/1` are also specific to this particular client-server application, as you will probably not find them in a window manager or a key-value store (and if they did happen to share the same name, the functions would be doing something completely different). Although starting the server, spawning the server process, and registering it are generic, the registered name and module containing the `init` function are considered specific.

The arguments passed to the `init` function are also specific. In our example, we are not passing any arguments (hence the arity 0), but that could change in other client-server implementations. The expressions in the `init/0` function are used to initialize the process state. Initializing the state is different from one implementation to another. Various applications might initialize window settings and display the window, create an empty key-value store, and upload a persistent backup, or, in this example, generate a tuple containing the list of available frequencies.

When the process state has been initialized, it is bound to a variable. Storing the process state is considered generic, but the contents of the state itself are specific. In the code example that follows, we highlight the `Frequency` variable as specific. This means that the content of the variable is specific, whereas the mechanism of passing it to the process loop is generic. Finally, the `get_frequencies/0` call used in `init/0` is also specific. In a real-world implementation, we would probably read the frequencies from a configuration file or a persistent database, or through a query to the base stations. For the sake of this example, we've been lazy and hardcoded them in the module.

Let's highlight the specific code:

```
-module(frequency).
-export([start/0, stop/0, allocate/0, deallocate/1]).
-export([init/0]).

start() ->
    register(frequency, spawn(frequency, init, [])).

init() ->
    Frequencies = {get_frequencies(), []},
    loop(Frequencies).

get_frequencies() -> [10,11,12,13,14,15].
```

Are you seeing the pattern and line of thought we are emphasizing? Let's continue doing the same with the rest of the module, starting with the client functions.

The Client Functions

We refer to the functions called by client processes to control and access the services of a server process as the *client API*. It is always good practice, for readability and maintainability, to hide message passing and protocol in a functional interface. The client functions in the running example do exactly this. In fact, we've taken it a step further here, encapsulating the sending of requests and receiving of replies in the call/1 and reply/2 functions. They contain code that otherwise would have to be cloned for every message sent and received:

```
stop()           -> call(stop).
allocate()       -> call(allocate).
deallocate(Freq) -> call({deallocate, Freq}).

call(Message) ->
    frequency ! {request, self(), Message},
    receive {reply, Reply} -> Reply end.

reply(Pid, Reply) ->
    Pid ! {reply, Reply}.
```

The stop/0 function sends the atom stop to the server. The server, upon receiving stop in its receive-evaluate loop, interprets it and takes appropriate action. For readability and maintainability reasons, it is good practice to use keywords that describe what we are trying to do, but for all it matters, we could have used the atom foobar, as it is not the name of the atom but the meaning we give it in our program that is important. In our case, stop ensures a normal termination of the process. We will see how it is handled later in the example.

The client functions `allocate/0` and `deallocate/1` are called and executed in the scope of the client process. The client sends a message to the server by executing one of the client functions in the `frequency` module. The message is passed as an argument to the `call/1` function and bound to the `Message` variable. The `Message` is in turn inserted in a tuple of the form {request, Pid, Message}, where the pid is the client process identifier, retrieved by calling the `self()` BIF and used by the server as the destination for a response in the format {reply, Reply}. We refer to this extra padding as the "protocol" between the client and the server (see Figure 3-5).

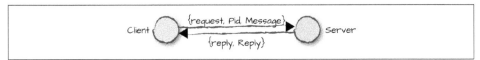

Figure 3-5. The message protocol

The server receives the request, handles it, and sends a reply using the `reply/2` call. It passes the pid sent in the client request as the first argument and its reply message as the second. This message is pattern matched in the `receive` clause of the `call/1` function, returning the contents of the variable `Reply` as a result. This will be the result returned by the client functions. A sequence diagram with the exchange of messages between the cell phones and the frequency server is shown in Figure 3-6.

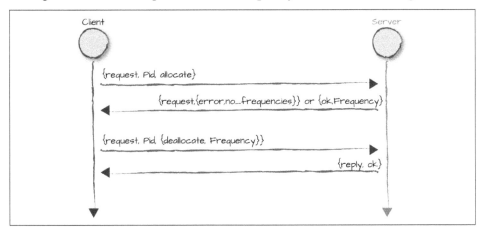

Figure 3-6. The frequency server messages

So, which parts of the code are generic? Which will not change from one client-server implementation to another? First in line is the `stop/0` function, used whenever we want to inform the server that it has to terminate. This code can be reused, as it is universal in what it does. Every time we want to send a message, we use `call/1`. There is a catch, however, as this function is not completely generic. Have a look at the code and try to spot the anomaly:

```
stop()           -> call(stop).
allocate()       -> call(allocate).
deallocate(Freq) -> call({deallocate, Freq}).

call(Message) ->
    frequency ! {request, self(), Message},
    receive
        {reply, Reply} -> Reply
    end.

reply(Pid, Reply) ->
    Pid ! {reply, Reply}.
```

We are sending a message to a registered process frequency. This name will change
from one server implementation to the next. However, everything else in the call is
generic. The function reply/2, called by the server process, is also completely
generic. So what remains specific in the client functions are the client functions
themselves, their message content to the server, and the name of the server:

```
stop()           -> call(stop).
allocate()       -> call(allocate).
deallocate(Freq) -> call({deallocate, Freq}).

call(Message) ->
    frequency ! {request, self(), Message},
    receive
        {reply, Reply} -> Reply
    end.

reply(Pid, Reply) ->
    Pid ! {reply, Reply}.
```

By hiding the message protocol in a functional interface and abstracting it, we are
able to change it without affecting the code outside of the frequency module, client
calls included. We show how this comes in handy later in the chapter, when we start
dealing with some of the common error patterns that occur when working with concurrent programming.

The Server Loop

Server processes iterate in a receive-evaluate loop. They wait for client requests, handle them, return a result, and loop again, waiting for the next message to arrive. With
every iteration, they may update their process state and might generate side effects:

```
loop(Frequencies) ->
    receive
        {request, Pid, allocate} ->
            {NewFrequencies, Reply} = allocate(Frequencies, Pid),
            reply(Pid, Reply),
            loop(NewFrequencies);
        {request, Pid , {deallocate, Freq}} ->
```

```
        NewFrequencies = deallocate(Frequencies, Freq),
        reply(Pid, ok),
        loop(NewFrequencies);
    {request, Pid, stop} ->
        reply(Pid, ok)
end.
```

In our frequency server example the `loop/1` function receives the `allocate`, `{deallocate, Frequency}`, and `stop` commands. Allocating a frequency is done through the helper function `allocate/2`, which, given the loop data and the pid of the client, moves a frequency from the available list to the allocated list. Deallocating a frequency invokes the `deallocate/2` call to do the opposite, moving the frequency from the list of allocated frequencies to the available list.

Both calls return the pair of updated frequency lists that make up the process state; this new state is bound to the variable `NewFrequencies` and passed to the tail-recursive `loop/1` call. In both cases, a reply is sent back to the clients. When allocating a frequency, the contents of the variable `Reply` are either `{error, no_frequency}` or `{ok, Frequency}`. When deallocating a frequency, the server sends back the atom ok.

When stopping the server, we acknowledge having received the message through the ok response, and by the lack of a call to `loop/1` we make the process terminate normally, as opposed to an abnormal termination that results from a runtime error. In this example, there is nothing to clean up, so we don't do anything other than acknowledge the `stop` message. Had this server handled some resource such as a key-value store, we could have ensured that the data was safely backed up on a persistent medium. Or in the case of a window server, we'd close the window and release any allocated objects associated with it.

With all of this in mind, what functionality do you think is generic?

For starters, looping is generic. The protocol used to send and receive messages is generic, but the messages and replies themselves aren't. Finally, stopping the server is generic, as is acknowledging the `stop` message. The generic parts of the code are highlighted here:

```
loop(Frequencies) ->
    receive
        {request, Pid, allocate} ->
            {NewFrequencies, Reply} = allocate(Frequencies, Pid),
            reply(Pid, Reply),
            loop(NewFrequencies);
        {request, Pid, {deallocate, Freq}} ->
            NewFrequencies = deallocate(Frequencies, Freq),
            reply(Pid, ok),
            loop(NewFrequencies);
        {request, Pid, stop} ->
```

```
            reply(Pid, ok)
    end.
```

We have not highlighted the variables Frequencies and NewFrequencies used to store the process state. Although storing the process state is generic, the state itself is specific. That is, the type of the state and the particular value that this variable has are specific, but not the generic task of storing the variable itself.

With the generic contents out of the way, the specifics include the loop data, the client messages, how we handle the messages, and the responses we send back as a result:

```
loop(Frequencies) ->
    receive
        {request, Pid, allocate} ->
            {NewFrequencies, Reply} = allocate(Frequencies, Pid),
            reply(Pid, Reply),
            loop(NewFrequencies);
        {request, Pid, {deallocate, Freq}} ->
            NewFrequencies = deallocate(Frequencies, Freq),
            reply(Pid, ok),
            loop(NewFrequencies);
        {request, Pid, stop} ->
            reply(Pid, ok)
    end.
```

Had there been specific code to be executed when stopping the server, it would also have been marked as specific. This code is usually placed in a function called terminate, which, given the reason for termination and the loop data, handles all of the cleaning up.

Functions Internal to the Server

The functions that actually perform the work of allocating or deallocating a frequency within the server are not "visible" outside the server module itself, and so we call them *internal* to the server. The allocate/1 call returns a tuple with the new frequencies and the reply to send back to the client. If there are no available frequencies, the first function clause will pattern match because the list is empty. The frequencies are not changed, and {error, no_frequency} is returned to the client. If there is at least one frequency, the second function clause will match.

The available frequency list is split into a head and a tail, where the head contains the available frequency, and the tail (a possibly empty list) contains the remaining available frequencies. The frequency with the client pid is added to the allocated list, and the response {ok, Freq} is sent back to the client.

When deallocating a frequency in the `deallocate/2` function, we delete it from the allocated list and add it to the available one. Have a look at the functions and try to figure out what is generic and what is specific:[2]

```
allocate({[], Allocated}, _Pid) ->
    {{[], Allocated}, {error, no_frequency}};
allocate({[Freq|Free], Allocated}, Pid) ->
    {{Free, [{Freq, Pid}|Allocated]}, {ok, Freq}}.

deallocate({Free, Allocated}, Freq) ->
    NewAllocated = lists:keydelete(Freq, 1, Allocated),
    {[Freq|Free], NewAllocated}.
```

This should have been an easy question to answer, as these internal functions are all specific to our frequency server. When did you last allocate and deallocate frequencies when working with a key-value store or a window manager?

The Generic Server

Now that we've gone through this example and distinguished the generic from the specific code, let's get to the core of this chapter, namely the separation of the code into two separate modules. Figure 3-7 shows we can now put all of the generic code into the `server` module and all of the specific code into `frequency`. Despite these changes, we maintain the same functionality and interface. Calling the `frequency` module in our new implementation should be no different from the trial run we did in "Extracting Generic Behaviors" on page 60.

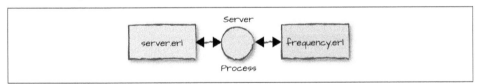

Figure 3-7. The frequency and server modules

The `server` module is in control, managing the process activities. Whenever it has to handle specific functionality it does not know how to execute, it hands over to the callback functions in the `frequency` module. Let's start with the generic code in the `server` module that starts and initializes the server:

```
-module(server).                          % server.erl
-export([start/2, stop/1, call/2]).
-export([init/2]).

start(Name, Args) ->
```

---

2 Warning, this is a trick question.

```
    register(Name, spawn(server, init, [Name, Args])).

init(Mod, Args) ->
    State = Mod:init(Args),
    loop(Mod, State).
```

Spawning a process, registering it, and calling the init function are all generic, whereas the alias with which we register the process, the name of the callback module, and the arguments we pass to the init function are all specific. We pass this specific information as parameters to the server:start/2 function, using them where needed. Name is used both as the registered name of the frequency process and as the name of the callback module. Args is passed to the init function and is used to initialize the process state.

We keep the client functions in the frequency module, using it as a wrapper around the server. By doing so, we are hiding implementation details, including the very use of the server module. Just like in our previous example, we start the server using frequency:start/0, resulting in a call to server:start/2. The newly spawned server, through the Mod:init/1 call, invokes the init/1 callback function in the frequency module, initializing the process state by creating the tuple containing the available and allocated frequencies. Mod is bound to the callback module frequency and Args is bound to []. The frequency tuple gets bound to the State variable, which along with Mod is passed as an argument to the loop in the server module:

```
-module(frequency).                        % frequency.erl
-export([start/0, stop/0, allocate/0, deallocate/1]).
-export([init/1, terminate/1, handle/2]).

start() -> server:start(frequency, []).

init(_Args) ->
    {get_frequencies(), []}.

get_frequencies() -> [10,11,12,13,14,15].
```

The init/1 callback is required to return the initial process state, stored and used in the server receive-evaluate loop. In the init/1 callback function, note that we are not using the value of the _Args parameter. Because init/1 is a callback function, we have to follow the required protocol and functional interface for that callback API. In the general case, init/1 requires an argument because there might be server implementations that need data at startup. This particular example doesn't, so we pass the empty list and ignore it.

Let's jump back to the server module. When a client process wants to send a request to the server, it does so by calling server:call(frequency, Msg). The server, when responding, does so using the reply/2 call. We are, in effect, hiding all of the message passing behind a functional interface.

Another generic function is `server:stop/1`. We distinguish this function from `call/2` because we want to fix its meaning and therefore differentiate it from `server:call(frequency, {stop, self()})`, which could be treated by the developer as a specific call rather than as a generic server control message. Instead, by calling `stop`, we invoke the `terminate/1` callback function, which is given the process state and will contain all of the specific code executed when shutting down the server. In our case, we have kept the example to a minimum. Note, however, that we could have chosen to terminate all of the client processes that had been allocated a frequency:

```
stop(Name) ->                          % server.erl
    Name ! {stop, self()},
    receive {reply, Reply} -> Reply end.

call(Name, Msg) ->
    Name ! {request, self(), Msg},
    receive {reply, Reply} -> Reply end.

reply(To, Reply) ->
    To ! {reply, Reply}.
```

To ensure that we maintain the same interface, we export exactly the same functions in our new implementation of the `frequency` module:

```
stop()           -> server:stop(frequency).            % frequency.erl
allocate()       -> server:call(frequency, {allocate, self()}).
deallocate(Freq) -> server:call(frequency, {deallocate, Freq}).
```

These functions send requests and stop messages to the server. When the process receives the messages, the relevant callback functions in the `frequency` module are invoked. In the case of the stop message, it is the function `terminate/1`. It takes the process state as an argument and its return value is sent back to the client, becoming the return value of the `stop/1` call:

```
loop(Mod, State) ->                    % server.erl
    receive
        {request, From, Msg} ->
            {NewState, Reply} = Mod:handle(Msg, State),
            reply(From, Reply),
            loop(Mod, NewState);
        {stop, From}  ->
            Reply = Mod:terminate(State),
            reply(From, Reply)
    end.
```

In the case of a call request, the `handle/2` callback is invoked. The call takes two arguments, the first being the message bound to the variable `Msg` and the second the process state bound to the variable `State`. Pattern matching on the `Msg` picks the function clause that handles the message. The callback has to return a tuple in the format {NewState, Reply}, where NewState contains the updated frequencies and Reply is the reply sent back to the client. Have a look at the implementation of allocate/2. It returns exactly that: a tuple where the first element is the updated process state and the second element either {ok, Frequency} or {error, no_frequency}.

The first clause of the receive in loop/2 takes the return value from handle/2, sends back a reply to the client using reply/2, and loops with the new state, awaiting the next request:

```erlang
terminate(_Frequencies) ->                  % frequency.erl
    ok.

handle({allocate, Pid}, Frequencies) ->
    allocate(Frequencies, Pid);
handle({deallocate, Freq}, Frequencies) ->
    {deallocate(Frequencies, Freq), ok}.

allocate({[], Allocated}, _Pid) ->
    {{[], Allocated}, {error, no_frequency}};
allocate({[Freq|Free], Allocated}, Pid) ->
    {{Free, [{Freq, Pid}|Allocated]}, {ok, Freq}}.

deallocate({Free, Allocated}, Freq) ->
    NewAllocated = lists:keydelete(Freq, 1, Allocated),
    {[Freq|Free], NewAllocated}.
```

The same applies to the deallocate request. The frequency is deallocated, the handle/2 call returns a tuple with the new state returned by the deallocate/2 call, and the response, the atom ok, is sent back to the client.

So what we now have is our frequency example split up into a generic library module we call server and a specific callback module we call frequency. This is all there is to understanding Erlang behaviors. It is all about splitting up the code into generic and specific parts, and packaging the generic parts into reusable libraries to hide as much of the complexity as possible from the developers. We've kept this example simple to show our point, and barely scratched the surface of the corner cases that are handled behind the scenes in the proper behavior libraries. We cover these details in the next section, and introduce them as we talk about the individual behavior library modules.

Message Passing: Under the Hood

Concurrent programming is not easy. You need to deal with race conditions, deadlocks, and critical sections as well as many corner cases. Despite this, you rarely hear Erlang developers complain, let alone discuss these problems. The reason is simple: most of these issues become nonissues as a result of the OTP framework. In this chapter, we extracted the generic code from a particular client-server system, but in doing so we kept our example as simple as possible. There are many error conditions in a scenario like this that are handled behind the scenes by the behavior library modules we cover in the next chapter. Just to emphasize the point, they are handled without the programmer having to be aware of them. Race conditions, especially with multicore architectures, have become more common, but they should be picked up with appropriate modeling and testing tools such as Concuerror, McErlang, PULSE, and QuickCheck.

Having said that, let's look at an example of how behavior libraries help us hide a lot of the tricky cases an inexperienced developer might not think of when first implementing a concurrent system. We use the call/2 function from the previous example, expanding it as we go along:

```
call(Name, Message) ->
    Name ! {request, self(), Message},
    receive
        {reply, Reply} -> Reply
    end.

reply(Pid, Reply) ->
    Pid ! {reply, Reply}.
```

We send a message to the server of the format {request, Pid, Message} and wait for a response of the format {reply, Reply}. When we receive the reply, as shown in Figure 3-8, how can we be confident that the reply is actually a reply from the server, and not a message sent by another process but also complying with the protocol?

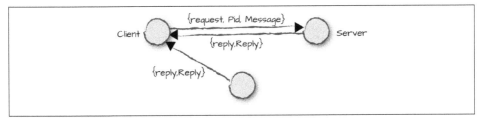

Figure 3-8. Message race conditions

Given this implementation, we can't. The solution to this problem is to use references. By creating a unique reference with the make_ref() BIF, adding it to the message, and including it in the reply, we will be guaranteed that the response is actually the reply to our request, and not just a message that happens to comply with our protocol. Adding references, our code looks like this:[3]

---

3 Minor changes are also needed to the code in order to get the stop call to work. We skip them in this example.

```
call(Name, Msg) ->
    Ref = make_ref(),
    Name ! {request, {Ref, self()}, Msg},
    receive {reply, Ref, Reply} -> Reply end.

reply({Ref, To}, Reply) ->
    To ! {reply, Ref, Reply}.
```

Note how Ref is already bound when entering the receive clause, ensuring replies are the result of the original message. This solves the problem, but is this enough? What happens if the server crashes before we send a request? If Name is an alias, we are covered because the client process will terminate when trying to send a message to a nonexistent registered process. But if Name is a pid, the message will be lost and the client will hang in the receive clause of the call function. Or similarly, what happens if the server crashes between receiving the message and sending the reply? This could be as a result of our request, or as the result of another client request it might be handling. Having a registered process will not cover this case either, as the process is alive when the message is sent.

The solution is to monitor the server. In doing so, let's use the monitor BIF instead of a link, because links are bidirectional and might cause side effects on the server if the child process were to be killed during the request. While the client wants to monitor termination of the server, terminating the client should not affect the server. The monitor BIF returns a unique reference, so we can drop the make_ref() BIF and use the monitor reference to tag our messages:

```
call(Name, Msg) ->
    Ref = erlang:monitor(process, Name),
    Name ! {request, {Ref, self()}, Msg},
    receive
        {reply, Ref, Reply} ->
            erlang:demonitor(Ref),
            Reply;
        {'DOWN', Ref, process, _Name, _Reason} ->
            {error, no_proc}
    end.
```

Have we covered everything that can go wrong? No, not really. By monitoring the process, we are now exposing ourselves to another race condition. Consider the following sequence of events:

1. The client monitors the server.

2. The client sends a request to the server.

3. The server receives the request and handles it.

4. The server sends back a response to the client.

5. The server crashes as the result of another request.

---

6. The client receives a DOWN message as a result of the monitor.

7. The client extracts the server response from its mailbox.

8. The client demonitors the (now defunct) server.

We are stuck with a DOWN message in the client mailbox containing a reference that will never match. Now, what are the chances of that happening? Do you really think someone would think of that particular test case where the server terminates right after it sends the client its reply, but before the client executes the erlang:demonitor/2 call? While this is an extreme corner case, we still need to handle the DOWN message as it might cause a memory leak. We do this by passing the [flush] option to the second argument in the demonitor/2 call, ensuring that any DOWN messages belonging to that monitor are not left lingering in the process mailbox.

Are we there yet? No, not really: what if Name is not an alias of a registered process? We need a catch to trap any exception raised as a result of the client sending a message to a nonexistent registered process. We don't really care about the result of the catch—if we did, we would have used try-catch instead—because if the server does not exist, monitor/1 will send a DOWN message. Our new code now looks like this:

```
call(Name, Msg) ->
    Ref = erlang:monitor(process, Name),
    catch Name ! {request, {Ref, self()}, Msg},
    receive
        {reply, Ref, Reply} ->
            erlang:demonitor(Ref, [flush]),
            Reply;
        {'DOWN', Ref, process, _Name, _Reason} ->
            {error, no_proc}
    end.
```

Unfortunately, though, these changes are still not enough. What happens if process A does a synchronous call to B at the same time as process B calls A? By "synchronous call," we mean an Erlang message exchange where the sending process expects a response, and the message and response are each sent as asynchronous messages. Process A enters the receive clause right after sending its request matching on a unique reference sent with the request, and B does the same. Back to answering our original question, if two processes synchronously call each other using this code, we get a deadlock. While deadlocks are a result of a design flaw, they might happen in live systems, and a recovery mechanism (preferably a generic one) needs to be put in place. The easiest way to resolve deadlocks is through a timeout in your receive statement, terminating the process. We go into more detail on deadlocks and timeouts and show you how OTP solves this problem in the next chapter.

Summing Up

In this chapter, we've covered the principles behind concurrency design patterns, introducing the concept of behavior libraries. We hope we have made our point about the importance and power of behavior libraries, as understanding them is fundamental to understanding the underlying principles of OTP. Decades of experience in process-oriented programming are reflected in them, removing the burden from the developers, reducing their code bases, and ensuring that corner cases are handled in a consistent, efficient, and correct manner. Be honest: how many of the corner cases discussed in this example would you have handled in a first iteration? What about your colleagues? Imagine testing and maintaining a system where everyone has reinvented the wheel with their own representation of these concurrent conditions and corner cases! The bottom line is that standard OTP behaviors handle all of these issues; that is why you should use them.

If you have the time, pick a simple client-server example you might have written when learning Erlang. It could be a key-value store, a chat server, or any other process that receives and handles requests. If you do not have any examples at hand, use the mobile subscriber database example from the ETS and DETS chapter of the *Erlang Programming* book. You can download the code from the authors' GitHub repositories (*https://github.com/francescoc/scalabilitywitherlangotp*).

Another useful exercise is to extend the `call` function with an `after` clause, making the process exit with reason `timeout`. Create a new function:

```
call(Name, Message, Timeout)
```

which, given a `Timeout` integer value in milliseconds or the atom `infinity`, allows users to set their own timeouts. Keep the `call/2` call, setting the default to 5 seconds. If the server does not respond within the given timeout value, make the client process terminate abnormally with the reason `timeout`. Don't forget to clean up before exiting, as the exit signal might be caught in a `try-catch` expression in the code using the server library.

What's Next?

In the next chapters, we introduce the library modules that together give us the OTP behaviors. We start with the `gen_server` library, and then later use a similar approach to introduce FSMs, event handlers, supervisors, and applications. We have not yet covered deadlocks, timeouts, and error cases that can arise when dealing with distribution or messages that never match. These are all topics we discuss when covering the individual behavior libraries.

## CHAPTER 4

Generic Servers

Having broken up the radio frequency allocator into generic and specific modules and investigated some of the corner cases that can occur when dealing with concurrency, you will have figured out there is no need to go through this process every time you have to implement a client-server behavior. In this chapter, we introduce the gen_server OTP behavior, a library module that contains all of the generic client-server functionality while handling a large number of corner cases. Generic servers are the most commonly used behavior pattern, setting the foundations for other behaviors, all of which can be (and in the early days of OTP were) implemented using this module.

Generic Servers

The gen_server module implements the client-server behavior we extracted in the previous chapter. It is part of the standard library application and available as part of the Erlang/OTP distribution. It contains the generic code that interfaces with the callback module through a set of *callback functions*. The *callback module*, in our example containing the code specific to the frequency server, is implemented by the programmer. The callback module has to export a series of functions that follow naming and typing conventions, so that their inputs and return values conform to the protocol required by the behavior.

As seen in Figure 4-1, the functions of both the behavior and callback module execute within the scope the same server process. In other words, a process loops in the generic server module, invoking the callback functions in the callback module as needed.

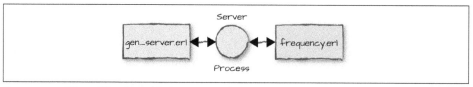

Figure 4-1. The callback and behavior modules

The gen_server library module provides functions to start and stop the server. You supply callback code to initialize the system, and in the case of either normal or abnormal process termination, it is possible to call a function from your callback module to clean up the state prior to termination. In particular, you no longer need to send messages to your process. Generic servers encapsulate all message passing in two functions—one for sending synchronous messages and one for sending asynchronous messages. These handle all of the borderline cases we discussed in the previous chapter, and many others we probably hadn't even realized could be an issue or cause a race condition. There is also built-in functionality for software upgrades, where you are able to suspend your process and migrate data from one version of your system to the next. Generic servers also provide timeouts, both on the client side when sending requests, and on the server side when no messages are received in a predetermined time interval.

We now cover all of the callback functions required when using generic servers. They include:

- The init/1 callback function initializes a server process created by the gen_server:start_link/4 call.

- The handle_call/3 callback function handles synchronous requests sent to the server by gen_server:call/2. When the request has been handled, call/2 returns a value computed by handle_call/3.

- Asynchronous requests are taken care of in the handle_cast/2 callback function. The requests originate in the gen_server:cast/2 call, which sends a message to a server process and immediately returns.

- Termination is handled when any of the server callback functions return a stop message, resulting in the terminate/2 callback function being called.

We look at these functions in more detail including all of their arguments, return values, and associated callbacks as soon as we've covered the module directives.

Behavior Directives

When we are implementing an OTP behavior, we need to include behavior directives in our module declarations.

```
-module(frequency).
-behavior(gen_server).

-export([start_link/1, init/1, ...]).

start_link(...) -> ...
```

The behavior directive is used by the compiler to issue warnings about callback functions that are not defined, not exported, or defined with the wrong arity. The *dialyzer* tool also uses these declarations for checking type discrepancies. An even more important use of the behavior directive is for the poor souls[1] who have to support, maintain, and debug your code long after you've moved on to other exciting and stimulating projects. They will see these directives and immediately know you have been using the generic server patterns. If they want to see the initialization of the server, they go to the `init/1` function. If they want to see how the server cleans up after itself, they jump to `terminate/3`. This is a great improvement over a situation in which every company, project, or developer reinvents their own, possibly buggy, client-server implementations. No time is wasted understanding this framework, allowing whoever is reading the code to concentrate on the specifics.

Behavior Versus Behaviour

You might have noticed that we are using the American spelling when adding the behavior directive in the callback module. British chums, don't despair. When defining your behavior directives, both the American "behavior" and British "behaviour" spellings are honored:

```
-behavior(tcp_wrapper).
-behaviour(tcp_wrapper).
```

The same applies when defining your `behavior_info/1` callback function. Many moons ago, if you did not stick to the British spelling, swallowing your pride and forcing yourself to type in that extra letter, you would get an unknown behavior warning when compiling your callback module. Many have been caught out and spent endless hours trying to figure out the problem and resolve it.

In our example code, compiler warnings come as a result of the `-behavior(gen_server).` directive because we omit the `code_change/3` function, a callback we cover in Chapter 12 when discussing release upgrades. In addition to this directive, we sometimes use a second, optional directive, `-vsn(Version)`, to keep track of module versions during code upgrade (and downgrade). We cover versions in more detail in Chapter 12.

---

1 At the risk of sounding repetitious, be nice to them, as it might be you someday.

Starting a Server

With the knowledge of our module directives, let's start a server. Generic servers and other OTP behaviors are started not with the spawn BIFs, but with dedicated functions that do more behind the scenes than just spawn a process:

```
gen_server:start_link({local,Name},Mod,Args,Opts) ->
    {ok, Pid} | ignore | {error, Reason}
```

The start_link/4 function takes four arguments. The first tells the gen_server module to register the process locally with the alias Name. Mod is the name of the callback module, where the server-specific code and the callback functions will be found. Args is an Erlang term passed to the callback function that initializes the server state. Opts is a list of process and debugging options we cover in Chapter 5. For the time being, let's keep it simple and pass the empty list for Opts. If a process is already registered with the Name alias, {error, {already_started, Pid}} is returned. Keep a vigilant eye on which process executes which functions. You can note them in Figure 4-2, where the server bound to the process Pid is started by the supervisor. The supervisor is denoted by a double ring as it is trapping exits.

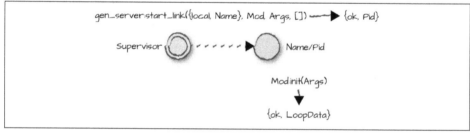

Figure 4-2. Starting a generic server

When the gen_server process has been spawned, it is registered with the alias Name, subsequently calling the init/1 function in the callback module Mod. The init/1 function takes Args, the third parameter to the start_link call, as an argument, irrespective of whether it is needed. If no arguments are needed, the init/1 function can ignore it with the don't care variable. Keep in mind that Args can be any valid Erlang term; you are not bound to using lists.

 If Args is a (possibly empty) list, the list will be passed to init/1 as a list, and not result in an init of a different arity being called. For example, if you pass [foo, bar], init([foo,bar]) will be called, not init(foo, bar). This is a common mistake developers make when transitioning from Erlang to OTP, as they confuse the properties of spawn and spawn_link with those of the behavior start and start_link functions.

The init/1 callback function is responsible for initializing the server state. In our example, this entails creating the variable containing the lists of available and allocated frequencies:

```
start() ->                                                    % frequency.erl
    gen_server:start_link({local, frequency}, frequency, [], []).

init(_Args) ->
    Frequencies = {get_frequencies(), []},
    {ok, Frequencies}.

get_frequencies() -> [10,11,12,13,14,15].
```

If successful, init/1 callback function returns {ok, LoopData}. If the startup fails but you do not want to affect other processes started by the same supervisor, return ignore. If you want to affect other processes, return {stop, Reason}. We cover ignore in Chapter 8 and stop in "Termination" on page 89.

In our example, start_link/4 passes the empty list [ ] to init/1, which in turn uses the _Args don't care variable to ignore it. We could have passed any other Erlang term, as long as we make it clear to anyone reading the code that no arguments are needed. The atom undefined or the empty tuple {} are other favorites.

By passing {timeout, Ms} as an option in the Opts list, we allow our generic server Ms milliseconds to start up. If it takes longer, start_link/4 returns the tuple {error, timeout} and the behavior process is not started. No exception is raised. We cover options in more detail in Chapter 5.

Starting a generic server behavior process is a synchronous operation. Only when init/1 callback function returns {ok, LoopData} to the server loop does the gen_server:start_link/4 function return {ok, Pid}. It's important to understand the synchronous nature of start_link and its importance to a repeatable startup sequence. The ability to deterministically reproduce an error is important when troubleshooting issues that occur at startup. You could asynchronously start all of the processes, checking each afterward to make sure they all started correctly. But as a result of changing scheduler implementations and configuration values running on multi-core architectures, deploying to different hardware or operating systems, or even the state of the network connectivity, the processes would not necessarily always initialize their state and complete the startup sequence in the same order. If all goes well, you won't have an issue with the variability inherent in an asynchronous startup approach, but if race conditions manifest themselves, trying to figure out what went wrong and when, especially in production environments, is not for the faint of heart. The synchronous startup approach implemented in start_link clearly ensures through its simplicity that each process has started correctly before moving on to the next one, providing determinism and reproducible startup errors on a single node. If startup errors are influenced by external factors such as networks, external databases, or the state of the underlying hardware or OS, try to contain them. In the cases where determinism does not help, a controlled startup procedure removes any element of doubt as to where the issue might be.

Message Passing

Having started our generic server and initialized its loop data, we now look at how communication works. As you might have understood from the previous chapter, sending messages using the ! operator is out of fashion. OTP uses functional interfaces that provide a higher level of abstraction. The gen_server module exports functions that allow us to send both synchronous and asynchronous messages, hiding the complexity of concurrent programming and error handling from the programmer.

Synchronous Message Passing

While Erlang has asynchronous message passing built in as part of the language, there is nothing stopping us from implementing synchronous calls using existing primitives. This is what the gen_server:call/2 function does. It sends a synchronous Message to the server and waits for a Reply while the server handles the request in a callback function. The Reply is passed as the return value to the call. The message and reply follow a specific protocol and contain a unique tag (or reference), matching the message and the response. Let's have a look at the gen_server:call/2 function in more detail:

```
gen_server:call(Name, Message) -> Reply
```

Name is either the server pid or the registered name of the server process. The Message is an Erlang term that gets forwarded as part of the request to the server. Requests are received as Erlang messages, stored in the mailbox, and handled sequentially. Upon receiving a synchronous request, the handle_call(Message, _From, LoopData) callback function is invoked in the callback module. The first argument is the Message passed to gen_server:call/2. The second argument, _From, contains a unique request identifier and information about the client. We will ignore it for the time being, binding it to a don't care variable. The third argument is the LoopData originally returned by the init/1 callback function. You should be able to follow the call flow in Figure 4-3.

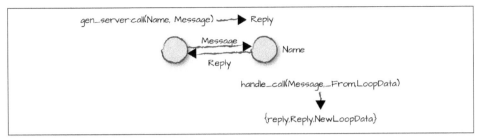

Figure 4-3. Synchronous message passing

The handle_call/3 callback function contains all the code required to handle the request. It is good practice to have a separate handle_call/3 clause for every request and to use pattern matching to pick the right one, instead of using a case statement to single out the individual messages. In the function clause, we would execute all of the code for that particular request and, when done, return a tuple of the format {reply, Reply, NewLoopData}. A callback module uses the atom reply to tell the gen_server that the second element, Reply, has to be sent back to the client process, becoming the return value of the gen_server:call/2 request. The third element, New LoopData, is the callback module's new state, which the gen_server passes into the next iteration of its tail-recursive receive-evaluate loop. If LoopData does not change in the body of the function, we just return the original value in the reply tuple. The gen_server merely stores it without inspecting it or manipulating its contents. Once it sends the reply tuple back to the client, the server is then ready to handle the next request. If no messages are queued up in the process mailbox, the server is suspended waiting for a new request to arrive.

In our frequency server example, allocating a frequency needs a synchronous call because the reply to the call must contain the allocated frequency. To handle the request, we call the internal function allocate/2, which you might recall returns {NewFrequencies, Reply}. NewFrequencies is the tuple containing the lists of allocated and available frequencies, while the Reply is the tuple {ok, Frequency} or {error, no_frequency}:

```erlang
allocate() ->                                        % frequency.erl
    gen_server:call(frequency, {allocate, self()}).

handle_call({allocate, Pid}, _From, Frequencies) ->
    {NewFrequencies, Reply} = allocate(Frequencies, Pid),
    {reply, Reply, NewFrequencies}.
```

Once completed, the allocate/0 function called by the client process returns {ok, Frequency} or {error, no_frequency}. The updated loop data containing available and allocated frequencies is stored in the generic server receive-evaluate loop awaiting the next request.

Asynchronous Message Passing

If the client needs to send a message to the server but does not expect a reply, it can use asynchronous requests. This is done using the gen_server:cast/2 library function:

```
gen_server:cast(Name, Message) -> ok
```

Name is the pid or the locally registered alias of the server process. Message is the term the client wants to send to the server. As soon as the cast/2 call has sent its request, it returns the atom ok. On the server side, the request is stored in the process mailbox and handled sequentially. When it is received, the Message is passed on to the handle_cast/2 callback function, implemented by the developer in the callback module.

The handle_cast/2 callback function takes two arguments. The first is the Message sent by the client, while the second is the LoopData previously returned by the init/1, handle_call/3, or handle_cast/2 callbacks. This can be seen in Figure 4-4.

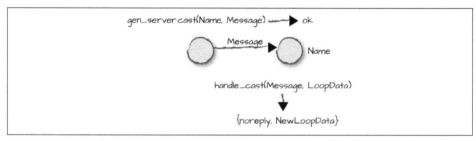

Figure 4-4. Asynchronous message passing

The handle_cast/2 callback function has to return a tuple of the format {noreply, NewLoopData}. The NewLoopData will be passed as an argument to the next call or cast request.

In some applications, client functions return a hardcoded value, often the atom ok, relying on side effects executed in the callback module. Such functions could be implemented as asynchronous calls. In our frequency example, did you notice that frequency:deallocate(Freq) always returns the atom ok? We don't really care if handling the request is delayed because the server is busy with other calls, making it a perfect candidate for an example using a generic server cast:

```
deallocate(Frequency) ->                                  % frequency.erl
    gen_server:cast(frequency, {deallocate, Frequency}).

handle_cast({deallocate, Freq}, Frequencies) ->
    NewFrequencies = deallocate(Frequencies, Freq),
    {noreply, NewFrequencies};
```

The client function `deallocate/1` sends an asynchronous request to the generic server and immediately returns the atom `ok`. This request is picked up by the `handle_cast/2` function, which pattern matches the `{deallocate, Frequency}` message in the first argument and binds the loop data to `Frequencies` in the second. In the function body, it calls the helper function `deallocate/2`, moving `Frequency` from the list of allocated frequencies to the list of available ones. The return value of `deallocate/2` is bound to the variable `NewFrequencies`, returned as the new loop data in the `noreply` control tuple.

Note that we said that only in some applications do client functions ignore return values from server functions with side effects. Pinging a server to make sure it is alive, for example, would rely on `gen_server:call/2` raising an exception if the server had terminated or if there were a delay, possibly as a result of heavy load, in handling the request and sending the response. Another example where synchronous calls are used is when there is a need to throttle requests and control the rate at which messages are sent to the server. We discuss the need to throttle messages in Chapter 15.

As with pure Erlang, calls and casts should be abstracted in a functional API if used from outside the module. This gives you greater flexibility to change your protocol and hide private implementation-related information from the caller of the function. Place the client functions in the same module as the process, as this makes it easier to follow the message flow without jumping between modules.

Other Messages

OTP behaviors are implemented as Erlang processes. So while communication should ideally occur through the protocols defined in the `gen_server:call/2` and `gen_server:cast/2` functions, that is not always the case. As long as the pid or registered name is known, there is nothing stopping a user from sending a message using the `Name ! Message` construct. In some cases, Erlang messages are the only way to get information across to the generic server. For example, if the server is linked to other processes or ports but has called the `process_flag(trap_exit, true)` BIF to trap exits from those processes or ports, it might receive `EXIT` signal messages. Also, communication between processes and ports or sockets is based on message passing. And finally, what if we are using a process monitor, monitoring distributed nodes or communicating with legacy, non-OTP-compliant code?

These examples all result in our server receiving Erlang messages that do not comply with the internal OTP messaging protocol of the server. Compliant or not, if you are using features that can generate messages to your server, then your server code has to be capable of handling them. Generic servers provide a callback function that takes care of all of these messages. It is the `handle_info(_Msg, LoopData)` callback. When called, it has to return either the tuple {noreply, NewLoopData} or, when stopping, {stop, Reason, NewLoopData}:

```erlang
handle_info(_Msg, LoopData) ->                              % frequency.erl
    {noreply, LoopData}.
```

It is common practice, even if you are not expecting any messages, to include this callback function. Not doing so and sending the server a non-OTP-compliant message (they arrive when you least expect them!) would result in a runtime error and the server terminating, as the handle_info/2 function would be called in the callback module, resulting in an undefined function error.

We've kept our frequency server example simple. We ignore any message coming in, returning the unchanged LoopData in the noreply tuple. If you are certain you should not be receiving non-OTP messages, you could log such messages as errors. If we wanted to print an error message every time a process the server was linked to terminated abnormally, the code would look like this (we are assuming that the server in question is trapping exits):

```erlang
handle_info({'EXIT', _Pid, normal}, LoopData) ->
    {noreply, LoopData};
handle_info({'EXIT', Pid, Reason}, LoopData) ->
    io:format("Process: ~p exited with reason: ~p~n",[Pid, Reason]),
    {noreply, LoopData};
handle_info(_Msg, LoopData) ->
    {noreply, LoopData}.
```

 One of the downsides of OTP is the overhead resulting from the layering of the various behavior modules and the data overhead required by the communication protocol. Both will affect performance. In an attempt to shave a few microseconds from their calls, developers have been known to bypass the gen_server:cast function and use the Pid ! Msg construct instead, or, even worse, embed receive statements in their callback functions to receive these messages. Don't do this! You will make your code hard to debug, support, and maintain, lose many of the advantages OTP brings to the table, and get the authors of this book to stop liking you. If you need to shave off microseconds, optimize only when you know from actual performance measurements that your program is not fast enough.

Unhandled Messages

Erlang uses selective receives when retrieving messages from the process mailbox. But allowing us to extract certain messages while leaving others unhandled comes with the risk of memory leakages. What happens if a message type is never read? Using Erlang without OTP, the message queue would get longer and longer, increasing the number of messages to be traversed before one is successfully pattern matched. This message queue growth will manifest itself in the Erlang VM through high CPU usage as a result of the traversal of the mailbox, and by the VM eventually running out of memory and possibly being restarted through *heart*, which we cover in Chapter 11.

All of this is valid if we are using pure Erlang, but OTP behaviors take a different approach. Messages are handled in the same order in which they are received. Start your frequency server, and try sending yourself a message you are not handling:

```
1> frequency:start().
{ok,<0.33.0>}
2> gen_server:call(frequency, foobar).

=ERROR REPORT==== 29-Nov-2015::18:27:45 ===
** Generic server frequency terminating
** Last message in was foobar
** When Server state == {data,[{"State",
                              {{available,[10,11,12,13,14,15]},
                               {allocated,[]}}}]}
** Reason for termination ==
** {function_clause,[{frequency,handle_call,
                        [foobar,
                         {<0.44.0>,#Ref<0.0.4.112>},
                         {[10,11,12,13,14,15],[]}],
                        [{file,"frequency.erl"},{line,63}]},
                   {gen_server,try_handle_call,4,
                        [{file,"gen_server.erl"},{line,629}]},
                   {gen_server,handle_msg,5,
                        [{file,"gen_server.erl"},{line,661}]},
                   {proc_lib,init_p_do_apply,3,
                        [{file,"proc_lib.erl"},{line,240}]}]}
```

This is probably not what you were expecting. The frequency server terminated with a function_clause runtime error, printing an error report.[2] When you call a function, one of the clauses always has to match. Failure to do so results in a runtime error. When doing a gen_server call or cast, the message is always retrieved from the mailbox in the generic server loop, and the handle_call/3 or handle_cast/2 callback function is invoked. In our example, handle_call(foobar, _From, LoopData) doesn't match any of the clauses, causing the function clause error we've just viewed. The same would happen with a cast.

How do we avoid such errors? One option is to have a catch-all, where unknown messages are pattern matched to a don't care variable and ignored. This is specific to the application, and may or may not be the answer. A catch-all might be the norm

---

2 If you run this example in the shell, you will also get an error report from the shell itself terminating as a result of the exit signal propagating through the link.

with the handle_info/2 callback when dealing with ports, sockets, links, monitors, and monitoring of distributed nodes where there is a risk of forgetting to handle a particular message not needed by the application. When dealing with calls and casts, however, all requests should originate from the behavior callback module and any unknown messages should be caught in the early stages of testing.

If in doubt, don't be defensive, and instead make your server terminate when receiving unknown messages. Treat these terminations as bugs, and either handle the messages or correct them at the source. If you do decide to ignore unknown messages, don't forget to log them.

Synchronizing Clients

What happens in a situation where two clients each send a synchronous request to a server, but instead of immediately responding to each individually, the server has to wait for both requests before responding to the first? We demonstrate this in Figure 4-5. This could be done for synchronization purposes or because the server needs the data from both requests.

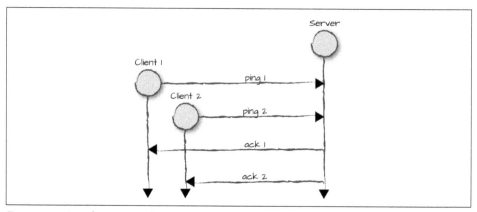

Figure 4-5. Rendezvous with generic servers

The solution to this problem is simple. Do you remember the From field in the handle_call(Message, From, State) callback function? Instead of returning a reply back to the behavior loop, we return {noreply, NewState}. We then use the From attribute and the function:

    gen_server:reply(From, Reply)

to later send back the reply to the client when it suits us. In the case of having to synchronize two clients, it could be in the second handle_call/3 callback, where the From value for the first client is stored between the calls either as part of the NewState or in a table or database.

You can also use reply/2 if a synchronous request triggers a time-consuming computation and the only response the client is interested in is an acknowledgment that the request has been received and is in the process of being fulfilled, without having to wait for the whole computation to be completed. To send an immediate acknowledgment, the gen_server:reply/2 call can be used in the callback itself:

```
handle_call({add, Data}, From, Sum) ->
    gen_server:reply(From, ok),
    timer:sleep(1000),
    NewSum = add(Data, Sum),
    io:format("From:~p, Sum:~p~n",[From, NewSum]),
    {noreply, NewSum}.
```

Let's run this code, assuming it is a generic server implemented in the from callback module. The call timer:sleep/1 will suspend the process, allowing the shell process to handle the response from gen_server:reply/2 before the io:format/2 call:

```
1> gen_server:start({local, from}, from, 0, []).
{ok,<0.53.0>}
2> gen_server:call(from, {add, 10}).
ok
From:{<0.55.0>,#Ref<0.0.3.248>}, Sum:10
```

Note the value and format of the From argument we are printing in the shell. It is a tuple containing the client pid and a unique reference. This reference is used in a tag with the reply sent back to the client, ensuring that it is in fact the intended reply, and not a message conforming to the protocol sent from another process. Always use From as an opaque data type; don't assume it is a tuple, as its representation might change in future releases.

Termination

What if we want to stop a generic server? So far, we've seen the callback functions init/1, handle_call/3, and handle_cast/2 return {ok, LoopData}, {reply, Reply, LoopData}, and {noreply, LoopData}, respectively. Stopping the server requires the callbacks to return different tuples:

- init/1 can return {stop, Reason}
- handle_call/3 can return {stop, Reason, Reply, LoopData}
- handle_cast/2 can return {stop, Reason, LoopData}
- handle_info/2 can return {stop, Reason, LoopData}

These return values terminate with the same behavior as if exit(Reason) were called. In the case of calls and casts, before exiting, the callback function terminate(Reason, LoopData) is called. It allows the server to clean up after itself before being shut down. Any value returned by terminate/2 is ignored. In the case of init, stop should be returned if something fails when initializing the state. As a result, terminate/2 will not be called. If we return {stop, Reason} in the init/1 callback, the start_link function returns {error, Reason}.

In our frequency server example, the stop/0 client function sends an asynchronous message to the server. Upon receiving it, the handle_cast/2 callback returns the tuple with the stop control atom, which in turn results in the terminate/2 call being invoked. Have a look at the code:

```
stop() -> gen_server:cast(frequency, stop).                    % frequency.erl

handle_cast(stop, LoopData) ->
    {stop, normal, LoopData}.

terminate(_Reason, _LoopData) ->
    ok.
```

To keep the example simple, we've left terminate empty. In an ideal world, we would probably have killed all of the client processes that were allocated a frequency, thereby terminating their tasks using those frequencies and ensuring that upon a restart, all frequencies are available.

Look at the message gen_server:cast/2 sends to the frequency server. You'll notice it is the atom stop, pattern matched in the first argument of the handle_cast/2 call. The message has no meaning other than the one we give to it in our code. We could have sent any atom, like gen_server:cast(frequency, donald_duck). Pattern matching donald_duck in the handle_cast/2 would have given us the same result. The only stop that has special meaning is the one that occurs in the first element of the tuple returned by handle_cast/2, as it is interpreted in the receive-evaluate loop of the generic server.

If you are shutting down your server as part of your normal workflow (e.g., the socket it is handling has been closed, or the hardware it controls and monitors is shutting down), it is good practice to set your Reason to normal. A non-normal reason, while perfectly acceptable, will result in error reports being logged by the SASL logger. These entries might overshadow those of real crashes. (The SASL logger is another freebie you get when using OTP. We cover it in Chapter 9.)

Although servers can be stopped normally by returning the stop tuple, there might be cases when they terminate as the result of a runtime error. In these cases, if the generic server is trapping exits (by having called the process_flag(trap_exit, true) BIF), terminate/2 will also be called, as shown in Figure 4-6. If you are not trapping exits, the process will just terminate *without* calling terminate/2.

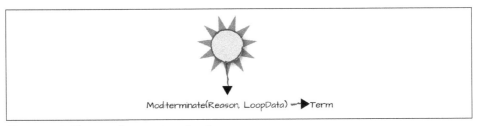

Figure 4-6. Abnormal server termination

If you want the `terminate/2` function to execute after abnormal terminations, you have to set the `trap_exit` flag. If it is not set, a supervisor or linked process might bring the server down without allowing it to clean up.

Having said this, always check the context for termination. If a runtime error has occurred, clean up the server state with extreme care, as you might end up corrupting your data and so set your system up for more runtime errors after the server restarts. When restarting, you should aim to recreate the server state from correct (and unique) sources of data, not a copy you stored right before the crash, as it might have been corrupted by the same fault that caused the crash.

Call Timeouts

When sending synchronous messages to your server using a `gen_server` call, you should expect a response within milliseconds. But what if there is a delay in sending the response? Your server might be extremely busy handling thousands of requests, or there might be bottlenecks in external dependencies such as databases, authentication servers, IP networks, or any other resource or API taking its time to respond. OTP behaviors have a built-in timeout of 5 seconds in their synchronous `gen_server:call` APIs. This should be enough to cater to most queries in any soft real-time system, but there are borderline cases that need to be handled differently. If you are sending a synchronous request using OTP behaviors and have not received a response within 5 seconds, the client process will raise an exception. Let's try it out in the shell with the following callback module:

```
-module(timeout).
-behavior(gen_server).

-export([init/1, handle_call/3]).

init(_Args) ->
    {ok, undefined}.

handle_call({sleep, Ms}, _From, LoopData) ->
    timer:sleep(Ms),
    {reply, ok, LoopData}.
```

In the gen_server:call/2 function, we send a message of the format {sleep, Ms}, where Ms is a value used in the timer:sleep/1 call executed in the handle_call/3 callback. Sending a value larger than 5,000 milliseconds should cause the gen_server:call/2 function to raise an exception, as such a value exceeds the default timeout. Let's try it out in the shell. We assume that the timeout module is already compiled, so as to avoid the compiler warnings from the callback functions we have omitted:

```
1> gen_server:start_link({local, timeout}, timeout, [], []).
{ok,<0.66.0>}
2> gen_server:call(timeout, {sleep, 1000}).
ok
3> catch gen_server:call(timeout, {sleep, 5001}).
{'EXIT',{timeout,{gen_server,call,[timeout,{sleep,5001}]}}}
4> flush().
Shell got {#Ref<0.0.0.300>,ok}
5> gen_server:call(timeout, {sleep, 5001}).
** exception exit: {timeout,{gen_server,call,[timeout,{sleep,5001}]}}
     in function  gen_server:call/2
6> catch gen_server:call(timeout, {sleep, 1000}).
{'EXIT',{noproc,{gen_server,call,[timeout,{sleep,1000}]}}}
```

We start the server, and in shell command 2, we send a synchronous message telling the server to sleep for 1,000 milliseconds before replying with the atom ok. As this is within the 5-second default timeout, we get our response back. But in shell command 3, we raise the timeout to 5,001 milliseconds, causing the gen_server:call/2 function to raise an exception. In our example, shell command 3 catches the exception, allowing the client function to handle any special cases that might arise as a result of the timeout.

If you decide to catch exceptions arising as the result of a timeout, be warned: if the server is alive but busy, it will send back a response after the timeout exception has been raised. This response has to be handled. If the client is itself an OTP behavior, the exception will result in the handle_info/2 call being invoked. If this call has not been implemented, the client process will crash.

If the call is from a pure Erlang client, the exception will be stored in the client mailbox and never handled. Having unread messages in your mailbox will consume memory and slow down the process when new messages are received, as the littering messages need to be traversed before new ones will be pattern matched. Not only that, but sending a message to a process with a large number of unread messages will slow down the sender, because the send operation will consume more reductions. This will have a knock-on effect, potentially triggering more timeouts and further growing the number of littering messages in the client mailbox.

The performance penalty when sending messages to a process with a long message queue does not apply to behaviors synchronously responding to the process where the request originated. If the client process has a long message queue, thanks to compiler and virtual machine optimizations, the receive clause will match the reply without having to traverse the whole message queue.

We see the proof of this memory leak in shell command 4, where unread messages are flushed. Had we not flushed the message, it would have remained in the shell's mailbox. Throughout this book, we keep reminding you not to handle corner cases and unexpected errors in your code, as you run the risk of introducing more bugs and errors than you actually solve. This is a typical example where side effects resulting from these timeouts will probably manifest themselves only under extreme load in a live system.

Now have a look at shell command 5 and Figure 4-7. We have a call that causes the client process to crash, because it is executed outside the scope of a try-catch statement. In a majority of cases, if your server is not responding for any (possibly unknown) reason, making the client process terminate and letting the supervisor deal with it is probably the best approach. In this example, the shell process terminates and is immediately restarted. The timeout server sends a response to the old client (and shell) pid after 5,001 milliseconds. As this process does not exist anymore, the message is discarded. So why does shell command 6 fail with reason noproc? Have a look at the sequence of shell commands and see if you can figure it out before reading on.

Figure 4-7. Server timeouts

When we started the server, we linked it to the shell, making the shell process act as both the client and the parent. The timeout server terminated after we executed a gen_server:call/2 call outside of the scope of a try-catch in shell command 5. Because the server is not trapping exits, when the shell terminated, the EXIT signal propagated to the server, causing it to also terminate. In normal circumstances, the client and the parent of the server that links to it would not be the same process, so this would not occur. These issues tend to show up when testing behaviors from the shell, so keep them in mind when working on your exercises.

So, how do we supply something other than the 5-second default timeout value in behaviors? Easy: we set our own timeout. In generic servers, we do this using the following function call:

```
gen_server:call(Server, Message, TimeOut) -> Reply
```

where TimeOut is either the desired value in milliseconds or the atom infinity.

A client call will often consist of a chain of synchronous requests to several, potentially distributed, behavior processes. They might in turn send requests to external resources. More often than not, choosing timeout values becomes tricky, as these processes are accessing services and APIs provided by third parties completely out of your control. Systems that have been known to respond in milliseconds to the majority of the requests can take seconds or even minutes under extreme loads. The throughput of your system counted in operations per second might still be the same, but when there is a higher load—possibly many orders of magnitude higher—going through it, the latency of the individual requests will be higher.

The only way to answer the question of what TimeOut you should set is to start with your external requirements. If a client specifies a 30-second timeout, start with it and work your way through the chain of requests. What are the guaranteed response times of your external dependencies? How will disk access and I/O respond under extreme load? What about network latency? Spend lots of time stress testing your system on the target hardware and fine-tune your values accordingly. When you're unsure, start with the 5,000-millisecond default value. Use the value infinity with extreme care, avoiding it altogether unless there's no other alternative.

Deadlocks

Picture two generic servers in a badly designed system. server1 does a synchronous call to server2. server2 receives the request, and through a series of calls in other modules ends up (possibly unknowingly) executing a synchronous callback to server1. Observing Figure 4-8, this problem is resolved not through complex deadlock prevention algorithms, but through timeouts.

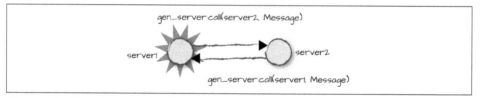

Figure 4-8. Generic server deadlocks

If server1 has not received a response within 5,000 milliseconds, it terminates, causing server2 to terminate as well. Depending on what gets there first, the termination is triggered either through the monitor signal or through a timeout of its own. If more processes are involved in the deadlock, the termination will propagate to them as well. The supervisor will receive the EXIT signals and restart the servers accordingly. The termination is stored in a log file where it is hopefully detected, resulting in the bug leading to the deadlock being fixed.

Despite the ease of creating deadlocks, they are extremely rare, no matter how complex the program might be. This has to do with how the systems are architected, the concurrency is modeled, and dependencies among processes and applications are handled. The lack of shared memory and critical sections helps remove the danger of deadlocks. Experienced Erlang programmers will by default ensure that their programs are designed to avoid deadlocks, often without having to think about it. Newbies, however, need to find a suitable strategy in the initial design phase of the system and stick to it. A standard practice when dealing with static processes that are not started and terminated dynamically is to allow synchronous calls to be made only to processes that were started before the process making the call. Calls from older processes to younger ones may only be asynchronous. If a reply is required from the younger process, it sends it back through a (possibly asynchronous) callback function. The start order of static processes is defined in supervision trees, which also happens to be the order used with dynamic processes. This will become clear when we cover supervision trees and restart orders in Chapter 8. You need to keep it in mind when processes are grouped into supervision trees, when supervision trees are grouped into applications, and when application start orders are defined.

In 17 years of working with Erlang, I've come across only one deadlock.[3] Process A synchronously called process B, which in turn did a remote procedure call to another node that resulted in a synchronous call to process C. Process C synchronously called process D, which did another remote procedure call back to the first node. This call resulted in a synchronous callback to process A, which was still waiting for a response back from B. We discovered this deadlock when integrating the two nodes for the first time, and it took us 5 minutes to solve. Process A should have called B asynchronously, and process B should have responded back to A with an asynchronous callback. So while there is a risk of deadlocks, if you approach the problem right, it is minimal, as the largest cause of deadlocks occurs when controlling execution and failure in critical sections—something for which the shared-nothing approach in Erlang provides plenty of alternatives.

Generic Server Timeouts

Picture a generic server whose task is to monitor and communicate with a particular hardware device. If the server has not received a message from the device within a predefined timeout, it should send a ping request to ensure the device is alive. These

---

3 I'm the author who in the previous book caused the nationwide data outage in a mobile network.

ping requests can be triggered by internal timeouts, created by adding a timeout value in the control tuples sent back as a result of the behavior callback functions:

```
init/1        -> {ok, LoopData, Timeout}
handle_call/3 -> {reply, Reply, LoopData, Timeout}
handle_cast/2 -> {noreply, LoopData, Timeout}
handle_info/2 -> {noreply, LoopData, Timeout}
```

The value Timeout is either an integer in milliseconds or the atom infinity. If the server does not receive a message in Timeout milliseconds, it receives a timeout message in its handle_info/2 callback function. Returning infinity is the same as not setting a timeout value. Let's try it with a simple example where every 5,000 milliseconds, we generate a timeout that retrieves the current time and prints the seconds. We can pause the timer and restart it by sending the synchronous messages start and pause:

```
-module(ping).
-behavior(gen_server).

-export([init/1, handle_call/3, handle_info/2]).
-define(TIMEOUT, 5000).

init(_Args) ->
    {ok, undefined, ?TIMEOUT}.

handle_call(start, _From, LoopData) ->
    {reply, started, LoopData, ?TIMEOUT};
handle_call(pause, _From, LoopData) ->
    {reply, paused, LoopData}.

handle_info(timeout, LoopData) ->
    {_Hour,_Min,Sec} = time(),
    io:format("~2.w~n",[Sec]),
    {noreply, LoopData, ?TIMEOUT}.
```

Assuming the ping module is compiled, we start it and generate a timeout every 5 seconds. We can suspend the timeout by sending it the pause message, which when handled in the second clause of the handle_call/3 function does not include a timeout in its return tuple. We turn it back on with the start message:

```
1> gen_server:start({local, ping}, ping, [], []).
{ok,<0.38.0>}
22
27
2> gen_server:call(ping, pause).
paused
3> gen_server:call(ping, start).
started
51
56
4> gen_server:call(ping, start).
```

```
started
4
```

Because we set a relatively high timeout, we do not generate a timeout message at 5,000-millisecond intervals. We send a timeout message *only* if a message has not been received by the behavior. If a message is received, as is happening with shell command 4 in our example, the timer is reset.

If you need timers that may not be reset or have to run at regular intervals irrespective of incoming messages, use functions such as `erlang:send_after/3` or those provided by the `timer` module, including `apply_after/3`, `send_after/2`, `apply_interval/4`, and `send_interval/2`.

Hibernating Behaviors

If instead of a timeout value or the atom `infinity` we return the atom `hibernate`, the server will reduce its memory footprint and enter a wait state. You will want to use `hibernate` when servers that receive intermittent, memory-intensive requests are causing the system to run low on memory. Using `hibernate` will discard the call stack and run a full-sweep garbage collection, placing everything in one continuous heap. The allocated memory is then shrunk to the size of the data on the heap. The server will remain in this state until it receives a new message.

 There is a cost associated with hibernating processes, as it involves a full-sweep garbage collection prior to hibernating and one soon after the process wakes up. Use hibernation only if you do not expect the behavior to receive any messages in the foreseeable future and need to economize on memory, not for servers receiving frequent bursts of messages. Using it as a preemptive measure is dangerous, especially if your process is busy, as it might (and probably will) cost more to hibernate the process than to just leave it as is. The only way to know for sure is to benchmark your system under stress and demonstrate a gain in performance along with a substantial reduction in memory usage. Add it as an afterthought only if you know what you are doing. If in doubt, don't do it!

Going Global

Behavior processes can be registered locally or globally. In our examples, they have all been registered locally using a tuple of the format {`local`, `ServerName`}, where `ServerName` is an atom denoting the alias. This is equivalent to registering the process using the `register(ServerName, Pid)` BIF. But what if we want location transparency in a distributed cluster?

Globally registered processes piggyback on the global name server, which makes them transparently accessible in a cluster of (possibly partitioned) distributed nodes. The name server stores local replicas of the names on every node and monitors node health and changes in connectivity, ensuring there is no central point of failure. You register a server globally by using the {global, Name} tuple as an argument to the server name field. It is equivalent to registering the process using the function global:register_name(Name, Pid). Use the same tuple in your synchronous and asynchronous calls:

```
gen_server:start_link({global,Name},Mod,Args,Opts) ->
    {ok, Pid} | ignore | {error, Reason}
gen_server:call({global, Name}, Message) -> Reply
gen_server:cast({global, Name}, Message) -> ok
```

There is an API that allows you to replace the global process registry with one you have implemented yourself. You can create your own when the functionality provided by the global module is not enough, or when you want a different behavior that caters for different network topologies. You need to provide a callback module—say, Module—that exports the same functions and return values defined in the global module, namely register_name/2, unregister_name/1, whereis_name/1, and send/2. Name registration then uses the tuple {via, Module, Name}, and starting your process using {via, global, Name} is the same as registering it globally using {global, Name}. For globally registered processes, the Name does not have to be an atom; rather, any Erlang term is valid. Once you have your callback module, you can start your process and send messages using:

```
gen_server:start_link({via, Module, Name},Mod,Args,Opts) -> {ok, Pid}
gen_server:call({via, Module, Name}, Message) -> Reply
gen_server:cast({via, Module, Name}, Message) -> ok
```

In the remainder of the book, we aggregate {via, Module, Name}, {local, Name}, and {global, Name} using NameScope. Most servers are registered locally, but depending on the complexity of the system and clustering strategies, global and via are used as well.

When communicating with behaviors, you can use their pids instead of their registered aliases. Registering behaviors is not mandatory; not registering allows multiple instances of the same behavior to run in parallel. When starting the behaviors, just omit the name field:

```
gen_server:start_link(Mod, Args, Opts) ->
    {ok, Pid} | ignore | {error, Reason}
```

If you broadcast a request to all servers within a cluster of nodes, you can use the generic server multi_call/3 call if you need results back and abcast/3 if you don't:

```
gen_server:multi_call(Nodes, Name, Request [, Timeout]) ->
    {[{Node,Reply}], BadNodes}
gen_server:abcast(Nodes, Name, Request) -> abcast
```

On the servers of the individual nodes, requests are handled in the handle_call/3
and handle_cast/2 callbacks, respectively. When broadcasting asynchronously with
abcast, no checks are made to see whether or not the nodes are connected and still
alive. Requests to nodes that cannot be reached are simply thrown away.

Linking Behaviors

When you start behaviors in the shell, you link the shell process to them. If the shell
process terminates abnormally, its EXIT signal will propagate to the behaviors it
started and cause them to terminate. Generic servers can be started without linking
them to their parent by calling gen_server:start/3 or gen_server:start/4. Use
these functions with care, and preferably only for development and testing purposes,
because behaviors should always be linked to their parent:

```
gen_server:start(NameScope,Mod,Args,Opts)
gen_server:start(Mod,Args,Opts) ->
    {ok, Pid} | {error, {already_started, Pid}}
```

Erlang systems will operate for years in the absence of rebooting the computers they
run on. They can continue even during software upgrades for bug fixes, feature
enhancements, and new functionality, and through behaviors terminating abnormally and being restarted. When shutting down a subsystem, you need to be 100%
certain that all processes associated with that subsystem are terminated, and avoid
leaving any orphan processes lingering. The only way to do so with certainty is using
links. We go into more detail when we cover supervisor behaviors in Chapter 8.

Summing Up

In this chapter, we have introduced the most important concepts and functionality in
the generic server behavior, the behavior behind all behaviors. You should by now
have a good understanding of the advantages of using the gen_server behavior
instead of rolling your own. We have covered the majority of functions and associated callbacks needed when using this behavior. Although you do not need to understand everything that goes on behind the scenes, we hope you now have an idea and
appreciation that there is more than meets the eye. The most important functions we
have covered are listed in Table 4-1.

Table 4-1. gen_server callbacks

gen_server function or action	gen_server callback function
gen_server:start/3, gen_server:start/4, gen_server:start_link/3, gen_server:start_link/4	Module:init/1
gen_server:call/2, gen_server:call/3, gen_server:multi_call/2, gen_server:multi_call/3	Module:handle_call/3
gen_server:cast/2, gen_server:abcast/2, gen_server:abcast/3	Module:handle_cast/2
Pid ! Msg, monitors, exit messages, messages from ports and sockets, node monitors, and other non-OTP messages	Module:handle_info/2
Triggered by returning {stop, ...} or when terminating abnormally while trapping exits	Module:terminate/2

When compiling behavior modules, you will have seen a warning about the missing code_change/3 callback. We cover it in Chapter 11 when looking at release handling and software upgrades. In the next chapter, while using the generic server behavior as an example, we look at advanced topics and behavior-specific functionality that comes with OTP.

At this point, you will want to make sure you review the manual pages for the gen_server module. If you are feeling brave, read the code in the *gen_server.erl* source file, and the source for the gen helper module. Having read this and the previous chapter and understood the corner cases, you will discover the code is not as cryptic as it might first appear.

What's Next?

The next chapter contains odds and ends that allow you to dig deeper into behaviors. We start investigating the built-in tracing and logging functionality we get from using them. We also introduce you to the Opts flags in the start functions. The flags allow you to fine-tune performance and memory usage, as well as start your behavior with trace flags enabled. So read on, as interesting things are in store in the next chapter.

## CHAPTER 5

Controlling OTP Behaviors

We have in the previous chapters covered the highlights of the gen_server behavior. You should by now have implemented your first client-server application and started to build an idea of how OTP behaviors help you to reduce your code base by allowing you to focus on the specifics of what your system has to do. This chapter digs deeper into behaviors, exploring some of the advanced topics intermixed with built-in functionality. While we are focusing on generic servers, most of what we write will apply to many of the other behaviors, including those you could implement yourself. Read with care, as we reference this chapter often in the remainder of this book.

The sys Module

We've mentioned many times the built-in functionality you get as a result of using OTP behaviors and the ease with which you can add your own features. Most of what we cover is accessed through the sys module, allowing you to generate trace events, inspect and manipulate behavior state, as well as send and receive system messages. All of this functionality works on the standard OTP behaviors, but also, as we show in Chapter 10, you can reuse it when defining your own behaviors.

Tracing and Logging

Let's find out how built-in tracing works by running a little example. Start your frequency server in the shell and, using the sys module, try the following:

```
1> frequency:start().
{ok,<0.35.0>}
2> sys:trace(frequency, true).
ok
3> frequency:allocate().
*DBG* frequency got call {allocate,<0.33.0>} from <0.33.0>
```

```
*DBG* frequency sent {ok,10} to <0.33.0>,
      new state {[11,12,13,14,15],[{10,<0.33.0>}]}
{ok,10}
4> frequency:deallocate(10).
*DBG* frequency got cast {deallocate,10}
ok
*DBG* frequency new state {[10,11,12,13,14,15],[]}
5> sys:trace(frequency, false).
ok
```

By turning on the trace flags for our frequency allocator, we are able to generate printouts of system events, including messages and state changes. Our example pipes the messages out to the shell. If we instead use the sys:log/2 call, we store them in the server loop. They can be displayed using the print flag or can be retrieved as an Erlang data structure through the get flag:

```
6> sys:log(frequency, true).
ok
7> {ok, Freq} = frequency:allocate(), frequency:deallocate(Freq).
ok
8> sys:log(frequency, print).
*DBG* frequency got call {allocate,<0.33.0>} from <0.33.0>
*DBG* frequency sent {ok,10} to <0.33.0>,
      new state {[11,12,13,14,15],[{10,<0.33.0>}]}
*DBG* frequency got cast {deallocate,10}
*DBG* frequency new state {[10,11,12,13,14,15],[]}
ok
9> sys:log(frequency, get).
{ok,[{{in,{'$gen_call',{<0.33.0>,#Ref<0.0.4.59>},
                        {allocate,<0.33.0>}}},
      frequency,#Fun<gen_server.0.40920150>},
     {{out,{ok,10},<0.33.0>,{[11,12,13,14,15],[{10,<0.33.0>}]}},
      frequency,#Fun<gen_server.6.40920150>},
     {{in,{'$gen_cast',{deallocate,10}}},
      frequency,#Fun<gen_server.0.40920150>},
     {{noreply,{[10,11,12,13,14,15],[]}},
      frequency,#Fun<gen_server.4.40920150>}]}
10> sys:log(frequency, false).
ok
```

When you use the sys:log/2 call to store trace events in the server loop, the default number of events stored is 10. You can override this number by passing the {true, Int} flag when enabling logging. Int is an integer denoting the new default number of events you want to store. When you plan to deal with large volumes of debug messages, or leave debugging turned on for a long time, use sys:log_to_file/2 to pipe the messages to a text file.

System Messages

Have a look at the return value of shell command 9 in the previous example. If we pass the get flag to sys:log/2, we get back a list of system events. The forms of the events in the log depend on the processes producing them, but generally each event contains a system message with one the following forms:

{in, Msg}
> This system message is triggered when a message (including a timeout) is sent to the gen_server. Msg includes any construct that is part of the OTP message protocol, e.g., {'$gen_cast', Msg} for casts and {'$gen_call',{Pid, Ref}, Msg} for calls. For any regular Erlang term sent as a message to a gen_server process, Msg will simply be that term.

{out, Msg, To, State}
> This system message is generated when replying to the client using the {reply, Reply, NewState} control tuple, but is not generated for replies sent via gen_server:reply/2. Msg is the reply sent to the client, and To is the pid of the client. State is the same as NewState specified in the reply tuple.

term()
> System messages of any format are allowed. For example, the return value of shell command 9 includes the message {noreply,{[10,11,12,13,14,15],[]}}, which is the result of handle_cast/2 after handling the deallocate cast. The second element of the noreply tuple is the new state of the gen_server.

Note that the documentation at the time of writing (up to and including Erlang 18) for the sys module also specifies {in, Msg, From} and {out, Msg, To} as valid system messages, but these are not used by any standard behaviors.

Your Own Trace Functions

You can implement your own trace functions by implementing your own fun that gets triggered in conjunction with a system event. You can pattern match on the events, taking any course of action you like. Trace functions can be used to generate your own debug printouts, turn on low-level traces using *dbg* or the trace BIFs, enable logging of particular information, run diagnostic functions, or execute any other code you might need (or none at all).

The following example keeps a counter for every time a client is refused a frequency and prints a warning message.[1] Note how we achieve this without touching the original frequency code:

```
11> F = fun(Count,{out, {error, no_frequency}, Pid, _LoopData}, ProcData) ->
              io:format("*DBG* Warning, Client ~p refused frequency! Count:~w~n",
              [Pid, Count]), Count + 1;
           (Count,  _, _) ->
              Count
         end.
#Fun<erl_eval.18.54118792>
12> sys:install(frequency, {F, 1}).
ok
13> frequency:allocate(), frequency:allocate(), frequency:allocate(),
    frequency:allocate(), frequency:allocate(), frequency:allocate().
{ok,15}
14> frequency:allocate().
*DBG* Warning, Client <0.33.0> refused frequency! Count:1
{error,no_frequency}
15> frequency:allocate().
*DBG* Warning, Client <0.33.0> refused frequency! Count:2
{error,no_frequency}
16> sys:remove(frequency, F).
false
17> frequency:allocate().
{error,no_frequency}
```

Let's look at this example in more detail. We create a fun F that takes three arguments. The first, Count, is the state of the debug function, passed between calls. Count, in this example, acts like a state variable, as we've chosen to count the number of times the first function clause is matched. Other trace functions might use more complicated states. The second argument is the system message, in which we pattern match on outbound messages of the format {error, no_frequency}. The third argument, ProcData, is specific to the behavior being traced; for example, for a gen_server it's either the registered name of the process or its pid, whereas for a gen_fsm it is a tuple of the process name or pid and the current state name of the FSM (we cover the gen_fsm behavior in Chapter 6). All other system messages are ignored due to the second clause of the F function. We set the state of the debug function Count to the integer 1 in the second element of the tuple of the sys:install/2 call in shell command 12. In this command, we also pass the fun F to the frequency server, enabling the debug printout. We continue by calling frequency:allocate/0 enough times to run out of frequencies, triggering the debug printout twice and increasing the counter. Every time it is executed, F returns the Count state variable,

---

1 The io:format/2 executed in the fun attaches itself to the group leader of the traced behavior, causing warnings to be printed in the local shell. If you connect from a remote shell, you will not be able to see them.

incremented by 1 if the first clause pattern matches or unchanged if the second clause matches. Returning the atom done in the debug function is equivalent to disabling the function by calling sys:remove/2, as shown in command line 16.

Statistics, Status, and State

The sys module also lets you collect general statistics on behaviors as well as retrieve information about their internal state, including loop data, without having to reinvent the wheel or implement anything new:

```
18> sys:statistics(frequency, true).
ok
19> frequency:allocate().
{error,no_frequency}
20> sys:statistics(frequency,get).
{ok,[{start_time,{{2015,11,29},{20,10,54}}},
     {current_time,{{2015,11,29},{20,12,9}}},
     {reductions,33},
     {messages_in,1},
     {messages_out,0}]}
21> sys:statistics(frequency, false).
ok
22> sys:get_status(frequency).
{status,<0.35.0>,
        {module,gen_server},
        [[{'$ancestors',[<0.33.0>]},
          {'$initial_call',{frequency,init,1}}],
         running,<0.33.0>,[],
         [{header,"Status for generic server frequency"},
          {data,[{"Status",running},
                 {"Parent",<0.33.0>},
                 {"Logged events",[]}]},
          {data,[{"State",
                 {{available,[]},
                  {allocated,[{15,<0.33.0>},
                              {14,<0.33.0>},
                              {13,<0.33.0>},
                              {12,<0.33.0>},
                              {11,<0.33.0>},
                              {10,<0.33.0>}]}}}]}]]}
```

While sys:statistics/2 returns a list of self-explanatory tagged values, the tuple returned by sys:get_status/1 is not as obvious. It returns a tuple of the format:

```
{status, Pid, {module,Mod}, [ProcessDictionary, SysState, Parent, Dbg, Misc]}
```

where Pid and Mod are the behavior's process identifier and callback module, respectively. The ProcessDictionary is a list of key-value tuples. Note that while we do not use the process dictionary in our frequency server example, the gen_server library module and other behaviors we have yet to cover all do.

SysState tells us whether the behavior's state is running or suspended. By calling sys:suspend/1 and sys:resume/1, we can stop the behavior from handling normal messages, in which case only system messages are handled. Usually you suspend a process when upgrading software using the OTP-specified upgrade capabilities or when testing edge conditions. You might also suspend a process when defining your own behaviors, but most probably not when using standard behaviors. The only way you should suspend Erlang processes in the business logic of your programs is by using receive clauses when none of the messages in the mailbox match. Using the sys:suspend/1 call in your code is a no-no!

Parent is the parent pid, needed by behavior processes that trap exits. If the parent terminates, the behavior processes have to terminate as well. In this example, Parent is the shell process ID. DbgFlag holds the trace and statistics flags, which at the time we retrieved the status had all been turned off (hence the empty list).

Finally, Misc is a list of tagged tuples that contain behavior-specific information. The contained items vary among behaviors, and you are able to override them yourself by providing an optional callback function in your behavior callback module. When working with generic servers, the most important information in Misc is the loop data. You can influence the contents of the Misc value yourself by providing an optional callback function in your behavior callback module, using the function to format the {data, [{"State", ...}]} field to a value the end user might find simpler, more meaningful, or more helpful:

```
...
-export([format_status/2]).
...

format_status(Opt, [ProcDict, {Available, Allocated}]) ->
    {data, [{"State", {{available, Available}, {allocated, Allocated}}}]}.
```

If Opt is the atom normal, it tells us the status is being retrieved as a result of the sys:get_status/1 call. If the behavior is terminating abnormally and the status is being retrieved to incorporate it in an error report, Opt is set to terminate.

ProcDict is a list of key-value tuples containing the process dictionary. In the earlier example, the new state would be:

```
{data,[{"State", {{available, []},{allocated, [{15,<0.33.0>}, {14,<0.33.0>},
                                                {13,<0.33.0>}, {12,<0.33.0>},
                                                {11,<0.33.0>}, {10,<0.33.0>}]}}}]}
```

While it is not mandatory to return a tuple of the format {data, [{"State", State}]}, it is recommended in order to stay consistent with what is currently in use.

To examine just the loop data stored in the behavior process by the callback module, use sys:get_state/1:

```
23> {Free, Alloc} = sys:get_state(frequency).
{[],
 [{15,<0.33.0>}, {14,<0.33.0>}, {13,<0.33.0>}, {12,<0.33.0>},
  {11,<0.33.0>}, {10,<0.33.0>}]}
```

This handy method allows you to avoid having to extract the loop data from the results of `sys:get_status/1`, something that's often difficult to do while debugging interactively in the shell. The `sys:get_state/1` call is intended only for debugging, in fact, as is the corresponding function `sys:replace_state/2`, which allows you to replace the loop state of a running behavior process. For example, imagine you are debugging in the shell and you want to quickly add a few frequencies. You could do it by recompiling the code and restarting the server—something that's simple to do when there are only a few frequencies available, as in our example, but much more difficult if you are in the middle of a test with thousands of allocated frequencies and need to retain the state:

```
24> sys:replace_state(frequency, fun(_) -> {[16,17], Alloc} end).
{[16,17],
 [{15,<0.33.0>}, {14,<0.33.0>}, {13,<0.33.0>}, {12,<0.33.0>},
  {11,<0.33.0>}, {10,<0.33.0>}]}
25> frequency:allocate().
{ok,16}
```

Replacing the loop data requires passing a function that receives the current value of the loop data and returns a new value. This allows you to easily modify only the necessary portions of a complex loop data value. In this example, we replace the empty list of available frequencies with a list of two new frequencies while keeping the list of allocated frequencies. The `sys:replace_state/2` function returns the new loop data. Since the new value in our example adds available frequencies, the next call to `frequency:allocate/0`, which previously was returning {error, no_frequency}, now returns {ok,16}.

The sys Module Recap

To sum up, let's take another look at the functions in the `sys` module we have seen. Note the notation we are using for [,Timeout] in our function descriptions. It means an optional argument to the call, defining functions of arity 2 and 3. Because these functions are nothing other than synchronous calls to our behavior, using Timeout allows us to override the 5-second default timeout time with a value more suited for our application. The functions we've covered are:

```
sys:trace(Name,TraceFlag [,Timeout]) -> ok

sys:log(Name,LogFlag [,Timeout]) -> ok | {ok, EventList}
sys:log_to_file(Name,FileFlag [,Timeout]) -> ok | {error, open_file}

sys:install(Name,{Func,FuncState} [,Timeout]) -> ok
sys:remove(Name,Func [,Timeout])
```

```
sys:statistics(Name,Flag [,Timeout]) -> ok | {ok, Statistics}.

sys:get_status(Name [,Timeout]) -> {status, Pid, {module, Mod}, Status}

sys:get_state(Name [,Timeout]) -> State

sys:replace_state(Name,ReplaceFun [,Timeout]) -> State

sys:suspend(Name [,Timeout]) -> ok
sys:resume(Name [,Timeout]) -> ok
```

To print trace events to the shell, use trace/2. When logging the events for later retrieval, use log/2. Turn logging on and off by setting LogFlag to true or false. By default, the last 10 events are stored; you can override this value by turning on logging using {true, Int}, where Int is a non-negative integer.

Events can be retrieved using the print and get flags. When using log_to_file/2, events are stored in textual format. The FileFlag is a string denoting the absolute or relative filename, or the atom false to turn it off. Use sys:install/2 to write your own triggers and trace functions in conjunction with system events and sys:remove/2 to recall them.

When using statistics/2, turn the gathering of statistics on and off by setting Flag to true or false, respectively. Use get_state/1 to examine loop data and replace_state/2 to replace it. And finally, get_status/1 returns all the available data relative to the internal behavior state. The get_state/1, replace_state/2, and get_status/1 functions are incredibly helpful when debugging and troubleshooting live systems.

Remember the Opts parameter passed as the last argument to the gen_server start functions? We used the empty list as a placeholder. You can enable tracing, logging, and statistics when starting your behavior by using the Opts field. If you pass [{debug, DbgList}], where DbgList contains one or more of the entries trace, log, statistics, and {log_to_file, FileName}, these flags are enabled as soon as the behavior process is started.

Spawn Options

When starting a behavior, you can change the default memory and garbage collector settings to address performance and memory utilization. The settings you pass are the same ones taken by the spawn_opt/4 BIF, but passed as an argument of the format [{spawn_opts, OptsList}] along with the debug options in the behavior Opts field.

Use your spawn options with care! The only way to be sure you have performance issues and bottlenecks related to memory management is by profiling and benchmarking your systems. In doing so, you need to understand how the underlying heaps, memory allocation, and garbage collection mechanisms work. Premature optimization is the root of all evil (after shared memory and mutable state). If you do not believe us, you will soon learn that attempts to optimize memory management often have the opposite effect and make your programs slower. The vast majority of cases do not call for performance tuning, but those that do will greatly benefit being spawned with a larger heap or more (or less) frequent garbage collection cycles.

Memory Management and Garbage Collection

If you suspect that your performance issues can be addressed through memory management, benchmark your system while manipulating the heap and the garbage collector settings. Memory-related options that can be changed include:

min_heap_size
: Sets the size the process heap will grow to before the garbage collector (gc) is triggered. This name is misleading, though, as it is in fact the *maximum* size the heap is allowed to grow to before triggering the gc.

min_bin_vheap_size
: Sets the initial and minimal value of the space this process is allowed to use in the shared binary heap before triggering a garbage collection on the binaries.

fullsweep_after
: Determines the number of generational garbage collections that have to be executed before a complete garbage collection pass.

How BEAM's Garbage Collection Works

Erlang's garbage collection can be described, in technical terms, as a *per-process generational semispace copying collector that uses Cheney's copy collection algorithm together with a global large object space*. Using less fancy words, whenever a process has used up all the memory allocated in its heap, the BEAM virtual machine triggers a garbage collection that copies all of the live data (data still in use) to a new heap, freeing up all of the previously held space.

The garbage collector is called generational because live data in the heap that survives two sweeps is copied from an area called the *young heap* to an area called the *old heap*. Data is moved to the old heap under the assumption that, having survived two garbage collections, it will most likely survive future ones. The garbage collector always starts by traversing data on the young heap, copying live data that has survived a previous garbage collection to the old heap, and creating a new young heap to hold the rest. All the memory in the original young heap gets freed. If the garbage collec-

---

tion of the young heap has been unable to free enough memory (or there is not enough memory to copy the data from the young heap), a *full-sweep garbage collection* is triggered. This will inspect and free all data no longer referenced in the old heap as well as the young one.

If there still is not enough memory after the full sweep, the heap size is increased by allocating memory chunks based on a Fibonacci recurrence series with a starting base of 12 words and 38 words. Each successive increase is the sum of 1 and the previous two word counts, so the next size would be 38+12+1, or 51 words. This continues to a size of 833,026 words, after which it is increased by 20% of its current size.

A full-sweep collection is also triggered after a predefined number of generational garbage collections. Because of periods of little activity and a large allocated heap, long-lived processes might be holding on to data that is no longer needed. This can be addressed by configuring the number of generational garbage collections that trigger a full sweep or by hibernating the process (see "Hibernating Behaviors" on page 97).

Not all process data and state is stored in the respective process heaps. Binaries larger than 64 bytes are stored in a shared binary heap used by all processes. They are accessed by a reference, which, through message passing, can be shared among processes. Using a reference makes message passing of large binaries efficient, because they do not have to be copied. A reference counter increments for every reference pointing to the binary, and decrements when the reference is removed. When this counter reaches 0, the binary can be garbage collected.

A *virtual binary heap* is local to every process, and is not shared globally. Garbage collection is triggered when any process exceeds its virtual binary heap size and needs to free up more space. Binaries smaller than 64 bytes are stored on the normal heap and are copied to the virtual heap when sent as a part of a message to other processes or during garbage collection. Garbage collection of the process and virtual binary heaps is done on a per-process basis, reducing the disruption created by memory management while retaining the soft real-time properties of the system.

In the following example, we start the frequency server and trace events related to the garbage collector. We use the *dbg* tracer to measure how many microseconds the process spends garbage collecting. When allocating five frequencies, the total was 9 microseconds (911,345–911,336):

```
1> dbg:tracer().
{ok,<0.35.0>}
2> {ok, Pid} = frequency:start().
{ok,<0.38.0>}
3> dbg:p(Pid, [garbage_collection, timestamp]).
{ok,[{matched,nonode@nohost,1}]}
4> frequency:allocate(), frequency:allocate(), frequency:allocate(),
    frequency:allocate(), frequency:allocate().
```

```
{ok,14}
(<0.38.0>) gc_start [{old_heap_block_size,0},
 {heap_block_size,233},
 {mbuf_size,0},
 {recent_size,0},
 {stack_size,12},
 {old_heap_size,0},
 {heap_size,213},
 {bin_vheap_size,0},
 {bin_vheap_block_size,46422},
 {bin_old_vheap_size,0},
 {bin_old_vheap_block_size,46422}] (Timestamp: {1448,829619,911336})
(<0.38.0>) gc_end [{old_heap_block_size,0},
 {heap_block_size,233},
 {mbuf_size,0},
 {recent_size,44},
 {stack_size,12},
 {old_heap_size,0},
 {heap_size,44},
 {bin_vheap_size,0},
 {bin_vheap_block_size,46422},
 {bin_old_vheap_size,0},
 {bin_old_vheap_block_size,46422}] (Timestamp: {1448,829619,911345})
```

If we now spawn the frequency server, setting the minimum heap size to 1,024 words
(a smaller size would have been enough), we have enough memory to allocate the frequencies without triggering the garbage collector:

```
1> dbg:tracer().
{ok,<0.35.0>}
2> {ok, Pid} = gen_server:start_link({local, frequency}, frequency, [],
                                     [{spawn_opt, [{min_heap_size, 1024}]}]).
{ok,<0.38.0>}
3> dbg:p(Pid, [garbage_collection, timestamp]).
{ok,[{matched,nonode@nohost,1}]}
4> frequency:allocate(), frequency:allocate(), frequency:allocate(),
   frequency:allocate(), frequency:allocate().
{ok,14}
```

Process heap

By increasing the {min_heap_size, Size} to an appropriate value in a short-lived
process, you can allow the process to execute without triggering the garbage collector
or having to allocate more memory to further increase the heap size. This is ideal if a
process is created and has a burst of memory- and CPU-intensive activity, after
which it terminates. Upon termination, all the memory is efficiently released in one
operation. Use this option with care, though, as picking too large a size will increase
memory consumption and might slow down your program.

Size is measured in *words*, a unit size of data used by a particular processor architecture. In a 32-bit architecture, a word is 4 bytes (32 bits), and in a 64-bit architecture, 8

bytes (64 bits). You could set the minimum heap size for all processes using the +hms flag when you start the Erlang runtime system using *erl*. Using the +hms flag is advisable only if you have relatively few processes running in your system and, of course, only if benchmarks show an increase in performance. As a rule of thumb, it is always better to set the minimum heap size on a per-process basis, and only if benchmarks show benefits. Because heap size increases are based on the Fibonacci series, the minimum heap size set will be the next value in the sequence larger than or equal to Size.

Virtual binary heap

One spawn option related to garbage collection and useful for performance tuning is {min_bin_vheap_size, VSize}, used to configure the minimum binary virtual heap size. The virtual binary heap size is the space a process is allowed to use before triggering the garbage collector and freeing the space taken up by binaries that are no longer referenced. This size refers to binaries larger than 64 bytes in size. These are accessed through binary references, which can be used by all processes. You can set the virtual binary heap size for all processes using the +hmbs flag when you start your system with *erl*, but just like with the regular heap, use this option with restraint, and preferably only on specific processes, not on all of them.

Full sweep of the heap

By setting the {fullsweep_after, Number} spawn option, you can specify the number of generational garbage collections that take place before executing a full sweep. Setting Number to 0 disables the generational garbage collection mechanism, freeing all unused data in both the young heap and the old heap every time it is triggered. This will help in environments with little RAM where memory has to be strictly managed. The zero setting may also be useful when a lot of large binaries that are no longer referenced collect in the old heap and you want to remove them frequently. Setting a small value will be suitable if your data is short-lived and benchmarks demonstrate that it is cluttering up your heap. The Erlang documentation suggests a value of 10 or 20, but you should pick your own based on the properties displayed by your system. The default value is much larger!

A full-sweep garbage collection is also triggered every time you hibernate your process. This might help reduce the memory footprint when working with processes that have memory-intensive computations but little overall activity. You can set the full-sweep value globally for all processes using the erlang:system_flag/2 call, but we recommend you don't. You can use the process_info/2 BIF to get information on the settings you change:

```
5> process_info(Pid, garbage_collection).
{garbage_collection,[{min_bin_vheap_size,46422},
                     {min_heap_size,1598},
```

```
{fullsweep_after,65535},
{minor_gcs,0}]}
```

Note the default setting of `fullsweep_after`, a value much higher than you might expect. We had set the `min_heap_size` to 1024, but in shell prompt 5, it appears to be 1598. We requested 1,024 words, but 1,598 is the first value greater than 1,024 in the Fibonacci recurrence sequence of heap sizes the VM uses, so that value is selected instead of 1,024.

If you start playing with the heap size and garbage collection settings, keep in mind that memory is freed only when the garbage collector is triggered. There might be cases where the process heap contains binary references to potentially large binaries in the shared heap. Each reference to a binary is relatively small, so even if the process does not refer to these binaries anymore, potentially huge amounts of memory can be consumed without the garbage collector being triggered, because there is still plenty of space on the process heap. That is why the per-process virtual binary heap is there, calculating the total amount of memory used up by the binaries in the shared heap and helping ensure they get garbage collected more promptly. Under these circumstances, hibernating the process or triggering garbage collection using the `erlang:garbage_collect()` BIF might prove more useful.

Another potential risk is running out of memory. As an example, having a large `min_heap_size` and using the dangerously high default `fullsweep_after` value of 65535 might result in the old heap growing because garbage collections are far apart, resulting in your system running out of memory before the first full sweeps are triggered. Always stress test your systems, and let soak test runs span days, if not weeks.

Spawn Options to Avoid

The following options should be avoided because they either do not work with behaviors or are considered to be bad programming practice. Although `monitor` can be passed as an option when using the `spawn_opt/3` BIF, it is disallowed in generic servers and will result in the process terminating with a `badarg`. While you are allowed to use `link` as an option, starting the behaviors with `start_link` is preferred.

Process priorities should never be set using the {`priority`, `Level`} option, where `Level` is the atom `low`, `normal`, or `high`. Changing process priorities is even more dangerous than meddling with memory and garbage collection, as it can upset the VM's balance and have serious repercussions on the soft real-time properties of your system. Changing priorities can cause the VM's schedulers to behave strangely and unfairly; processes with a higher priority have been known to starve when the ratio between them and those with a lower priority reached certain limits. Furthermore, processes with a lower priority have caused the runtime system to run out of memory when, under heavy load, messages were not consumed as fast as they were produced. You obviously never notice these issues when testing your system; rather, they tend to come back and bite you when the live system comes under heavy load. Let the runtime system decide on your behalf, especially when dealing with hundreds of thousands of processes. You have been warned!

Timeouts

If you want to limit the time a behavior spends in its `init` function, include the option `{timeout,Timeout}`. If after `Timeout` milliseconds the `init` callback function is still executing, the process is terminated and the start function returns `{error,timeout}`. This option is useful in very specific circumstances, often in a running system with dynamic children responsible for a particular transient resource. We don't recommend using it when starting your system, though; we instead suggest that you try to minimize the amount of work executed in the `init` function so as to not slow down the startup procedure.

Summing Up

There are many options to control and monitor your behaviors. Start with built-in tracing and logging functionality. You can then dynamically add generic trace and debug triggers or change your process state using funs and the `sys` module, during runtime and without the need to recompile your code. This is a priceless feature, as you can use it on systems you have never seen that have been running for years on end without the need to restart them. You can read more about this in the `sys` module's reference manual page.

Optimizing processes through the use of the memory flags in their options is trickier, as it requires you to benchmark your system and base your optimizations on the information you extract as a result of your tests. It is rare that you will have to manipulate the default garbage collector settings or play with your heap sizes. But if and when you are having performance problems, you will be grateful you have read this far in this chapter. If you need more information, look at the documentation of the `spawn_opt` BIF in the `erlang` module's manual page.

What's Next?

We park online tracing for now, until we implement our own behaviors (learning how it all works behind the scenes) in Chapter 10, and ignore performance tuning until we reach Chapter 13. In the next chapters, we focus on the remaining behaviors, starting with FSMs, followed by event managers, supervisors, and applications.

Remember that they are all built on the same foundations, so the sys module and all of the spawn and debug options we have discussed in this chapter will be valid.

## CHAPTER 6

Finite State Machines

Now that we've become experts at writing generic servers, the time has come to master our next behavior. When prototyping systems with what eventually became Erlang, language inventors Joe Armstrong, Mike Williams, and Robert Virding were implementing a soft telephony switch allowing them to phone each other and say hello.[1] Each phone accessing the switch was prototyped as a process acting as an FSM. At any one time, the function would represent the state the phone was in (on hook, off hook, dialing, ringing, etc.) and receive events associated with that state (incoming call, dial, off hook, on hook, etc.).

One of the outcomes of this prototyping activity was to ensure that Erlang became a language suited for and optimized for building nontrivial and scalable FSMs, a key component in many complex systems. Developers use FSMs to program protocol stacks, connectors, proxies, workflow systems, gaming engines, and simulations, to mention but a few examples. So it was no surprise that when OTP behaviors came along, they included generic FSMs.

In this chapter, we introduce FSMs implemented in pure Erlang. We break an example up into generic and specific code, migrating it to the gen_fsm behavior. The good news is that all the borderline cases relating to concurrency and error handling that apply to generic servers also apply to FSMs. So while we might mention some of them, there will be no need for us to go into the same level of detail. After all, an FSM implementation is essentially a special variant of a generic server.

---

1 Movie fans will have seen this switch in the blockbuster production of *Erlang the Movie*. It was filmed when the language was still evolving, so observant fans will have noticed the old syntax in some of the examples. If you have not viewed it, look for it on YouTube. It is a must-see!

Finite State Machines the Erlang Way

Before diving into our examples, let's get a bit of automata theory out of the way. An FSM is an abstract model consisting of a finite number of states and incoming events. When the program is in each state, it can receive certain events from the environment—and only those events. When an event arrives and the FSM is in a certain state, the program executes some predetermined actions associated with that state and transitions to a new state. The FSM then waits for a new event, in the new state.

For instance, in the FSM shown in Figure 6-1, the state *day* can handle events *eclipse* and *sunset*. *eclipse* keeps the FSM in its current state, while event *sunset* causes a transition to state *night*. In state *night*, event *sunrise* causes a transition back to state *day*. Any other events coming out of sequence (such as *sunrise* when in state *day*) are handled only after a transition to a state where they can be dealt with.

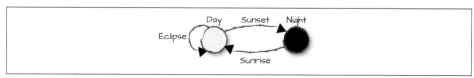

Figure 6-1. Erlang FSM

In Erlang, each state is represented within a tail-recursive function and events are represented as messages. So for Figure 6-1, the code for state *day* would look as follows:

```
day() ->
    receive
        eclipse -> day();
        sunset  -> night()
    end.
```

Upon receiving an incoming event, the FSM executes one or more actions before transitioning to its next state. The state transition is achieved by calling the next function, determined by the combination of the current state and inbound event. In the following example, the combination of the event *sunrise* in state *night* will result in the action defined in the function make_roosters_crow/0, followed by a transition to state *day*. Note how we are not allowing solar eclipses to take place at night. If the FSM receives an *eclipse* event, it remains in the process mailbox until the FSM transitions to a state that can handle it:

```
night() ->
    receive
        sunrise ->
            make_roosters_crow(),
            day()
    end.
```

When you start an FSM, you need to give it a starting state and initialize it. As in the next code example, we could initialize the FSM by spawning the init/0 function and create the Earth there[2] before moving on to state *day*:

```
start() ->
    spawn(?MODULE, init, []).

init() ->
    create_earth(),
    day().
```

This is how we do FSMs in Erlang. The keys to keeping FSMs simple are selective receives, tail-recursive functions, and the ability to initialize the FSM when spawning the process.

You should completely design your FSM, perhaps by drawing out a diagram like the ones in this chapter, before you start coding. You want to know what your states, events, actions, and state transitions are. If they get complex, see whether your FSM can be split up into smaller FSMs that, during execution, pass the flow between each other. They will be easier to both implement and maintain.

FSMs Versus Generic Servers

Beware of the common beginner error where instead of using a generic FSM, you use a generic server and unknowingly store the FSM state in the loop data. Ask yourself when designing the system whether you need an FSM or a client-server behavior. The answer is usually obvious if you consider the question in the design phase of the project.

Coffee FSM

To keep our Java aficionados happy, let's use a coffee vending machine as an FSM example. It will be an embedded application interfacing the hardware through a specific hardware module. The implementation we are about to study has three states:

- *Selection*, allowing the customer to select the desired coffee brew
- *Payment*, allowing the customer to insert coins and pay for the selected item
- *Remove*, a state where the FSM waits for the user to remove the drink from the machine

---

2 This would be an interesting function to benchmark.

These states are linked by four events that trigger actions and transitions to next states. Events triggered by the customer include:

- Making a coffee *selection*
- Dropping a coin of any value in the slot to *pay* for the selection
- Pressing the *cancel* button
- Successful *removal* of the cup of coffee from the machine

Note that most of these events can be triggered in most states. If the FSM is in the *payment* state, there is nothing stopping a user from pressing the coffee selection buttons, or if we are in state *selection*, the user can always insert a coin. If the events can be triggered, they have to be managed regardless of the state. When events are received in a particular state, actions can be executed before transitioning to the next state. The actions in our example include:

- *Display* text in the coffee machine's LED display
- *Return change* or inserted coins to the client
- *Drop the cup* in the machine
- *Prepare* the selected drink
- *Reboot* the coffee machine (not user-initiated)

A simplified version of the FSM can be seen in Figure 6-2. Note that it does not depict a complete set of events and actions. Coins can be inserted in states other than *payment*, the cancel button can be pressed in the *selection* or *remove* states, or the hardware could be reset when starting the FSM. The figure does, however, provide an overview of all the state transitions and events that trigger them. The figure annotates each transition with the actions that are executed when that transition is taken. Actions appear in brackets (<>) and events are in bold.

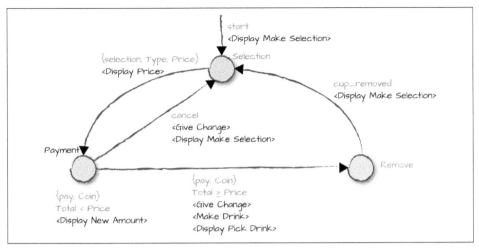

Figure 6-2. Coffee machine FSM

With this model in mind, let's start by stepping through a pure Erlang implementation of the FSM. After that, we migrate the implementation to the generic FSM behavior module.

The Hardware Stub

Embedded systems that require sensors and hardware interactions include device drivers written in C interfacing to the Erlang code. To keep the example simple, we have stubbed this interaction in the *hw.erl* module. We use this module in both the Erlang implementation and the generic FSM behavior implementation:

```
-module(hw).
-compile(export_all).

display(Str, Arg)         -> io:format("Display:" ++ Str ++ "~n", Arg).
return_change(Payment)    -> io:format("Machine:Returned ~w in change~n",[Payment]).
drop_cup()                -> io:format("Machine:Dropped Cup.~n").
prepare(Type)             -> io:format("Machine:Preparing ~p.~n",[Type]).
reboot()                  -> io:format("Machine:Rebooted Hardware~n").
```

You will see calls to this module in the FSM implementations. Functions being called as a result of the sensors in the coffee machine call the client functions in the *coffee.erl* module directly. For testing purposes, we instead call them from the shell. With this out of the way, let's start looking at the implementation itself.

The Erlang Coffee Machine

In this section we create the Erlang part of the application, keeping in mind throughout how the FSM in this example can be generalized and made into a reusable behavior in OTP.

Starting

We start the FSM using the `start_link/0` function. It spawns a new process that starts executing in the `init/0` function and registers itself using the name `coffee`, the same name as the module. Here, we use the `?MODULE` preprocessor construct to refer to the module name rather than using the module name explicitly, which we did for clarity in previous chapters. The `init/0` function reboots the coffee machine and shows *Make Your Selection* in the display. We then enter into our first state by calling the tail-recursive function `selection/0`. Have a look at it and try to split it up into generic and specific code:

```
-module(coffee).
-export([tea/0, espresso/0, americano/0, cappuccino/0,
         pay/1, cup_removed/0, cancel/0]).
-export([start_link/0, init/0]).

start_link() ->
    {ok, spawn_link(?MODULE, init, [])}.

init() ->
    register(?MODULE, self()),
    hw:reboot(),
    hw:display("Make Your Selection", []),
    selection().
```

The generic code, highlighted in this example, includes spawning the process that runs in the `init/0` function, registering it, and transitioning to the first state. The code specific to the coffee machine is the process name, the callback module, and the hardware-specific operations executed in `init/0`, along with any arguments we pass on to that call. The first state is also specific, as is any loop data we might pass on to that state. In our example, there is no state needed at startup.

The events

Two sets of client functions generate events that are passed on to the coffee FSM as asynchronous calls. The first four functions inform the FSM of the drink selection the user made, together with the price. The `cup_removed` event is triggered by hardware sensors when a cup is removed. If a coin is inserted, `pay/1` is called, with the value of the coin passed as an argument. Finally, `cancel` is called when the cancel button is pressed. As we mentioned earlier, these events can be triggered in any state. There is nothing stopping a user from pressing the cancel button when the drink is being prepared, or inserting a coin without having made a selection. The client functions are as follows:

```
%% Client Functions for Drink Selections

tea()        -> ?MODULE ! {selection, tea,       100}.
espresso()   -> ?MODULE ! {selection, espresso,  150}.
americano()  -> ?MODULE ! {selection, americano, 100}.
cappuccino() -> ?MODULE ! {selection, cappuccino,150}.

%% Client Functions for Actions

cup_removed() -> ?MODULE ! cup_removed.
pay(Coin)     -> ?MODULE ! {pay, Coin}.
cancel()      -> ?MODULE ! cancel.
```

In these client functions, the tags and any data (such as the price) associated with the events are specific. What is generic are the sending of the events to the FSM and the possibility of having synchronous and asynchronous calls. In our example, the calls are all asynchronous. Had some of them been synchronous, the return value would also have been specific, but the protocol and the `receive` statement receiving the reply would have been generic.

The selection state

In the `init/0` function, after having initialized the coffee machine, we make the transition to our first state. This is the *selection* state, where the customer picks a drink. Upon receiving the event {selection, Type, Price}, we display the price of the drink and move to the next state, *payment*. In this state, we pass the arguments Type, Price, and amount Paid, initially set to 0. These three arguments are the loop data needed in the *payment* state.

If a customer inserts a coin without having made a selection, we have to return it. If the customer presses the cancel button, we need to remove the event from the process mailbox, ensuring that it is not accidentally received in a later state:

```
%% State: drink selection

selection() ->
    receive
        {selection, Type, Price} ->
            hw:display("Please pay:~w",[Price]),
            payment(Type, Price, 0);
        {pay, Coin} ->
            hw:return_change(Coin),
            selection();
        _Other ->    % cancel
            selection()
    end.
```

Every combination of state and event will result in a specific set of actions and a transition to the next state. The generic code consists of the sections receiving events, handling state transitions, and storing the loop data. The specific code relates to handling the events, namely updating the display, returning the coins, and deciding on the next state.

The payment state

When the customer has picked a drink, it is time to either pay for it or cancel the selection. Every coin inserted will result in the event {pay, Coin} being generated, where Coin is the amount that has been inserted. This amount is added to the total. If the total is greater than or equal to the price of the drink, the code will trigger actions terminating with the transition to the *remove* state. If not enough money has been inserted, the remaining amount to be paid is updated and the FSM remains in the *payment* state. If the cancel button is pressed, any payment made is returned to the user and the FSM returns to the *selection* state. Any other event—more specifically, pressing any of the selection buttons—is ignored. The way we ignore an event is to reinvoke the current state:

```
%% State: payment

payment(Type, Price, Paid) ->
    receive
        {pay, Coin} ->
            if
                Coin + Paid >= Price ->
                    hw:display("Preparing Drink.",[]),
                    hw:return_change(Coin + Paid - Price),
                    hw:drop_cup(), hw:prepare(Type),
                    hw:display("Remove Drink.", []),
                    remove();
                true ->
                    ToPay = Price - (Coin + Paid),
                    hw:display("Please pay:~w",[ToPay]),
                    payment(Type, Price, Coin + Paid)
            end;
        cancel ->
            hw:display("Make Your Selection", []),
            hw:return_change(Paid),
            selection();
        _Other -> %selection
            payment(Type, Price, Paid)
    end.
```

As in the *selection* state, the generic code includes receiving events, state transitions, and storing the loop data. Specific code includes the events themselves, the actions executed as a result, and the next state. Storing the loop data could have been done in one variable containing a record, but as different states need a different number of arguments, this solution is cleaner for this particular example.

The remove state

The FSM enters the *remove* state when the coffee is paid for and has been brewed. It is a state of its own because the machine cannot be used to brew other beverages until the user removes the cup. When that happens, sensors will trigger the cup_removed event and reset the display. This allows us to transition to the *selection* state, where the activity can start all over again. There is nothing stopping the customer from inserting coins, and if this happens, they have to be returned. The same applies to the customer pressing the cancel or selection buttons, events that have to be ignored:

```
%% State: remove cup

remove() ->
    receive
        cup_removed ->
            hw:display("Make Your Selection", []),
            selection();
        {pay, Coin} ->
            hw:return_change(Coin),
            remove();
        _Other ->    % cancel/selection
            remove()
    end.
```

Before starting the next section about the FSM behavior, download the code and stub modules and try it out. When doing so, take a moment to think of other possible implementations of an Erlang-based FSM. What parts of them are specific and what parts are generic? Of the generic parts, how would you package the generics into a callback-based library module?

Generic FSMs

To separate the generic from the specific functionality in an FSM, we'll take the same course we took with generic servers. Table 6-1 lists the major generic and specific parts of the FSM.

Table 6-1. FSM generic and specific code

Generic	Specific
• Spawning the FSM	• Initializing the FSM state
• Storing the loop data	• The loop data
• Sending events to the FSM	• The events
• Sending synchronous requests	• Handling events/requests
• Receiving replies	• The FSM states
• Timeouts	• State transitions
• Stopping the FSM	• Cleaning up

Spawning the FSM, ensuring it has started correctly, and registering it do not change from one implementation to another. What do change are the local or global registered name of the process (if registered at all), debugging options, and arguments needed for the initialization. Initializing the FSM is specific, including determining the initial state and binding the loop data. Both are returned to the generic FSM receive-evaluate loop, which generically stores the data and state.

Sending both synchronous and asynchronous events and requests to the FSM is generic, as is receiving replies. What is specific are the contents of the events and requests and how they are handled based on the FSM state.

The states are all specific, as are the actions that have to be executed, choosing the next state to transition the FSM to, and updating loop data. Handling of timeouts, within both the client and the FSM itself, is generic. What happens when the timeout is triggered, on the other hand, is specific. Finally, stopping the FSM is generic, while cleaning up prior to termination is specific.

We can view the FSM as an extension of the generic server, with state handling added on top. Messages become events and callback functions that receive the messages become states. All of the generic code is placed in a library module called gen_fsm, while all of the specifics are placed in a callback module. The architecture is illustrated in Figure 6-3, which you can compare to Figure 4-1.

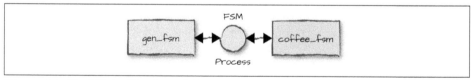

Figure 6-3. The FSM callback module

A Behavior Example

Using the coffee machine example, let's have a look at all the library APIs and associated callback functions of the gen_fsm behavior module. We explore starting and stopping the generic FSM, as well as synchronous and asynchronous events. When stepping through the code, compare the gen_fsm behavior with gen_server. If you want to take it for a practice run, download the code from the book's repository (*https://github.com/francescoc/scalabilitywitherlangotp*).

Starting the FSM

Every behavior callback module starts with module, behavior, and export directives. It also contains all of the state callback functions. While not mandatory, it is good practice to also include all of the client functions that generate the events in one place. Our coffee_fsm module looks like this:

```erlang
-module(coffee_fsm).
-behavior(gen_fsm).

-export([start_link/0, stop/0]).
-export([init/1, terminate/3, handle_event/3]).    % Callback functions
-export([selection/2, payment/2, remove/2]).       % States
-export([americano/0, cappuccino/0, tea/0, espresso/0, % Client functions
         pay/1, cancel/0, cup_removed/0]).
```

The -behavior directive specifies the atom gen_fsm, used for compile-time warnings if callback functions are not implemented or exported. Exported functions include the start and stop functions with their respective callbacks, the client functions, and state callback functions.

The coffee machine is started using the gen_fsm:start_link/4 call, which spawns the FSM and links it to the parent. It returns the tuple {ok, Pid}, where Pid identifies the spawned process, or {error, Reason} if something goes wrong. We cover possible error reasons later; for now, let's focus on the example.

As with all OTP behaviors, we prefer to wrap the start_link/4 call in a client function, located in the callback module. In our example, we've called this function coffee_fsm:start_link/0, but it could take on any name you like. What is important is that it eventually calls gen_fsm:start_link and returns whatever this call returns: most commonly {ok, Pid} or {error, Reason}, as seen in Figure 6-4, or the atom ignore. These values become relevant when we look at supervisors in Chapter 8.

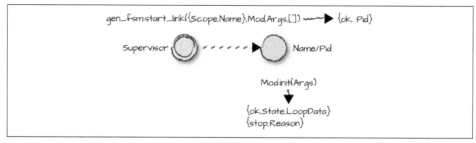

Figure 6-4. Starting a gen_fsm

As soon as the generic FSM process has been spawned, the `init/1` function in the callback module is invoked. Just as with generic servers, this function contains all the specific initialization code. In our example, it will reboot the hardware, reset the display, and return a tuple of the format {ok, StartState, LoopData}, where Start State denotes the state the FSM will be in when it receives its first event. LoopData contains the data passed to the state callback functions. We are also trapping exits in this example, for reasons that will become obvious when we look at termination:

```
start_link() ->
    gen_fsm:start_link({local, ?MODULE}, ?MODULE, [], []).

init([]) ->
    hw:reboot(),
    hw:display("Make Your Selection", []),
    process_flag(trap_exit, true),
    {ok, selection, []}.
```

In our example, the StartState is selection and the LoopData is not used, so we simply return the empty list value, []. When the init/1 callback returns control to the generic module, the synchronous gen_fsm:start_link call returns.

We register the process locally and set the callback module using the ?MODULE macro, which at compile time is replaced with the atom coffee_fsm. We pass [] as an argument to the init/1 callback function and set no options.

The following functions, identical to the ones exported by the generic server module, start an FSM:

```
gen_fsm:start_link(NameScope,Mod,Args,Opts)
gen_fsm:start(NameScope,Mod,Args,Opts)
gen_fsm:start_link(Mod, Args, Opts)
gen_fsm:start(Mod, Args, Opts) -> {ok, Pid}
                                  {error, Error}
                                  ignore

Mod:init/1 -> {ok, NextState, LoopData}
              {stop, Reason}
              ignore
```

NameScope defines how we register our behavior. Just as with generic servers, it can be set to {local, Name}, {global, Name}, or {via, Module, ViaName}, where the via tuple points to a user-defined process registry exporting the same API as the global module, all previously covered in "Going Global" on page 97. We can use the start functions to avoid linking the FSM process to its parent, and we can also decide not to register it. Opts (covered in Chapter 5) can also be passed. They include time-out, debug, and spawn options. Here, we just pass an empty list for Opts.

If something goes wrong in the init/1 callback, you can either terminate abnormally or return the tuple {stop, Reason}. It will propagate the error to the parent process calling the gen_fsm start function (typically via one of the callback module's start functions), causing it to terminate as well. If the parent process happens to be a supervisor, it will in turn terminate all of its children and abort the startup procedure. Although things can go wrong when the system is running, by default, the system cannot recover from a fault in the init/1 callback function.

The most common failure reason you will encounter when testing your FSM from the shell is {error, {already_started, Pid}}. It occurs if another process with the same registered name already exists:

```
1> coffee_fsm:start_link().
Machine:Rebooted Hardware
Display:Make Your Selection
{ok,<0.38.0>}
2> coffee_fsm:start_link().
{error,{already_started,<0.38.0>}}
```

If you want to let the supervisor continue to start workers when init/1 fails, return the atom ignore. Instead of aborting the startup procedure, the supervisor will store the child specification and continue starting other behaviors. We cover the ignore and stop options in more detail in Chapter 8 when we look at supervisors.

Until then, the following example should give you an overview of the different behaviors. Pay particular attention to what causes the process calling the start and start_link functions to terminate. We've omitted the module headers from this example. If you want to view them, download the *test_fsm.erl* module from the book's code repository:

```
start_link(TimerMs, Options) ->
    gen_fsm:start_link(?MODULE, TimerMs, Options).
start(TimerMs, Options) ->
    gen_fsm:start(?MODULE, TimerMs, Options).

init(0) ->
    {stop, stopped};
init(1) ->
    {next_state, selection, []};
init(TimerMs) ->
```

```
    timer:sleep(TimerMs),
    ignore.
```

Let's run the code. In the first set of tests, we stop the FSM by returning {stop, Reason}:

```
1> test_fsm:start_link(0, []).
** exception exit: stopped
2> test_fsm:start(0, []).
{error,stopped}
```

Note the difference when the shell is linked to the behavior and when it is not.

In shell commands 3 and 4, we initialize the FSM with the test_fsm:init(1) call, which accidentally specifies next_state instead of ok as the first element of the return tuple in the callback function. This results in an invalid return value not recognized by the FSM back-end module, a mistake the authors have made many times:

```
3> test_fsm:start_link(1, []).
** exception exit: {bad_return_value,{next_state,selection,{}}}
4> test_fsm:start(1, []).
{error,{bad_return_value,{next_state,selection,{}}}}
```

A behavior module will terminate with the reason bad_return_value whenever you return a control tuple that does not follow the predefined protocol.

When reading through this example, make sure you understand the effect of the EXIT signal propagation when the shell process is linked to the FSM and when it is not. In shell command 5, we pass a 1,000-millisecond argument to init/1 to cause it to sleep for that long, but set the timeout option to 100 milliseconds; this triggers a timeout in the startup process that results in the {error, timeout} tuple. This will be returned whether or not the process is linked to the shell process:

```
5> test_fsm:start_link(1000, [{timeout, 100}]).
{error,timeout}
```

In our last set of tests, in shell commands 6 and 7, our init/1 function returns ignore. This does not result in the behavior terminating abnormally, and as a result, does not propagate further:

```
6> test_fsm:start_link(2, []).
ignore
7> test_fsm:start(2, []).
ignore
```

Although these examples specifically use the gen_fsm behavior, they are valid for all OTP workers.

Enough on starting and initializing our FSMs. Let's move on to important things in life and figure out how to get this coffee brewed.

Sending Events

Having started our coffee FSM, we need to be able to define the states and send both synchronous and asynchronous events. When handled, they trigger state transitions. Events are usually sent in client functions defined in the callback module. Let's start looking at asynchronous events in our FSM and see how they are handled in the different states.

Asynchronous events

Asynchronous events are sent using the gen_fsm:send_event(Name, Event) library function. This sends the Event to the FSM, which handles it in the callback function State(Event, LoopData) in the callback module. After handling the request, the State/2 function returns the new loop data with the next_state or the stop reason (Figure 6-5).

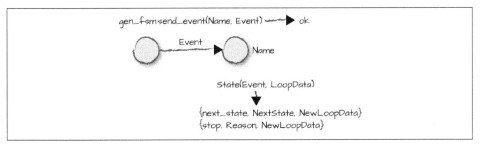

Figure 6-5. Sending events

Our FSM event functions are split into two categories. The first are customer drink selections. These send events of the format {selection, Type, Price}, where Type is one of the atoms tea, espresso, americano,[3] or cappuccino. Price is either 100 or 150 units:

```
tea()       -> gen_fsm:send_event(?MODULE,{selection,tea,100}).
espresso()  -> gen_fsm:send_event(?MODULE,{selection,espresso,100}).
americano() -> gen_fsm:send_event(?MODULE,{selection,americano,150}).
cappuccino()-> gen_fsm:send_event(?MODULE,{selection,cappuccino,150}).
```

The second set of events include actions where the user inserts a coin, presses the cancel button, or removes a cup. There are no rules stating that events must comprise only static values. Note how in the pay/1 function we pass a variable as part of our event—the value of the inserted coin is bound to Coin and passed through the event {pay, Coin}:

---

3 An Americano coffee is an espresso topped up with water—it could not be omitted as it is our favorite.

```
pay(Coin)       -> gen_fsm:send_event(?MODULE,{pay, Coin}).
cancel()        -> gen_fsm:send_event(?MODULE,cancel).
cup_removed()   -> gen_fsm:send_event(?MODULE,cup_removed).
```

Defining states

States in FSMs are defined in callback functions, where the name of the function is the name of the state, Event is the first argument, and LoopData is the second one. Remember that state callback functions are defined in the callback module and have to be exported. The first state we look at is *selection*, where the customer is prompted to choose a drink. It was the start state returned by the init/1 function when we started the FSM:

```
selection({selection,Type,Price}, _LoopData) ->
    hw:display("Please pay:~w",[Price]),
    {next_state, payment, {Type, Price, 0}};
selection({pay, Coin}, LoopData) ->
    hw:return_change(Coin),
    {next_state, selection, LoopData};
selection(_Other, LoopData) ->
    {next_state, selection, LoopData}.
```

Upon choosing a drink, one of the functions tea/0, espresso/0, americano/0, or cappuccino/0 is called. This sends an asynchronous event of the format {selection, Type, Price} to the FSM. Regardless of which drink the customer chooses or its price, the selection gets handled generically. This event is pattern matched in the first clause of the state callback function, displaying the price the customer has to pay. By returning the tuple {next_state, NextState, NewLoopData}, we return the control to the gen_fsm module and wait for the next event. In this case, NextState is bound to the *payment* state and LoopData to a tuple denoting the selection (Type), the price, and the amount paid so far, which is initially set to 0. Note how we ignore the incoming loop data, set to the empty list in the init/1 callback function, but create it for the next state.

What happens if a customer walks up to the coffee machine when it is in the *selection* state and inserts a coin? In our example, we programmed the FSM to return the coin using the hw:return_change/1 call, remaining in the *selection* state and not changing the loop data (which is set to the empty list anyhow). If you prefer to keep the coin, just delete that line of code. Or, if you are implementing a deluxe variant of a coffee machine, add functionality to block the coin insert facility until the selection has been entered.

When in the *selection* state, clients can generate events that do not require any actions or state changes. They include pressing the cancel button or setting off the cup removed sensors, events that need to be handled but can be ignored in the sense that they change neither the current state nor the loop data. Had we not included the third function, a customer pressing the cancel button would have triggered a call to

---

selection(cancel, []), causing a runtime error, because none of the function clauses would have matched.

If the customer selects an Americano coffee, the FSM displays the amount owed and moves to the state *payment*, eagerly awaiting the next event:

```
payment({pay, Coin}, {Type,Price,Paid}) when Coin+Paid < Price ->
    NewPaid = Coin + Paid,
    hw:display("Please pay:~w",[Price - NewPaid]),
    {next_state, payment, {Type, Price, NewPaid}};
payment({pay, Coin}, {Type,Price,Paid}) when Coin+Paid >= Price ->
    NewPaid = Coin + Paid,
    hw:display("Preparing Drink.",[]),
    hw:return_change(NewPaid - Price),
    hw:drop_cup(), hw:prepare(Type),
    hw:display("Remove Drink.", []),
    {next_state, remove, null};
payment(cancel, {_Type, _Price, Paid}) ->
    hw:display("Make Your Selection", []),
    hw:return_change(Paid),
    {next_state, selection, null};
payment(_Other, LoopData) ->
    {next_state, payment, LoopData}.
```

The customer now has to pay for the coffee. Every time a coin is inserted, the {pay, Coin} event is generated. We add the value in Coin to the amount Paid, and, if the sum is less than the price of the drink, we display the remaining amount to pay. By returning payment as the next state, we keep the FSM in that state, changing the loop data to reflect the amount paid so far.

If the customer has inserted enough change to pay for the drink, we trigger a chain of actions that start by changing the display, indicating we are preparing the drink. We return any change and drop the cup. We brew the drink, returning from the synchronous hw:prepare(Type) call only when the drink is finished. At this point, we tell the customer to remove the drink and return the control to the gen_fsm control loop, indicating that the next state is *remove*.

While paying for their coffee, customers could change their minds and press the cancel button. If they do, we change the display to "Make Your Selection," return any coins they might have paid, and indicate that the next state is *selection*. Finally, if a customer triggers the cup removed sensors or presses any of the drink selection buttons, we ignore the event and remain in the state *payment*.

Let's assume the customer has paid for a drink and received the appropriate change, and the drink has been brewed. The FSM would at this stage be in the state *remove*:

```
remove(cup_removed, LoopData) ->
    hw:display("Make Your Selection", []),
    {next_state, selection, LoopData};
remove({pay, Coin}, LoopData) ->
```

```
        hw:return_change(Coin),
        {next_state, remove, LoopData};
    remove(_Other, LoopData) ->
        {next_state, remove, LoopData}.
```

Sensors in the coffee machine will be triggered when the customer removes the cup. This will trigger the `coffee_fsm:cup_removed()` call, resulting in the `cup_removed` event being handled in the first clause. The coffee machine updates its display to "Make Your Selection" and the function returns, setting the next state to *selection*. In the *remove* state, customers can also insert coins, which we return in the second function clause, or they can press the cancel or drink selection buttons, which we ignore in the third clause.

The moment of truth has arrived. Will we get our coffee? Let's test our program and see if it works. When compiling your behavior, as we saw in "Generic Servers" on page 77, you get a warning over the missing `code_change/3` callback when compiling the code in this chapter. We cover this in Chapter 12 when looking at software upgrades.

To better understand what is going on, we'll use the debug options built into OTP and described in "Tracing and Logging" on page 101. We start the FSM, select tea, change our mind to an Americano coffee, and insert two 100-unit coins. We get our change, and while waiting to remove the cup, we insert a 50-unit coin just for the sake of testing out the FSM. As you step through the example, you can distinguish the code you input by the prompts (such as `1>`), and debugger printouts by the `*DBG*` prefix. Output from `io:format/2` in the *hw.erl* module starts with a hint of what parts of the system it represents (`Display:` or `Machine:`), and the rest of the output is actual return values from the function calls:

```
1> {ok, Pid} = coffee_fsm:start_link().
Display:Make Your Selection
{ok,<0.68.0>}
2> sys:trace(Pid, true).
ok
3> coffee_fsm:cancel().
*DBG* coffee_fsm got event cancel in state selection
ok
*DBG* coffee_fsm switched to state selection
4> coffee_fsm:tea().
*DBG* coffee_fsm got event {selection,tea,100} in state selection
ok
Display:Please pay:100
*DBG* coffee_fsm switched to state payment
5> coffee_fsm:cancel().
*DBG* coffee_fsm got event cancel in state payment
ok
Display:Make Your Selection
Machine:Returned 0 in change
*DBG* coffee_fsm switched to state selection
```

```
6> coffee_fsm:americano().
*DBG* coffee_fsm got event {selection,americano,150} in state selection
ok
Display:Please pay:150
*DBG* coffee_fsm switched to state payment
7> coffee_fsm:pay(100).
*DBG* coffee_fsm got event {pay,100} in state payment
ok
Display:Please pay:50
*DBG* coffee_fsm switched to state payment
8> coffee_fsm:pay(100).
*DBG* coffee_fsm got event {pay,100} in state payment
ok
Display:Preparing Drink.
Machine:Returned 50 in change
Machine:Dropped Cup.
Machine:Preparing americano.
Display:Remove Drink.
*DBG* coffee_fsm switched to state remove
9> coffee_fsm:pay(50).
*DBG* coffee_fsm got event {pay,50} in state remove
ok
Machine:Returned 50 in change
*DBG* coffee_fsm switched to state remove
10> coffee_fsm:cup_removed().
*DBG* coffee_fsm got event cup_removed in state remove
ok
Display:Make Your Selection
*DBG* coffee_fsm switched to state selection
11> sys:trace(Pid, false).
ok
```

It seems to work; time for a break!

Timeouts

We are not sure if this has ever happened to you, but imagine you're standing patiently in line to buy your coffee. While doing so, you decide what you want and prepare the exact change, and are ready to go. But the person in front of you is apparently not in the same rush. After spending ages reading through all the options, they make their selection and get shown the price. Only then do they dip into their purse or pocket and start looking not just for change, but for the exact change. They insert a penny and go back in looking for another one, until they find no more. After which they start looking for nickels and dimes. It can be aggravating, and not only for impatient authors. Luckily, we control the coffee machine now, so we can take advantage of that to implement punishment and revenge to discourage this type of behavior.

Timeouts can be specified within the FSM as an integer in milliseconds or as the atom infinity. We can include them in the init/1 and State callback functions. When a timeout is triggered, the event is sent to the state the FSM is currently in. As we are controlling the code for the coffee machine, let's put a bit of stress into the lives of those who do not have any by triggering a timeout if a user waits more than 10 seconds between one coin insertion and another. First, let's refactor the *payment* state by adding a timeout:

```erlang
-define(TIMEOUT, 10000).
...

selection({selection,Type,Price}, _LoopData) ->
    ...
    {next_state, payment, {Type, Price, 0}, ?TIMEOUT};

payment({pay, Coin}, {Type,Price,Paid}) when Coin+Paid >= Price ->
    ...
    {next_state, remove, []};
payment({pay, Coin}, {Type,Price,Paid})
  when Coin+Paid < Price ->
    ...
    {next_state, payment, {Type, Price, NewPaid}, ?TIMEOUT};
payment(timeout, {Type, Price, Paid}) ->
    hw:display("Make Your Selection", []),
    hw:return_change(Paid),
    {next_state, selection, []};
payment(_Other, LoopData) ->
    {next_state, payment, LoopData, ?TIMEOUT}.
```

Customers inserting coins will now have to hurry. If they take longer than 10 seconds to insert a coin, their selections will be canceled and their money returned. There is a risk that they'll figure that out that by pressing one of the drink selection buttons they will get an extra 10 seconds, but let's assume for now that they are too wrapped up looking for their next penny to work this out.

In place of a timeout value, we can alternatively return hibernate if we want to reduce the generic FSM's memory footprint. Use hibernate only if you are not expecting the FSM to receive events for a while, with benchmarks showing you have memory issues. We can also stop the FSM, something we cover later in this chapter:

```erlang
gen_fsm:send_event(NameScope ,Event) -> ok

Mod:State/2 -> {next_state, NextState,NewLoopData}
               {next_state ,NextState,NewLoopData, Timeout}
               {next_state, NextState,NewLoopData, hibernate}
               {stop, Reason, NewLoopData}
```

Asynchronous events to all states

If you want to send an asynchronous event but are not concerned about the state in which it is received, you can use the send_all_state_event/2 call. This could be useful if you want to execute actions such as formatting and printing the loop data or stopping the FSM. Events are passed as the first argument to the handle_event/3 callback function, which executes the actions and then returns the {next_state, NextState, NewLoopData} tuple back to the gen_fsm control loop (Figure 6-6).

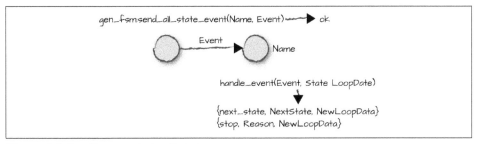

Figure 6-6. Sending events to all states

As with generic servers, the handle_info/3 callback function takes care of all non-OTP-compliant messages such as exit signals, monitors, and messages sent using the Pid!Msg construct. The handle_info/3 callback returns the same range of control tuples as handle_event/3 and State/2:

```
gen_fsm:send_all_state_event(NameScope ,Event) -> ok

Mod:handle_info/3,
Mod:handle_event/3 -> {next_state, NextState,NewLoopData}
                      {next_state ,NextState,NewLoopData, Timeout}
                      {next_state, NextState,NewLoopData, hibernate}
                      {stop, Reason, NewLoopData}
```

Selective Receives

Selective receives are one thing the OTP gen_fsm behavior module does not provide. In complex FSMs running across unreliable distributed networks, events occasionally arrive out of sequence. Imagine receiving a sunset event when you are in state *night*! You can either buffer these events in your loop data and handle them when you reach a state that knows how to deal with them, or add an extra state, turning the out-of-sequence events into valid ones. Both solutions cause unnecessary complexity when compared to the simplicity of using a selective receive, leaving the events in the process mailbox until they are matched in a state that can actually handle them.

This lack of functionality arises from a conscious design decision in behaviors, where messages are handled in the order they arrive, ensuring no memory leaks occur as a result of any message not being matched. Events in the gen_fsm behavior are handled on a first-in, first-out (FIFO) basis, and are removed from the receiving process's mailbox when read.

There are two approaches if you want to avoid the increase in complexity resulting from messages arriving out of sequence. You could implement your own selective FSM behavior, which we explain how to do in Chapter 10. Or you can use a selective

FSM behavior someone else has already implemented. At the time of writing, the most commonly used implementation is plain_fsm by Ulf Wiger. It follows all OTP principles and can be included in supervision trees. The plain_fsm source code and examples are available on GitHub (*https://github.com/uwiger/plain_fsm*).

Synchronous events

Although all the events sent in our FSM examples were asynchronous, sometimes we want to ensure clients can't generate a new event until their previous one is handled. For example, a diagnostic client might want to ask the FSM to set a particular value into a hardware register and take no further action until the FSM indicates the setting was successful. As illustrated in Figure 6-7, this is when we use the sync_send_event/2 (or sync_send_all_state_event/2) call.

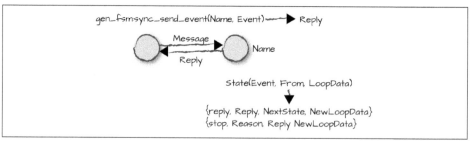

Figure 6-7. Synchronous events

This call and its callback are a middle ground between using the call/2 and handle_call/3 functions in the generic server and using asynchronous events and event handling in FSMs. Events are handled in the State(Event, From, LoopData) callback, where From is a tuple denoting the client and the request reference. Instead of returning the next_state tuple, the callback returns a tuple of the format {reply, Reply, NextState, NewLoopData}. Reply is sent back to the client and becomes the return value of the gen_fsm:sync_send_event/2 call.

Just as with generic servers, we can use the From in a gen_fsm:reply(From, Reply) call to send Reply back to the original caller identified by From, returning {next_state, NextState, NewLoopData} in the State/3 callback function itself.

The gen_fsm:sync_send_all_state_event/2 function (Figure 6-8) sends synchronous requests to the FSM regardless of its current state. The event is handled in the handle_sync_event/4 callback function, which returns a Reply sent back to the original caller, either through the use of From or in the control tuple sent back to the gen_fsm module.

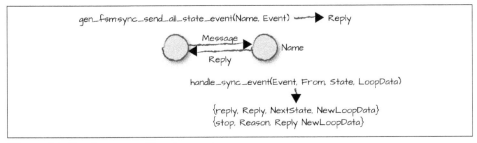

Figure 6-8. Synchronous all state events

```
gen_fsm:sync_send_event(NameScope, Event) -> Reply
gen_fsm:sync_send_event(NameScope, Event, Timeout) -> Reply

gen_fsm:sync_send_all_state_event(NameScope, Event) -> Reply
gen_fsm:sync_send_all_state_event(NameScope, Event, Timeout) -> Reply

Mod:State/3,
Mod:handle_sync_event/4 -> {reply,Reply,NextState,NewLoopData}
                           {reply,Reply,NextState,NewLoopData,Timeout}
                           {reply,Reply,NextState,NewLoopData,hibernate}
                           {next_state,NextState,NewLoopData}
                           {next_state,NextState,NewLoopData,Timeout}
                           {next_state,NextState,NewLoopData,hibernate}
                           {stop,Reason,Reply,NewLoopData}
                           {stop,Reason,NewLoopData}
```

Let's use the sync_send_all_state_event/2 function to trigger the actions for normal termination of our coffee machine. After all, it doesn't really matter what state it is in, as long as it stops.

Termination

Our coffee machine can terminate for two reasons. It is either stopped normally, or the process terminates abnormally if the exit BIFs are used or a runtime error occurs. For abnormal termination, if the FSM is trapping exits as a result of a process_flag(trap_exit, true) call, terminate/3 (Figure 6-9) is invoked in the callback module. If the FSM is not trapping exits, the FSM terminates and its exit signal propagates to other processes linked to it.

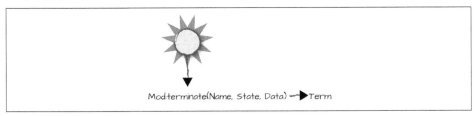

Figure 6-9. Termination

If a stop event is sent using sync_send_all_state_event/2, the event is handled in handle_sync_event/4. Note that unlike the stop atom returned in the tuple, the stop we pass through the sync_send_all_state_event/2 call has no meaning other than one given to it in the program. This also contrasts with the stop parameter in {stop, Reason, LoopData}, which is interpreted and used by the gen_fsm module to terminate the FSM. This is exactly the same principle we discussed when we looked at generic server termination in "Termination" on page 89:

```
stop() -> gen_fsm:sync_send_all_state_event(?MODULE, stop).

handle_sync_event(stop, _From, _State, LoopData) ->
    {stop, normal, LoopData}.

terminate(_Reason, payment, {_Type,_Price,Paid}) ->
    hw:return_change(Paid);
terminate(_Reason, _StateName, _LoopData) ->
    ok.
```

Note also how, in the terminate function, we handle the cleanup for the states individually. If customers have started paying for their drinks, they should receive a refund. By doing this in terminate/3, we are also able to refund users after an abnormal termination. Here's an example of what happens:

```
1> {ok, Pid} = coffee_fsm:start_link().
Display:Make Your Selection
{ok,<0.35.0>}
2> coffee_fsm:americano().
Display:Please pay:150
ok
3> coffee_fsm:pay(100).
Display:Please pay:50
ok
4> exit(Pid, crash).
Display:Shutting Down
true
Machine:Returned 100 in change

=ERROR REPORT==== 3-Mar-2013::12:01:25 ===
** State machine coffee_fsm terminating
** Last message in was {'EXIT',<0.33.0>,crash}
** When State == payment
**       Data  == {americano,150,100}
** Reason for termination =
** crash
** exception exit: crash
```

Summing Up

We've now introduced the principles behind the generic FSM behavior. Although it might not be the most commonly used behavior, when it fits your application it will greatly simplify your task, making your code more readable and easier to maintain. Table 6-2 lists the most important functions we covered in this chapter.

Table 6-2. gen_server callbacks

gen_fsm function or action	gen_fsm callback function
gen_fsm:start/3, gen_fsm:start/4, gen_fsm:start_link/3, gen_fsm:start_link/4	Module:init/1
gen_fsm:send_event/2	Module:StateName/2
gen_fsm:send_all_state_event/2	Module:handle_event/3
gen_fsm:sync_send_event/2, gen_fsm:sync_send_event/3	Module:StateName/3
gen_fsm:sync_send_all_state_event/2, gen_fsm:sync_send_all_state_event/3	Module:handle_sync_event/4
Pid ! Msg, monitors, exit messages, messages from ports and socket, node monitors, and other non-OTP messages	Module:handle_info/2
Triggered by returning {stop, ...} or when terminating abnormally while trapping exits	Module:terminate/3

Review the manual pages for the gen_fsm module. You can find the code implementing the behavior library in the *gen_fsm.erl* source file. If you previously looked at the *gen_server.erl* code, pay particular attention to how they both interact with the *gen.erl* helper module, since other behaviors use it as well.

Get Your Hands Dirty

Before moving on to the next chapter, why not have a go at implementing an FSM to get a feel for the process of designing, coding, and testing it? If you are not up to coding, download the code (*https://github.com/francescoc/scalabilitywitherlangotp*) from the Chapter 8 examples, read through it, and take it for a trial run, since we use the controller in future examples. What makes this example interesting is that different instances of the behaviors, each representing a cell phone, will speak to each other. It is a typical example of a massively concurrent application where processes are used to represent and control resources or devices. The cell phones use the home location register, the database that maps users registered on the network to unique phone numbers that we implemented in "ETS: Erlang Term Storage" on page 45 in the hlr module.

The Phone Controllers

In our cellular system, there is no central switch. Instead, for every phone attached to the network, we create a phone controller that interacts with other controllers. Each controller is a process implemented as an FSM holding the state of a single phone. All communication between the phone controllers must be asynchronous so as to prevent blocking of the system. Fulfill the following API to implement the phone controllers in the *phone_fsm.erl* module:

start_link(PhoneNumber) -> {ok, FsmPid}.
:   Starts a new phone controller FSM process for the phone number linked to the calling process. This should also attach the phone controller process to its phone number in the home location register (HLR).

stop(FsmPid) -> ok.
:   Stops a phone controller FSM at FsmPid. This should also detach it from its phone number in the HLR.

connect(FsmPid) -> ok., disconnect(FsmPid) -> ok.
:   Called by a phone to attach itself to a phone controller FSM process. This must be done so that the phone controller knows where to send the phone replies that provide information about incoming and outgoing calls. The connect function call usually occurs when a phone is started, or when it is connecting to another FSM process. Note that we connect to an FSM process by its pid and not its number. The disconnect function detaches a phone from a phone controller FSM process.

action(FsmPid, Action) -> ok.
:   Sends an action from the phone to the phone controller at FsmPid. The legal actions are:

    {outbound,PhoneNumber}
    :   Try to connect to another phone.

    accept
    :   Accept a call request.

    reject
    :   Reject a call request.

    hangup
    :   Hang up an ongoing call.

The following calls send events between the phone controllers inside the switch:

`busy(FsmPid) -> ok.`
> Sends a `busy` event to `FsmPid`, generally as a reply to an inbound request indicating that this phone is busy and can't accept the call

`reject(FsmPid) -> ok.`
> Sends a `reject` event to `FsmPid`, generally as a reply to an inbound request indicating that we refuse the call

`accept(FsmPid) -> ok.`
> Sends an `accept` event to `FsmPid`, generally as a reply to an inbound request indicating that we accept the call

`hangup(FsmPid) -> ok.`
> Sends a `hangup` event to `FsmPid` to terminate an ongoing call

`inbound(FsmPid) -> ok.`
> Sends an `inbound` event to `FsmPid` requesting that a call be set up

Given this API, Figure 6-10 shows what the controller FSM might look like. Note that the FSM is not complete: events can come out of sequence as a result of race conditions or go missing in action as a result of network or software errors. Before coding, make sure you have reviewed it and added the missing events and state transitions. You'll figure out what they are when reviewing the interfaces.

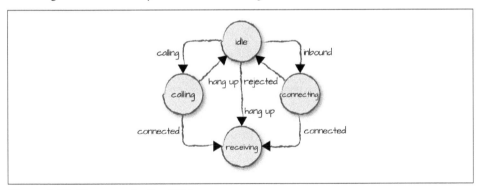

Figure 6-10. Phone controller FSM

Let's Test It

Each phone controller is connected to a mobile phone. You do not have to write the code for the phone. It is provided in the module *phone.erl* and has the following API:

`start_link(PhoneNumber) -> {ok, PhonePid}.`

Starts a new phone for number `PhoneNumber`, which is linked to the calling process.

`stop(PhonePid) -> ok.`

Stops the phone at `PhonePid`.

`action(PhonePid, Action) -> ok.`

Performs an action requested by the phone user for the phone at `PhonePid`. The legal actions are:

`{call,PhoneNumber}`
> Start a call to `PhoneNumber`.

`accept`
> Accept a call request.

`reject`
> Reject a call request.

`hangup`
> Hang up an ongoing call.

Calling an action will result in events being sent to the phone's phone controller using the API for the phone controller that we defined in the previous section.

`reply(PhonePid, Reply) -> ok.`

Sends a reply event from the phone controller to the phone. The legal reply events are:

`{inbound,PhoneNumber}.`
> An inbound call has arrived from `PhoneNumber`.

`accept`
> An outbound call has been accepted.

`invalid`
> An outbound call was attempted to an invalid number.

`reject`
> An outbound call has been rejected.

`busy`
> An outbound call was attempted to a busy phone.

`hangup`
> An outbound call has hung up.

These reply events will result in the phone process printing information on the console of the format *PhonePid*: *PhoneNumber*: *Event*. For example:

```
<0,459,0>: 103618: hangup
```

You should start your phones in a different node from those running the hlr and the phone controllers. The ultimate test is for a phone to call itself and return a busy signal. Here is a trial test run with three phones:

```
1> hlr:new().
{ok,<0.34.0>}
2> phone_fsm:start_link("123").
{ok,<0.36.0>}
3> phone_fsm:start_link("124").
{ok,<0.38.0>}
4> phone_fsm:start_link("125").
{ok,<0.40.0>}
5> {ok,P123}=phone:start_link("123").
{ok,<0.42.0>}
6> {ok,P124}=phone:start_link("124").
{ok,<0.44.0>}
7> {ok,P125}=phone:start_link("125").
{ok,<0.46.0>}
8> phone:action(P123, {call,"124"}).
<0.44.0>: 124: inbound call from 123
ok
9> phone:action(P124, accept).
<0.42.0>: 123: call accepted
ok
10> phone:action(P125, {call,"123"}).
<0.46.0>: 125: busy
ok
11> phone:action(P125, {call,"124"}).
<0.46.0>: 125: busy
ok
```

What's Next?

In the next chapter, we look at another worker behavior, the generic event manager. It is a slightly different from a generic server and an FSM in that a single instance of an event manager is allowed to have multiple callback modules. These callback modules are called *handlers*, and if implemented generically, they can be reused across multiple managers. We use them to add visibility into what is going on in our base station controller.

## CHAPTER 7

Event Handlers

The mobile frequency server your company produces hits the market and appears to be extremely popular. Having no visibility into its performance and uptime, you have been asked to implement monitoring software that not only collects statistics and logs important things that happen, but also warns you when things go wrong. And that is where the problem begins. When you are in the office, you want a widget to start flashing on your screen. When you leave your desk, you might want to keep the widget, but also have the system send you an email. And if you leave the office, you want an SMS or pager message but no emails. Your other colleagues on call might prefer a phone call, as an SMS or pager message would not wake them up in the middle of the night. So, the same event types must trigger different actions at different times, all dependent on external factors. This is where the event handler behavior comes to the rescue.

Events

An *event* represents a state change in the system. It could be a high CPU load, a hardware failure, or a trace event resulting from the activity in a port. An *event manager* is an Erlang process that receives a specific type of event, which could be alarms, warnings, equipment state changes, debug traces, or issues related to network connectivity. When generated, events are sent to the manager in the form of a message, as shown in Figure 7-1. For every event generated, the system might want to take a specific set of actions, as discussed earlier: generate SNMP traps; send emails, SMSs, or pager messages; collect statistics; print messages to a console; or log the event to a file. We call these processes that generate events *producers* and processes receiving and handling these events *consumers*.

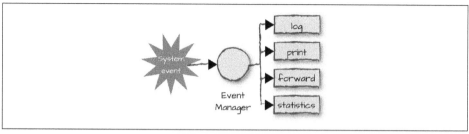

Figure 7-1. Event managers and handlers

Event handlers are behavior callback modules that handle these types of actions. They subscribe to events sent to a manager, allowing different handlers to subscribe to the same events. Different managers handling different event types can use the same event handler. If a handler allows you to log events to a file, another allows you to print them to a console, and a third collects statistics, they could be all be used both by the event manager dealing with debug traces and the event manager handling equipment state changes. Functionality to add, remove, query, and upgrade handlers during runtime is provided in the code implementing the event manager. If you were to implement the code managing events and handlers, what would be generic to all Erlang systems and what would be specific to your application? Table 7-1 shows the breakdown.

Table 7-1. Event handler and manager generic and specific code

Generic	Specific
• Starting/stopping the event manager	• The events
• Sending events	• The event handlers
• Sending synchronous requests	• Initializing event handlers
• Forwarding events/requests to handlers	• Event handler loop data
• Adding/deleting handlers	• Handling events/requests
• Upgrading handlers	• Cleaning up

Starting and stopping the event manager processes is generic, as is registering them with an alias. The process name and events sent to the manager are specific, but the producer sending them, the manager receiving them, and the act of calling a handler are generic. The event handlers themselves are specific, as well as what we do to initialize them, along with cleaning up when they are removed (or when the event manager is stopped). How the handlers deal with the events is specific, as is their loop data. And finally, upgrading the handlers is generic, but what the individual handlers have to do to hand over their state is specific.

Let's have a look at the event behavior module. While the generic server still acts as its foundation, it is very different from the behaviors we've looked at so far.

Generic Event Managers and Handlers

Generic event handlers and managers are part of the standard library application, and like all other behaviors, are split up into generic and specific code. The gen_event module contains all of the generic code. The process running this code is often referred to as the event manager. The callback modules subscribing to the events and handling them through a set of callback functions are called the event handlers. Each handler solves a specific event-driven task and is part of the specific code. Unlike other behaviors, which allow only one callback module per instance, an event manager can take care of zero or more event handlers, as shown in Figure 7-2. But despite the possibility of there being multiple handlers, they will all be executed in a single event manager process.

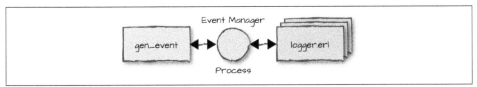

Figure 7-2. Handler callback module

Starting and Stopping Event Managers

The gen_event:start_link(NameScope) function starts a new event manager. Name Scope specifies the *local* or *global* process name or the via module, first explained in "Going Global" on page 97. Should you not want to register the process, use start_link/0 and communicate with it using its pid. Unlike with other behaviors, start_link/0 accepts no callback modules, arguments, or options. Nor does it invoke any callback functions. All the manager does is set its handler list to the empty list:

```
gen_event:start()
gen_event:start(NameScope)
gen_event:start_link()
gen_event:start_link(NameScope) -> {ok,Pid}
                                    {error,{already_started,Pid}}
gen_event:stop(NameScope) -> ok
```

Because you are not calling an init/1 callback function that can return stop or ignore, or even generate a runtime error, not much can go wrong here unless an event manager or process with the same name is already registered.

Stop the event manager using the gen_event:stop/1 call.

Adding Event Handlers

Now that we can start and stop our manager, let's implement a handler and add it. Event handlers are added to and removed from the event manager process dynamically, at runtime. They are considered more generic than other behaviors because you can implement an event handler that can not only handle different event types, but do so in different event managers.

In our logger example, we implement an event handler that logs events and unexpected messages to standard I/O or a file, depending on which parameters are provided when it is added to the manager. As with our other generic behaviors, we start with the behavior directive and export our callback functions:

```
-module(logger).
-behavior(gen_event).
-export([init/1, terminate/2, handle_event/2, handle_info/2]).

init(standard_io)  ->
    {ok, {standard_io, 1}};
init({file, File}) ->
    {ok, Fd} = file:open(File, write),
    {ok, {Fd, 1}};
init(Args) ->
    {error, {args, Args}}.
```

If we call the gen_event:add_handler(Name, Mod, Args) function, the handler implemented in the Mod module is added to the event manager. The event manager calls the Mod:init(Args) callback function, returning {ok, LoopData}, where the LoopData refers to that particular handler. In our example, our loop data contains a tuple with either the file descriptor or the atom standard_io and the integer 1, a counter incremented every time we receive an event. If we pass the standard_io atom as an argument, all events will be printed to the shell. Passing {file, File}, where file is an atom and File is a string containing the filename, will log all events to that file.

To manage multiple events, the event manager stores its handlers and their loop data in a list. Figure 7-3 shows our handler instance and its loop data getting added to the list of other handlers stored by the event manager.

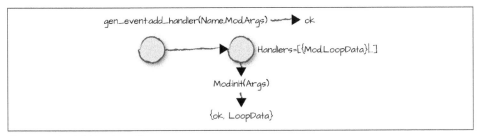

Figure 7-3. Adding handlers

You can not only add many handlers to a manager, but also add the same handler many times, storing different instances of the loop data. In our case, we could add two logger handlers, one saving everything to a file and the other printing the events in the shell. Alternatively, the Mod parameter can be specified as {Module, Id}, where Id can be any Erlang term. If Id is unique, it allows client functions to differentiate between multiple handlers using the same callback module in a particular manager.

```
gen_event:add_handler(NameScope, Mod, Args) -> {'EXIT',Reason}
                                               ok
                                               Term

Mod:init/1 -> {ok, LoopData}
              {ok, LoopData, hibernate}
              Term
```

Adding a nonexistent event handler will result in the event manager failing to call Mod:init/1 and returning {'EXIT', Reason}, where Reason is the undef runtime error (the undefined function). Should the evaluation of any expression in the init/1 callback function fail, {'EXIT', Reason} will be returned. Keep in mind that {'EXIT', Reason} is the tuple caught within the scope of a try-catch expression, and not an exception.

If the init/1 callback returns a Term other than {ok, LoopData}, the Term itself is returned. This includes the case where the Term is the atom ok without the LoopData, a common beginner error. Whenever init/1 does not return {ok, LoopData}, the event handler is not added to the manager. This means just returning ok without LoopData will not work as you might at first think, as the handler is not added.

In our example, if the handler is started with arguments that fail pattern matching in the first two clauses, init/1 returns {error, {args, Args}} and the manager does not add it to its list of handlers. So, while init/1 can return any term, be careful and stick to return values of the format {ok, LoopData} and {error, Reason} to avoid confusion.

Just like other behaviors, you can make your event manager hibernate in between events. It is enough for one handler to return hibernate for this to happen. Use hibernation with care, and only if events will be intermittent. Hibernating your process will trigger a full-sweep garbage collection before you hibernate and right after waking up. This is not a behavior you want when receiving a large number of events at short intervals.

Deleting an Event Handler

Now that we have added a handler, let's see what we need to do in order to delete it. The logger callback module exports the terminate(Args, LoopData) callback function. This function is invoked whenever gen_event:delete_handler(Name, Mod, Args) is called. Name identifies the specific event manager process where our handler is registered; it is either its pid, or its local Name if registered locally. But when using name servers, {global, Name} has to be passed, or if you are using your own name server, pass {via, Name, Module}. Mod specifies the handler you want to delete and Args is any valid Erlang term passed as the first argument to terminate/2. Args could be the reason for termination or just a parameter with instructions needed in the cleanup (Figure 7-4).

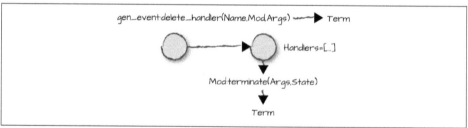

Figure 7-4. Deleting handlers

In our example, if we were to remove the logger handler, we would have to cater for the cases where we are printing the logs to standard I/O or to a file:

```
terminate(_Reason, {standard_io, Count}) ->
    {count, Count};
terminate(_Reason, {Fd, Count}) ->
    file:close(Fd),
    {count, Count}.
```

When the terminate/2 function returns, the handler is deleted from the list of handlers in the specific event manager process identified by the Name argument to delete_handler/3. Other managers using the same handler are not affected. If multiple handlers are registered using the same Mod, such as one for logging to standard_io and another for logging to a file, they are deleted in the reverse order of their addition. If you stop the manager using gen_event:stop/1, all handlers are deleted with reason stop.

Note how `terminate/2` returns `Term`. This becomes the return value of the `delete_handler/3` call. In our example, we return the log counter, `{count, Count}`, which lets the caller of `delete_handler/3` know how many events came through the handlers before they were terminated. But if we were upgrading the handler, `Term` might be all of the loop data. We cover upgrades later in this chapter.

Attempting to delete a handler that isn't registered results in a return value of `{error, module_not_found}`. Both adding and deleting a handler in a nonexistent event manager, irrespective of whether the manager is referenced using a pid or a registered alias, will result in the calling process terminating with reason `noproc`.

```
gen_event:delete_handler(NameScope, Mod, Args) -> {error,module_not_found}
                                                  {'EXIT',Reason}
                                                  Term

Mod:terminate/2 -> Term
```

Sending Synchronous and Asynchronous Events

Events can be sent to the manager and forwarded to the handlers synchronously or asynchronously depending on the need to control the rate at which producers generate events. Events are handled by the manager process, which invokes all added handlers sequentially, one at a time. If you send multiple events to the event manager and they need to be handled by several—potentially slow—event handlers, your message queue might grow and result in a reduction of throughput as described in "Synchronous versus asynchronous calls" on page 417, so make sure your handler does not become a bottleneck. We discuss techniques to handle large volumes of messages in "Balancing Your System" on page 414.

The `gen_event:notify/2` function sends an asynchronous event to all handlers and immediately returns `ok`. The callback function `Mod:handle_event/2` is called for every handler that has been added to the manager, one at a time. `gen_event:sync_notify/2` also invokes the `Mod:handle_event/2` callback function for all handlers. The difference from its asynchronous variant is that `ok` is returned only when all callbacks have been executed.

Let's consider how we might implement the `handle_event/2` callback function for our logger:

```
handle_event(Event, {Fd, Count}) ->
    print(Fd, Count, Event, "Event"),
    {ok, {Fd, Count+1}}.

print(Fd, Count, Event, Tag) ->
    io:format(Fd, "Id:~w Time:~w Date:~w~n"++Tag++":~w~n",
              [Count,time(),date(),Event]).
```

The handle_event/2 callback, illustrated in Figure 7-5, receives an event together with either the atom standard_io or the file descriptor of the file opened in the init/1 callback. The print/4 function invokes io:format/3 to output the counter value, the current date and time, and the Event tag value followed by the event itself.

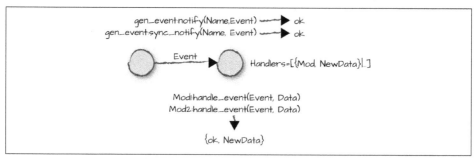

Figure 7-5. Notifications

If our event handler receives any non-OTP-compliant events originating from links, trapping exits, process monitors, monitoring distributed Erlang nodes, or messages resulting from Pid!Msg, they are handled in the handle_info/2 callback function of the event handlers:

```
handle_info(Event, {Fd, Count}) ->
    print(Fd, Count, Event, "Unknown"),
    {ok, {Fd, Count+1}}.
```

The implementation of handle_info/2 for the logger is almost identical to handle_event/2, except that it passes the tag value "Unknown" to the print function to indicate that it doesn't know the source of the event.

```
gen_event:notify(NameScope, Event)
gen_event:sync_notify(Name, Event) -> ok

Mod:handle_event(Event, Data)
Mod:handle_info(Event, Data) -> {ok, NewData}
                                {ok, NewData, hibernate}
                                remove_handler
                                {swap_handler,Args1,NewData,Handler2,Args2}
```

If a handler returns remove_handler from its handle_event/2 or handle_info/2 function, Mod:terminate(remove_handler, Data) is called and the handler is deleted. We look at swapping handlers later in this chapter. Until then, let's make sure that the code in the event handler we have written so far works.

In shell command 1, we start the event manager without registering or linking it to its parent. Should the shell process crash, the event manager process will not be affected. We proceed by adding a handler and sending two notifications, one synchronous and one asynchronous:

```
1> {ok, P} = gen_event:start().
{ok,<0.35.0>}
2> gen_event:add_handler(P, logger, {file, "alarmlog"}).
ok
3> gen_event:notify(P, {set_alarm, {no_frequency, self()}}).
ok
4> gen_event:sync_notify(P, {clear_alarm, no_frequency}).
ok
```

Note how both calls return the atom ok. The semantic difference is that shell command 4 does not return ok until all the handlers have executed their handle calls.

In shell command 5, we add a second instance of the handler, this time directing events to standard I/O. In shell command 6, we send a non-OTP-compliant message that is logged and printed to the shell by the handle_info/2 callback function of our two event handler instances:

```
5> gen_event:add_handler(P, logger, standard_io).
ok
6> P ! sending_junk.
Id:1 Time:{18,59,25} Date:{2013,4,26}
Unknown:sending_junk
sending_junk
```

In shell commands 7 and 8, we read the binary contents of the *alarmlog* file and print them out in the shell. We see the first two events we sent asynchronously and synchronously, as well as the unknown message received by the handle_info/2 call:

```
7> {ok, Binary} = file:read_file("alarmlog").
{ok,<<"Id:1 Time:{18,59,10} Date:{2013,4,26}\nEvent:{set_alarm,{no_frequency,...
8> io:format(Binary).
Id:1 Time:{18,59,10} Date:{2013,4,26}
Event:{set_alarm,{no_frequency,<0.32.0>}}
Id:2 Time:{18,59,14} Date:{2013,4,26}
Event:{clear_alarm,no_frequency}
Id:3 Time:{18,59,25} Date:{2013,4,26}
Unknown:sending_junk
ok
9> gen_event:delete_handler(P, freq_overload, stop).
{error,module_not_found}
10> gen_event:stop(P).
ok
```

We wrap up this example by trying to delete freq_overload, an event handler that has not been added to this event manager. As expected, this returns the error module_not_found. Finally, we stop the event manager, by default terminating all of the event handlers.

Download the logger handler from the book's code repository (*https://github.com/ francescoc/scalabilitywitherlangotp*) and take it for a spin. Test sending it synchronous and asynchronous messages when the event manager has been stopped (or has crashed), and start it using `start_link` and make the shell crash. Finally, try to figure out what happens if you provide an invalid filename when adding the handler.

Retrieving Data

Let's implement another event handler, one that stores metrics. Every time we log an event, we also bump up a counter in an ETS table that tells us how many times this event has been logged. If it is the first occurrence of the event, we create a new entry in the table. Have a look at the code, and if necessary, refer to the manual pages of the ets module:

```
-module(counters).
-behavior(gen_event).
-export([init/1, terminate/2, handle_event/2, handle_info/2]).
-export([get_counters/1, handle_call/2]).

get_counters(Pid) ->
    gen_event:call(Pid, counters, get_counters).

init(_) ->
    TableId = ets:new(counters, []),
    {ok, TableId}.

terminate(_Reason, TableId) ->
    Counters = ets:tab2list(TableId),
    ets:delete(TableId),
    {counters, Counters}.

handle_event(Event, TableId) ->
    try ets:update_counter(TableId, Event, 1) of
        _ok -> {ok, TableId}
    catch
        error:_ -> ets:insert(TableId, {Event, 1}),
                   {ok, TableId}
    end.

handle_call(get_counters, TableId) ->
    {ok, {counters, ets:tab2list(TableId)}, TableId}.

handle_info(_, TableId) ->
    {ok, TableId}.
```

Of interest in this example is how we retrieve the counters. Using `gen_event:sync_event/2` would not have worked, as despite it being synchronous, it forwards the event to all handlers and returns ok. We need to specify the handler to which we want to send our synchronous message, and we do so using the `gen_event:call(NameScope, Mod, Message)` function.

As Figure 7-6 shows, the event handler synchronously receives the request in the Mod:handle_call/2 callback and returns a tuple of the format {ok, Reply, New Data}, where Reply is the return value of the request.

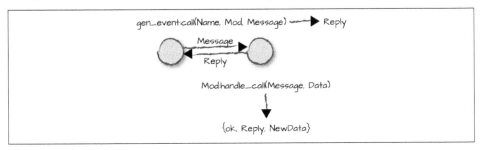

Figure 7-6. Calls

```
gen_event:call(NameScope, Mod, Request)
gen_event:call(NameScope, Mod, Request, Timeout)  -> Reply
                                                     {error, bad_module}
                                                     {error, {'EXIT', Reason}}
                                                     {error, Term}


Mod:handle_call(Event, Data) -> {ok, Reply, NewData}
                                Term
```

The default timeout in gen_event:call/3 is 5,000 milliseconds. It can be overridden by passing either a Timeout value as an integer in milliseconds or the atom infinity. If Mod is not an event handler that has been added to NameScope, {error, bad_mod ule} is returned. If the callback function handle_call/2 terminates abnormally when handling the request, expect {error, {'EXIT', Reason}}. And finally, if handle_call/2 returns any term other than {ok, Reply, NewData}, the return value of gen_event:call will be {error, Term}. In both of these error cases, the handler is removed from the list managed by the event manager without affecting the other handlers.

```
1> {ok, P} = gen_event:start().
{ok,<0.35.0>}
2> gen_event:add_handler(P, counters, {}).
ok
3> gen_event:notify(P, {set_alarm, {no_frequency, self()}}).
ok
4> gen_event:notify(P, {event, {frequency_denied, self()}}).
ok
5> gen_event:notify(P, {event, {frequency_denied, self()}}).
ok
6> counters:get_counters(P).
{counters,[{{event,{frequency_denied,<0.33.0>}},2},
          {{set_alarm,{no_frequency,<0.33.0>}},1}]}
```

Handling Errors and Invalid Return Values

It is not just when its handle_call/2 terminates abnormally or returns an invalid reply that a handler gets deleted. An abnormal termination in any of its callbacks will also result in deletion. The event manager and other handlers are not affected. This differs from other behaviors in that the event handler is silently removed, without any notifications being sent to the event manager's supervisor. What also differs from other behaviors is that the event manager will by default trap exits. The assumption is that event managers are added and removed dynamically and independently of each other, and as a result, a crash should not affect anything in its surrounding environment (see Figure 7-7). While fault isolation is a good property, failing silently isn't.

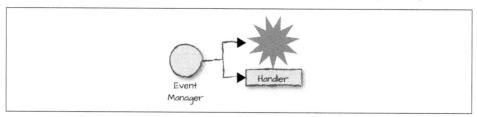

Figure 7-7. Handler crash

To better understand how abnormal termination in event handlers works, let's use the following code snippet as an example:

```
-module(crash_example).
-behavior(gen_event).
-export([init/1, terminate/2, handle_event/2]).

init(normal) -> {ok, []};
init(return) -> error;
init(ok)     -> ok;
init(crash)  -> exit(crash).

terminate(_Reason, _LoopData) -> ok.

handle_event(crash,  _LoopData) -> 1/0;
handle_event(return, _LoopData) -> error.
```

Depending on what parameters we send to the event handler when adding it to the event manager and notifying it of an event, we can generate runtime errors and return invalid values. Step through the shell commands in the following example, mapping all requests to the error conditions that occur:

```
1> {ok,P}=gen_event:start().
{ok,<0.35.0>}
2> gen_event:which_handlers(P).
[]
3> gen_event:add_handler(P, crash_example, return).
error
```

```
4> gen_event:which_handlers(P).
[]
5> gen_event:add_handler(P, crash_example, normal).
ok
6> gen_event:which_handlers(P).
[crash_example]
7> gen_event:notify(P, crash).
ok
=ERROR REPORT==== 27-Apr-2013::09:27:49 ===
** gen_event handler crash_example crashed.
** Was installed in <0.35.0>
** Last event was: crash
** When handler state == []
** Reason == {badarith,
                 [{crash_example,handle_event,2,
                     [{file,"crash_example.erl"},{line,13}]},
                  ...]}
8> gen_event:which_handlers(P).
[]
9> gen_event:add_handler(P, crash_example, normal).
ok
10> gen_event:notify(P, return).
ok
=ERROR REPORT==== 27-Apr-2013::09:28:41 ===
** gen_event handler crash_example crashed.
** Was installed in <0.35.0>
** Last event was: return
** When handler state == []
** Reason == error
11> gen_event:which_handlers(P).
[]
```

While error reports are generated (these are covered in more detail in "The SASL Application" on page 231), no runtime errors occur, and as a result, no EXIT signals are generated. Sending notifications can fail silently, resulting in the handler being deleted without any processes or humans noticing.

You get around this problem by connecting a handler to the calling process using gen_event:add_sup_handler/3. It works in the same way as add_handler/3, with the side effect that the calling process is now monitoring the handler, and the calling process is being monitored by the newly added instance of the handler in the manager. If an exception occurs or an incorrect return value is returned in callbacks handling events, a message of the format {gen_event_EXIT, Mod, Reason} is sent to the process that added the handler. Reason can be one of the following:

- normal if a callback function returned remove_handler or the handler was removed using delete_handler/3

- shutdown if the event manager is being stopped, either by its supervisor or by the stop/1 call

- {'EXIT', Term} if a runtime error occurred

- Term if the callback returned anything other than {ok, LoopData} or {ok, Reply, LoopData}

- {swapped, NewMod, Pid}, where Pid has swapped the handler

We look into swapping handlers in the next section.

Monitoring goes two ways. If the process that added the handler terminates, the handler is removed with {stop, Reason} as an argument. This ensures that multiple instances of the handler are not included in the manager should the handler be added by a behavior stuck in a cyclic restart.

Fail Loudly!

If you are writing a system with requirements on high availability and fault tolerance, the last thing you want is a handler being silently deleted or failing in init/1 and not being added at all. Always check the return value of the add_handler/3 and add_sup_handler/3 calls. If you have to use add_handler, ensure that you execute any code that might fail as a result of a bug, external dependencies (such as a disk full error), or corrupt data within the scope of a try-catch expression. Where possible, use add_sup_handler/3, pattern matching on its return value to ensure that the handler has been properly added, and pay attention to all exception messages you receive as a result. You don't want your alarm system to fail without raising any alarms!

Swapping Event Handlers

The event manager provides functionality to swap handlers during runtime. It allows a handler to pass its state to a new handler, ensuring that no events are lost in the process. The second parameter of the gen_event:swap_handler/3 call is a tuple containing the name of the handler callback module we want to replace, together with the arguments passed to its terminate function. The third parameter is a tuple containing the callback module of the new handler and the arguments passed to its init function. Figure 7-8 shows these parameters along with the steps that take place when swapping handlers.

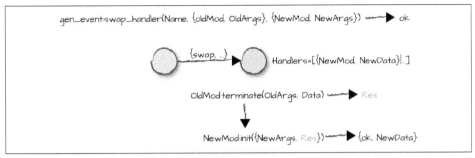

Figure 7-8. Swapping handlers

The `terminate` callback function in the old handler is first called. Its return value, `Res`, is passed in a tuple together with the arguments intended for the `init` function of the new handler. It couldn't be simpler! If you want to swap the handler and start supervising the connection between the handler and the calling process, use `gen_event:swap_sup_handler/3`. The handler you are swapping does not have to be supervised.

An example is probably the best way to demonstrate swapping. Let's extend our logger handler to be able to flip between logging to a file and printing to standard I/O. We extend our `terminate` function to handle the reason `swap`, returning `Res`, a tuple of the format `{Type, Count}`. `Type` is either the file descriptor or the atom `standard_io`, and `Count` is the unique ID for the next item to be logged. As we do not know what the logger we are swapping to wants to do with the events, we do not close the file and instead let the handler deal with it in its `init/1` call.

In the `init/1` call, we add two cases where we accept the same `Args` as when we are adding the handler, but also the results sent back from `terminate`. So, if we are logging to a file and want to swap to standard I/O, we close the file and return `{ok, {standard_io, Count}}`. If we are printing to standard I/O, we open the file and start writing events in it. In both cases, we retain whatever value `Count` is set to:

```
init({standard_io, {Fd, Count}}) when is_pid(Fd) ->
    file:close(Fd),
    {ok, {standard_io, Count}};
init({File, {standard_io, Count}}) when is_list(File) ->
    {ok, Fd} = file:open(File, write),
    {ok, {Fd, Count}};
...

terminate(swap, {Type, Count}) ->
    {Type, Count};
...
```

If we test our code, starting the manager, adding the logger handler, raising an alarm, swapping the handlers, and raising a second alarm, we get the following results:

```
1> {ok, P} = gen_event:start().
{ok,<0.35.0>}
2> gen_event:add_handler(P, logger, {file, "alarmlog"}).
ok
3> gen_event:notify(P, {set_alarm, {no_frequency, self()}}).
ok
4> gen_event:swap_handler(P, {logger, swap}, {logger, standard_io}).
ok
5> gen_event:notify(P, {set_alarm, {no_frequency, self()}}).
Id:2 Time:{10,1,16} Date:{2013,4,27}
Event:{set_alarm,{no_frequency,<0.33.0>}}
ok
6> {ok, Binary}=file:read_file("alarmlog"), io:format(Binary).
Id:1 Time:{10,1,16} Date:{2013,4,27}
Event:{set_alarm,{no_frequency,<0.33.0>}}
ok
```

Wrapping It All Up

Now that we have a handler, let's wrap it in a module, hiding the event manager API in a more intuitive and application-specific set of functions. We do this in the freq_overload module, which is responsible for starting the manager along with providing an API for setting and clearing the no_frequency alarm and generating events when a client is denied a frequency. It also provides a wrapper around the functions used to add and delete handlers. We leave the handler-specific function calls, such as retrieving the counters or swapping from file to standard I/O, local to the handlers themselves:

```
-module(freq_overload).
-export([start_link/0, add/2, delete/2]).
-export([no_frequency/0, frequency_available/0, frequency_denied/0]).

start_link() ->
    case gen_event:start_link({local, ?MODULE}) of
        {ok, Pid} ->
            add(counters, {}),
            add(logger, {file, "log"}),
            {ok, Pid};
        Error ->
            Error
    end.


no_frequency() ->
    gen_event:notify(?MODULE, {set_alarm, {no_frequency, self()}}).
frequency_available() ->
    gen_event:notify(?MODULE, {clear_alarm, no_frequency}).
```

```
frequency_denied() ->
    gen_event:notify(?MODULE, {event, {frequency_denied, self()}}).

add(M,A) -> gen_event:add_sup_handler(?MODULE, M, A).
delete(M,A) -> gen_event:delete_handler(?MODULE, M, A).
```

Note how we are adding the counters in our freq_overload:start_link/0 call. This ensures that if the event manager is restarted, the counters and logger handlers will also be added. The downside is that we are unable to supervise the handlers from the event manager process in case it crashes. If you want another process to monitor the handlers, use freq_overload:add/2, which uses gen_event:add_sup_handler/3.

When setting alarms and raising events, we are also including the pid of the frequency allocator. This allows us to differentiate among different allocators (called the alarm or event originators), allowing operational staff to determine which servers are overutilized and need to be allocated a larger frequency pool. We want to raise an alarm every time the allocator runs out of frequencies and clear it when a frequency becomes available. If a client allocates the last frequency, we call freq_over load:no_frequency/0, setting the no_frequency alarm. If a frequency is deallocated in a state where there were no frequencies available, we clear the alarm by calling freq_overload:frequency_available/0. We also raise an event every time a user is denied a frequency by calling the function freq_overload:frequency_denied/0. We handle this as a separate event, as we might be out of frequencies but do not reject requests. The code additions to *frequency.erl* are straightforward:

```
allocate({[], Allocated}, _Pid) ->
    freq_overload:frequency_denied(),
    {{[], Allocated}, {error, no_frequency}};
allocate({[Res|Resources], Allocated}, Pid) ->
    case Resources of
        [] -> freq_overload:no_frequency();
        _  -> ok
    end,
    {{Resources, [{Res, Pid}|Allocated]}, {ok, Res}}.

deallocate({Free, Allocated}, Res) ->
    case Free of
        [] -> freq_overload:frequency_available();
        _  -> ok
    end,
    NewAllocated = lists:keydelete(Res, 1, Allocated),
    {[Res|Free], NewAllocated}.
```

Now that we have fixed other code in the frequency allocator and implemented our freq_overload event manager, let's add the logger and counters handlers to the event manager and run them alongside each other, as seen in Figure 7-9. Along with raising alarms, we also log them.

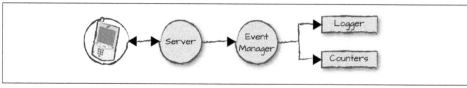

Figure 7-9. Handler example

We start the frequency server and the event manager and add a second logger event handler, this one printing to the shell. In our example, the frequency allocator had six frequencies. In shell command 4, we allocate all of them, raising a no_frequency alarm. This happens despite the last request being successful and returning {ok, 15}:

```
1> frequency:start_link().
{ok,<0.35.0>}
2> freq_overload:start_link().
{ok,<0.37.0>}
3> freq_overload:add(logger, standard_io).
ok
4> frequency:allocate(), frequency:allocate(), frequency:allocate(),
    frequency:allocate(), frequency:allocate(), frequency:allocate().
Id:1 Time:{10,41,25} Date:{2015,2,28}
Event:{set_alarm,{no_frequency,<0.35.0>}}
{ok,15}
5> frequency:allocate().
Id:2 Time:{10,41,46} Date:{2015,2,28}
Event:{event,{frequency_denied,<0.35.0>}}
{error,no_frequency}
6> frequency:allocate().
Id:3 Time:{10,42,0} Date:{2015,2,28}
Event:{event,{frequency_denied,<0.35.0>}}
{error,no_frequency}
7> frequency:deallocate(15).
Id:4 Time:{10,42,16} Date:{2015,2,28}
Event:{clear_alarm,no_frequency}
ok
8> counters:get_counters(freq_overload).
{counters,[{{set_alarm,{no_frequency,<0.35.0>}},1},
           {{clear_alarm,no_frequency},1},
           {{event,{frequency_denied,<0.35.0>}},2}]}
```

Having set the alarm, we then try to allocate two frequencies and fail both times. We clear the alarm when deallocating a frequency in shell command 7. When we retrieve the counters, we see that a frequency was denied twice and that the no_frequency alarm was set and cleared once.

The SASL Alarm Handler

We've been talking about alarm handlers in this chapter without giving a proper definition, but the time has come to set the record straight. An alarm handler is the part of the system that records ongoing issues and takes appropriate actions. If your system reaches a high memory mark or is running out of disk space (or frequencies), you will want to set (or raise) an alarm. When memory usage decreases or old log files are deleted, the respective alarms are cleared. At any point in time, it should be possible to inspect the list of active alarms and get a snapshot of ongoing issues.

The SASL alarm handler process is an event manager and handler that comes as part of the Erlang runtime system and provides this functionality. It is a very basic alarm handler you are encouraged to replace or complement in your own project when more functionality is required. The philosophy of developing Erlang systems is to start simple and add complexity as your system grows. That is exactly what has been done with the SASL alarm handler.

Depending on how you have installed Erlang on your computer, the SASL alarm handler might already have been started. Run `whereis(alarm_handler).` in your shell to find out. If you get back the atom `undefined`, start the alarm handler by typing `application:start(sasl).` in the shell. You might get some progress reports printed out in the shell, once again depending on how you installed Erlang. We cover the reports, alarming in general, and other useful tools and libraries in SASL in Chapter 9, Chapter 11, and Chapter 16. For now, don't worry about the reports.

If `whereis/1` returns a pid, the alarm handler is already running and you do not need to do anything other than try it out:

```
1> whereis(alarm_handler).
<0.41.0>
2> alarm_handler:set_alarm({103, fan_failure}).

=INFO REPORT==== 26-Apr-2013::08:23:27 ===
    alarm_handler: {set,{103,fan_failure}}
ok
3> alarm_handler:set_alarm({104, cabinet_door_open}).

=INFO REPORT==== 26-Apr-2013::08:23:43 ===
    alarm_handler: {set,{104,cabinet_door_open}}
ok
4> alarm_handler:clear_alarm(104).

=INFO REPORT==== 26-Apr-2013::08:24:04 ===
    alarm_handler: {clear,104}
ok
5> alarm_handler:get_alarms().
[{103,fan_failure}]
```

In our example, picture a rack in which the cooling fan fails. A system administrator goes to the rack, opens the cabinet door to inspect what is going on, closes it, and heads off to order a replacement fan. What we've done is raise two alarms with IDs 103 and 104. These IDs are used to clear the alarm, something that happens in shell command 4 when the cabinet door is closed. The wrapper around the SASL event manager and event handler exports the following functions:

```
alarm_handler:set_alarm({AlarmId, Description}) -> ok
alarm_handler:clear_alarm(AlarmId) -> ok
alarm_handler:get_alarms() -> [{AlarmId, Description}]
```

In a complex system, you might have hundreds of alarms of varying severities, where clearing one will by default clear half a dozen other ones dependent on it. You will want to keep accurate statistics, log everything, and in advanced systems run agents that take immediate action. In the case of the fan failure, for example, you would want to start shutting down all equipment in that cabinet to avoid overheating. The existing handler does none of this and will not scale. But to start off, it works and fits in with the iterative design, develop, and test cycles that are the norm when developing Erlang systems.

Replacing or complementing the existing handler is easy. You need to handle the events {set_alarm, {AlarmId, AlarmDescr}} and {clear_alarm, AlarmId}. If you want to swap the existing handler using swap_handler/3:

```
gen_event:swap_handler(alarm_handler,
                       {alarm_handler, swap}, {NewHandler, Args})
```

the init function in your new handler should pattern match the argument {Args, {alarm_handler, Alarms}}, where Args is passed in the swap_handler/3 call and {alarm_handler, Alarms} is the term returned from the terminate/2 call of the old handler. Alarms is a list of {AlarmId, Description} tuples.

Summing Up

In this chapter, we introduced how events are handled by the event manager behavior. You should by now have a good understanding of the advantages of using the gen_event behavior instead of rolling your own or increasing the complexity of one of your subsystems by integrating this functionality in it. The biggest difference between the event manager and other OTP behaviors is the one-to-many relationship, where you can associate many event handlers with one event manager. The most important functions and callbacks we have covered are listed in Table 7-2.

Table 7-2. gen_event callbacks

gen_event function or action	gen_event callback function
gen_event:start/0, gen_event:start/1, gen_event:start_link/0, gen_event:start_link/1	
gen_event:add_handler/3, gen_event:add_sup_handler/3	Module:init/1
gen_event:swap_handler/3, gen_event:swap_sup_handler/3	Module1:terminate/2, Module2:init/1
gen_event:notify/2, gen_event:sync_notify/2	Module:handle_event/2
gen_event:call/3, gen_event:call/4	Module:handle_call/2
gen_event:delete_handler/3	Module:terminate/2
gen_event:stop/1	Module:terminate/2
Pid ! Msg, monitors, exit messages, messages from ports and socket, node monitors, and other non-OTP messages	Module:handle_info/2

Before reading on, make sure you review the manual pages for the gen_event module. An example that complements the ones in this chapter is the alarm_handler module. Read through the code and you will notice how the developers have integrated the client functions to start and stop the event manager as well as the handler functions themselves.

What's Next?

The event manager is the last worker behavior we cover. Event managers, along with generic servers, FSMs, and behaviors you have written yourself, are started and monitored in supervision trees. The next chapter covers the supervisor behavior, responsible for starting, stopping, and monitoring other supervisors and workers. We show you how to write your own behaviors in Chapter 10. We go into more detail on the importance of alarms in ensuring the high availability and reliability of your systems when we cover monitoring and preemptive support in Chapter 16.

## CHAPTER 8

Supervisors

Now that we are able to monitor and handle predictable errors, such as running out of frequencies, we need to tackle unexpected errors arising as the result of corrupt data or bugs in the code. The catch is that unlike the errors returned to the client by the frequency allocator or alarms raised by the event managers, we will not know what the unexpected errors are until they have occurred. We could speculate, guess, and try to add code that handles the unexpected and hope for the best. Using automated test generation tools based on property-based testing, such as QuickCheck (*http://www.quviq.com/products/erlang-quickcheck/*) or PropEr (*https://github.com/manopapad/proper*), can definitely help create failure scenarios you would never devise on your own. But unless you have supernatural powers, you will never be able to predict every possible unexpected error that might occur, let alone handle it before knowing what it is.

Too often, developers try to cater for bugs or corrupt data by implementing their own error-handling and recovery strategies in their code, with the result that they increase the complexity of the code along with the cost of maintaining it (and, yet handle only a fraction of the issues that can arise, and more often than not, end up inserting more bugs in the system than they solve). After all, how can you handle a bug if you don't know what the bug *is*? Have you ever come across a C programmer who checks the return values of `printf` statements, but is unsure of what to do if an error actually occurs? If you've come to Erlang from another language that supports exception handling, such as Java or C++, how many times have you seen `catch` expressions that contain nothing more than *TODO* comments to remind the development team to fix the exception handlers at some point in the future—a point that unfortunately never arrives?

This is where the generic supervisor behavior makes its entrance. It takes over the responsibility for the unexpected-error-handling and recovery strategies from the developer. The behavior, in a deterministic and consistent manner, handles monitoring, restart strategies, race conditions, and borderline cases most developers would not think of. This results in simpler worker behaviors, as well as a well-considered error-recovery strategy. Let's examine how the supervisor behavior works.

Supervision Trees

Supervisors are processes whose only task is to monitor and manage children. They spawn processes and link themselves to these processes. By trapping exits and receiving EXIT signals, the supervisors can take appropriate actions when something unexpected occurs. Actions vary from restarting a child to not restarting it, terminating some or all the children that are linked to the supervisor, or even terminating itself. Child processes can be both supervisors and workers.

Fault tolerance is achieved by creating supervision trees, where the supervisors are the nodes and the workers are the leaves (Figure 8-1). Supervisors on a particular level monitor and handle children in the subtrees they have started.

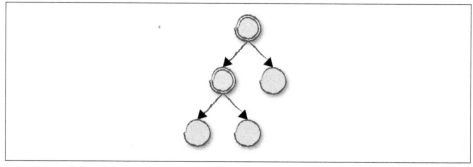

Figure 8-1. Supervision trees

Figure 8-1 uses a double ring to denote processes that trap exits. Only supervisors are trapping exits in our example, but there is nothing stopping workers from doing the same.

Let's start by writing our own simple supervisor. It will allow us to better appreciate what needs to happen behind the scenes before examining the OTP supervisor implementation. Given a list of child process specifications, our simple supervisor starts the children as specified and links itself to them. If any child terminates abnormally, the simple supervisor immediately restarts it. If the children instead terminate normally, they are removed from the supervision tree and no further action is taken. Stopping the supervisor results in all of the children being unconditionally terminated.

Here is the code that starts the supervisor and child processes:

```erlang
-module(my_supervisor).
-export([start/2, init/1, stop/1]).

start(Name, ChildSpecList) ->
    register(Name, Pid = spawn(?MODULE, init, [ChildSpecList])),
    {ok, Pid}.

stop(Name) -> Name ! stop.

init(ChildSpecList) ->
    process_flag(trap_exit, true),
    loop(start_children(ChildSpecList)).

start_children(ChildSpecList) ->
    [{element(2, apply(M,F,A)), {M,F,A}} || {M,F,A} <- ChildSpecList].
```

When starting my_supervisor, we provided the init/1 function with child specifications. This a list of {Module, Function, Arguments} tuples containing the functions that will spawn and link the child process to its parent. We assume that this function always returns {ok, Pid}, where Pid is the process ID of the newly spawned child. Any other return value is interpreted as a startup error.

We start each child in start_children/1 by calling apply(Module,Function,Args) within a list comprehension that processes the ChildSpecList. The result of the list comprehension is a list of tuples where the first element is the child pid, retrieved from the {ok, Pid} tuple returned from apply/3, and a tuple of the module, function, and arguments used to start the child. If Module does not exist, Function is not exported, and if Args contains the wrong number of arguments, the supervisor process terminates with a runtime exception. When the supervisor terminates, the runtime ensures that all processes linked to it receive an EXIT signal. If the linked child processes are not trapping exits, they will terminate. But if they are trapping exits, they need to handle the EXIT signal, most likely by terminating themselves, thereby propagating the EXIT signal to other processes in their link set.

It is a valid assumption that nothing abnormal should happen when starting your system. If a supervisor is unable to correctly start a child, it terminates all of its children and aborts the startup procedure. While we are all for a resilient system that tries to recover from errors, startup failures is where we draw the line.

```erlang
loop(ChildList) ->
    receive
        {'EXIT', Pid, normal} ->
            loop(lists:keydelete(Pid,1,ChildList));
        {'EXIT', Pid, _Reason} ->
            NewChildList = restart_child(Pid, ChildList),
            loop(NewChildList);
        stop ->
```

```
            terminate(ChildList)
    end.

restart_child(Pid, ChildList) ->
    {Pid, {M,F,A}} = lists:keyfind(Pid, 1, ChildList),
    {ok, NewPid} = apply(M,F,A),
    lists:keyreplace(Pid,1,ChildList,{NewPid, {M,F,A}}).

terminate(ChildList) ->
    lists:foreach(fun({Pid, _}) -> exit(Pid, kill) end, ChildList).
```

The supervisor loops with a tuple list of the format {Pid, {Module, Function, Argument}} returned from the start_children/1 call. This tuple list is the supervisor state. We use this information if a child terminates abnormally, mapping the pid to the function used to start it and needed to restart it. If we want to register supervisors with an alias, we pass it as an argument using the variable name. The reason for not hardcoding it in the module is that you will often have multiple instances of a supervisor in your Erlang node.

Having started all the children, the supervisor process enters the receive-evaluate loop. Notice how this is no different from the process skeleton described in "Process Skeletons" on page 53, and similar to the generic loop in servers, FSMs, and event handler processes. The only difference from the other behavior processes we have implemented in Erlang is that here we handle only EXIT messages and take specific actions when receiving the stop message.

In our supervisor, if a child process terminates with reason normal, it is deleted from the ChildSpecList and the supervisor continues monitoring other children. If it terminates with a reason other than normal, the child is restarted and its old pid is replaced with NewPid in the tuple {Pid, {Module, Function, Argument}} of the child specification list. If our supervisor receives the stop message, it traverses through its list of child processes, terminating each one.

Let's try out my_supervisor with the Erlang implementation of the coffee FSM. If you do the same, don't forget to compile *coffee_fsm.erl* and *hw.erl*. Actually, on second thought, don't compile *hw.erl*. Start your coffee FSM from the supervisor and see what happens if the *hw.erl* stub module is not available. When all of the error reports are being printed out, compile or load *hw.erl* from the shell, making it accessible:

```
1> my_supervisor:start(coffee_sup, [{coffee_fsm, start_link, []}]).
{ok, <0.39.0>}

=ERROR REPORT==== 4-May-2013::08:26:51 ===
Error in process <0.468.0> with exit value:
{undef,[{hw,reboot,[],[]},{coffee,init,0,[....]}]}

...<snip>...
```

```
=ERROR REPORT==== 4-May-2013::08:26:58 ===
Error in process <0.474.0> with exit value:
{undef,[{hw,reboot,[],[]},{coffee,init,0,[....]}]}

2> c(hw).
Machine:Rebooted Hardware
Display:Make Your Selection
{ok,hw}
3> Pid = whereis(coffee_fsm).
<0.476.0>
4> exit(Pid, kill).
Machine:Rebooted Hardware
Display:Make Your Selection
true
5> whereis(coffee).
<0.479.0>
6> my_supervisor:stop(coffee_sup).
stop
7> whereis(coffee).
undefined
```

What is happening? The coffee FSM, in its init function, calls hw:reboot/0, causing an undef error because the module cannot be loaded. The supervisor receives the EXIT signal and restarts the FSM. The restart becomes cyclic, because restarting the FSM will not solve the issue; it will continue to crash until the module is loaded and becomes available. Compiling the *hw.erl* module in shell command 2 also loads the module, allowing the coffee FSM to initialize itself and start correctly. This puts an end to the cyclic restart.

Cyclic restarts happen when restarting a process after an abnormal termination does not solve the problem, resulting in the process crashing and restarting again. The supervisor behavior has mechanisms in place to escalate cyclic restarts. We cover them later in this chapter. Now, back to our example.

In shell command 3, we find the pid of the FSM and use it to send an exit signal, which causes the coffee FSM to terminate. It is immediately restarted, something visible from the printouts in the shell generated in the init/0 function. We stop the supervisor in shell command 6, which, as a result, also terminates its workers.

Now comes the question we've been asking for every other behavior. Have a look at the code in *my_supervisor.erl* and, before looking at the answer in Table 8-1, ask yourself: what is generic and what is specific?[1]

---

1 If you are someone who reads footnotes, good for you, as you can now consider yourself warned that this is a trick question.

Table 8-1. Supervisor generic and specific code

Generic	Specific
• Spawning the supervisor	• What children to start
• Starting the children	• Specific child handling:
• Monitoring the children	— Start, restart
• Restarting the children	— Child dependencies
• Stopping the supervisor	• Supervisor name
• Cleaning up	• Supervisor behaviors

Spawning the supervisor and registering it will be the same, irrespective of what children the supervisor starts or monitors. Monitoring the children and restarting them are also generic, as are stopping the supervisor and terminating all of the children. In other words, all of the code in *my_supervisor.erl* is generic. All of the specific functionality is passed as variables. It includes the child spec list, the order in which the children have to be started, and the supervisor alias.

Although `my_supervisor` will cater for some use cases, it barely scratches the surface of what a supervisor has to do. We decided to keep our example simple, but could have added more specific parameters. We've already seen that child startup failures cause endless retries. Supervisors should provide the ability to specify the maximum number of restarts within a time interval so that rather than trying endlessly, they can take further action if the child does not start properly. And what about dependencies? If a child terminates, shouldn't the supervisor offer the option of terminating and restarting other children that depend on that child? These are some of the configuration parameters included in the OTP supervisor behavior library module, which we cover next.

OTP Supervisors

In OTP, we structure our programs with one or more supervision trees. We group together, under the same subtree, workers that are either similar in nature or have dependencies, starting them in order of dependency. When describing supervision trees, worker behaviors are usually represented as circles, while supervisors are represented as squares. Figure 8-2 shows what the supervision structure of the frequency allocator example we've been working on could look like.

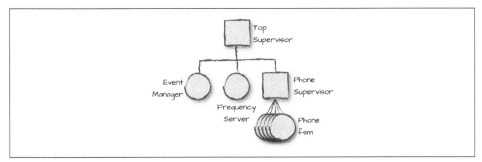

Figure 8-2. Supervision trees

Taking dependencies into consideration, the top supervisor first starts the event manager worker that handles alarms, because it is not dependent on any other worker. The top supervisor then starts the frequency allocator, because it sends alarms to the event manager. The last process on that level is a phone supervisor, which takes responsibility for starting and monitoring all of the FSMs representing the cell phones.

Note how we have grouped dependent processes together in one subset of the tree and related processes in another, starting them from left to right in order of dependency. This forms part of the supervision strategy of a system and in some situations is put in place not by the developer, who focuses only on what particular workers have to do, but by the architect, who has an overall view and understanding of the system and how the different components interact with each other.

The Supervisor Behavior

In OTP, the supervisor behavior is implemented in the supervisor library module. Like with all behaviors, the callback module is used for nongeneric code, including the behavior and version directives. The supervisor callback module needs to export a single callback function used at startup to configure and start the subset of the tree handled by that particular supervisor (Figure 8-3).

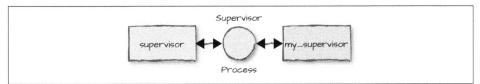

Figure 8-3. Generic supervisors

You may have guessed that the single exported function is the init/1 function, containing all of the specific supervisor configuration. The callback module usually also provides the function used to start the supervisor itself. Let's look at these calls more closely.

Starting the Supervisor

As a first step in getting our complete supervision tree in place, we create a supervisor that starts and monitors our frequency server and overload event manager. Because the frequency server calls the overload event manager, it has a dependency on the event manager. That means that the overload manager needs to be started before the frequency server, and if the overload manager terminates, we need to terminate the frequency server as well before restarting them both. Supervision tree diagrams, such as that in Figure 8-4, show not only the supervision hierarchy, but also dependencies and the order in which processes are started.

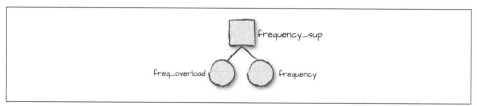

Figure 8-4. Frequency server supervision tree

Let's look at the code for the frequency supervisor callback module. Like with all other behaviors, you have to include the behavior directive. You start the supervisor using the start or start_link functions, passing the optional supervisor name, the callback module, and arguments passed to init/1. As with event managers, there is no Options argument allowing you to set tracing, logging, or memory fine-tuning options:

```
-module(frequency_sup).
-behavior(supervisor).

-export([start_link/0, init/1]).
-export([stop/0]).

start_link() ->
    supervisor:start_link({local,?MODULE},?MODULE, []).

stop() ->
    exit(whereis(?MODULE), shutdown).

init(_) ->
    ChildSpecList = [child(freq_overload), child(frequency)],
    {ok,{{rest_for_one, 2, 3600}, ChildSpecList}}.

child(Module) ->
    {Module, {Module, start_link, []},
     permanent, 2000, worker, [Module]}.
```

In our example, the [] in the start_link/3 call denotes the arguments sent to the init/1 callback, not the Options. You cannot set sys options in supervisors at

---

startup, but you can do so once the supervisor is started. Another difference from other behaviors is that supervisors do not expose built-in stop functionality to the developer. They are usually terminated by their supervisors or when the node itself is terminated. For those of you who do not want to write systems that never stop and insist on shutting down the supervisor from the shell, look at the `stop/0` function we've included; it simulates the shutdown procedure from a higher-level supervisor.

Calling `start_link/3` results in invocation of the `init/1` callback function. This function returns a tuple of the format {ok, `SupervisorSpec`}, where `Supervisor Spec` is a tuple containing the supervisor configuration parameters and the child specification list (Figure 8-5). This specification is a bit more complicated than our pure Erlang example, because more is happening behind the scenes. The next section provides a complete overview of `SupervisorSpec`. For now, we informally introduce it by walking through the example.

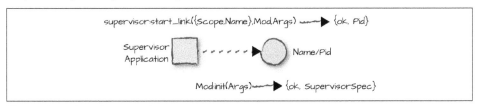

Figure 8-5. Generic supervisors

In our example, the first element of the `SupervisorSpec` configuration parameter tuple tells the supervisor that if a child terminates, we want to terminate all children that were started after it before restarting them all. In general this element is called the *restart strategy*, and to obtain the desired restart approach we need for this case, we specify the `rest_for_one` strategy. Following the restart strategy, the numbers 2 and 3600 in the tuple, called the *intensity* and *period*, respectively, tell the supervisor that it is allowed a maximum of two abnormal child terminations per hour (3,600 seconds). If this number is exceeded, the supervisor terminates itself and its children, and sends an exit signal to all the processes in its link set with reason `shutdown`. So, if this supervisor were part of a larger supervision tree, the supervisor monitoring it would receive the exit signal and take appropriate action.

The second element in the `SupervisorSpec` configuration parameter tuple is the child specification list. Each item in the list is a tuple specifying details for how to start and manage the static child processes. In our example, the first element in the tuple is a unique identifier within the supervisor in which it is started. Following that is the {`Module,Function,Arguments`} tuple indicating the function to start and link the worker to the supervisor, which is expected to return {ok,`Pid`}. Next, we find the restart directive; the atom `permanent` specifies that when the supervisor is restarting workers, this worker should always be restarted.

Following the restart directive is the shutdown directive, specified here as 2000. It tells the supervisor to wait 2,000 milliseconds for the child to shut down (including the time spent in the terminate function) after sending the EXIT signal. There is no guarantee that terminate is called, as the child might be busy serving other requests and never reach the EXIT signal in its mailbox.

Following that, the worker atom indicates that the child is a worker as opposed to another supervisor, and finally the single-element list [Module] specifies the callback module implementing the worker.

```
supervisor:start_link(NameScope, Mod, Args)
supervisor:start_link(Mod, Args) -> {ok, Pid}
                                     {error, Error}
                                     ignore

Mod:init/1 -> {ok,{{RestartStrategy,MaxR,MaxT},[ChildSpec]}}
              ignore
```

Because it can be difficult to remember the purpose and order of all the fields of the SupervisorSpec, Erlang 18.0 and newer allow it to be specified instead as a map. Here are implementations of init/1 and child/1 that return our SupervisorSpec as a map rather than a tuple:

```
init(_) ->
    ChildSpecList = [child(overload), child(frequency)],
    SupFlags = #{strategy => rest_for_one,
                 intensity => 2, period => 3600},
    {ok, {SupFlags, ChildSpecList}}.

child(Module) ->
    #{id => Module,
      start => {Module, start_link, []},
      restart => permanent,
      shutdown => 2000,
      type => worker,
      modules => [Module]}.
```

As you can see, the SupervisorSpec map code is much easier to read because unlike in the tuple, all the fields are named. If you're using Erlang 18.0 or newer, use maps for your supervisor specifications.

Supervisors, just like all other behaviors, can be registered or referenced using their pids. If registering the supervisor, valid values to NameScope include {local,Name} and {global,Name}. You can also use the name registry represented in the {via, Module, Name} tuple, where Module exports the same API defined in the global name registry.

The init/1 callback function normally returns the whole tuple comprising the restart tuple and a list of child specifications. But if it instead returns ignore, the supervisor

---

terminates with reason `normal`. Note how supervisors do not export `start/2,3` functions, forcing you to link to the parent. In the next section, we look at all the available options and restart strategies in more detail. We refer to these options and strategies as the *supervisor specification*.

The Supervisor Specification

The supervisor specification is a tuple containing two elements (Figure 8-6):

- The nongeneric information about the restart strategy for that particular supervisor
- The child specifications relevant to all static workers the supervisor starts and manages

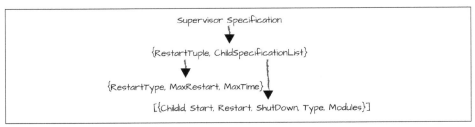

Figure 8-6. Supervisor specification

Let's look at these values in more detail, starting with the restart tuple.

The restart specification

The restart tuple, of the format:

```
{RestartType, MaxRestart, MaxTime}
```

specifies what happens to the other children in its supervision tree if a child terminates abnormally. By "child" we mean either a worker or another supervisor. Starting with Erlang 18.0, you can also use a map. The map defining the restart specification has the following type definition:

```
#{strategy  => strategy(),
  intensity => non_neg_integer(),
  period    => pos_integer()}
```

There are four different restart types: `one_for_one`, `one_for_all`, `rest_for_one`, and `simple_one_for_one`. Under the `one_for_one` strategy (Figure 8-7), only the crashed process is restarted. This strategy is ideal if the workers don't depend on each other and the termination of one will not affect the others. Imagine a supervisor monitoring the worker processes that control the instant messaging sessions of hundreds of thousands of users. If any of these processes crashes, it will affect only the user whose session is controlled by the crashed process. All other workers should continue running independently of each other.

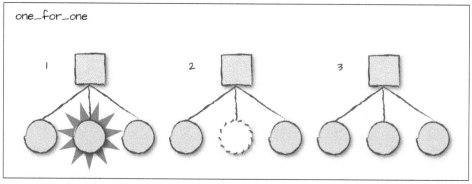

Figure 8-7. One for one

Under the one_for_all strategy shown in Figure 8-8, if a process terminates, all processes are terminated and restarted. This strategy is used if all or most of the processes depend on each other. Picture a very complex FSM handling a protocol stack. To simplify the design, the machine has been split into separate FSMs that communicate with each other asynchronously, and these workers all depend on each other. If one terminates, the others would have to be terminated as well. For these cases, pick the one_for_all strategy.

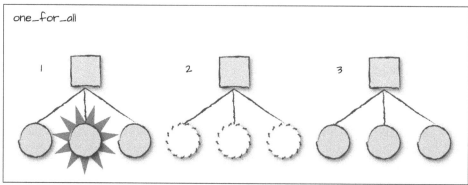

Figure 8-8. One for all

Under the rest_for_one strategy (Figure 8-9), all processes started *after* the crashed process are terminated and restarted. Use this strategy if you start the processes in order of dependency. In our frequency_sup example, we first start the overload event manager, followed by the frequency allocator. The frequency allocator sends requests to the overload event manager whenever it runs out of frequencies. So if the overload manager has crashed and is being restarted, there is a risk the frequency server might send it requests that get lost. Under such circumstances, we want to first terminate the frequency allocator, and then restart the overload manager and the frequency allocator in that order.

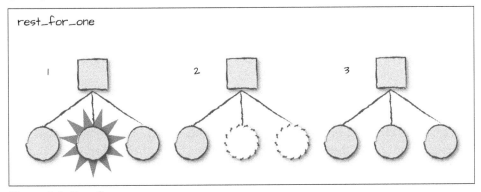

Figure 8-9. Rest for one

If losing the alarms sent to the frequency allocator did not matter (as the requests were asynchronous), we could have used the one_for_one strategy. Or we could have taken it a step further by making the raising and clearing of the alarms to the overload manager synchronous. In this case, if the overload manager had crashed and was being restarted, the frequency allocator would have also been terminated only when trying to make a synchronous call to it. Had the frequency allocator not run out of frequencies, thus not needing to raise or clear alarms, it could have continued functioning. As we have seen, there is no "one size fits all" solution; it all depends on the requirements you have and behavior you want to give your system.

There is one last restart strategy to cover: simple_one_for_one. It is used for children of the same type added dynamically at runtime, not at startup. An example of when we would use this strategy is in a supervisor handling the processes controlling mobile phones that are added to and removed from the supervision tree dynamically. We cover dynamic children and the simple_one_for_one restart strategy later in this chapter.

The last two elements in the restart tuple are MaxRestart and MaxTime. MaxRestart specifies the maximum number of restarts all child processes are allowed to do in MaxTime seconds. If the maximum number of restarts is reached in this number of seconds, the supervisor itself terminates with reason shutdown, escalating the termination to its higher-level supervisor. What is in effect happening is that we are giving the supervisor MaxRestart chances to solve the problem. If crashes still occur in Max Time seconds, it means that a restart is not solving the problem, so the supervisor escalates the issue to its supervisor, which will hopefully be able to solve it.

Look at the supervision tree in Figure 8-2. What if the phone FSMs under the phone supervisor are crashing because of corrupt data in the frequency handler? No matter how many times we restart them, they will continue to crash, because the problem lies in the frequency allocator, a worker supervised outside of our supervision sub-tree. We solve cyclic restarts of this nature through escalation. If we allow the phone supervisor to terminate, the top supervisor will receive the exit signal and restart the frequency server and event manager workers before restarting the phone supervisor. Hopefully, the restart can clear the corrupt data, allowing the phone FSMs to function as expected.

The key to using supervisors is to ensure you have properly designed your start order and the restart strategy associated with it. Though you will never be able to fully predict what will cause your processes to terminate abnormally, you can nevertheless try to design your restart strategy to recreate the process state from known-good sources. Instead of storing the state persistently and assuming it is uncorrupted such that it reading it after a crash will correctly restore it, retrieve the various elements that created your state from their original sources.

For example, if the corrupted data causing your worker to crash was the result of a transient transmission error, rereading it might solve the problem. The supervisor would restart the worker, which in turn would successfully reread the transmission and continue operating. And since the system would have logged the crash, the developer could look into its cause, modify the code to handle it appropriately, and prepare and deploy a new release to ensure that future similar transmission errors do not negatively impact the system.

In other cases, recovery might not be as straightforward. More difficult transmission errors might cause repeated worker crashes, in turn causing the supervisor to restart the worker. But since the restarts do not correct the problem, the client supervisor eventually reaches the restart threshold and terminates itself. This in turn affects the top-level supervisor, which eventually reaches its own restart threshold, and by terminating itself it takes the entire virtual machine down with it. When the virtual machine terminates, *heart*, a monitoring mechanism we cover in Chapter 11, detects that the node is down and invokes a shell script. The recovery actions in this script could be as simple as restarting the Erlang VM or as drastic as rebooting the computer. Rebooting might reset the link to the hardware that is suffering from transmission problems and solve the problem. If it doesn't, after a few reboot attempts the script might decide not to try again and instead alert an operator, requesting manual intervention.

Hopefully, a load balancer will already have kicked in to forward requests to redundant hardware, providing seamless service to end users. If not, this is when you receive a call in the middle of the night from a panicking first-line support engineer informing you there is an outage. In either case, the crash is logged, hopefully with enough data to allow you to investigate and solve the bug: namely, ensuring that data is checked before being introduced into your system so that data corrupted by transmission errors is not allowed in the first place. We look at distributed architectures and fault tolerance in Chapter 13. For now, let's stay focused on recovery of a single node. Next in line are child specifications.

The child specification

The child specification contains all of the information the supervisor needs to start, stop, and delete its child processes. The specification is a tuple of the format:

```
{Name,StartFunction,RestartType,ShutdownTime,ProcessType,Modules}
```

or, in Erlang 18.0 or newer, a map with the following type specification:

```
child_spec() = #{id => child_id(),      % mandatory
                 start => mfargs(),       % mandatory
                 restart => restart(),    % optional
                 shutdown => shutdown(),  % optional
                 type => worker(),        % optional
                 modules => modules()}    % optional
```

The elements of the tuple are:

Name

Any valid Erlang term, used to identify the child. It has to be unique within a supervisor, but can be reused across supervisors within the same node.

StartFunction

A tuple of the format {Module, Function, Args}, which, directly or indirectly, calls one of the behavior start_link functions. Supervisors can start only OTP-compliant behaviors, and it is their responsibility to ensure that the behaviors can be linked to the supervisor process. You cannot link regular Erlang processes to a supervision tree, because they do not handle the system calls.

RestartType

Tells the supervisor how to react to a child's termination. Setting it to permanent ensures that the child is always restarted, irrespective of whether its termination is normal or abnormal. Setting it to transient restarts a child only after abnormal termination. If you never want to restart a child after termination, set RestartType to temporary.

ShutdownTime

ShutdownTime is a positive integer denoting a time in milliseconds, or the atom infinity. It is the maximum time allowed to pass between the supervisor issuing the EXIT signal and the terminate callback function returning. If the child is overloaded and it takes longer, the supervisor steps in and unconditionally terminates the child process. Note that terminate will be called only if the child process is trapping exits. If you are feeling grumpy or do not need the behavior to clean up after itself, you can instead specify `brutal_kill`, allowing the supervisor to unconditionally terminate the child using `exit(ChildPid, kill)`.

Choose your shutdown time with care, and never set it to `infinity` for a worker, because it might cause the worker to hang in its `terminate` callback function. Imagine that your worker is trying to communicate with a defunct piece of hardware, the very reason for your system needing to be rebooted. You will never get a response because that part of the system is down, and this will stop the system from restarting. If you have to, use an arbitrarily large number, which will eventually allow the supervisor to terminate the worker. For children that are supervisors themselves, on the other hand, it is common but not mandatory to select `infinity`, giving them the time they need to shut down their potentially large subtree.

ProcessType *and* Modules

These are used during a software upgrade to control how and which processes are being suspended during the upgrade. `ProcessType` is the atom `worker` or `supervisor`, while `Modules` is the list of modules implementing the behavior. In the case of the frequency server, we would include `frequency`, while for our coffee machine we would specify `coffee_fsm`. If your behavior includes library modules specific to the behavior, include them if you are concerned that an upgrade of the behavior module will be incompatible with one of library modules. For example, if you changed the API in the `hw` interface module as well as the `coffee_fsm` behavior calling it, you would have to atomically upgrade both modules at the same time to ensure that `coffee_fsm` does not call the old version of `hw`. By listing both of these modules, you would be covered. But if you did not list `hw`, as in our example, you would have to ensure that any upgrade would be backward-compatible and handle both the old and the new APIs. We cover software upgrades in more detail in Chapter 12.

What if you don't know your `Modules` at compile time? Think of the event manager, which is started without any event handlers. When you do not know what will be running when you do a software upgrade, set `Modules` to the atom `dynamic`. When using dynamic modules, the supervisor will send a request to the behavior module and retrieve the module names when it needs them.

Before looking at the interface and callback details, let's test our example with what we've learned. Looking at their child specifications, we see that both the overload event manager and the frequency server are permanent worker processes given 2 seconds to execute in their `terminate` functions. We start the supervisor and its children, and see immediately that they have started correctly. In shell command 4, we stop the frequency server, but because it has its `RestartType` set to `permanent`, the supervisor will immediately restart it. We verify the restart in shell command 5 by retrieving the pid for the new frequency server process and noting that it differs from the pid of the original server returned from shell command 2. In shell command 6 we explicitly kill the frequency server, and shell command 7 shows that, once again, it restarted:

```
1> frequency_sup:start_link().
{ok,<0.35.0>}
2> whereis(frequency).
<0.38.0>
3> whereis(freq_overload).
<0.36.0>
4> frequency:stop().
ok
5> whereis(frequency).
<0.42.0>
6> exit(whereis(frequency), kill).
true
7> whereis(frequency).
<0.45.0>
8> supervisor:which_children(frequency_sup).
[{frequency,<0.45.0>,worker,[frequency]},
 {freq_overload,<0.36.0>,worker,[freq_overload]}]
9> supervisor:count_children(frequency_sup).
[{specs,2},{active,2},{supervisors,0},{workers,2}]
```

In shell command 8, which_children/1 returns a tuple list containing the ChildId its pid, worker or supervisor to denote its role, and the Modules list. Be careful when using this function if your supervisor has lots of children, because it will consume lots of memory. If you are calling the function from the shell, remember that the result will be stored in the shell history and not be garbage collected until the history is cleared.

```
supervisor:which_children(SupRef) -> [{Id, Child, Type, Modules}]
supervisor:count_children(SupRef) -> [{specs, SpecCount},
                                      {active, ActiveProcessCount},
                                      {supervisors, ChildSupervisorCount},
                                      {workers, ChildWorkerCount}]
supervisor:check_childspecs(ChildSpecs) -> ok
                                           {error, Reason}
```

The function count_children/1 returns a property list covering the supervisor's child specifications and managed processes. The elements are:

specs
> The total number of children, both those that are active and those that are not

active
> The number of actively running children

`workers` *and* `supervisors`

> The number of children of the respective type

And finally, `check_childspecs/1` is useful when developing and troubleshooting child specifications and startup issues. It validates a list of child specifications, returning an error if any are incorrect or the atom ok if it finds no problems.

Supervisor specifications are easy to write. And as a result, they are also *easy to get wrong*. Too often, programmers pick configuration values that do not reflect the reality and conditions under which the application is running, or copy specifications from other applications, or, even worse, use the default values from skeleton templates that different editors provide. You must take care to get your supervision structure right when designing your start and restart strategy, and must build in fault tolerance and redundancy. The tasks include starting your processes in order of dependency, and setting restart thresholds that will propagate problems to supervisors higher up in the hierarchy and allow them to take control if supervisors lower down in the supervision tree cannot solve the issue.

Dynamic Children

Having gone through the supervisor specification returned by the `init/1` callback function, you must have come to the realization that the only child type we have dealt with so far is static children started along with the supervisor. But another approach is viable as well: dynamically creating the child specification list in our `init/1` call when starting the supervisor. For instance, we could inspect the number of active mobile devices and start a worker for each of them. We have already handled the end of the worker's lifecycle (by making the worker `transient`, so that if the phone is shut off, the worker is terminated), but we don't yet have similar flexibility for the start of the lifecycle. What if a mobile device attaches itself to the network after we have started the supervisor? The solution to the problem is dynamic children, represented in Figure 8-10.

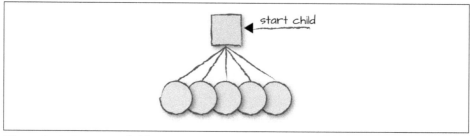

Figure 8-10. Dynamic children

Let's start an empty supervisor whose sole responsibility will be that of dynamically starting and monitoring the FSM processes controlling mobile devices. The FSM we'll be using is the one described but left as an exercise in "The Phone Controllers" on page 142. If you have not already solved it, download the code from the book's code repository. The code includes a phone simulator, *phone.erl*, which starts a specified number of mobile devices and lets them call each other. We'll make the phone supervisor a child of the frequency supervision tree. Let's take a look at the code for the phone_sup module:

```erlang
-module(phone_sup).
-behavior(supervisor).

-export([start_link/0, attach_phone/1, detach_phone/1]).
-export([init/1]).

start_link() ->
    supervisor:start_link({local, ?MODULE}, ?MODULE, []).

init([]) ->
    {ok, {{one_for_one, 10, 3600}, []}}.

attach_phone(Ms) ->
    case hlr:lookup_id(Ms) of
        {ok, _Pid}    ->
            {error, attached};
        _NotAttached ->
            ChildSpec = {Ms, {phone_fsm, start_link, [Ms]},
                         transient, 2000, worker, [phone_fsm]},
            supervisor:start_child(?MODULE, ChildSpec)
    end.

detach_phone(Ms) ->
    case hlr:lookup_id(Ms) of
        {ok, _Pid}    ->
            supervisor:terminate_child(?MODULE, Ms),
            supervisor:delete_child(?MODULE, Ms);
        _NotAttached ->
            {error, detached}
    end.
```

In the init/1 supervisor callback function we set the maximum number of restarts to 10 per hour, and because mobile devices run independently of each other, the one_for_one restart strategy will do. Note that since we intend to start all children dynamically, the return value from init/1 includes an empty list of child specifications. Further down in the module is the phone_sup:attach_phone/1 call, which, given a mobile device number Ms, checks whether the number is already registered on the network. If not, it creates a child specification and uses the supervisor:start_child/2 call to start it.

Let's experiment with this code. In shell commands 1 through 3 in the following interaction, we start the supervisors and initialize the home location register database, hlr (covered in "ETS: Erlang Term Storage" on page 45). We start two phones in shell commands 4 and 5, providing simple phone numbers as arguments. In shell command 6, we make phone 2, controlled by process P2, start an outbound call to the phone with phone number 1. Debug printouts are turned on for both phone FSMs, allowing you to follow the interaction between the phone FSMs and the phone simulator, implemented in the phone module. Following the debug printouts, we can see that phone 2 starts an outbound call to phone 1. Phone 1 receives the inbound call and rejects it, terminating the call and making both phones return to idle (as the simulator is based on random responses, you might get a different result when running the code):

```
1> frequency_sup:start_link().
{ok,<0.35.0>}
2> phone_sup:start_link().
{ok,<0.40.0>}
3> hlr:new().
ok
4> {ok, P1} = phone_sup:attach_phone(1).
{ok,<0.43.0>}
5> {ok, P2} = phone_sup:attach_phone(2).
{ok,<0.45.0>}
6> phone_fsm:action({outbound,1}, P2).
*DBG* <0.45.0> got {'$gen_sync_all_state_event',
                    {<0.33.0>,#Ref<0.0.4.55>},
                    {outbound,1}} in state idle
<0.45.0> dialing 1
*DBG* <0.45.0> sent ok to <0.33.0>
     and switched to state calling
*DBG* <0.43.0> got event {inbound,<0.45.0>} in state idle
*DBG* <0.43.0> switched to state receiving
ok
*DBG* <0.43.0> got event {action,reject} in state receiving
*DBG* <0.43.0> switched to state idle
*DBG* <0.45.0> got event {reject,<0.43.0>} in state calling
1 connecting to 2 failed:rejected
<0.45.0> cleared
*DBG* <0.45.0> switched to state idle
7> supervisor:which_children(phone_sup).
[{2,<0.45.0>,worker,[phone_fsm]},
 {1,<0.43.0>,worker,[phone_fsm]}]
8> supervisor:terminate_child(phone_sup, 2).
ok
9> supervisor:which_children(phone_sup).
[{2,undefined,worker,[phone_fsm]},
 {1,<0.43.0>,worker,[phone_fsm]}]
10> supervisor:restart_child(phone_sup, 2).
{ok,<0.53.0>}
11> supervisor:delete_child(phone_sup, 2).
{error,running}
12> supervisor:terminate_child(phone_sup, 2).
```

```
ok
13> supervisor:delete_child(phone_sup, 2).
ok
14> supervisor:which_children(phone_sup).
[{1,<0.43.0>,worker,[phone_fsm]}]
```

Have a look at the other shell commands in our example. You will find functions used to start, stop, restart, and delete children from the child specification list, some of which we use in our phone_sup module. Note how we get the list of workers when calling supervisor:which_children/1. We terminate the child in shell command 8, and note in the response to shell command 9 that it is still part of the child specification list but with the pid set to undefined. This means that the child specification still exists, but the process is not running. We can now restart the child using only the child Name in shell command 10.

Keep in mind that these function calls do not use pids, but only unique names identifying the child specifications. This is because children crash and are restarted, so their pids might change. Their unique names, however, will remain the same.

Once the supervisor has stored the child specification, we can restart it using its unique name. To remove it from the child specification list, we need to first terminate the child as shown in shell command 12, after which we call supervisor:delete_child/2 in shell command 13. Looking at the child specifications in shell command 14, we see that the specification of phone 2 has been deleted.

Simple one for one

The simple_one_for_one restart strategy is used when there is only one child specification shared by all the processes under a single supervisor. Our phone supervisor example fits this description, so let's rewrite it using this strategy. In doing so, we have added the detach_phone/1 function, which we explain later. Note how we have moved the hlr:new() call to the supervisor init function:

```
-module(simple_phone_sup).
-behavior(supervisor).

-export([start_link/0, attach_phone/1, detach_phone/1]).
-export([init/1]).

start_link() ->
    supervisor:start_link({local, ?MODULE}, ?MODULE, []).

init([]) ->
    hlr:new(),
    {ok, {{simple_one_for_one, 10, 3600},
        [{ms, {phone_fsm, start_link, []},
            transient, 2000, worker, [phone_fsm]}]}}.

attach_phone(Ms) ->
```

```
        case hlr:lookup_id(Ms) of
            {ok, _Pid}    ->
                {error, attached};
            _NotAttached ->
                supervisor:start_child(?MODULE, [Ms])
        end.

    detach_phone(Ms) ->
        case hlr:lookup_id(Ms) of
            {ok, Pid}    ->
                supervisor:terminate_child(?MODULE, Pid);
            _NotAttached ->
                {error, detached}
        end.
```

If you have looked at the code in detail, you might have spotted a few differences between the simple_one_for_one restart strategy and the one we used earlier for dynamic children. The first change is the arguments passed when starting the children. In the supervisor init/1 callback function, the {phone_fsm, start_link, ChildSpecArgs} in the child specification specifies no arguments (ChildSpecArgs is []), whereas the function phone_fsm:start_link(Args) in the earlier example takes one, Ms. As the children are dynamic, they are started via the function supervisor:start_child(SupRef, StartArgs). This function takes its second parameter, which it expects to be a list of terms, appends that list to the list of arguments in the child specification, and calls apply(Module, Function, ChildSpecArgs ++ StartArgs).

For the phone FSM, ChildSpecArgs in the child specification is empty, so the result of passing [Ms] as the second argument (StartArgs) to supervisor:start_child/2 is that it calls phone_fsm:start_link(Ms). It is also worth noting that we are initializing the ETS tables using the hlr:new() call in the init/1 callback, making the supervisor the owner of the tables.

The second difference is that in the simple_one_for_one strategy you do not use the child's name to reference it, you use its pid. If you study the detach_phone/1 function, you will notice this. You will also notice in the code that we are terminating the child without deleting it from the child specification list. We don't have to, as it gets deleted automatically when terminated. Thus, the functions supervisor:restart_child/1 and supervisor:delete_child/1 are not allowed. Only supervisor:terminate_child/2 will work. Testing the supervisor reveals no surprises:

```
1> frequency_sup:start_link().
{ok,<0.35.0>}
3> simple_phone_sup:start_link().
{ok,<0.40.0>}
4> simple_phone_sup:attach_phone(1), simple_phone_sup:attach_phone(2).
```

```
{ok,<0.43.0>}
5> simple_phone_sup:attach_phone(3).
{ok,<0.45.0>}
6> simple_phone_sup:detach_phone(3).
ok
7> supervisor:which_children(simple_phone_sup).
[{undefined,<0.42.0>,worker,[phone_fsm]},
 {undefined,<0.43.0>,worker,[phone_fsm]}]
```

Once we've detached the phone, it does not appear among the supervisor children. This is specific to the `simple_one_for_one` strategy, because with the other strategies, you need to both terminate and delete the children. Another difference is during shutdown; as `simple_one_for_one` supervisors often grow to have many children running independently of each other (often a child per concurrent request), when shutting down, they terminate the children in no specific order, often concurrently. This is acceptable, as determinism in these cases is irrelevant, and most probably not needed. Finally, `simple_one_for_one` supervisors scale better with a large number of dynamic children, as they use a `dict` key-value dictionary library module to store child specifications, unlike other supervisor types, which use a list. While other supervisors might be faster for small numbers of children, performance deteriorates quickly if the frequency at which dynamic children are started and terminated is high.

Keeping ETS Tables Alive

You will recall that an ETS table is linked to the process that creates it. If that process terminates, normally or abnormally, the ETS table is deleted. You could use the `heir` option when creating the table or call the `ets:give_away/3` function in your `terminate` function to transfer ownership instead when the owner terminates. An easier solution, however, is to place your ETS table not in its own process, but in a supervisor. Pick the supervisor that monitors the processes using the table, so if the supervisor is terminated, you are guaranteed that the processes using it have also terminated. This approach requires the table to have public access so that nonowning processes can both read and write to it. In our example, we have placed our ETS tables mapping pids to numbers and numbers to pids there. If the supervisor is terminated or shuts down, so will all of the processes accessing the table. The primary drawback to this approach is that if the data in the ETS table gets corrupted, you need to restart the supervisor to clear it. Keep this in mind if you use this approach.

This is quite a bit of information to absorb. Before going ahead, let's review the functional API used to manage dynamic children. Keep in mind that `terminate_child/2`, `restart_child/2`, and `delete_child/2` cannot be used with `simple_one_for_one` strategies:

```
supervisor:start_child(Name, ChildSpecOrArgs)   -> {ok, Pid}
                                                    {ok, Pid, Info}
                                                    {error, already_started |
                                                            {already_present,Id} |
                                                            Reason}
supervisor:terminate_child(Name, Id)   -> ok
                                          {error, not_found | simple_one_for_one}
supervisor:restart_child(Name, Id)   -> {ok, Pid}
                                         {ok, Pid, Info}
                                         {error, running | restarting |
                                                 not_found | simple_one_for_one}
supervisor:delete_child(Name, Id)   -> ok
                                       {error, running | restarting |
                                               not_found | simple_one_for_one |
                                               Reason}
```

Gluing it all together

Before wrapping up this example, let's create the top-level supervisor, bsc_sup, which starts both the frequency_sup and the simple_phone_sup functions. We will test the system using the *phone.erl* phone test simulator, which lets us specify the number of phones and the number of calls each phone should attempt, and then makes random calls, replying to and rejecting calls. The code for the top-level supervisor is as follows:

```
-module(bsc_sup).
-export([start_link/0, init/1]).
-export([stop/0]).

start_link() ->
    supervisor:start_link({local,?MODULE}, ?MODULE, []).

stop() -> exit(whereis(?MODULE), shutdown).

init(_) ->
    ChildSpecList = [child(freq_overload, worker),
                     child(frequency, worker),
                     child(simple_phone_sup, supervisor)],
    {ok,{{rest_for_one, 2, 3600}, ChildSpecList}}.

child(Module, Type) ->
    {Module, {Module, start_link, []},
     permanent, 2000, Type, [Module]}.
```

We pick the rest_for_one strategy because if the phones or the phone supervisor terminates, we do not want to affect the frequency allocator and overload handler. But if the frequency allocator or the overload handler terminates, we want to restart all of the phone FSMs. We allow a maximum of two restarts per hour, after which we escalate the problem to whatever is responsible for the bsc_sup supervisor.

Suppose that corrupted data in the frequency server is causing the phone FSMs to crash. After the `simple_phone_sup` has terminated three times within an hour, thus surpassing its maximum restart threshold, `bsc_sup` will terminate all of its children, bringing the frequency server down with it. The restart will hopefully clear up the problem, allowing the phones to function normally. We show how this escalation is handled in the upcoming chapters. Until then, let's use our *phone.erl* simulator and test our supervision structure and phone FSM by starting 150 phones, each attempting to make 500 calls:

```
1> bsc_sup:start_link().
{ok,<0.35.0>}
2> phone:start_test(150, 500).
*DBG* <0.107.0> got {'$gen_sync_all_state_event',
                    {<0.33.0>,#Ref<0.0.4.37>},
                    {outbound,109}} in state idle
<0.107.0> dialing 109

...<snip>...

*DBG* <0.92.0> switched to state idle
*DBG* <0.53.0> switched to state idle
3> counters:get_counters(freq_overload).
{counters,[{{event,{frequency_denied,<0.38.0>}},27},
          {{set_alarm,{no_frequency,<0.38.0>}},6},
          {{clear_alarm,no_frequency},6}]}
```

For the sake of brevity, we've cut out all but one of the debug printouts. Having run the test, we retrieve the counters and see that during the trial run, we ran out of available frequencies six times, raising and eventually clearing the alarm accordingly. During these six intervals, 27 phone calls could not be set up as a result. Examining the logs, we can get the timestamps when these calls were rejected. If a pattern emerges, we can use the information to improve the availability of frequencies at various hours.

Before moving on to the next section, if you ran the test just shown on your computer and still have the shell open, try killing the frequency server three times using `exit(whereis(frequency), kill)`. You will cause the top-level supervisor to reach its maximum restart threshold and terminate. Note how, when the phone FSM detaches itself in the FSM `terminate` function, you get a `badarg` error as a result of the `hlr` ETS tables no longer being present. The error reports originate in the `terminate` function if the supervisor has terminated before the phone FSM, taking the ETS tables with it. These error reports might shadow more important errors, so it is always a good idea within a `terminate` function to embed calls that might fail within a `try-catch` and, by default, return the atom `ok`.

Non-OTP-Compliant Processes

Child processes linked to an OTP supervision tree have to be OTP behaviors, or follow the behavior principles, and be able to handle and react to OTP system messages. There are, however, times when we want to bypass behaviors and use pure processes, either because of performance reasons or simply as a result of legacy code. We get around this problem by using supervisor bridges, implementing our own behaviors, or having a worker spawn and link itself to regular Erlang processes.

Supervisor bridges

In the mid-1990s, when major projects for the next generation of telecom infrastructure of that time were started at Ericsson, OTP was being implemented. The first releases of these systems, while following many of the design principles, were not OTP-compliant because OTP did not exist. When OTP R1 was released, we ended up spending more time in meetings discussing whether we should migrate these systems to OTP than it would actually have taken to do the job. It is at times like these, when no progress is made, that the supervisor_bridge behavior comes in handy.

The supervisor bridge is a behavior that allows you to connect a non-OTP-compliant set of processes to a supervision tree. It behaves like a supervisor toward its supervisor, but interacts with its child processes using predefined start and stop functions. In Figure 8-11, the right-hand side of the supervision tree consists of OTP behaviors, while the left-hand side of the supervision tree connects the non-OTP-compliant processes.

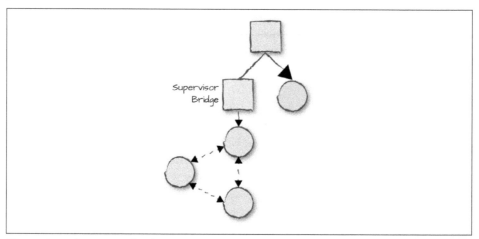

Figure 8-11. Supervisor bridges

Start a supervisor bridge using the supervisor_bridge:start_link/2,3 call, passing the optional NameScope, the callback Mod, and the Args. This results in calling the

---

init(Args) callback function, in which you start your Erlang process subtree, ensuring all processes are linked to each other. The init/1 callback, if successful, has to return {ok, Pid, State}. Save the State and pass it as a second argument to the terminate/2 callback.

If the Pid process terminates, the supervisor bridge will terminate with the same reason, causing the terminate/2 callback function to be invoked. In terminate/2, all calls required to shut down the non-OTP-compliant processes have to be made. At this point, the supervisor bridge's supervisor takes over and manages the restart. If the supervisor bridge receives a shutdown message from its supervisor, terminate/2 is also called. While the supervisor bridge handles all of the debug options in the sys module, the processes it starts and is connected to have no code upgrade and debug functionality. Supervision will be limited to what has been implemented in the subtree.

```
supervisor_bridge:start_link(NameScope, Mod, Args) ->
    {ok, Pid} | ignore | {error, {already_started,Pid}}


Mod:init(Args)                 -> {ok,Pid,State} | ignore | {error,Reason}
Mod:terminate(Reason, State) -> term()
```

Adding non-OTP-compliant processes

Remember that supervisors can accept only OTP-compliant processes as part of their supervision tree. They include workers, supervisors and supervisor bridges. There is one last group, however, that can be added: processes that follow a subset of the OTP design principles, the same ones standard behaviors follow. We call processes that follow OTP principles but are not part of the standard behaviors *special processes*. You can implement your own special processes by using the proc_lib module to start your processes and handle system messages in the sys module. With little effort, the sys, debug, and stats options can be added. Processes implemented following these principles can be connected to the supervision tree. We cover them in more detail in Chapter 10.

Scalability and Short-Lived Processes

Typical Erlang design creates one process for each truly concurrent activity in your system. If your system is a database, you will want to spawn a process for every query, insert, or delete operation. But don't get carried away. Your concurrency model will depend on the resources in your system, as in practice, you could have only one connection to the database. This becomes your bottleneck, as it ends up serializing your requests. In this case, is sending this process a message easier than spawning a new one? If your system is an instant messaging server, you will want a process for every inbound and outbound message, status update, or login and logout operation. We are talking about tens or possibly hundreds of thousands of simultaneous processes that are short-lived and reside under the same supervisor. At the time of writing, supervisors that have a large number of dynamic children starting and terminating at very short continuous intervals will not scale well because the supervisor becomes the bottleneck. The implementation of the simple_one_for_one strategy scales better, as unlike other supervisor types that store their child specifications in lists, it uses the dict key-value library module. But despite this, it will also have its limits. Giving a rule-of-thumb measure of the rate at which dynamic children can be started and terminated is hard, because it depends on the underlying hardware, OS, and cores, as well as the behavior of the processes themselves (including the amount of data that needs to be copied when spawning a process). These issues are rare, but if a supervisor message queue starts growing to thousands of messages, you know you are affected. There are two approaches to the problem.

The clean approach, shown in Figure 8-12, is to create a pool of supervisors, ensuring that each does not need to cater for more children than it can handle. This is a recommended strategy if the children have to interact with other processes and are often long-lived. The process on the left is the *dispatcher*, which manages coordination among the supervisors and, if necessary, starts new ones. You can pick a supervisor in the pool using an algorithm that best suits your needs, such as round robin, consistent hashing, or random.

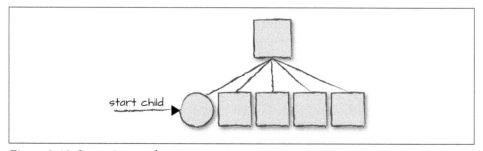

Figure 8-12. Supervisor pools

The second approach taken by many is to have a worker, more often than not a generic server, that spawn_links a non-OTP-compliant process for every request (Figure 8-13). You will often find this strategy in messaging servers, web servers, and databases. This non-OTP-compliant process usually executes a sequential, synchronous set of operations and terminates as soon as it has completed its task. This solution potentially sacrifices OTP principles for speed and scalability, but it ensures that your process is linked to the behavior that spawned it; if the process tree shuts down, the linked processes will also terminate.

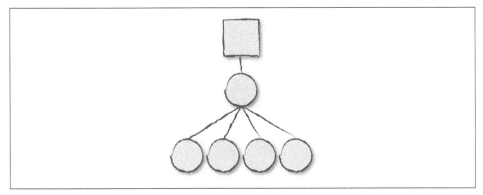

Figure 8-13. Linking to a worker

Why link? Don't forget that your system will run for years without being restarted. You can't predict what upgrades, new functionality, or even abnormal terminations will occur. The last thing you want is a set of dangling processes you can't control, left there after the last failed upgrade. Because you link the non-OTP-compliant children to their parent, if the parent terminates, so do the children.

Multiple Supervision Policies

Every child may be associated with one supervisor or parent. OTP supervision trees are not set up to handle cases where a behavior might belong to two process groups with different policies. If you come across such use cases where it might make sense to have multiple processes monitor the same behavior, use links and monitors, and ensure that only one of the behaviors is responsible for handling the restart strategy.

Synchronous Starts for Determinism

Remember that when you start behaviors with either the start or start_link calls, process creation and the execution of the init/1 function are synchronous. The functions return only when the init/1 callback function returns. The same applies to the supervisor behavior. A crash during the start of any behavior will cause the supervisor to fail, terminating all the children it has already started. Because starts are synchronous and if start and restart times are critical, try to minimize the amount of work done in the init/1 callback. You need to guarantee that the process has been restarted and is in a consistent state. If starting up involves setting up a connection toward a remote node or a database—a connection that can later fail as a result of a transient error—start setting up the connection in your init/1 function, but do not wait for the connection to come up.

A trick you can use to postpone your initialization is to set the timeout to 0 in your init/1 behavior callback function. Setting a timeout in this manner results in your callback module receiving a timeout message immediately after init/1 returns, allowing you to asynchronously continue initializing your behavior. This could involve waiting for node or database connections or any other noncritical parts over which your init/1 function does not provide guarantees. A more general alternative to a timeout is for init/1 to send a suitable asynchronous message to self(), which is handled after init/1 returns, in order to asynchronously proceed with initialization.

Repairing Mnesia Tables

Remember Mnesia, the distributed database introduced in the *Erlang Programming* book? An unexpected restart issue we had many times in live systems was for Mnesia to load and fix its tables during a restart, which can be caused after a node is shut down abnormally as the result of a VM crashing or it being killed, or after a power outage or hardware fault. Upon restarting, Mnesia loads its tables asynchronously, so as to not block other behaviors from starting. Fixing tables has been known to take a long time, as logs and backups are scanned. If you try to read a value from a table that has not been completely loaded, the call will raise an exception.

If a behavior is dependent on a set of tables, you can get around this problem by calling mnesia:wait_for_tables/2 when initializing your behavior. This will work without any issues in a test environment when tables are small, but in production systems, the data being loaded can be substantial. In fact, data sets in test environments are usually so small that you will probably get away without calling wait_for_tables/2. But in the worse case, in a live system after a major outage, can your supervisor startup handle waiting a couple of minutes for an Mnesia table being repaired as the result of an abnormal termination? Will it cause unwanted message queue growth elsewhere, or result in a knock-on effect? These are issues you have to validate when testing your system.

Why are synchronous starts important? Imagine first spawning all your child processes asynchronously and then checking that they have all started correctly. If something goes wrong at startup, the issue might have been caused by the order in which processes were started or the order the expressions in their respective init callbacks were executed. Recreating the race condition that resulted in the startup error might not be trivial. Your other option is to start a process, allow it to initialize, and start the next one only when the init function returns. This will give you the ability to reproduce the sequence that led to a startup error without having to worry about race conditions. Incidentally, this is the way we do it when using OTP, where the combination of applications (covered in Chapter 9), supervisors, and the synchronous startup sequence together provide a "simple core" that guarantees a solid base for the rest your system.

Testing Your Supervision Strategy

In this chapter, we've explained how to architect your supervision tree, group and start processes based on dependencies, and ensure that you have picked the right restart strategy. These tasks should not be overlooked or underestimated. Although you are encouraged to avoid defensive programming and let your behavior terminate if something unexpected happens, you need to make sure that you have isolated the error and are able to recover from this exception. You might have missed dependencies, picked the wrong restart strategy, or set your allowed number of restarts too high (or low) in a possibly incorrect time interval. How to you test these scenarios and detect these design anomalies?

Abnormal or Normal Termination?

One of this book's authors was involved in a project where each generic server managed by the supervisor owned a TCP connection. When the socket was closed as a result of a connectivity error, it would terminate the behavior abnormally, be restarted, and attempt to re-establish the connection. Each network connectivity error, although perfectly legitimate, would increment the counter for the number of abnormal terminations, occasionally resulting in shutting the node down. This was particularly evident when experiencing network connectivity issues as a result of a firewall misconfiguration, router and load balancer failures, or something as simple as a system administrator tripping over a network cable. On top of creating outages, other abnormal issues happening in the system were being lost in the sheer volume of error reports being generated. Because these actions can happen under normal operations, the socket closings that were not initiated by the program itself should have been handled as normal events and not resulted in abnormal termination.

All correctly written test specifications for Erlang systems will contain negative test cases where recovery scenarios and supervision strategies have to be validated by simulating abnormal terminations. You need to ensure that the system is not only able to start, but also to restart and self-heal when something unexpected happens.

In our first test system, `exit(Pid, Reason)` was used to kill specific processes and validate the recovery scenarios. In later years, we used Chaos Monkey (*https://github.com/Netflix/SimianArmy*), an open source tool that randomly kills processes, simulating abnormal errors. Try it while stress testing your system, complementing it with fault injections where hardware and network failures are being simulated. If your system comes out of it alive, it is on track to becoming production-ready.

Don't Tell the World You Are Killing Children!

While working on the R1 release of OTP, a group of us left the office and took the commuter train into Stockholm. We were talking about the ease of killing children, children dying, and us not having to worry about it, as supervisors would trap exits and restart them. We were very excited and vocal about this, as it was at the time a novel approach to software development, and one we were learning about as we went along. We were all so engrossed in this conversation that we failed notice the expressions of horror on the faces of some elderly ladies sitting next to us. I have never seen an expression of alarm turn so quickly into an expression of relief as when we finally got off the train. Pro Tip: when in public, talk about behaviors, not children, and do not kill them—terminate them instead. It will help you make friends, and you won't risk having to explain yourself to a law enforcement officer who probably has no sense of humor.

How Does This Compare?

How does the approach of nondefensive programming, letting supervisors handle errors, compare to conventional programming languages? The urban legend among us Erlang programmers boasted of less code and faster time to market. But the numbers we quoted were based on gut feelings or studies that were not public. The very first study, in fact, came from Ericsson, where a sizable number of features in the MD110 corporate switch were rewritten from PLEX (a proprietary language used at the time) to Erlang. The result was a tenfold decrease in code volume. Worried that no one would believe this result, the official stance was that you could implement the same features with four times less code. Four was picked because it was big enough to be impressive, but small enough not to be challenged. We finally got a formal answer when Heriot-Watt University in Scotland ran a study focused on rewriting C++ production systems to Erlang/OTP. One of the systems was Motorola's Data Mobility (DM), a system handling digital communication streams for two-way radio systems used by emergency services. The DM had been implemented in C++ with fault tolerance and reliability in mind. It was rewritten in Erlang using different approaches, allowing the various versions to be compared and contrasted.

Many academic papers and talks have been written on this piece of research. One of the interesting discoveries was an 85% reduction in code in one of the Erlang implementations. This was in part explained by noting that 27% of the C++ code consisted of error handling and defensive programming. The counterpart in Erlang, if you assumed OTP to be part of the language libraries, was a mere 1%!

Just by using supervisors and the fault tolerance built into OTP behaviors, you get a code reduction of 26% compared to other conventional languages. Remove the 11%

of the C++ code that consists of memory management, remove another 23% consisting of high-level communication—all features that are part of the Erlang semantics or part of OTP—and include declarative semantics and pattern matching, and you can easily understand how an 85% code reduction becomes possible. Read one or two of the papers[2] and have a look at the recordings of the presentations available online if you want to learn more about this study.

Summing Up

Building on previous chapters that covered OTP worker processes, this chapter explained how to group them together in supervision trees. We have looked at dependencies and recovery strategies, and how they allow you to handle and isolate failures generically. The bottom line is for you not to try to handle software bugs or corrupt data in your code. Focus on the positive cases and, in the case of unexpected ones, let your process terminate and have someone else deal with the problem. This strategy is what we refer to as *fail safe*.

In Table 8-2 we list the functions exported by the supervisor and supervisor bridge behaviors, together with their respective callback functions. You can read more about them in their respective manual pages.

Table 8-2. Supervisor callbacks

Supervisor function or action	Supervisor callback function
`supervisor:start_link/2, supervisor:start_link/3`	`Module:init/1`
`supervisor_bridge:start_link/2,` `supervisor_bridge:start_link/3`	`Module:init/1, Module:terminate/2`

Before reading on, you should also read through the code of the examples provided in this chapter and look for examples of supervisor implementations online. Doing so will help you understand how to design your system while keeping fault tolerance and recovery in mind.

What's Next?

In the next chapter, we cover how to package supervision trees into a behavior called an application. Applications contain supervision trees and provide operations to start and stop them. They are seen as the basic building blocks of Erlang systems. In Chapter 11, we look at how we group applications into a release, giving us an Erlang node.

---

2 The most comprehensive being Nyström, J. H., Trinder, P. W., and King, D. J. (2008), "High-level distribution for the rapid production of robust telecoms software: Comparing C++ and ERLANG," *Concurrency Computat.: Pract. Exper*, 20: 941–968. doi: 10.1002/cpe.1223.

## CHAPTER 9

Applications

In our previous chapters, we've looked at worker behaviors and how they can be grouped together to form a supervision tree. In this chapter, we explore the application behavior, which allows us to package together supervision trees, modules, and other resources into one semi-independent unit, providing the basic building blocks of large Erlang systems. An OTP application is a convenient way to package code and configuration files and distribute the result around the world for others to use.

An Erlang node typically consists of a number of loosely coupled OTP applications that interact with each other. OTP applications come from a variety of sources:

- Some are available as part of the standard Ericsson distribution, including *mnesia*, *sasl*, and *os_mon*.

- Other generic applications that are not part of the Ericsson distribution but are necessary for the functionality of many Erlang systems can be obtained commercially or as open source. Examples of generic applications include *elarm* for alarming, *folsom* or *exometer* for metrics, and *lager* for logging.

- Each node also has one or more nongeneric applications that contain the system's business logic. These are often developed specifically for the system, containing the core of the functionality.

- A final category of OTP applications are those that are full user applications themselves that, together with their dependencies, could run on a standalone basis in an Erlang node. The bundle of applications is referred to as a *release*. Examples include the Yaws web server, the Riak database, the RabbitMQ message broker, and the MongooseIM chat server. While not a common practice, inter-application throughput and overall performance can sometimes be improved by running business logic applications together on the same node with these types of full applications.

Regardless of their sources, though, OTP applications are generally structured the same way. We explore the details of this structure in the remainder of this chapter. In the rest of the book, we use the term "application" to refer specifically to an OTP application, and not an application in the broader sense of the word.

How Applications Run

One way to view an application is as a means of packaging resources into reusable components. Resources can consist of modules, processes, registered names, and configuration files. They could also include other non-Erlang source or executable code, such as bash scripts, graphics, or drivers. Though different OTP applications contain different resources and perform different functions or services, to the Erlang run-time system they all look the same; it doesn't distinguish between them in terms of how it loads and runs them, allows them to be accessed and invoked from other applications, or terminates them. Figure 9-1 shows how various components run together on the Erlang runtime.

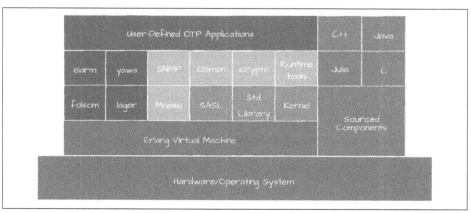

Figure 9-1. An Erlang release

Applications can be configured, started, and stopped as a whole. This allows a system to easily manage many supervision trees, running them independently of each other. One application can also depend on another one; for example, a server-side web application might depend on a web server application such as Yaws (*http://yaws.hyber.org/*). Supporting application dependencies means the runtime has to handle starting and stopping applications in the proper order. This provides a basis for cleanly encapsulating functionality and encourages reusability in a way that goes far beyond that of modules.

There are two types of applications: *normal applications* and *library applications*. Normal applications start a top-level supervisor, which in turn starts its children, forming the supervision tree. Library applications contain library modules but do not start a supervisor or processes themselves; the function calls they export are invoked by workers or supervisors running in a different application. A typical example of a library application is *stdlib*, which contains all of the OTP standard libraries such as supervisor, gen_event, gen_server, and gen_fsm.

Behind the scenes in the Erlang VM a process called the *application controller* starts on every node. For every OTP application, the controller starts a pair of processes called the *application master*. It is the master that starts and monitors the top-level supervisor and takes action if it terminates (Figure 9-2).

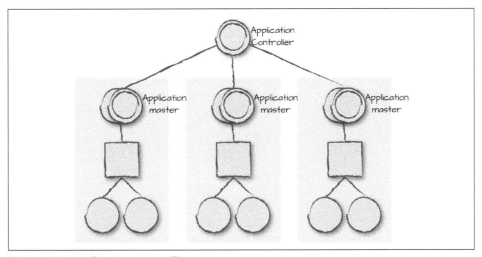

Figure 9-2. Application controller

When using releases (covered in Chapter 11), the Erlang runtime treats each application as a single unit; it can be loaded, started, stopped, and unloaded as a whole. When loading an application, the runtime system loads all modules and checks all its resources. If a module is missing or corrupt, startup fails and the node is shut down. When starting an application, the master spawns the top-level supervisor, which in turn starts the remainder of the supervision tree. If any of the behaviors in the supervision tree fail at startup, the node is also shut down. When stopped, the application master terminates the top-level supervisor, propagating the shutdown exit signal to all behavior processes in the supervision tree. Finally, when unloading an application, the runtime purges all modules for that application from the system.

Now that we have a high-level overview of how everything is glued together, let's start looking at the details.

The Application Structure

Applications are packaged in a directory that follows a special structure and naming convention. Tools depend on this structure, as do the release-handling mechanisms. A typical application directory has the structure shown in Figure 9-3, containing the *ebin*, *src*, *priv*, and *include* directories.

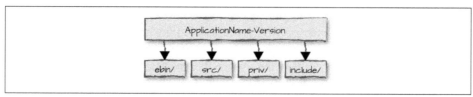

Figure 9-3. Application structure

The name of the application directory is the name of the application followed by its version number. This allows you to store different versions of the application in the same library directory, using the code search path to point to the one being used. Subdirectories of an application include:

ebin
> Contains the beam files and the application configuration file, also known as the app file

src
> Contains the Erlang source code files and include files that you do not want other applications to use

priv
> Contains non-Erlang files needed by the application, such as images, drivers, scripts, or proprietary configuration files

include
> Contains exported include files that can be used by other applications

Other nonstandard directories, such as *doc* for documentation, *test* for test cases, and *examples*, can also be part of your application. What sets nonstandard directories apart from the ones in the previous list is that the runtime system and tools allow you to access the standard directories by application name, without having to reference the version. For instance, when you load an application, the code search path for that application will point straight to the *ebin* directory of the version you are using. Or, if you want to include the *.hrl* file of another application, the include path in the makefiles will point to the correct version. This doesn't happen with nonstandard directories, and as such, you or your tools have to figure out the path.

Let's have a look at this structure in more detail by following an example in the OTP distribution. Remember that the directory structure of any OTP application in the Erlang distribution will be the same as those of the applications you are implementing in your system.

Go to the Erlang root directory, and from there, cd into the *lib* directory. If you are unsure where Erlang is installed, start a shell and determine the location of the *lib* directory by typing code:lib_dir().. The *lib* directory contains all of the applications included when installing Erlang. If you have upgraded your release or installed patches, you might find more than one version of some applications. The versions of the applications will differ from release to release, so what you see might differ from the examples in this chapter.

Let's have a look at the contents of the *lib* directory and the latest version of the runtime tools application *runtime_tools*, which should be included in every release:

```
1> code:lib_dir().
"/usr/local/lib/erlang/lib"
2> halt().
$ cd /usr/local/lib/erlang/lib
$ ls
...<snip>...
appmon-2.1.14.2       erts-5.7.5      public_key-0.18
asn1-1.6.13           erts-5.8.1      public_key-0.5
asn1-1.6.14.1         et-1.4          public_key-0.8
asn1-2.0.1            et-1.4.1        reltool-0.5.3
common_test-1.4.7     et-1.4.4.3      reltool-0.5.4
common_test-1.5.1     eunit-2.1.5     reltool-0.6.3
common_test-1.7.1     eunit-2.2.4     runtime_tools-1.8.10
compiler-4.6.5        gs-1.5.11       runtime_tools-1.8.3
compiler-4.7.1        gs-1.5.13       runtime_tools-1.8.4.1
...<snip>...
$ cd runtime_tools-1.8.10/
$ ls
doc     examples    info    src
ebin    include     priv
```

The *doc* directory and *info* file are nonstandard, and as such have nothing to do with OTP (the Ericsson OTP team uses them for documentation purposes). Erlang developers often add other application-specific directories and files, such as *test* and *examples*. No guarantees exist that these nonstandard directories and files will be retained between releases. If you look at different versions of the *runtime-tools* application, for example, you will see that earlier versions have an *info* file that is no longer present in later versions.

Let's focus on the OTP standard directories. If you cd into the *ebin* directory of the *runtime_tools* application and examine its contents, you will find *.beam* files, an *.app* file, and possibly an *.appup* file. The *.beam* files, as you likely already know, contain Erlang byte code. The *.app* file is a mandatory application resource file we explore in more detail in "Application Resource Files" on page 213. The *.appup* file might be there if you have at some point upgraded your application. We cover this file in more detail in Chapter 12 when looking at software upgrades.

The *src* directory contains the Erlang source code. If the modules in this directory use one or more *.hrl* files that are not exported to be used by other applications, put them here. The current working directory is by default always included in the include file search path, so when compiling, files you put here will be picked up. It is the responsibility of your build system to ensure that beam files resulting from compilation are moved from the *src* to the *ebin* directory. Makefiles and tools like *rebar3* (covered in "Rebar3" on page 303) normally do this for you.

Macros and records defined in include files are often part of interface descriptions, requiring modules in other applications to have access to these definitions. The *include* directory is used in the build process to provide access to the *.hrl* files stored in it. Without having to know the location of the include file directory or the application version, you can use the following directive:

```
-include_lib("Application/include/File.hrl").
```

where `Application` is the application name without the version and `File.hrl` is the name of the include file. The compiler will know which version of the application you are working with, find the directory, and automatically include the file without you having to change the version numbers between releases. Even if include files do not require the *.hrl* extension, it is good practice to always use it. Version dependencies are handled in release files, covered in Chapter 12.

If you run `grep ^-include_lib ssl*/src/*.erl` from your Erlang *lib* directory to examine the *src* directories of all the versions of the *ssl* application installed on your system, you will notice that some of the modules include *.hrl* files from other applications, such as *public_key* and *kernel*. There will also be a few include files stored directly in the *src* directory, which are used only by the *ssl* application itself.

The *priv* directory contains non-Erlang-specific resources. They could be linked-in drivers, shared libraries for native implemented functions (NIFs), executables, graphics, HTML pages, JavaScript, or application-specific configuration files—basically, any source the application needs at runtime that is not directly Erlang-related resides here. In the case of the *runtime_tools* application, the *priv* directory includes source and object code of its trace drivers. Because the path of the *priv* directory will differ based on the version of the application you are running, use `code:priv_dir(Applica tion)` in your code to generically find it.

The *ebin* and *priv* directories are usually the only ones shipped and deployed on target machines. This will probably answer your question as to why the mandatory application resource file is included in the *ebin* directory and not *src*. If you look at other applications shipped as part of the standard distribution, you will also notice that the *priv* directory is not mandatory if it is not used. The *sasl* application, for example, has no *priv* directory, and there are other such applications as well.

Although it is up to you whether you ship source code and documentation with your products, it is not a good idea to bundle them up with your release deployed on target machines, because once you've upgraded your beam files, no checks are made to ensure the source code is up to date. Once, when called in to resolve an outage, we were reading the code on the production machines until we realized it was the first release of the code, now woefully out of date as the sources had since been patched, rewritten, cleaned up, and redeployed. After all, those who deployed the new beam files knew the source code on the target machines was not up to date. They also knew that they were not always the ones supporting the system, but assumed we would be using the source code repository, or that we would just ask. Should you find yourself in a similar predicament, follow our words of wisdom and always start with the assumption that those supporting the systems you have written and deployed are antisocial axe murderers who know where you live. They will not speak to you in the middle of the night when called to deal with an outage caused by a bug in your code, but might come knocking on your door at dawn once the system is operational again.

And while we have your attention, please, never ever deploy the compiler application and your system source code with production systems. If you do, you are really asking for trouble, because you will end up changing and compiling the code on target machines in an attempt to resolve the issue. Assuming it is the correct version of the code (which it probably isn't), and assuming it actually solves the problem (which it probably won't), there is still the risk you will forget to commit the changes back to your actual source code repository. Don't forget all of this is happening at 3 AM, and all you want is to return to sleep. Code should be taken from the repository and tested in a test environment before deploying it to a live system. No matter how urgent the fix, don't cut corners, because you will risk paying the price later, irrespective of the time of day (or night).

The Callback Module

The application behavior is no different from other OTP behaviors. The module containing the generic code, `application`, is part of the `kernel` library, and a callback module contains all of the specific code (Figure 9-4).

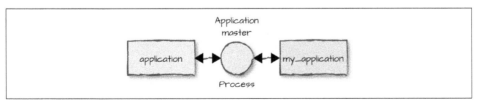

Figure 9-4. Application behavior

The behavior directive must be included in the callback module, along with the mandatory and optional callbacks. Of all behaviors, the application callback module is the simplest. Unless you are dealing with takeovers and failovers in distributed environments or complex startup strategies, expect your application callback module to require no more than a few simple lines of code.

Starting and Stopping Applications

The callback module is invoked when starting your application. You start it by calling `application:start(Application)`, where `Application` is the application name. This call loads all of the modules that are bundled with the application and starts the master processes, one of which calls the `Mod:start(StartType, StartArgs)` callback function in the application callback module. The `start/2` function has to return `{ok, Pid}`, where `Pid` is the process identifier of the top-level supervisor. If the application is not already loaded, `application:load(Application)` is called prior to starting the master processes. Our application callback module looks something like this:

```
-module(bsc).

-behavior(application).

%% Application callbacks
-export([start/2, stop/1]).

start(_StartType, _StartArgs) ->
    bsc_sup:start_link().

stop(_Data) ->
    ok.
```

The first argument, `_StartType`, is ignored by most applications; it is usually the atom `normal`, but if we're running distributed applications with automated failover and takeover, it could have the value `{takeover, Node}` or `{failover, Node}`. We look at these values later in the chapter. The second argument, `_StartArgs`, comes from the `mod` key of the application resource file, described in "Application Resource Files" on page 213.

Figure 9-5 shows how the application callback module starts the top-level supervisor. The application callback module's `start/2` function typically just calls the `start_link` function provided by the top-level supervisor. For example, the `bsc:start/2` function shown earlier simply calls `bsc_sup:start_link/0`.

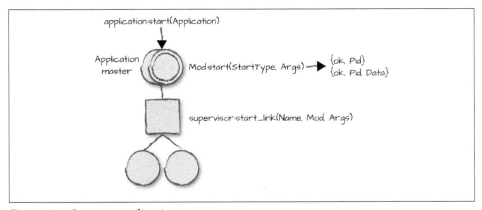

Figure 9-5. Starting applications

In our case, `bsc_sup:start_link/0` returns {ok, Pid}, which is also what `bsc:start/2` returns. Another valid return value is {ok, Pid, Data}, where the contents of `Data` are stored and later passed to the `stop/1` callback function (Figure 9-6). If you do not return any `Data`, just ignore the argument passed to `stop/1` (in case you're curious, it will be bound to [] in that case).

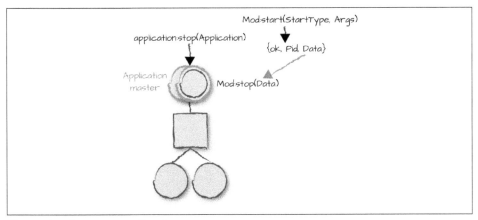

Figure 9-6. Stopping applications

To stop an application, use `application:stop(Application)`. This results in the callback function `Mod:stop/1` being called *after* the supervision tree has been terminated, including all workers and supervisors. `Mod:prep_stop/1` is an equally important but optional callback invoked before the processes are terminated. If you need to clean anything up before terminating your supervision tree, `prep_stop/1` is where you trigger it.

Let's try loading, starting, and stopping the *sasl* application from the standard OTP distribution. Depending on how you installed Erlang, *sasl* might or might not be

started automatically when you start the shell. You can find out by typing
application:which_applications().. In the following example, we do this in shell
command 1, getting back a list of tuples. The first element is the application name,
the second is a descriptive string,[1] and the third is a string denoting the application
version. When you start Erlang, its boot script determines which applications it
starts. If the *sasl* application is in there, first stop it before attempting to run the
example. In our installation of Erlang, it is not started:

Example 9-1. Loading an application

```
1> application:which_applications().
[{stdlib,"ERTS  CXC 138 10","2.0"},
 {kernel,"ERTS  CXC 138 10","3.0"}]
2> application:load(sasl).
ok
3> application:start(sasl).
ok
4>
=PROGRESS REPORT==== 17-Feb-2014::19:51:08 ===
          supervisor: {local,sasl_safe_sup}
             started: [{pid,<0.42.0>},
                       {name,alarm_handler},
                       {mfargs,{alarm_handler,start_link,[]}},
                       {restart_type,permanent},
                       {shutdown,2000},
                       {child_type,worker}]
...<snip>...

4> application:stop(sasl).

=INFO REPORT==== 17-Feb-2014::19:51:23 ===
    application: sasl
    exited: stopped
    type: temporary
ok
```

The system architecture support libraries (*sasl*) application is a collection of tools for
building, deploying, and upgrading Erlang releases. It is part of the minimal OTP
release; together with the *kernel* and *stdlib* applications, it has to be included in all
OTP-compliant releases. We cover all of this in more detail later.

In our example, we load *sasl* in shell command 2 and start it in shell command 3. You
will notice that when we start the application, a long list of progress reports is printed

---

1 In case you are wondering, CXC is an internal Ericsson product-numbering scheme. It is rumored that a copy
of every product with a CXC number is stored in a nuclear-proof bunker at a secret location somewhere in
the Swedish woods.

in the shell (we deleted all but the first one from our output). *sasl* starts its top-level supervisor, which in turn starts other supervisors and workers. These progress reports come from the supervisors and workers started as part of the main supervision tree. We stop the application in shell command 4. Before reading on, have a look at the source code of the `sasl` callback module, defined in the file *sasl.erl*. If you're unsure where to find it, use the shell command `m(sasl)`. It will tell you where the beam file is located. The source code is up a level, and then down again in a directory called *src*. The functions to look at in the source code are `start/2` and `stop/1`.

Application Resource Files

Every application must be packaged with a resource file, often referred to as the *app file*. It contains a specification consisting of configuration data, resources, and information needed to start the application. The specification is a tagged tuple of the format `{application, Application, Properties}`, where `Application` is an atom denoting the application name and `Properties` is a list of tagged tuples.

Let's step through the *sasl* application resource file before putting one together ourselves for the mobile phone example. This is version 2.3.3 of the application; be aware the contents of your app file might differ based on the release you downloaded. Looking at it, you should immediately spot `mod`, which points out the application callback module and arguments passed to the `start/2` callback function:

```
{application, sasl,
   [{description, "SASL  CXC 138 11"},
    {vsn, "2.3.3"},
    {modules, [sasl, alarm_handler, format_lib_supp, misc_supp, overload, rb,
               rb_format_supp, release_handler, release_handler_1, erlsrv,
               sasl_report, sasl_report_tty_h, sasl_report_file_h, si,
               si_sasl_supp, systools, systools_make, systools_rc,
               systools_relup, systools_lib]},
    {registered, [sasl_sup, alarm_handler, overload, release_handler]},
    {applications, [kernel, stdlib]},
    {env, [{sasl_error_logger, tty}, {errlog_type, all}]},
    {mod, {sasl, []}}]}.
```

Let's step through the properties in order. The property list contains a set of standard items. All items are optional—if an item is not included in the list, a default value is set—but there are a few that almost all applications set. The list of standard items includes:

`{description, Description}`
> where `Description` is a string of your choice. You will see the description string surface when you call `application:which_applications()` in the shell. The default value is an empty string.

`{vsn, Vsn}`

> where Vsn is a string denoting the version of the application. It should mirror the name of the directory and in automated build systems is set by scripts, not by hand. If omitted, the default value is an empty string.

`{modules, Modules}`

> where Modules is a list of modules defaulting to the empty list. The module list is used when creating your release and loading the application, with a one-to-one mapping between the modules listed here and the beam files included in the *ebin* directory. If your module beam file is in the *ebin* directory but is not listed here, it will not be loaded automatically.[2] This list is also used to check the module namespace for clashes between applications, ensuring names are unique.

> Each module is specified as an atom denoting the module name, as in the sasl example. Up to R15, it was also possible to specify the module version {Module, Vsn}, as it appeared in the -vsn(Vsn) directive in the module itself. This is no longer the case.

`{registered, Names}`

> where Names contains a list of registered process names running in this application. Including this property ensures that there will be no name clashes with registered names in other applications. Missing a name will not stop the process from running, but could result in a runtime error later when another application tries to register the same name. If omitted, the default value is the empty list.

`{applications, AppList}`

> where AppList is a list of application dependencies that must be started in order for this application to start. All applications are dependent on the *kernel* and *stdlib* applications, and many also depend on *sasl*. Dependencies are used when generating a release to determine the order in which applications are started. Sometimes, only an application such as *sasl* is provided, which in turn depends on *kernel* and *stdlib*. This will work, but it makes the system harder to maintain and understand. The default for this property is the empty list, but it is extremely unusual to omit it since doing so implies there are no dependencies on other applications.

`{env, EnvList}`

> where EnvList is a list of {Key, Value} tuples that set environment variables for the application. Values can be retrieved using functions from the application module: get_env(Key) or get_all_env() by processes in the application, or get_env(Application, Key) and get_all_env(Application) for processes that

---

2 The code server might load it later when you try to call it.

are not part of the application. Environment variables can also be set through other means covered later in this chapter. This property defaults to the empty list.

{mod, Start}

where `Start` is a tuple of the format `{Module, Args}` containing the application callback module and arguments passed to its start function. Each tuple results in a call to `Module:start(normal, Args)` when the application starts. Omitting this property will result in the application being treated as a library application, started by a supervisor or worker in another application, and no supervision tree will be created at startup.

Here are some other properties that are not included in the *sasl.app* file example but that are useful and are often included in other app files:

{id, Id}

where `Id` is a string denoting the product identifier. This property is used by overzealous configuration management trolls but, as you can see, not by the OTP team. The default value is the empty string.

{included_applications, Apps}

where `Apps` is a list of applications included as subapplications to the main one. The difference with included applications is that their top-level supervisors have to be started by one of the other supervisors. We cover included applications in more depth later in this chapter. Omitting this property will default it to the empty list.

{start_phases, Phases}

where `Phases` is a list of tuples of the format `{Phase, Args}`: `Phase` is an atom and `Args` is a term. This allows the application to be started in phases, allowing it to synchronize with other parts of the system and start workers in the background. Before `Module:start/2` returns, `Module:start_phase(StartPhase, StartType, Args)` will be called for every phase. `StartType` is the atom `normal`, or the tuples `{takeover, Node}` or `{failover, Node}`. We cover start phases in more detail later in this chapter.

The Base Station Controller Application File

Having looked at how app files are constructed, let's create one we can use in the base station controller. Alongside the `description` and application `vsn`, we list all of the `modules` that form the application. We follow that with a list of the `registered` worker and supervisor process names, and state in the `applications` list that the *bsc* application is dependent on *sasl*, *kernel*, and *stdlib*. We do not set any env variables, but explicitly keep the list empty for readability reasons. And finally, the application callback module mod is set to bsc, passing [] as a dummy argument:

```
{application, bsc,
   [{description, "Base Station Controller"},
    {vsn, "1.0"},
    {modules, [bsc, bsc_sup, frequency, freq_overload,
               logger, simple_phone_sup, phone_fsm]},
    {registered, [bsc_sup, frequency, frequency_sup,
                  overload, simple_phone_sup]},
    {applications, [kernel, stdlib, sasl]},
    {env, []},
    {mod, {bsc, []}}]}.
```

With the app file completed, all that remains is to place it in the *ebin* directory, compile the source code, and make sure the resulting *beam* files are placed in the ebin directory.

Starting an Application

When starting the Erlang emulator, include the path to your application *ebin* directory. This is a good habit when testing; *bsc* might be one of the many applications we have written and for which we need a load path, so starting Erlang directly from the *ebin* directory might not always be an option. Adding a path will no longer be a problem when implementing a release, but do it for now, as it is not set automatically. In our example, we add the path when starting Erlang using:

```
erl -pa bsc-1.0/ebin
```

but you could also use code:add_patha/1 to add the path within the Erlang shell.

Let's try starting the *bsc* application. In shell prompt 1, we fail because *sasl*, one of the applications *bsc* depends on, has not been started. We could have avoided that by using application:ensure_all_started/1, which starts up an application's dependencies and then starts the application itself, but here we simply resolve it by starting *sasl* in shell command 2 and then starting *bsc* again in shell command 3. For every child started by our top-level supervisor bsc_sup, we get a progress report from *sasl*. This is all happening behind the scenes as a result of using OTP behaviors:

```
1> application:start(bsc).
{error,{not_started,sasl}}
2> application:start(sasl).

...<snip>...

=PROGRESS REPORT==== 9-Jan-2016::18:47:09 ===
         application: sasl
          started_at: nonode@nohost
ok
```

```
3> application:start(bsc).

=PROGRESS REPORT==== 9-Jan-2016::18:47:40 ===
          supervisor: {local,bsc}
             started: [{pid,<0.51.0>},
                       {id,freq_overload},
                       {mfargs,{freq_overload,start_link,[]}},
                       {restart_type,permanent},
                       {shutdown,2000},
                       {child_type,worker}]

=PROGRESS REPORT==== 9-Jan-2016::18:47:40 ===
          supervisor: {local,bsc}
             started: [{pid,<0.53.0>},
                       {id,frequency},
                       {mfargs,{frequency,start_link,[]}},
                       {restart_type,permanent},
                       {shutdown,2000},
                       {child_type,worker}]

=PROGRESS REPORT==== 9-Jan-2016::18:47:40 ===
          supervisor: {local,bsc}
             started: [{pid,<0.54.0>},
                       {id,simple_phone_sup},
                       {mfargs,{simple_phone_sup,start_link,[]}},
                       {restart_type,permanent},
                       {shutdown,2000},
                       {child_type,worker}]

=PROGRESS REPORT==== 9-Jan-2016::18:47:40 ===
          application: bsc
          started_at: nonode@nohost
ok
4> l(phone), phone:start_test(150, 500).
*DBG* <0.123.0> got {'$gen_sync_all_state_event',
                     {<0.34.0>,#Ref<0.0.5.140>},
                     {outbound,109}} in state idle
<0.123.0> dialing 109
...<snip>...
```

After starting the base station, we took it for a test run by starting a few hundred phones that randomly call each other. Because the phone module is not part of the application, we load it before calling phone:start_test/2. In our case, not doing this would not make a difference, but it might if we were running in embedded mode in production, where modules are not loaded automatically. We cover different start modes when looking at release handling in Chapter 11.

If you have run this example, keep the Erlang shell open, type observer:start()., and read on.

The Observer Tool

The *observer* is a graphical tool that provides an overview of Erlang-based systems. It replaces and complements deprecated utilities that you might have come across in older versions of Erlang, including the process manager *pman*, the table visualizer *tv*, and *appmon*, the application monitor. To reduce performance overhead in live systems, you should start the observer tool in a separate hidden node, connecting to the cluster you want to observe through distributed Erlang. Because our *bsc* application is still in development mode, we can be lazy and get away with starting the observer locally.

The observer window opens up in the System tab, where you can view general information such as the hardware architecture, version of the runtime system, and operating system-specific data. You will also find details of the CPUs and schedulers, memory usage, and general runtime statistics. The Load Charts tab will plot memory usage, scheduler utilization, and I/O usage in real time. Although the observer will not replace proper metrics and monitoring or store historical data, it helps you understand the behavior of a system under development.

The Applications tab contains a list of applications sorted in alphabetical order (Figure 9-7). Click on any of the applications and you will see the respective supervision trees, showing how workers and supervisors are linked to each other. Narrow down on the *bsc* app. The first thing you should notice is the two application master processes. Note how one of them is linked to the *bsc* top-level supervisor, which in turn is linked to the other worker and supervisor processes it started.

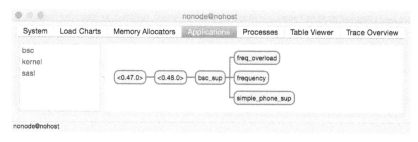

Figure 9-7. The observer

Click on any of the processes and you will get a window containing information on the process itself, the message queue, the dictionary, and the stack trace. You can view the same window from the Processes tab. The Table Viewer is a port of the table visualizer, allowing you to inspect Mnesia and ETS tables. Finally, the Trace Overview is a graphical interface to the trace BIFs and *dbg*. You can read more about all these options in the Observer User's Guide and Reference Manual.

Environment Variables

Erlang uses environment variables mainly to obtain configuration parameters when initializing the application behaviors. You can set, inspect, and change these variables. Start an Erlang shell, make sure the *sasl* application is running, and type `application:get_all_env(sasl)..` Don't worry about the meaning of the environment variables for now—we explain them later, when we cover *sasl* reports—but be aware that they are not the same as the environment variables supported by your operating system shells. For now, we focus just on how they are set and retrieved.

If you ran the `get_all_env(sasl)` call as we suggested, you saw that it returns the environment variables belonging to the *sasl* application. If you want a specific variable, say `errlog_type`, use `application:get_env(sasl, errlog_type)`. If the process retrieving the environment variables is part of an application's supervision tree, you can omit the application name and just call `application:get_all_env()` or `application:get_env(Key)`.

Using functionality similar to that in the `application:get_application()` call, OTP uses the Erlang process group leader to determine the application to which the process belongs. In our examples we are using the shell, which is not part of the *sasl* application supervision tree, so we have to specify the application.

Where are these environment variables set? If you look at the *sasl.app* file, you will find them in the env attribute of the application resource file. The app file usually contains default values you might want to override on a case-by-case basis, depending on the system and use of the application. This is best done using the system configuration file. It is a plain-text file with the *.config* suffix containing an Erlang term of the format:

```
[{Application1, [{Key1, Value1}, {Key2, Value2}, ...]},
 {Application2, [{Key2, Value2}|...}].
```

Tell the application controller which configuration file to read when starting the Erlang VM by using:

```
erl -config filename
```

where `filename` is the name of the system configuration file, with or without the *.config* suffix.

If prototyping, testing, or troubleshooting, you can override values set in the app and config files at startup in the command-line prompt using:

```
erl -application key value
```

Although convenient, this approach should not be used to set values in production systems. For the sake of clarity, stick to app and config files, as they will be the first point of call for anyone debugging or maintaining the system.

With this knowledge at hand, let's write our own *bsc.config* file containing the frequencies for our frequency allocator example and override some of the *sasl* environment variables:

```
[{sasl, [{errlog_type, error}, {sasl_error_logger, tty}]},
 {bsc, [{frequencies, [1,2,3,4,5,6]}]}].
```

This file overrides the errlog_type and sasl_error_logger environment variables set in the app file. To test the configuration parameters from the shell, start the Erlang node and provide it with the name of the configuration file, placed in the same directory where you start Erlang. In production systems, config files are placed in specific release directories. We look at them in more detail in Chapter 11.

In the following command starting the *erl* shell, we take configuration a step further and override sasl_error_logger, setting its value to false. We do this in the remainder of our examples to suppress the progress reports:

```
$ erl -config bsc.config -sasl sasl_error_logger false -pa bsc-1.0/ebin
Erlang/OTP 18 [erts-7.2] [smp:8:8] [async-threads:10] [kernel-poll:false]

Eshell V7.2  (abort with ^G)
1> application:start(sasl).
ok
2> application:get_all_env(sasl).
[{included_applications,[]},
 {errlog_type,error},
 {sasl_error_logger,false}]
3> application:start(bsc).
ok
4> application:get_env(bsc, frequencies).
{ok,[1,2,3,4,5,6]}
5> application:set_env(bsc, frequencies, [1,2,3,4,5,6,7,8,9]).
ok
6> application:get_env(bsc, frequencies).
{ok,[1,2,3,4,5,6,7,8,9]}
```

In shell command 1, we start *sasl*, retrieving all of its environment variables in shell command 2. Note the final values of the environment variables:

- errlog_type is set in the *bsc.config* file, overriding the value set in the app file.

- included_applications comes from the app file. Not originally an environment variable, it is converted into one by the application controller.

- sasl_error_logger is set in the app file, overridden in the config file, and overridden again on the Unix prompt level when starting Erlang.

The frequencies environment variable can be used in the get_frequencies() call of the frequency server to retrieve the frequencies. Note how we do not have to specify the application name in the code, because the runtime can determine the application from the group leader of the process making the call. In earlier versions of the frequency module, the get_frequencies/0 function had a hardcoded list of frequencies. In this example, the code will work with or without the *bsc.config* file:

```
get_frequencies() ->
    case application:get_env(frequencies) of
        {ok, FreqList} -> FreqList;
        undefined      -> [10,11,12,13,14,15]
    end.
```

In shell command 5 in our example interaction, we set environment variables directly in the Erlang shell, retrieving them in shell command 6. The application name is optional; if not provided, the environment variables set and retrieved will be those of the application belonging to the process executing the call. In our example, we provided the application because the shell process is not part of the *bsc* application.

 Although there is nothing stopping you from setting environment variables in the shell using the application:set_env functions, it is advisable to do so only for applications you have written yourself or know well. For third-party applications, including those that are part of the Erlang distribution, changing environment variables once the application has been started is dangerous. As you do not know when and where the application reads these environment variables, changing them may cause it to enter an inconsistent state and behave unexpectedly. You are also not guaranteed your changes will survive a restart. Do this at your own risk, and only if you know how the values are read and refreshed by the applications using them.

Application Types and Termination Strategies

When we stopped the *sasl* application in Example 9-1, we got the following info report:

```
=INFO REPORT==== 17-Feb-2014::19:51:23 ===
    application: sasl
    exited: stopped
    type: temporary
```

Did you notice that the application type was set to temporary? The type determines what happens to the virtual machine and to other applications within it when your application terminates. The temporary type is the default assigned when you start an application using application:start(Name). Three application types exist:

temporary
> When an application of this type terminates, no matter what the reason, it does not affect other running applications or the virtual machine.

transient

>   If an application of this type terminates with reason `normal`, other applications
>   are not affected. For abnormal terminations, other applications are terminated,
>   together with the virtual machine. This option is relevant only when writing your
>   own supervisor behavior (see Chapter 10), because supervisors use reason `shut
>   down` to terminate.

permanent

>   If a permanent application terminates for whatever reason, normal or abnormal,
>   all other running applications are also terminated together with the virtual
>   machine.

These options become relevant when creating our own releases, as they can be set in
the start scripts. In proper OTP releases, all applications tend to be permanent. Top-
level supervisors in an application should never terminate. When they do, they
assume that your restart strategy failed, so the whole node is taken down. Stopping an
application with `application:stop/1`, however, has no effect on other applications,
irrespective of type.

Distributed Applications

OTP comes with a convenient distribution mechanism for migrating applications
across nodes. It can handle the majority of cases where you need an instance of an
application running in your cluster, and can act as a stopgap measure until a more
complex solution can be put in place. The majority of cases assume reliable networks,
so use with care and make sure you have covered your edge cases should a network
partition occur.

Distributed applications are managed by a process called the *distributed application
controller*, implemented in the `dist_ac` module and registered with the same name.
You will find an instance of this process in the kernel supervision tree running on
every distributed node.

To run your distributed application, all you need to do is configure a few environment variables in the *kernel* application, ensure that requests are transparently forwarded to the node where the applications are running, and then test, test, and test
again. You have to specify the precedence order for the nodes where you want the
application to run. If the node on which an application is running fails, the application will fail over to the next node in the precedence list. If a newly started or connected node with higher precedence appears in the cluster, the application will be
migrated to that node in what OTP calls a *takeover*.

Let's assume our system consists of a cluster of four nodes, *n1@localhost*, *n2@local-
host*, *n3@localhost*, and *n4@localhost*. Let's create a configuration file, *dist.config*, setting the kernel environment variables distributing our *bsc* application across them:

```
[{kernel, [{distributed, [{bsc, 1000, [n1@localhost,{n2@localhost,n3@localhost},
                                       n4@localhost]}]},
           {sync_nodes_mandatory, [n1@localhost]},
           {sync_nodes_optional, [n2@localhost,n3@localhost,n4@localhost]},
           {sync_nodes_timeout, 15000}]},
  {bsc,  [{frequencies, [1,2,3,4,5,6]}]}]].
```

Note that if you intend to run the distributed *bsc* example, you may need to replace all occurrences of the string "localhost" in the *dist.config* file with your own computer's host name.

Of the environment variables in the *kernel* application, the first we need to set is distributed. It consists of a list of tuples containing the application we want to distribute, a timeout value, and the distributed list of nodes and node tuples, which defines the order of precedence of nodes on which we want the application to run. So, this list:

```
[{bsc, 1000, [n1@localhost,{n2@localhost,n3@localhost},n4@localhost]}]
```

specifies bsc as the application, 1000 (measured in milliseconds) as the time to wait for the node to come back up, and the following node precedence:

```
[n1@localhost,{n2@localhost,n3@localhost},n4@localhost]
```

The precedence specifies that the application will start on n1. Should that node fail or be shut down, the distributed application controller will wait 1 second and then fail the application over to either n2 or n3. They have been given the same precedence by being grouped into the same tuple. If both n2 and n3 fail, the controller will check to see whether n1 has come back up and, if it is still down, will fail the application over to n4. If one of the other nodes comes back up, the application is later moved via a takeover to the node with the highest precedence.

The sync_nodes_mandatory and sync_nodes_optional environment variables specify the nodes to be connected into the distributed system. When starting the system, the distributed application controller tries to connect the specified nodes, waiting for the number of milliseconds specified in the {sync_nodes_timeout, Timeout} environment variable. If you omit the timeout when defining the nodes in your kernel environment variables, the timeout defaults to 0.

The {sync_nodes_mandatory, NodeList} environment variable defines the nodes with which the distributed application controller *must* synchronize; the system will start only if all of these nodes are started and connected to each other within Timeout milliseconds.

The environment variable {sync_nodes_optional, NodeList} specifies nodes that can also be connected at system startup, but unlike mandatory nodes, the failure of any of these nodes to join the cluster within the specified Timeout does not prevent the system from starting up.

The best way to understand the environment variable settings is to play with the *dist.config* configuration file. Let's first start node *n2* on its own:

```
$ erl -sname n2@localhost -config dist -pa bsc-1.0/ebin
```

This node will wait the 15 seconds set in the sync_nodes_timeout value for n1 to come up. If the node fails to connect to n1 within that time frame, it will terminate, regurgitating a long and to the untrained eye incomprehensible error message. Nodes n3 and n4 are optional, so assuming n1 comes up within the timeout period, n2 will also wait for these two nodes within the same period, after which it starts normally whether or not n3 and n4 have connected.

Let's try again, but this time, before starting n2, start n1 and n3:

```
$ erl -sname n1@localhost -config dist -pa bsc-1.0/ebin
$ erl -sname n3@localhost -config dist -pa bsc-1.0/ebin
```

The nodes will wait 15 seconds for the optional nodes to come up. If they don't, the nodes will start regardless. You can try deleting n4 from the config file (or decide to start it), avoiding the timeout if the other nodes are up.

When all nodes are up, let's start the *sasl* and *bsc* applications on all nodes, starting with n3, followed by n2 and n1. Type the following in all three Erlang shells and pay attention to when the shell command returns:

```
application:start(sasl), application:start(bsc).
```

You will notice that the shell will hang in n2 and n3, returning only when the *bsc* application is started in n1, as it is the node running with the highest priority. If you start the observer and inspect the Applications tab on the different nodes, you will notice that the supervision tree is started only on n1. Looking at the progress reports for n2 and n3, you will notice that the *bsc* application is also started, but without its supervision tree.

Keeping an eye on nodes n2 and n3, shut down node n1 using the halt() shell command.

The application controller will wait 1,000 milliseconds for n1 to restart. If it doesn't, you will see the progress reports for the *bsc* app being started on either n2 and n3. In our config file, because both n2 and n3 have the same precedence, either one will be chosen nondeterministically. In Figure 9-8, we assume that the chosen node is n2.

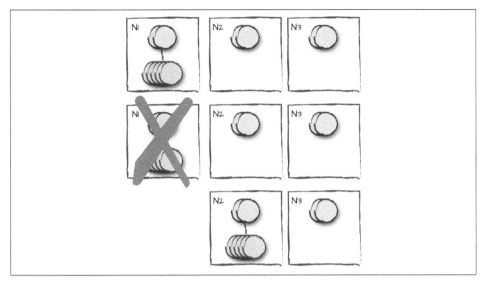

Figure 9-8. Failing over with different precedence

Now that *n1* is down, let's shut down *n2* (or *n3* if the *bsc* application was started on it instead). You will see that application fail over to the remaining node (Figure 9-9). Use the observer to check that the supervision tree has started correctly (Figure 9-7). Restart the node you just shut down and observe what happens. You will notice that it hangs for 15 seconds, waiting for *n1* to restart. Because *n1* is mandatory and has not restarted, the node fails to restart.

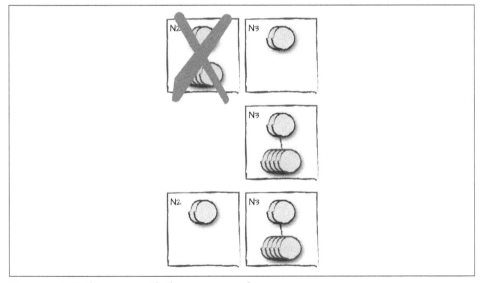

Figure 9-9. Failing over with the same precedence

Restart both *n1* and *n2* (or *n3* if it was the node that shut down) within 15 seconds of each other. Both will wait 15 seconds for the nonmandatory node *n4* to start. After the timeout, start both *sasl* and *bsc* on *n2* using `application:start/1`. Just as the first time you started the cluster, the application hangs waiting for *bsc* to start on *n1* so that the nodes can coordinate among each other. When you start *bsc* on *n1*, there will be a takeover from *n3*, where the behaviors are terminated and the supervision tree is taken down (Figure 9-10).

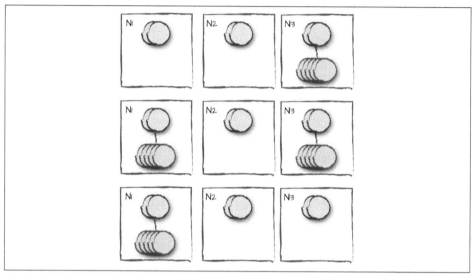

Figure 9-10. Application takeover

This is a limited approach that might cover some use cases and not others. The moral of the story if you go down this route is to pick your mandatory nodes with care. When designing your system with no single point of failure, you should not assume or require any of the nodes to be up at any one time. If there are services you require for a failover or a takeover to be successful, do the checks in start phases when starting the applications or in the worker processes themselves. While this layer can be thin and consist of only a couple hundred lines of code, it is application dependent. Make sure you've thought through your design. We look at other approaches to distributed architectures when discussing clusters in Chapter 13.

Start Phases

Some systems are so complex that it is not enough to start each application one at a time. In such systems, applications need to be started in phases and synchronized with each other. Imagine a node that is part of a cluster handling instant messaging:

1. In a first phase, as a background task, you might want to start loading all of the Mnesia tables containing routing and configuration data. This could take time, as some of the tables might have to be restored because of an abrupt shutdown or node crash.

2. Once the tables load, the next phase gets your system to a state where you are ready to start accepting configuration requests. We refer to this as enabling the *administration state*. This might include checking links toward other clusters in the federation that users might want to connect to, configuring hardware, and waiting for all of the other parts of the system, such as the authentication server or logging facility, to start correctly.

3. When this phase completes, you will be able to inspect and configure the system, but not allow any users to initiate sessions. Your final start phase might be to provide the go-ahead and start allowing users to log on and traffic to run through this node. We refer to this phase as enabling the *operational state*.

If we add the following parameter in our *bsc.app* file, we allow three start phases:

```
{start_phases, [{init, []}, {admin, []}, {oper, []}]}
```

In our application callback module source file, *bsc.erl*, we need to export and define the callback function start_phase(StartPhase, StartType, Args). This function will be called for every phase defined in the app file, after the supervision tree has been started but before application:start(Application) returns. The StartPhase argument reflects which phase is currently being processed. So, in our example, if we added:

```
start_phase(StartPhase, StartType, Args) ->
    io:format("bsc:start_phase(~p,~p,~p).~n", [StartPhase, StartType, Args]).
```

to our application callback module *bsc.erl* and ran it with the updated *bsc.app* file, we would get the following sequence of events when starting the application. Both these files are in the *start_phases* directory of the code repository:

```
$ erl -pz bsc-1.0/ebin/ -pa start_phases/ -sasl sasl_error_logger false
Erlang/OTP 18 [erts-7.2] [smp:8:8] [async-threads:10] [kernel-poll:false]

Eshell V7.2  (abort with ^G)
1> application:start(sasl), application:start(bsc).
bsc:start_phase(init,normal,[]).
bsc:start_phase(admin,normal,[]).
bsc:start_phase(oper,normal,[]).
ok
```

Here, the StartType argument is always the atom normal, indicating this is a normal startup. Each phase invokes a synchronous or asynchronous call that triggers certain operations, as well as setting the internal state that allows or disallows requests to be handled by the node.

When shutting down the system, we can disable the operational state, stopping new requests from executing but allowing all existing requests to execute to completion. This could make the system reject user login attempts while allowing existing sessions to expire. When there are no more requests going through the node, the operational state can be disabled and the node shut down. This could happen when all the users have logged out, or after a timeout, where the system times out the remaining sessions and disables the operational state. To shut down the node, disable the operational state. A simple example using start phases appears in the next section.

Included Applications

In your app resource file, you have the option of specifying the parameter included_applications. The directory structure of included applications should be placed in the *lib* directory, alongside all other applications in that release. When the main application is started, all included applications are loaded but not started. It is up to the top-level supervisor of the main application to start the included applications' supervision trees. You could start them as dynamic children or as static ones by returning the child specification in the supervisor init/1 callback function.

When starting your application, you can either call the start/2 function in the application callback module, assuming it returns {ok, Pid} (and not {ok, Pid, Data}, since it is not possible for us to pass that data to the callback module's prep_stop/1 callback function as it expects when it is stopped), or directly call the start_link function of the top-level supervisor. There is no more to it; it's as simple as that!

In every node, included applications may be included only once by other applications. This restriction avoids clashes in the application namespace, ensuring that each module and registered process (local or global) is unique. If you need to start several identical supervision trees in the same node, place the code in a standalone library application. Do not include this application anywhere else other than by dependency and ensure that there are no name clashes with the locally and globally registered processes.

You might be asking yourself, why go through the hassle of included applications when we can instead have a flat application structure, starting the applications individually? The answer lies in start phases.

Start Phases in Included Applications

You can use start phases to synchronize your included applications at startup. As the included application supervision trees are started by the main application, you need to follow a few steps to invoke the start_phase/3 callback function in the application callback module.

First, in your included application app files, make sure you have included the mod and start_phases parameters. The callback module is used to determine where the start_phase/3 call is made. The arguments are ignored, because the ones in the start_phases item are used.

Finally, in your top-level application, alongside your start phases, you need to change your mod parameter to:

```
{mod, {application_starter,[Mod,Args]}}
```

passing the application callback module Mod and Args as arguments. The OTP application_starter module provides the logic to start your top-level application and coordinate the start phases of the included applications.

The process is straightforward. The top-level application's supervision tree starts the included applications. The first start_phase/3 function is called in the callback module of the top-level application, after which all included applications are traversed in the order they are defined. If one or more of the included applications have the same phase defined as the one in the top-level application, start_phase/3 is called for each of these included applications.

The next start phase in the top-level application is recursively triggered. Start phases defined in the included applications but not in the top-level application are never triggered.

All of what we've described is best shown in an example. We create a top-level application, *top_app*, that includes the *bsc* application. The top_app callback module is responsible for starting the supervision tree of the included *bsc* application:

```
-module(top_app).
-behavior(application).
-export([start/2, start_phase/3, stop/1]).

start(_Type, _Args) ->
    {ok, _Pid} = bsc_sup:start_link().

start_phase(StartPhase, StartType, Args) ->
    io:format("top_app:start_phase(~p,~p,~p).~n", [StartPhase, StartType, Args]).

stop(_Data) ->
    ok.
```

In our top application's *top_app.app* file, we define the start, admin, and stop phases. They are different from the start phases in *bsc*, which in "Start Phases" on page 226, our previous example, were set to init, admin, and oper. Note also the included_applications and the value we give the mod attribute:

```
{application, top_app,
    [{description, "Included Application Example"},
```

```
      {vsn, "1.0"},
      {modules, [top_app]},
      {applications, [kernel, stdlib, sasl]},
      {included_applications, [bsc]},
      {start_phases, [{start, []}, {admin, []}, {stop, []}]},
      {mod, {application_starter, [top_app, []]}}
    ]
}.
```

The start phases work as follows. The top application is started, which in turn starts
the *bsc* supervision tree. Once that is successful, the first start phase in *top_app*,
start, is triggered. If any of the included applications, in the order they appear in the
included_applications list, also has this phase, it is also called. If you are trying this
on your computer, do not forget to compile the contents of the *top_app* directory,
and use the *bsc.app* file in the *start_phases* directory of this chapter's code repository:

```
$ erl -pz bsc-1.0/ebin/ -pa start_phases/ \
      -pa top_app/  -sasl sasl_error_logger false
Erlang/OTP 18 [erts-7.2] [smp:8:8] [async-threads:10] [kernel-poll:false]

Eshell V7.2  (abort with ^G)
1> application:start(sasl), application:start(top_app).
top_app:start_phase(start,normal,[]).
top_app:start_phase(admin,normal,[]).
bsc:start_phase(admin,normal,[]).
top_app:start_phase(stop,normal,[]).
ok
```

We have kept the example simple so as to demonstrate the principles without getting
lost in the business logic. In our example, we call all of the start phases in the top
application, but only admin in the included one, as it is the only phase they both have
in common.

Combining Supervisors and Applications

Some supervisor callback modules contain only a few lines of code. And if your application does not have to deal with complex initialization procedures, start phases, and
distribution, but needs only to start the top-level supervisor, it will be just as compact. A common practice is to combine the two callback modules, as their callback
function names do not overlap. While some people will strongly disagree with this
practice, you are bound to come across it when reading other people's code—even
code that is part of the standard Ericsson distribution.

For example, cd into the *sasl* directory of your OTP installation and have a look at the
sasl.erl file. At the time of writing, version 2.6.1 of the *sasl* application combined the
supervisor init/1 callback function in its application module together with the
application start/2 and stop/1 callback functions. In this example, the developers
included only the -behavior(application). directive, but there is nothing stopping

---

you from including the -behavior(supervisor). directive as well. The only side effect is a compiler warning telling you about two behavior directives in the same callback module. We recommend including both directives, because it facilitates the understanding of the purpose of the callback module. Here is a simple example of what combining the `supervisor` and `application` callback modules would look like in our *bsc* example:

```erlang
-module(bsc).
-behavior(application).
-behavior(supervisor).

-export([start/2, start_phase/3, stop/1, init/1]).

start(_Type, _Args) ->
    {ok, Pid} = supervisor:start_link({local,?MODULE},?MODULE, []).

start_phase(Phase, Type, Args) ->
    io:format("bsc:start_phase(~p,~p,~p).",[Phase, Type, Args]).

stop(_Data) ->
    ok.

%% Supervisor callbacks

init(_) ->
    ChildSpecList = [child(freq_overload),
                     child(frequency),
                     child(simple_phone_sup)],
    {ok,{{rest_for_one, 2, 3600}, ChildSpecList}}.

child(Module) ->
    {Module, {Module, start_link, []},
     permanent, 2000, worker, [Module]}.
```

The SASL Application

Throughout this chapter, we've been telling you to look at the SASL callback module, app file, directory structure, and supervision tree, but we have yet to tell you what SASL actually does.

SASL stands for system architecture support libraries. The SASL application (*sasl*) is a container for useful items needed in large-scale software design. It is one of the mandatory applications (along with *kernel* and *stdlib*) required in a minimal OTP release. It is mandatory because it contains all of the common library modules used for release handling and software upgrades.

We cover releases in Chapter 11 and software upgrades in Chapter 12. SASL doesn't stop, however, at handling releases and software upgrades. In "The SASL Alarm Handler" on page 165, we looked at the alarm handler, a simple alarm manager and handler that is started by default when you start any OTP-based system. SASL also has a very basic way, through its overload library module, to regulate CPU load in the system. We cover load regulation in more detail in Chapter 13, when we discuss the architecture of a typical Erlang node. Have patience.

What we concentrate on in this chapter are the SASL reports used to monitor the activity in supervision trees when processes are started, terminated, and restarted. You will have come across SASL reports in the previous chapters of this book. They are the printouts you see in the shell when starting applications, supervisors, and worker processes. You might have noticed that they appeared only when the SASL application was started and the sasl_error_logger environment variable was not set to false.

SASL starts an event handler that receives the following reports:

Supervisor reports
    Issued by a supervisor when one of its children terminates abnormally.

Progress reports
    Issued by a supervisor when starting or restarting a child or by the application master when starting the application.

Error reports
    Issued by behaviors upon abnormal termination.

Crash reports
    Issued by processes started with the proc_lib library, which by default include behaviors. We cover proc_lib in the next chapter.

Default settings print reports to standard I/O. You can override this by setting environment variables, which allow you to send the reports to wraparound binary logs as well as to limit which reports are forwarded. The formats of the reports vary depending on the version of the OTP release you are running. Let's have a look at the SASL environment variables that allow you to control the reports:

sasl_error_logger
    Defaults to tty and installs the sasl_report_tty_h handler module, which prints the reports to standard output. If you instead specify {file,FileName}, where FileName is a string containing the relative or absolute path of a file, the sasl_report_file_h handler is installed, storing all reports in FileName. If this environment variable is set to false, no handlers are installed, and as a result, no SASL reports are generated.

errlog_type

> Can take the values error, progress, or all, the default if you omit the variable. Use this variable to restrict the types of error or progress reports printed or logged to file by the installed handler.

utc_log

> An optional environment variable that, if set to true, will convert all timestamps in the reports to Universal Coordinated Time (UTC).

The following configuration file stores all the SASL reports in a text file called *SASL-logs*. We do this by setting the sasl_error_logger environment variable to {file, "SASLlogs"}. We also enable UTC time with the utc_log environment variable:

```
[{sasl, [{sasl_error_logger, {file, "SASLlogs"}},
        {utc_log, true}]},
 {bsc,  [{frequencies, [1,2,3,4,5,6]}]}].
```

If you start the *sasl* and *bsc* applications in a local, nondistributed node, you will find all of the logs stored as plain text in the running directory. In our example, we show just the first and last reports. Note how the UTC tag is appended to the timestamp:

```
$ erl -pa bsc-1.0/ebin/ -config logtofile.config
Erlang/OTP 18 [erts-7.2] [smp:8:8] [async-threads:10] [kernel-poll:false]

Eshell V7.2  (abort with ^G)
1> application:start(sasl), application:start(bsc).
ok
2> halt().
$ cat SASLlogs

=PROGRESS REPORT==== 9-Jan-2016::10:09:25 UTC ===
          supervisor: {local,sasl_safe_sup}
             started: [{pid,<0.40.0>},
                       {name,alarm_handler},
                       {mfargs,{alarm_handler,start_link,[]}},
                       {restart_type,permanent},
                       {shutdown,2000},
                       {child_type,worker}]

...<snip>...

=PROGRESS REPORT==== 9-Jan-2016::10:09:33 UTC ===
         application: bsc
          started_at: nonode@nohost
```

Text files might be good during your development phase, but when moving to production, it is best to move to wraparound logs that store events in a searchable binary format. Because text and binary formats are implemented by different handlers, they can be added and run alongside each other. To install the binary log handler, error_logger_mf_h, you have to set three environment variables. If any of these are disabled, the handler will not be added. The environment variables needed are:

error_logger_mf_dir
> A string specifying the directory that stores the binary logs. The default is a period ("."), which specifies the current working directory. If this environment variable is set to false, the handler is not installed.

error_logger_mf_maxbytes
> An integer defining the maximum size in bytes of each log file.

error_logger_mf_maxfiles
> An integer between 1 and 256 specifying the maximum number of wraparound log files that are generated.

Sticking to our *bsc* example, let's try storing the SASL logs in a binary file using the *rb.config* configuration file found in the book's code repository. Note how we are explicitly turning off the events sent to the shell by setting the sasl_error_logger environment variable to false and the frequencies to the atom crash, rather than a list of integers, ensuring that the process fails when we try to allocate a frequency:

```
[{sasl, [{sasl_error_logger, false},
        {error_logger_mf_dir, "."},
        {error_logger_mf_maxbytes, 20000},
        {error_logger_mf_maxfiles, 5}]},
  {bsc,  [{frequencies, crash}]}].
```

We start the *bsc* application in shell command 1, and cause a crash of the frequency server in shell command 2 when we try to pattern match the atom crash into a head and a tail in the allocate/2 function of the frequency module:

```
$ erl -pa bsc-1.0/ebin -config rb.config
Erlang/OTP 18 [erts-7.2] [smp:8:8] [async-threads:10] [kernel-poll:false]

Eshell V7.2  (abort with ^G)
1> application:start(sasl), application:start(bsc).
ok
2> frequency:allocate().

=ERROR REPORT==== 9-Jan-2016::19:24:30 ===
** Generic server frequency terminating
** Last message in was {allocate,<0.34.0>}
** When Server state == {data,[{"State",{{available,crash},{allocated,[]}}}]}
** Reason for termination ==
** {function_clause,[{frequency,allocate,
                                [{crash,[]},<0.34.0>],
                                [{file,"bsc-1.0/src/frequency.erl"},
                                 {line,99}]},
...<snip>...
```

```
3> rb:start().
rb: reading report...done.
{ok,<0.56.0>}
4> rb:list().
  No                Type   Process      Date     Time
  ==                ====   =======      ====     ====
  14            progress   <0.37.0> 2016-01-09 19:24:26
  13            progress   <0.37.0> 2016-01-09 19:24:26
  12            progress   <0.37.0> 2016-01-09 19:24:26
  11            progress   <0.37.0> 2016-01-09 19:24:26
  10            progress   <0.24.0> 2016-01-09 19:24:26
   9            progress   <0.46.0> 2016-01-09 19:24:26
   8            progress   <0.46.0> 2016-01-09 19:24:26
   7            progress   <0.46.0> 2016-01-09 19:24:26
   6            progress   <0.24.0> 2016-01-09 19:24:26
   5               error   <0.46.0> 2016-01-09 19:24:30
   4        crash_report   frequency 2016-01-09 19:24:30
   3   supervisor_report   <0.46.0> 2016-01-09 19:24:30
   2            progress   <0.46.0> 2016-01-09 19:24:30
   1            progress   <0.46.0> 2016-01-09 19:24:30
ok
```

Try it out yourself in the shell, as it will help you understand how applications and supervision trees work. The first thing you will notice is that, even though we set sasl_error_logger to false, we still get an error report. This is because all the environment variable controls are *supervisor*, *crash*, and *progress* reports. *Error* reports are printed out irrespective of configuration file settings. We've reduced the size of this particular error report in the trial run, because our focus is on the report browser.

Having caused a crash, we start the report browser using rb:start() in shell command 3. After it reads in all of the reports, we list them in shell command 4 with rb:list(). If at any time you do not recall the report browser commands, rb:help() will list them. The progress reports 14–6 (they are listed in reverse order, with the oldest having the highest number) are the ones starting the application and its supervision tree. Let's start by inspecting reports 1–5:

- The frequency server generates reports 4 and 5 as a result of its abnormal termination. The reports contain complementary information needed for postmortem debugging and troubleshooting.

- The supervisor generates report 3 as a result of the termination. It contains the information stored by the supervisor of that particular child.

- Reports 1 and 2 are issued by the children being restarted. In our case, it is the frequency server that crashed and the simple_phone_sup supervisor that was terminated and restarted as a result of the rest_for_all strategy of the top-level bsc_sup supervisor.

Progress Reports

Progress reports are issued by a supervisor when starting a child, worker or supervisor alike. These reports include the name of the supervisor and the child specification of the child being started. They are also issued by the application master when starting or restarting an application. In this case, the report shows the application name and the node on which it is started. Here's an example:

```
5> rb:show(6).

PROGRESS REPORT  <0.7.0>                                2016-01-09 19:24:26
===========================================================================
application                                                             bsc
started_at                                                    nonode@nohost

ok
```

The progress report in our example is the one telling us that the *bsc* application was started correctly. Note how we are using rb:show/1 to view individual reports.

Error Reports

Error reports are raised by behaviors upon abnormal termination. In our case, the frequency server generates the report when terminating abnormally. You can generate your own error reports using the error_logger:error_msg(String, Args) call, but we advise against this. Use this command sparingly and only for unexpected errors, as too many user-generated reports will hide serious issues and clutter the logs, making it harder to find important details when you are looking for crash reports and other real errors. Here's the error report from our example:

```
6> rb:show(5).

ERROR REPORT  <0.51.0>                                  2016-01-09 19:24:30
===========================================================================

** Generic server frequency terminating
** Last message in was {allocate,<0.34.0>}
** When Server state == {data,[{"State",{{available,crash},{allocated,[]}}}]}
** Reason for termination ==
** {function_clause,[{frequency,allocate,
                                 [{crash,[]},<0.34.0>],
                                 [{file,"bsc-1.0/src/frequency.erl"},
                                  {line,99}]},
                     {frequency,handle_call,3,
                                 [{file,"bsc-1.0/src/frequency.erl"},
                                  {line,66}]},
                     {gen_server,try_handle_call,4,
                                 [{file,"gen_server.erl"},{line,629}]},
                     {gen_server,handle_msg,5,
                                 [{file,"gen_server.erl"},{line,661}]},
```

```
                    {proc_lib,init_p_do_apply,3,
                              [[file,"proc_lib.erl"},{line,240}]]}]}
ok
7> error_logger:error_msg("Error in ~w. Division by zero!~n", [self()]).
ok

=ERROR REPORT==== 9-Jan-2016::19:28:19 ===
Error in <0.57.0>. Division by zero!
```

Crash Reports

Crash reports are issued by processes started with the proc_lib library. If you look at the exit reason in our example, you will realize that this applies to all behaviors, which are started from that library. A try-catch in the main behavior loop will trap abnormal terminations and generate a crash report. No reports are generated if the behavior or process terminates with reason normal or when the supervisor terminates the behavior with reason shutdown. A crash report contains information on the crashed process, including exit reason, initial function, and message queue, as well as other process information typically found using the process_info BIFs. The crash report from our example looks like this:

```
8> rb:show(4).

CRASH REPORT  <0.51.0>                                  2016-01-09 19:24:30
===========================================================================
Crashing process
    initial_call                        {frequency,init,['Argument__1']}
    pid                                                         <0.51.0>
    registered_name                                            frequency
    error_info
        {exit,
          {function_clause,
            [{frequency,allocate,
                [{crash,[]},<0.34.0>],
                [{file,"bsc-1.0/src/frequency.erl"},{line,99}]},
             {frequency,handle_call,3,
                [{file,"bsc-1.0/src/frequency.erl"},{line,66}]},
             {gen_server,try_handle_call,4,
                [{file,"gen_server.erl"},{line,629}]},
             {gen_server,handle_msg,5,
                [{file,"gen_server.erl"},{line,661}]},
             {proc_lib,init_p_do_apply,3,
                [{file,"proc_lib.erl"},{line,240}]}]},
           [{gen_server,terminate,7,[{file,"gen_server.erl"},{line,826}]},
            {proc_lib,init_p_do_apply,3,
                [{file,"proc_lib.erl"},{line,240}]}]}]}
    ancestors                                          [bsc,<0.47.0>]
    messages                                                       []
    links                                                   [<0.48.0>]
    dictionary                                                     []
```

```
        trap_exit                                                           false
        status                                                            running
        heap_size                                                             987
        stack_size                                                             27
        reductions                                                            412

    ok
```

Supervisor Reports

Supervisor reports are issued by supervisors upon abnormal child termination. They usually follow the error reports issued by the children themselves. The supervisor report contains the name of the reporting supervisor and the phase of the child in which the error occurred:

9> rb:show(3).

```
SUPERVISOR REPORT   <0.48.0>                              2016-01-09 19:24:30
=============================================================================
Reporting supervisor                                              {local,bsc}

Child process
    errorContext                                           child_terminated
    reason
          {function_clause,
             [{frequency,allocate,
                 [{crash,[]},<0.34.0>],
                 [{file,"bsc-1.0/src/frequency.erl"},{line,99}]]},
              {frequency,handle_call,3,
                 [{file,"bsc-1.0/src/frequency.erl"},{line,66}]]},
              {gen_server,try_handle_call,4,
                 [{file,"gen_server.erl"},{line,629}]]},
              {gen_server,handle_msg,5,[{file,"gen_server.erl"},{line,661}]]},
              {proc_lib,init_p_do_apply,3,
                 [{file,"proc_lib.erl"},{line,240}]]}]}
    pid                                                              <0.51.0>
    id                                                              frequency
    mfargs                                              {frequency,start_link,[]}
    restart_type                                                    permanent
    shutdown                                                             2000
    child_type                                                         worker

    ok
```

If you look close to the top of the example output, you will find the report phase of the child when the error occurred: one of start_error, child_terminated, or shutdown_error. In our case, the termination happened because of a runtime error, resulting in the report phase being child_terminated. It is followed with the reason for termination and the child specification.

You can look at the last two progress reports on your own. They are the progress reports generated when the frequency server and phone supervisor are restarted. Use rb:help(), and spend some time experimenting with the commands in the report browser, especially the filters and regular expressions.

The SASL Logs Will Bail You Out

The SASL logs should by default be enabled on all nodes in production, as they will be your first point of call when investigating a node crash or trying to restart a node. In the majority of cases, the error, crash, and supervisor reports will contain enough information to figure out what happened. Always have a separate start script that allows you to start Erlang (and *sasl*) on its own, using the command rb:start([{report_dir, Dir}]) to load the logs, because there is a good chance the Erlang node with your release will not be able to restart. Do not rely on the Erlang node you are investigating to read them, as it most likely will not start. If you have an external alarm and monitoring system, it is always a good idea to generate notifications when you receive error, crash, and supervisor reports to ensure you investigate them. With many nodes in production—potentially thousands—aggregating these notifications in one place will make life much easier for you. You can easily forward them to third-party tools by writing your own event handler and hooking it into the SASL event manager.

Summing Up

In this chapter, we covered the behavior that allows us to package code, resources, configuration files, and supervision trees into what we call an application. Applications are the reusable building blocks of your systems; they are loaded, started, and stopped as a single unit. They provide functionality such as start phases, synchronization, and failover in distributed clusters, as well as basic monitoring and logging services.

Table 9-1 lists the major functions used to control applications.

Table 9-1. Application callbacks

Application function or action	Application callback function
application:start/1, application:start/2	Module:start/2, Module:start_phase/3
application:stop/1	Module:prep_stop/1, Module:stop/2

You can read more about applications in the application (*http://bit.ly/erlang-app*) manual pages, and about resource files in the *app (http://erlang.org/doc/man/ app.html)* manual page. The OTP Design Principles User's Guide, which comes with the standard Erlang documentation, has sections covering general, included, and distributed applications. To learn more about the tools we've covered, consult the manual pages for the report browser, rb (*http://bit.ly/erlang-rb*), as well as the observer (*http://bit.ly/erlang-observer*). Read through the code of the examples provided in this chapter and see how applications in the Erlang distribution are packaged and configured.

What's Next?

Now that we know how to create our applications, the basic building blocks for Erlang systems, next we look at how to group them together in a release and start our systems using boot files. But first, we look at some of the libraries used to implement special processes, and using that knowledge to define our own behaviors. What are special processes, I hear you say? They are processes that, despite not being OTP behaviors that come as part of the *stdlib* application, can be added to OTP supervision trees. Read on to find out more.

## CHAPTER 10

Special Processes and Your Own Behaviors

OTP behaviors, in the vast majority of cases, provide you with the concurrency design patterns you need in your projects. There might, however, be occasions where you want to create an OTP-compliant application while attaching processes that are not standard behaviors to your supervision tree. For instance, existing behaviors might have performance impacts caused by the overhead of the layers added as a result of abstracting out the generic parts and error handling. You may want to write new behaviors after separating your code into generic and specific modules. Or you might want to do something as simple as adding pure Erlang processes to a supervision tree, making your release OTP compliant beyond the capabilities provided by supervision bridges. For instance, you might have to preserve that proof of concept you wrote when you first started exploring Erlang that, against your better judgment, wound up in production.[1]

We refer to a process that can be added to an OTP supervision tree and packaged in an application as a *special process*. This chapter explains how to write your own special processes, providing you with the flexibility of pure Erlang while retaining all of the advantages of OTP. We also explain how you can take your special processes a step further, turning them into OTP behaviors by splitting the code into generic and specific modules that interface with each other through predefined callback functions. If you are not planning on implementing your own behaviors or are uninterested in how they work behind the scenes, feel free to jump to the next chapter (or go to the pub) without a bad conscience. You can always come back and read this chapter

---

1 For those of you working in large companies, we're referring to the projects where we've spent more time in meetings discussing and trying to get approval for a migration to OTP than it would have actually taken to refactor the code.

when you need to. If, on the other hand, we've piqued your curiosity, keep on reading.

Special Processes

In order for a process to be considered a special process, and as such be part of an OTP supervision tree, it must:

- Be started using the `proc_lib` module and link to its parent
- Be able to handle system messages, system events, and shutdown requests
- Return the module list if running dynamic modules, as we did with event managers when defining their child specs

While optional, it is useful if the process is also capable of handling debug flags and generating trace messages.

We show you how to implement special processes by walking through an example where we implement a mutex, serializing access to critical resources.

The Mutex

Mutex stands for mutual exclusion. It ensures only one process is allowed to execute the code in the critical section at any one time. A critical resource could be a printer, shared memory, or any other device for which requests must be serialized because it can handle only one client at a time. A process executing code that accesses this resource is said to be in the critical section. It needs to finish executing all the code in the critical section and exit it before a new process is allowed to enter.

In Erlang, programmers can implement a mutex as an FSM, serializing client requests through a process and managing the request queue using the mailboxes and selective receives. Because we are implementing an FSM, you must be asking yourself why we are not using the `gen_fsm` behavior module. The reason is that the `gen_fsm` behavior, and any of the other standard OTP behaviors, for that matter, does not allow us to selectively receive messages through pattern matching. Instead, the standard behaviors force us to handle events in the order in which they arrive. In contrast, by using the process mailbox and selective receives to manage the queue of client processes waiting for the mutex, we simplify our code because we have to handle only one client request at a time, without having to worry about the others waiting in the queue.

Mutexes are FSMs with two states, *free* and *busy*. A client wanting to enter the critical section does so by calling the client function `mutex:wait(Name)`, where `Name` is the variable bound to the registered name associated with the mutex. The `wait` call is synchronous, returning only when the calling process is allowed to enter the critical section. When that occurs, the FSM transitions to state *busy*.

Requests are stored in the mailbox and handled on a first in, first out basis. If the mutex is being blocked by another process in state *busy*, the request is left in the mailbox and handled when the mutex returns to state *free*. When the busy process is ready to leave the critical section, it calls `mutex:signal(Name)`, an asynchronous call that releases the mutex. When that occurs, the FSM transitions back to state *free*, ready to handle the next request. Figure 10-1 shows the state transitions of a mutex.

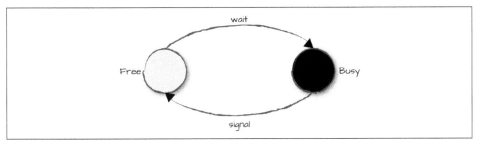

Figure 10-1. State transitions in a mutex

Let's have a look at the `mutex` module, starting with the client functions (other exported functions will be defined shortly):

```
-module(mutex).
-export([start_link/1, start_link/2, init/3, stop/1]).
-export([wait/1, signal/1]).

wait(Name) ->
    Name ! {wait,self()},
    Mutex = whereis(Name),
    receive
        {Mutex,ok} -> ok
    end.

signal(Name) ->
    Name ! {signal,self()},
    ok.
```

Lots of borderline cases are handled gracefully in standard OTP behaviors and are often taken for granted by the programmer. You might have seen them yourself when looking at the code in the `gen_server` or `gen_fsm` modules. When implementing special processes, however, you need to decide which borderline cases to handle and take care of them yourself. In our example, we've opted for simplicity and do not cover any of them. But to give you an idea of what we are talking about, have a look at the `wait/1` function, where we do not check if `Name` exists. We do not monitor whether the mutex terminates while the client process is suspended in its `receive` clause. Nor are we handling the case where the mutex terminates right before `whereis/1` and is restarted and reregistered immediately, leaving wait/1 in a receive clause waiting for a message from a live process it will never receive. Nor have we implemented any timeouts if the mutex process is deadlocked or hanging.

Starting Special Processes

When starting special processes, use the start and spawn functions defined in the proc_lib library module instead of Erlang's standard spawn and spawn_link BIFs. The proc_lib functions store the process's name, identity, parent, ancestors, and initial function call in the process dictionary. If the process terminates abnormally, SASL crash reports are generated and forwarded to the error logger. They contain all the process info stored at startup, together with the reason for termination. And like with other behaviors, there is functionality allowing for a synchronous startup with an init phase.

A common error is to attach a process that doesn't implement a behavior to the supervision tree. There are no warnings at compile time or runtime for this, as the only check made by the supervisor is to ensure the tuple {ok, Pid} is returned. No checks are made on Pid either. You will notice things going wrong only after a crash, restart, or upgrade. And because these processes do not follow standard behaviors, unless you've tested your restart strategy, hunting down the issue will resemble more of a wild goose chase than a routine and civilized troubleshooting session. For non-OTP-compliant processes, use supervisor bridges, covered in "Supervisor bridges" on page 194. This chapter shows you how to create an OTP-compliant process.

Basic template for starting a special process

The recommended approach to starting a special process is to use the proc_lib:start_link(Mod, Fun, Args) call instead of the spawn_link/3 BIF. Given a module, a function, and a list of arguments, it synchronously spawns a process and waits for this process to notify that it has correctly started through the proc_lib:init_ack(Value) call. Value is sent back to the parent process, becoming the return value of the start_link/3 call. Note how we are passing optional DbgOpts debug option parameters in our start_link call. We covered them in Chapter 5. For now, assume DbgOpts is an empty list. Note also how we are passing the Parent process ID to the init/3 function; we need it in our main loop. It is the result of the self() BIF in the start_link/2 call.

```
start_link(Name) ->
    start_link(Name, []).

start_link(Name, DbgOpts) ->
    proc_lib:start_link(?MODULE, init, [self(), Name, DbgOpts]).

stop(Name) -> Name ! stop.
```

```
init(Parent, Name, DbgOpts) ->
    register(Name, self()),
    process_flag(trap_exit, true),
    Debug = sys:debug_options(DbgOpts),
    proc_lib:init_ack({ok,self()}),
    free(Name, Parent, Debug).
```

When initializing the process state, we first register the mutex with the alias Name. We set the trap_exit flag so we can receive exit signals from processes in our linked set (we use links instead of monitors to notify or terminate the caller if the mutex fails). And finally, we initialize the debug trace flags using the sys:debug_options(DbgOpts) call. The return value of debug_options/1 is passed as loop data and stored in the process state. It will be needed whenever the special process has to generate a trace message or receives a system message requesting it to update its trace flags.

As illustrated in Figure 10-2, once the state is initialized, we call proc_lib:init_ack(Value) to inform the parent that the special process has started correctly. Value is sent back and becomes the return value of the proc_lib:start_link/3 call. Although it isn't mandatory, it is common practice to return {ok, self()} because supervisors expect their children's start functions to return {ok, Pid}. If any part of the initialization fails before calling init_ack/1, proc_lib:start_link/3 terminates with the same reason. Have a look at the last line of the init/3 function and differentiate between the function call free, which points to the FSM's first state, and Name, Parent, and Debug, which is the process state.

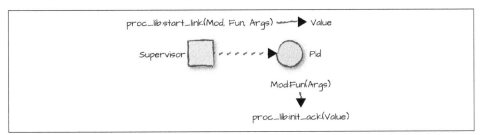

Figure 10-2. Starting special processes

The calls you can use to synchronously start a special process are:

```
proc_lib:start(Module, Function, Args)
proc_lib:start(Module, Function, Args, Time)
proc_lib:start(Module, Function, Args, Time, SpawnOpts) -> Ret
proc_lib:start_link(Module, Function, Args)
proc_lib:start_link(Module, Function, Args, Time)
proc_lib:start_link(Module, Function, Args, Time, SpawnOpts) -> Ret
```

```
proc_lib:init_ack(Ret)
proc_lib:init_ack(Parent, Ret) -> ok
```

The Ret return value of the start/3,4,5 and start_link/3,4,5 functions comes from the init_ack/1,2 call. As with other behaviors, SpawnOpts is a list containing all options the spawn BIFs accept, monitor excluded. If within Time milliseconds init_ack is not called, the start function returns {error, timeout}. If you use spawn or spawn_opt, do not forget to link the child to the parent process, either through the link/1 BIF or by passing the link option in SpawnOpts.

Asynchronously starting a special process

The following variations on the standard spawn and spawn_link functions are used in situations where you need asynchronous starts, such as the simultaneous launch of hundreds of new processes. They spawn the child process and immediately return its pid:

```
proc_lib:spawn(Fun)
proc_lib:spawn_link(Fun)
proc_lib:spawn_opt(Fun, SpawnOpts) -> Pid
proc_lib:spawn(Module, Function, Args)
proc_lib:spawn_link(Module, Function, Args)
proc_lib:spawn_opt(Node, Function, SpawnOpts) -> Pid
```

Other options to synchronously start special servers include spawning a process using a fun and spawning a process with the spawn options SpawnOpts.

Use asynchronous spawning with care, because the functions might cause multiple processes to run in parallel, resulting in race conditions that make your program nondeterministic. The same arguments we put forward in "Starting a Server" on page 80 when discussing generic servers are valid here. A startup error might be hard to reproduce if it is dependent on a certain number of concurrent events happening in a specific order, an issue that is becoming more evident with multicore architectures. To be able to deterministically reproduce a startup error, create your process synchronously.

Regardless of how you start your special processes, they always have to be linked to their parent (by default, the supervisor). This happens automatically if you use start_link, spawn_link, or pass the link option in SpawnOpts. However, no checks are made to ensure that the process is actually linked to the supervisor, so even here, omissions of this type can be difficult to troubleshoot and detect.

The Mutex States

As we saw, a mutex has two states, *free* and *busy*, that are implemented as tail-recursive functions. The synchronous `wait` and asynchronous `signal` events are sent as messages together with the client pid. The combination of state and event dictates the actions and state transitions. Note how when in the *free* state, we accept only the `wait` event, informing the client through the message `{self(), ok}` that it is allowed to enter the critical section. The mutex will then transition to the *busy* state, where the only event that will pattern match is `signal`, sent by `Pid`. You should have noticed that `Pid` was bound in the function head to the client holding the mutex. Upon receiving the `signal` event, the mutex transitions back to the *free* state:

```
free(Name, Parent, Debug) ->
    receive
        {wait,Pid} ->
            Pid ! {self(),ok},
            busy(Pid, Name, Parent, Debug);
        stop ->
            ok
    end.

busy(Pid, Name, Parent, Debug) ->
    receive
        {signal,Pid} ->
            free(Name, Parent, Debug)
    end.
```

Note how we accept the `stop` message only if the mutex is in the *free* state. If you stop the mutex in the *busy* state, you'll leave the client executing the code in its critical section in an unknown and possibly corrupt state, because the mutex might have been restarted and blocked by other client processes. By stopping the mutex only in the *free* state, you can guarantee a clean shutdown.

So far, so good. We are going back to Erlang 101 with the basics of FSMs. Let's now start expanding the states to handle the system messages required by special processes.

Handling Exits

If the parent of your special process terminates, your process must terminate as well. If your process does not trap exit signals, the runtime will take care of this for you because you should be linked to your parent. Non-`normal` exit signals propagate to all processes in the link set, terminating them with the same reason that terminated the original process. An exit with reason `normal` doesn't propagate, but in OTP, the supervisor guarantees that a parent will never terminate with that reason, so you don't have to worry about it.

Special processes that trap exits have to monitor their parents, as they might receive messages of the format:

```
{'EXIT', Parent, Reason}
```

where Parent is the parent pid and Reason is the reason for termination. If they do, they should clean up after themselves, possibly in their terminate or cleanup function, followed by a call to the exit(Reason) BIF.

In our previous example, the mutex is trapping exits, so we have to monitor parent termination. Let's expand the state functions, handling the EXIT messages from the parent process by calling terminate/2. We also call terminate/2 when receiving the stop message. If the parent terminates in state *busy*, we terminate the process holding the mutex before calling terminate/2:

```
free(Name, Parent, Debug) ->
    receive
        {wait,Pid} ->
            link(Pid),
            Pid ! {self(),ok},
            busy(Pid, Name, Parent, Debug);
        stop ->
            terminate(shutdown, Name);
        {'EXIT',Parent,Reason} ->
            terminate(Reason, Name)
    end.

busy(Pid, Name, Parent, Debug) ->
    receive
        {signal,Pid} ->
            free(Name, Parent, Debug);
        {'EXIT',Parent,Reason} ->
            exit(Pid, Reason),
            terminate(Reason, Name)
    end.

terminate(Reason, Name) ->
    unregister(Name),
    terminate(Reason).
terminate(Reason) ->
    receive
        {wait,Pid} ->
            exit(Pid, Reason),
            terminate(Reason)
    after 0 ->
            exit(Reason)
    end.
```

The first thing terminate/2 does is unregister the mutex, ensuring that any processes that try to send it requests terminate with reason badarg. The mutex goes on to terminate all processes in the queue by traversing its mailbox and extracting wait requests. When done, it knows no client processes are kept hanging and terminates itself with reason `Reason`.

System Messages

In addition to monitoring parents, special processes need to manage system messages of the format:

```
{system, From, Msg}
```

where `From` is the request originator and `Msg` is the system message itself. They could be messages originating from the supervisor used to suspend and resume processes during software upgrades or from a client manipulating or retrieving trace outputs using the `sys` module. What they are, however, is irrelevant to you as a developer, as you handle them as opaque data types and just pass them on.

No matter what the request is, these calls are handled behind the scenes in the `sys:handle_system_message(Msg, From, Parent, Mod, Dbg, Data)` function, as seen in Figure 10-3. The arguments to the `sys:handle_system_message/6` call, although numerous, are straightforward:

- `Msg` and `From` are provided by the system message.
- `Parent` is the parent pid, passed when spawning the special process.
- `Mod` is the name of the module implementing the special process.
- `Dbg` is the debug data, initially returned by the `sys:debug_options/1` call.
- `Data` is used to store the loop data of the process.

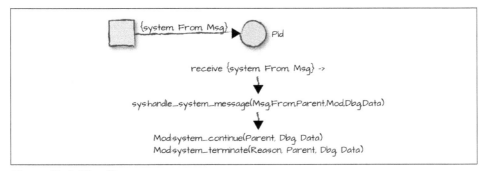

Figure 10-3. Handling system messages

The functions in the special process module that executes the call must be tail recursive as they never return. Not making them tail recursive will cause a memory leak every time a system message is received. Control is handed back to the special process in the `Mod` module by calling one of the following callback functions:

```
Mod:system_continue(Parent, Debug, Data)
Mod:system_terminate(Reason, Parent, Debug, Data)
```

If control is returned through the system_continue/3 callback function, your special process needs to return to its main loop. If system_terminate/4 is instead called, probably as a result of the parent ordering a shutdown, the special process needs to clean up after itself and terminate with reason Reason. We show you all of this in the mutex example, but first, let's understand how debug printouts work.

Trace and Log Events

When we covered the start functions earlier in this chapter, we discussed the SpawnOpts argument, which among other options allows us to pass debug flags to special processes. In our mutex:start_link/2 call, we can pass these debug options in the second argument, binding them to the DbgOpts variable. DbgOpts contains zero or more of the trace, log, statistics, and {log_to_file, FileName} flags described in Chapter 5. This list is passed by the special process to the sys:debug_options(DbgOpts) call, which initiates the debug routines. Unrecognized or unsupported debug options are ignored. The return value of the call, stored in the variable Debug in our example, is kept in the special process loop data passed to all system calls. Remember the example in "Tracing and Logging" on page 101 where we turned the trace and logs on or off during runtime, printing them in the shell and diverting them to a file? If everything is initialized correctly, you can generate similar trace logs with your special processes, turning the options on and off at runtime. All requests originating from calls such as sys:trace/3 or sys:log/2 are received and handled as system messages. What might change in between calls are the contents of the Debug list, returned as part of the system_continue/3 callback function.

Generating trace events is a straightforward operation done by calling this function:

```
sys:handle_debug(Debug, DbgFun, Extra, Event)
```

where:

- Debug is the initialized debug options.
- DbgFun is a fun of arity 3 that formats the trace event.
- Extra is data that can be used when formatting the event, usually the process name or the loop data.
- Event is the trace event you want to print out.

DbgFun is a fun that formats the event, sometimes by calling another function to do so. The arguments passed to it by the sys module include the I/O device you are writing to, which can be either the standard_io or standard_error atom or the pid returned by the `file:open` call. `Extra` and `Event` come from the arguments to the `handle_debug/4` call:

```
fun(Dev, Extra, Event) ->
    io:format(Dev, "mutex ~w: ~w~n", [Extra,Event])
end
```

You can also add your own trace functions at runtime using the `sys:install/2` call, using pattern matching in the fun head to examine events and decide on the flow of execution. With system messages and trace outputs in place, let's see how it all fits together by adding them to our mutex example.

Putting It Together

For your convenience, we've put the whole mutex example in one place. Note how we've expanded the *free* and *busy* states to include trace messages and system messages. Let's focus on this functionality, starting with trace messages.

When we receive the `wait` and `signal` events, we call `sys:handle_debug(Debug, fun debug/3, Name, Event)`, where `Event` is either `{wait, Pid}` or `{signal, Pid}`. This call hands control over to the `sys` module, which eventually calls the debug fun. In our case, it is the local function `debug/3`. Have a look at it, paying special attention as to how the I/O device, extra arguments, and events passed to it are used. `handle_debug/4` returns `NewDebug`, which is passed as an argument to the next state. When reviewing the example, remember the mutex process does not implement the services it protects. It just implements the semaphore that gives other processes access to these services. The complete mutex example looks like this:

```
-module(mutex).

-export([start_link/1, start_link/2, init/3, stop/1]).
-export([wait/1, signal/1]).
-export([system_continue/3, system_terminate/4]).

wait(Name) ->
    Name ! {wait,self()},
    Mutex = whereis(Name),
    receive
        {Mutex,ok} -> ok
    end.

signal(Name) ->
    Name ! {signal,self()},
    ok.

start_link(Name) ->
    start_link(Name, []).

start_link(Name, DbgOpts) ->
```

```
        proc_lib:start_link(?MODULE, init, [self(), Name, DbgOpts]).

stop(Name) -> Name ! stop.

init(Parent, Name, DbgOpts) ->
    register(Name, self()),
    process_flag(trap_exit, true),
    Debug = sys:debug_options(DbgOpts),
    proc_lib:init_ack({ok,self()}),
    NewDebug = sys:handle_debug(Debug, fun debug/3, Name, init),
    free(Name, Parent, NewDebug).

free(Name, Parent, Debug) ->
    receive
        {wait,Pid} ->  %% The user requests.
            NewDebug = sys:handle_debug(Debug, fun debug/3, Name, {wait,Pid}),
            Pid ! {self(),ok},
            busy(Pid, Name, Parent, NewDebug);
        {system,From,Msg} ->    %% The system messages.
            sys:handle_system_msg(Msg, From, Parent,
                                  ?MODULE, Debug, {free, Name});
        stop ->
            terminate(stopped, Name, Debug);
        {'EXIT',Parent,Reason} ->
            terminate(Reason, Name, Debug)
    end.

busy(Pid, Name, Parent, Debug) ->
    receive
        {signal,Pid} ->
            NewDebug = sys:handle_debug(Debug, fun debug/3, Name, {signal,Pid}),
            free(Name, Parent, NewDebug);
        {system,From,Msg} ->    %% The system messages.
            sys:handle_system_msg(Msg, From, Parent,
                                  ?MODULE, Debug, {busy,Name,Pid});
        {'EXIT',Parent,Reason} ->
            exit(Pid, Reason),
            terminate(Reason, Name, Debug)
    end.

debug(Dev, Event, Name) ->
    io:format(Dev, "mutex ~w: ~w~n", [Name,Event]).

system_continue(Parent, Debug, {busy,Name,Pid}) ->
    busy(Pid, Name, Parent, Debug);
system_continue(Parent, Debug, {free,Name}) ->
    free(Name, Parent, Debug).

system_terminate(Reason, _Parent, Debug, {busy,Name,Pid}) ->
    exit(Pid, Reason),
    terminate(Reason, Name, Debug);
system_terminate(Reason, _Parent, Debug, {free,Name}) ->
```

```
        terminate(Reason, Name, Debug).

    terminate(Reason, Name, Debug) ->
        unregister(Name),
        sys:handle_debug(Debug, fun debug/3, Name, {terminate, Reason}),
        terminate(Reason).
    terminate(Reason) ->
        receive
            {wait,Pid} ->
                exit(Pid, Reason),
                terminate(Reason)
        after 0 ->
                exit(Reason)
        end.
```

When the free and busy functions receive {system, From, Msg}, they tail recursively invoke sys:handle_system_msg(Msg, From, Parent, ?MODULE, Debug, {State, LoopData}), handing control over to the sys module. The system message is handled behing the scenes, after which the function returns by calling either system_continue/3 or system_terminate/4 in the mutex module. If the function is not tail recursive, there will be, as we mentioned earlier, a memory leak for every system message received.

In our example, if system_continue is called, we just return to the state we were in, determined by the Name loop data in state *free* and the {Name, Pid} loop data in *busy*, where we wait for the next event or system call. In the case of system_terminate, if in state *busy*, we terminate the process that held the mutex (potentially leaving the system in an inconsistent state), followed by calling terminate/2. If in state *free*, we just call terminate/2. In both cases, we employ pattern matching on the final argument to ensure we take the correct actions for continuation and termination.

System messages and debug options are straightforward to handle in your own special processes. All you need to do is reuse the code from this example, ensuring that when you get handed back the control, you go back into your loop or state with a tail-recursive function. Before looking at the trial run of the mutex, read through the code one more time and make sure you understand the what, why, and hows of special processes.

In our trial run, we create a child specification for our special process, starting it as a dynamic child in a supervisor mutex_sup. We've not included the supervisor code in this example, as it is boilerplate code. All init/1 does is return the supervisor specification with a restart tuple with a one_for_one strategy allowing a maximum of five restarts per hour and an empty child list. You can find the source code in the book's GitHub repository.

Note how in the mutex:start_link/2 arguments of the child specification, we turn on the trace flag. This leads to the trace printout when the mutex is started as a result of shell command 3. We turn on other debug options using the sys module in shell commands 4 and 5:

```
1> ChildSpec = {mutex, {mutex, start_link, [printer, [trace]]},
                    transient, 5000, worker, [mutex]}.
{mutex,{mutex,start_link,[printer,[trace]]},
        transient,5000,worker,
        [mutex]}
2> mutex_sup:start_link().
{ok,<0.35.0>}
3> supervisor:start_child(mutex_sup, ChildSpec).
mutex printer: init
{ok,<0.37.0>}
4> sys:log(printer, {true,10}).
ok
5> sys:statistics(printer, true).
ok
6> mutex:wait(printer), mutex:signal(printer).
mutex printer: {wait,<0.32.0>}
mutex printer: {signal,<0.32.0>}
ok
7> sys:log(printer, get).
{ok,[{{wait,<0.32.0>},printer,#Fun<mutex.1.94496536>},
     {{signal,<0.32.0>},printer,#Fun<mutex.2.94496536>}]}
8> sys:log(printer, print).
mutex printer: {wait,<0.32.0>}
mutex printer: {signal,<0.32.0>}
ok
9> sys:get_status(printer).
{status,<0.37.0>,
        {module,mutex},
        [[{'$ancestors',[mutex_sup,<0.32.0>]},
          {'$initial_call',{mutex,init,3}}],
         running,<0.35.0>,
         [{statistics,{{{2014,1,6},{8,50,36}},{reductions,66},0,0}},
          {log,{10,
                [{{signal,<0.32.0>},printer,#Fun<mutex.2.94496536>},
                 {{wait,<0.32.0>},printer,#Fun<mutex.1.94496536>}]}},
          {trace,true}],
         {free,printer}]}
10> exit(whereis(printer), kill).
mutex printer: init
true
11> exit(whereis(mutex_sup), shutdown).
mutex printer: {terminate,shutdown}
** exception exit: shutdown
```

In shell command 6, we wait for the mutex and then signal for it to be released, and each request generates a trace event. In shell commands 7, 8, and 9, we retrieve some of the trace and status information through the sys module, followed by some tests with termination and restarts in shell commands 10 and 11.

Do some tests of your own, experimenting with multiple clients, the SASL report browser, and other sys commands such as suspending and restarting the modules.

Dynamic Modules and Hibernating

You might recall from Chapter 8 that we need to provide the list of modules implementing the behavior in the child specification. They are used to determine which processes to suspend during software upgrades. There are occasions, as is the case with event managers and handlers, where the modules are not known at compile time. In the supervisor child specification module list, these behaviors were tagged with the atom dynamic. Special processes can also have dynamic modules.

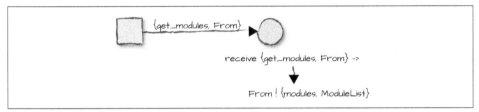

Figure 10-4. Retrieving dynamic modules

If your special process modules are tagged as dynamic in the child specification, then as Figure 10-4 illustrates, you need to handle the system message {get_modules, From}. From is the pid of the supervisor, used to return the list of modules in the From ! {modules, ModuleList} expression.

If you need to hibernate your special processes, instead of the BIF, use:

```
proc_lib:hibernate(Mod, Fun, Args)
```

It hibernates the process just like the BIF and the standard OTP behavior return values, but as an added feature, it also ensures that logging and debugging still function when the process wakes up.

Your Own Behaviors

Now that you understand special processes, let's take the concept further by splitting the code into generic and specific parts to implement our own behaviors. You will want to implement your own behaviors when several processes follow a pattern that cannot be expressed using existing OTP behaviors. Generic servers, FSMs, and event managers cater to most programmers' needs, so don't get caught up in the excitement and start writing new behaviors in every project. Chances are you are overengineering a solution that could easily be abstracted in a simple library module.

Having said that, there will be times when there are good reasons to implement your own behaviors. Patterns can be abstracted in generic and specific modules, when the generic part is substantial enough to make it worthwhile. If you go down this route, chances are good that your behavior (or library) can be built on top of generic servers. If not, or if you prefer to avoid generic servers because of the performance overhead, make sure your behavior follows the design rules required by special processes using the `sys` and `proc_lib` modules.

> If you are into software archeology and have an interest in the evolution of software, try to get your hands on the source code of the early versions of Erlang/OTP. Skim through the old behavior code and you will find that most of the behaviors were built on top of generic servers. Current OTP behaviors, generic servers included, are built using a module called gen. It is a wrapper on top of the `sys` and `proc_lib` modules, handling a lot of the tricky and borderline cases associated with concurrent and distributed programming we've discussed in previous chapters. Look for it in the source directory of your *stdlib* application and look through the code. If you are implementing your own behaviors and do not want to get caught out, you might want to use gen instead of rolling your own. Be warned, however, as it is undocumented, and it might change in between releases with little or no notice.

Rules for Creating Behaviors

The steps to creating your own behavior are straightforward, requiring you to break up your code into generic and specific modules and define the callback functions and their return values. When doing so, you need to follow these simple rules:

- The name of the generic module has to be the same as the behavior name.
- You need to list the callback functions in the behavior module.
- In your callback module, include the `-behavior(BehaviorName).` directive.

Once you've compiled your generic behavior code, compiling your callback modules with the behavior directives will result in warnings should you omit any callbacks.

An Example Handling TCP Streams

Let's have a look at some parts of an example in which we implement our own behavior, focusing on the code specific to our behavior's implementation. We've omitted functions not relevant to the example, marking them with ... in the code. If you want to look at the whole module, you can find it in the code repository (*https://github.com/francescoc/scalabilitywitherlangotp*) with the book's examples. There is no need, however, to view the full example if you are interested only in understanding the specifics of implementing your own behavior.

Our example is a wrapper that encapsulates activities associated with TCP streams, including connections, configuration, and error handling, exposing only the stream of data being received. Upon receiving a socket accept request, the behavior spawns a new process that is kept alive for as long as the socket is open. The behavior receives the packets, forwarding them to the callback module as they arrive. The socket can be closed by the callback module through a return value of a callback function, or indirectly when the TCP client closes its side of the connection.

The callback functions in the callback module consist of an initialization function called once when the socket is opened, a data handling call invoked for every packet received, and a termination function called when the socket is closed:

```
-module(tcp_print).
-export([init_request/0, get_request/2, stop_request/2]).
-behavior(tcp_wrapper).


init_request() ->
    io:format("Receiving Data~n."),
    {ok,[]}.
get_request(Data, Buffer)->
    io:format("."),
    {ok, [Data|Buffer]}.
stop_request(_Reason, Buffer) ->
    io:format("~n"),
    io:format(lists:reverse(Buffer)),
    io:format("~n").
```

The callback function init_request/0 returns {ok, LoopData}. The get_request/2 function receives the TCP packet bound to the variable Data and the LoopData, returning either {ok, NewLoopData} or {stop, Reason, NewLoopData}. In this example, LoopData is a buffer of received TCP packets bound to the variable Buffer. Upon closing the socket, stop_request/2 is given the Reason for termination and the LoopData, and has to return the atom ok.

Note how we have included the -behavior(tcp_wrapper). directive in the code. This points to the tcp_wrapper module, where the behavior is implemented.

When starting the tcp_wrapper behavior, we pass the callback module Mod and the Port number. We spawn a process that initializes the behavior state, opens a listener socket, and eventually makes its way to the accept/4 function. For every concurrent stream, we accept a connection on the listener socket, spawn a new process that starts executing in the init_request/2 function, and handle the stream through the callback module. In the accept call, we specify a timeout to keep from blocking infinitely so we can yield control back to the main loop (not shown in the example) every second, ensuring we can handle system messages and the EXIT signal from the parent process. We also export the cast/3 call, which allows us to create a connection and send a request asynchronously to the server:[2]

```
-module(tcp_wrapper).
-export([start_link/2, cast/3]).
-export([init/3, system_continue/3, system_terminate/4, init_request/2]).

-callback init_request() -> {'ok', Reply :: term()}.
-callback get_request(Data :: term(),
                      LoopData :: term()) ->
    {'ok', Reply :: term()} |
    {'stop', Reason :: atom(), LoopData :: term()}.
-callback stop_request(Reason :: term(), LoopData :: term()) -> term().

start_link(Mod, Port) ->
    proc_lib:start_link(?MODULE, init, [Mod, Port, self()]).

cast(Host, Port, Data) ->
    {ok, Socket} = gen_tcp:connect(Host, Port, [binary, {active, false},
                                                {reuseaddr, true}]),
    send(Socket, Data),
    ok = gen_tcp:close(Socket).

send(Socket, <<Chunk:1/binary,Rest/binary>>) ->
    gen_tcp:send(Socket, [Chunk]),
    send(Socket, Rest);
send(Socket, <<Rest/binary>>) ->
    gen_tcp:send(Socket, Rest).

init(Mod, Port, Parent) ->
    {ok, Listener} = gen_tcp:listen(Port, [{active, false}]),
    proc_lib:init_ack({ok, self()}),
    loop(Mod, Listener, Parent, sys:debug_options([])).

loop(Mod, Listener, Parent, Debug) ->
    receive
        {system,From,Msg} ->
            sys:handle_system_msg(Msg, From, Parent,
                                  ?MODULE, Debug, {Listener, Mod});
        {'EXIT', Parent, Reason} ->
            terminate(Reason, Listener, Debug);
        {'EXIT', Child, _Reason} ->
            NewDebug = sys:handle_debug(Debug, fun debug/3,
                                        stop_request, Child),
            loop(Mod, Listener, Parent, NewDebug)
    after 0 ->
            accept(Mod, Listener, Parent, Debug)
```

---

2 An alternative to this timeout approach is to use the `prim_inet:async_accept/2` function, which sends the calling process a message when a new connection is accepted, but that function is intended to be private to Erlang/OTP and so is not part of its documented and supported set of API functions.

```erlang
    end.

accept(Mod, Listener, Parent, Debug) ->
    case gen_tcp:accept(Listener, 1000) of
        {ok, Socket} ->
            Pid = proc_lib:spawn_link(?MODULE, init_request, [Mod, Socket]),
            gen_tcp:controlling_process(Socket, Pid),
            NewDebug = sys:handle_debug(Debug, fun debug/3, init_request, Pid),
            loop(Mod, Listener, Parent, NewDebug);
        {error, timeout} ->
            loop(Mod, Listener, Parent, Debug);
        {error, Reason} ->
            NewDebug = sys:handle_debug(Debug, fun debug/3, error, Reason),
            terminate(Reason, Listener, NewDebug)
    end.

system_continue(Parent, Debug, {Listener, Mod}) ->
    loop(Mod, Listener, Parent, Debug).

system_terminate(Reason, _Parent, Debug, {Listener, _Mod}) ->
    terminate(Reason, Listener, Debug).

terminate(Reason, Listener, Debug) ->
    sys:handle_debug(Debug, fun debug/3, terminating, Reason),
    gen_tcp:close(Listener),
    exit(Reason).

debug(Dev, Event, Data) ->
    io:format(Dev, "Listener ~w:~w~n", [Event,Data]).

init_request(Mod, Socket) ->
    {ok, LoopData} = Mod:init_request(),
    get_request(Mod, Socket, LoopData).

get_request(Mod, Socket, LoopData) ->
    case gen_tcp:recv(Socket, 0) of
        {ok, Data} ->
            case Mod:get_request(Data, LoopData) of
                {ok, NewLoopData} ->
                    get_request(Mod, Socket, NewLoopData);
                {stop, Reason, NewLoopData} ->
                    gen_tcp:close(Socket),
                    stop_request(Mod, Reason, NewLoopData)
            end;
        {error, Reason} ->
            stop_request(Mod, Reason, LoopData)
    end.

stop_request(Mod, Reason, LoopData) ->
    Mod:stop_request(Reason, LoopData).
```

The generic code handling the TCP stream is straightforward. It is a process loop that initializes the stream state, receives the packets, and terminates when the callback module returns a stop tuple, or when the TCP client decides to close its side of the connection. For initialization, receiving packets, and termination, appropriate callback functions in the Mod callback module are called.

One item that stands out in our behavior implementation—probably the most important one alongside the calling of the callback functions—is the callback specification. It lists the callback functions that need to be exported in the callback module, following the directives set out in the Erlang type and function specifications. The callback specifications are mapped to the behavior_info(callbacks) function, which returns a list of the form {Function, Arity}. You can bypass the callback specifications altogether, directly implementing and exporting the behavior_info/1 call in your generic behavior module (which is how behaviors were required to be implemented with older releases of Erlang/OTP prior to R15B). Compare the callback specifications to the callback functions in the tcp_print module. Do they match?

```
-module(tcp_wrapper).
...
-export([behavior_info/1]).

behavior_info(callbacks) ->
    [{init_request, 0}, {get_request, 2}, {stop_request, 2}].
...
```

The advantages of using callback specifications over the behavior_info/1 function is that the *dialyzer* tool will find discrepancies between your callback modules and the specs, a welcome addition to the undefined callback function compiler warnings. The *dialyzer* enables behavior callback warnings by default. Remember to compile your generic behavior module and make it available in the code search path before compiling your callback module, or else you will get an undefined behavior warning.

Summing Up

In this chapter, we've introduced you to the ins and outs of implementing special processes, making them OTP compliant and including them as part of OTP supervision trees. We've also taken special processes a step further, allowing you to split the code into generic and specific modules and turning them into behaviors complete with callback modules, behavior directives, and associated compiler warnings.

When starting and hibernating special processes, instead of the standard BIFs, you must use the functions in the proc_lib module, listed in Table 10-1.

Table 10-1. Starting special process with the proc_lib module

Function call	Callback function or action
proc_lib:spawn_link/1,2,3,4	None
proc_lib:spawn_opt/2,3,4,5	None
proc_lib:start/3,4,5	proc_lib:init_ack(Parent, Reply), proc_lib:init_ack(Reply)
proc_lib:start_link/3,4,5	proc_lib:init_ack(Parent, Reply), proc_lib:init_ack(Reply)
proc_lib:hibernate/3	None

The system message calls in Table 10-2 and their respective callbacks need to be managed by your process, either by responding directly to the process sending the request or by using the sys module.

Table 10-2. System requests and messages

Message	Callback function or action
{system, From, Request}	Mod:system_continue(Parent, Debug, LoopData), Mod:system_terminate(Reason, Parent, Debug, LoopData)
{'EXIT', Parent, Reason}	exit(Reason)
{get_modules, From}	From ! {modules, ModuleList}

You can read more about the sys and proc_lib modules in their respective manual pages. There is an example covering special processes and user-defined behaviors in the "sys and proc_lib" section of the OTP Design Principles User's Guide. And finally, you can find more information on type and function specifications used in defining your own callback definitions in the Erlang Reference Manual and User's Guide.

If you feel like coding, we suggest you download the mutex example from the book's code repository and implement some of the edge cases that can occur in concurrent applications. In your client function, when requesting the mutex, add references guaranteeing the validity of your reply together with optional timeouts. You will also want to monitor the mutex in case it terminates abnormally while you are executing in the critical section.

What's Next?

Special processes and user-defined behaviors are the foundations used to build existing and new behaviors, allowing us to glue them together in a supervision tree and package them in an application. In the next chapter, on release handling and system principles, we group applications in a release and see how we can configure, start, and stop an Erlang node as a whole.

## CHAPTER 11

System Principles and Release Handling

Now that we know how to implement and use existing OTP behaviors, organize them in supervision trees with special processes, and package them in applications, the time has come to group these applications together into an Erlang node that can be started up as one unit. In many programming languages, packaging is a problem handled by the operating system. In Erlang, this is handled in OTP by creating a `release`, where a system consists of one or more possibly different releases. Each node runs a release, either on a single host or in a distributed environment. Standard releases allow your system to follow a generic structure that not only is target independent, but can be managed and upgraded with tools independent of the underlying operating system. So, while Erlang's release process might appear complicated, it is as easy to create a release (if not easier) as it would be to create a non-Erlang package. If we think of the packaging hierarchy in Erlang, we start with a *function*, followed by a *module* bundled in an *application*. An Erlang node consists of a set of loosely coupled applications, grouped together in a release.

You might not have realized it, but when you installed Erlang on your computer, you installed the standard release. What differs between a standard release and the ones you create yourself are the applications that are loaded and started together, along with their configuration parameters. The underlying Erlang runtime system does not differentiate between user-defined applications and applications that come as part as the Erlang/OTP distribution, but rather treats them in the same manner. Releases have the same directory structure, their own copy of the virtual machine, and manage release and configuration files in a similar way. Because of this, it should not come as a surprise that Erlang releases you start with the `erl` command are created with the same underlying tools, structure, and principles you use when defining your own releases.

In this chapter, we walk you through the steps needed to build a target release, explaining how it all hangs together. We cover the different release types, from simple and interactive target systems, which give you the flexibility of loading modules and easily starting applications at runtime, to embedded target systems, where applications are loaded and started at startup under strict version control. To create target systems, we cover systools, an Erlang library used when integrating the creation of releases in an existing tool chain or build process, and the use of *rebar3* for greenfield projects or when dependency management becomes complicated.

System Principles

An Erlang release is defined as a standalone node consisting of:

- A set of OTP applications written or reused as part of the project, typically containing the system's business logic. The applications can be proprietary, open source, or a combination thereof.

- The OTP applications from the standard distribution that the aforementioned applications depend on.

- A set of configuration and boot files, together with a start script.

- The Erlang runtime system, including a copy of the virtual machine.

There are tools that help you create and package a standalone node, but before introducing them, we cover all the components in detail and step you through a build manually. This will help you better understand how a release is structured and how it works, along with what options you have available.

The simplest way to start an Erlang node is using the erl command. You can start your program from the Erlang shell itself by typing in the module and function name or by passing the -s flag to erl:

```
$ erl -s module function arg1 arg2 ...
```

The *function* and arguments are optional. If only the module is listed, the command will invoke *module*:start(). If the module and function are listed, the command will invoke *module*:*function*(). We refer to this method of starting your node as a *basic target system*, where you create a Unix shell script that initializes your state and calls the erl -s command. This approach should be used only when coding, for basic proofs of concepts, or for quick hacks. Using basic target systems in production is not recommended, as you lose a lot of the benefits that come with OTP. There are better alternatives.

Do not ship basic target systems unless they are proofs of concepts or quick hacks. If your program is started by a script that invokes `erl -s myprojectsup -noshell`, you lose all of the benefits gained by OTP applications and their startup, supervision, and upgrade procedures. You have everything to gain from using boot files and shipping your systems as embedded target systems.

The next way of starting your node is as a *simple target system*. It makes use of a boot script and tools shipped with the *sasl* application, facilitating controlled software upgrades at runtime. To understand how simple target systems work, let's start by examining your Erlang installation and investigating its directory structure and all the files and scripts associated with it. You need to create some of these files yourself when generating the release, using tools such as *systools*, *reltool*, or *relx*, while you can just copy other files from a repository or the installation in your target environment.

Start by finding the top-level directory, often called the *Erlang root directory*. It is the location where you (or the scripts you used) installed Erlang. If you don't know that location, start an Erlang node and call `code:root_dir().`:

```
$ erl
Erlang/OTP 18 [erts-7.2] [smp:8:8] [async-threads:10] [kernel-poll:false]

Eshell V7.2  (abort with ^G)
1> code:root_dir().
"/usr/local/lib/erlang"
2> q().
ok
$ cd /usr/local/lib/erlang
$ ls
Install    erts-6.4    erts-7.1    misc
bin        erts-6.3    erts-7.2    releases
erts-6.2   erts-7.0    lib         usr
```

The contents of the directory are the output of creating a release. They vary depending on how (and from where) you installed Erlang, the number of upgrades you've done throughout the years, and the customizations made by those who built the release. There is, however, a set of basic files and directories that are required and will always be there, appearing with your first installation.

Release Directory Structure

In this section we explore the files needed for a release. Your own releases will have the same directories and file structures as the Erlang root, so we spend some time looking at that. The only differences between the root and your own releases are the applications that are loaded and started, their versions, and the version of the runtime system. This becomes evident in the next few sections, where we create our own base station controller release that follows these very principles.

Four directories are mandatory in every OTP release, as shown in Figure 11-1. We have already looked at *lib*, which contains all of the applications with their version numbers appended to their directory names. You rummaged through it in "The Application Structure" on page 206 when reading about applications and their directory structures. After upgrades, you could end up with multiple versions of a single application, differentiated by a version number in the application directory name. With multiple instances, the code search path defined when creating the release usually points to the *ebin* directory of the latest version of the application.

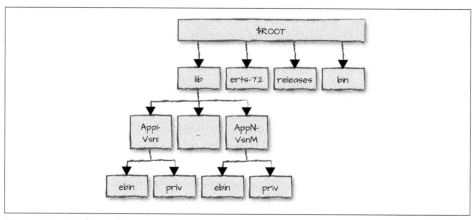

Figure 11-1. Release directory structure

The *erts* directory contains binaries for the Erlang runtime system. Even here, if you have at some point upgraded your installation, you might find multiple instances of the directory, distinguished by the *erts* version number appended to the directory name. In *erts* the most interesting subdirectory is *bin*. It contains executables and shell scripts related not only to the virtual machine, but also to all the tools that can be invoked from the shell. Look around in the directory and you will find the following:

erl

A script or program (depending on the target environment) that starts the runtime system and provides an interactive shell.

erlexec

The binary executable called by the *erl* script.

erlc

A common way to run Erlang-specific compilers. The compiler chosen depends on the extension of the file you are trying to compile.

epmd

The Erlang port mapper daemon. It acts as a name server in distributed Erlang environments, mapping Erlang nodes to IP addresses and port numbers.

escript

Allows you to execute short Erlang programs as if they were scripts, without having to compile them.

start

Starts an embedded Erlang target system in Unix environments. This kind of release runs as a daemon job without a shell window. We look at embedded target systems in "Creating a Release Package" on page 283.

run_erl

The binary called by *start* to start Unix-based embedded systems, where I/O is streamed to pipes.

to_erl

Connects to the Erlang I/O streams with nodes started by *run_erl* in an embedded target system.

werl

Starts the runtime system in Windows environments, in a separate window from the console.

start_erl

Part of the chain of commands to start embedded target systems, setting the boot and config files in Unix systems. In Windows environments, this is similar to the Unix *start* command previously described.

erlsrv

Similar to *run_erl* but for Windows environments, allowing Erlang to be started without the need for the user to log in.

heart

Monitors the heartbeat of the Erlang runtime system and calls a script if the heartbeat is not acknowledged.

dialyzer

A static analysis tool for beam files and Erlang source code. It finds, among other things, type discrepancies and dead or unreachable code. The *dialyzer* should be part of everyone's build process.

typer

Infers variable types in Erlang programs based on how the variables are used. It adds type specifications derived from your source code and provides input data to the *dialyzer*.

Programmers use several of the executables listed in the *bin* directory when creating and starting an Erlang release. The ones we list are the most important and most relevant to what we cover in more detail later in this chapter. But the list is nowhere near complete, as the full contents depend on the Erlang/OTP version and operating system you are running.

These contents of the *erts-version/bin* directory are similar to those of *bin* in the Erlang root directory. The version-specific directory contains links and copies to the scripts and executables of the *bin* directory of the Erlang runtime version you start by default. This directory is needed because you might have several versions of a release installed and running at any one time. Although typing erl would point to the script in the *bin* directory, environment variables would redirect it to the *erts-version/bin* version you are using. Let's have a look at the contents of the *erl* script. With release 18.2 on a Mac running OS X Yosemite, it looks like this:

```
#!/bin/sh
#
# %CopyrightBegin%
#
# Copyright Ericsson AB 1996-2012. All Rights Reserved.
#
# Licensed under the Apache License, Version 2.0 (the "License");
# you may not use this file except in compliance with the License.
# You may obtain a copy of the License at
#
#     http://www.apache.org/licenses/LICENSE-2.0
#
# Unless required by applicable law or agreed to in writing, software
# distributed under the License is distributed on an "AS IS" BASIS,
# WITHOUT WARRANTIES OR CONDITIONS OF ANY KIND, either express or implied.
# See the License for the specific language governing permissions and
# limitations under the License.
#
# %CopyrightEnd%
#
ROOTDIR="/usr/local/lib/erlang"
BINDIR=$ROOTDIR/erts-7.2/bin
EMU=beam
PROGNAME=`echo $0 | sed 's/.*\///'`
export EMU
export ROOTDIR
export BINDIR
export PROGNAME
exec "$BINDIR/erlexec" ${1+"$@"}
```

ROOTDIR and BINDIR, along with other environment variables, are set when installing or upgrading Erlang. Note how BINDIR points to the *$ROOTDIR/erts-7.2/bin* directory we inspected at the beginning of this section and ends up executing *erlexec*. Look in the *erts-7.2/bin* directory for *erl.src* and you will find the source file used to create the *erl* script. Similar source files exist for *start_erl* and *start*. We cover *.src* files in "Creating a Release" on page 273.

If you enter the *releases* directory, also located in the Erlang root directory, you will find a subdirectory for every release you've installed on your machine. There should be a one-to-one mapping to the *erts* directories, because most new releases come with a new version of the runtime system. Inspect the contents of any of the *start_erl.data* files and you will see two numbers, the first referring to the emulator version used in the current installation of Erlang and the second referring to the directory of the OTP release being used:

```
$ cd releases
$ ls
17 18 RELEASES RELEASES.src start_erl.data
$ cat start_erl.data
7.2 18
$ ls 18
OTP_VERSION                           start.boot              start_sasl.boot
installed_application_versions  start.script            start_sasl.rel
no_dot_erlang.boot                   start_all_example.rel  start_sasl.script
no_dot_erlang.rel                    start_clean.boot
no_dot_erlang.script                 start_clean.rel
```

If you list the contents of the directory specified in *start_erl.data*—we've picked version 18 in our example—you will find files with *.rel*, *.script*, and *.boot* extensions. Files with the *.rel* suffix list the versions of the applications and runtime system for a particular release. The *.boot* file is a binary representation of the *.script* file, which contains commands to load and start applications when the system is first started. Enter the subdirectory of the latest release and look at any of the *.rel* and *.script* files to get a feel for what they might do. We create our own scripts in an upcoming section.

You can override the default location of the *releases* directory by setting the *sasl* application configuration variable `releases_dir` or the OS environment variable `RELDIR`. The Erlang runtime system must have write permissions to this directory for upgrades to work, as it updates the *RELEASES* file in conjunction with upgrades.

Release Resource Files

All your project's OTP applications, including those that come as part of the standard distribution, and proprietary as well as open source applications, are bundled up in a release specification containing their versions. This specification also includes the system release version and name, together with the version of the runtime system. The build system uses this information to do sanity checks, create the boot files, and create the target directory structure.

The minimal (and default) release consists of the *kernel* and *stdlib* applications, but most releases also include and start *sasl* because it contains all of the tools required for a software upgrade. You might not think about upgrades when creating your first release, but you'll probably need to do so at a later date. You are given the option of including *sasl* by default when installing Erlang from source, but if you are using third-party binaries, this choice will have already been made for you.

Let's look at the rel files more closely. If, from the Erlang root directory, you enter into the *releases* directory and from there move into any of the subdirectories, you will find at least one file with the *.rel* suffix. As an example, we've picked the *releases/18/start_sasl.rel* file, stripping out the comments:

```
{release, {"Erlang/OTP","18"}, {erts, "7.2"},
 [{kernel,"4.1.1"},
  {stdlib,"2.7"},
  {sasl, "2.6.1"}]}.
```

As we can see, this release will run emulator version 7.2, starting *kernel* version 4.1.1, *stdlib* version 2.7, and *sasl* version 2.6.1. The name of the release is "Erlang/OTP" and its version is "18." Other examples and versions of the rel files and corresponding boot and script files in the directory specify how other systems are grouped together.

What Applications Do You Include in a Standard Release?

In our base station release file, we kept it simple and included only the *bsc* application. Production systems often include monitoring, logging, and debugging applications that will not affect the code of your base applications, but provide insight and visibility when you are troubleshooting a live system. We have already seen a basic form of logging and alarming in the *sasl* application. The *os_mon* application provides the ability to inspect the underlying operating system, including disk and memory supervision along with CPU load and utilization.

The *runtime_tools* application is often overlooked and omitted. It includes the *dbg* debugger and the `system_information` module, as well as other tools needed for real-time profiling of the virtual machine. You never know when these tools and the visibility they bring with them will come in handy (especially *dbg*), so we recommend you include them.

Let's create a release file named *basestation.rel* to use in our base station controller example. The release name is "basestation" and we've given it version "1.0." Along with the standard included applications, we'll include version 1.0 of *bsc*. The file is fairly straightforward and differs very little from the previous example:

```
{release,
 {"basestation","1.0"},
 {erts, "7.2"},
 [{kernel, "4.1.1"},
  {stdlib, "2.7"},
```

```
  {sasl, "2.6.1"},
  {bsc, "1.0"}]}.
```

The resource file is by convention named *ReleaseName.rel*. Following this convention is not mandatory, but doing so makes life easier for those supporting and maintaining your code. The resource file contains a tuple with four elements: the release atom, a tuple of the format {ReleaseName, RelVersion}, a tuple of the format {erts, ErtsVersion}, and a list of tuples containing information about the applications and their versions. The application tuples we've seen so far were of the format {Application, AppVersion}, but as the following shows, other formats exist as well:

```
{release,
 {ReleaseName, RelVersion},
 {erts, ErtsVersion},
 [{Application, AppVersion},
  {Application, AppVersion, Type},
  {Application, AppVersion, IncludedAppList},
  {Application, AppVersion, Type, IncludedAppList}]
}.
```

All of the version fields for the various elements in the tuple are strings. In your application tuple, you can also add an application Type. You can include the types we covered in "Application Types and Termination Strategies" on page 221, as well as load and none:

load
: Loads the application but does not start it.

none
: Loads the modules in the application, but not the application itself.

permanent
: Shuts down the node when the top-level supervisor terminates. When the application terminates, all other applications are cleanly taken down with it. This is the default chosen if no restart type is specified.

transient
: Shuts down the node when the top-level supervisor terminates with a non-normal reason. This is useful only for library applications that do not start their own supervision trees, because top-level supervisors will always terminate with the non-normal reason shutdown, yielding the same outcome as a permanent application.

temporary
: Applications that terminate, normally or abnormally, are reported in the SASL logs, but do not affect other applications in the release.

Finally, you can specify a list of included applications in `IncludedAppList`. The list must be a subset of the applications specified in the application app file.

Release and Application Versions

An OTP version is a set of specific application versions listed in the rel file that have been tested together with an emulator version. But this does not mean you cannot swap and change application and emulator versions; all it says is that they have not been tested together. As the test cases for OTP releases are part of its source repository, there is nothing stopping you from running them yourself with your proprietary applications as part of your development process. An application version is a set of module versions and resources, listed in the app file or contained in the *priv* directory.

Starting with OTP 17, application and OTP versions share the same numbering scheme. They consist of three integers of the format *<Major>.<Minor>.<Patch>*, where major releases include substantial, possibly non–backwards-compatible changes, minor releases are incremented when new functionality is added, and the patch number is incremented as a result of bug fixes. Incrementing the version of a major release will set the minor and patch levels to 0, while incrementing a minor release will reset the patch level to 0. Trailing 0s are usually removed from the version number, so a version 17.1.0 is equivalent to version 17.1.

Higher versions, starting with major releases, include features and bug fixes from minor and patch releases. Aside from backward-incompatible changes and features that might have been removed, you can assume that higher versions contain all of the bug fixes and enhancements of the lower versions.

Versions can have more than three parts. This allows one to specify branches of a particular release created in order to deliver compatible patches in older releases. There is no limit to how many branched versions you can have. As an example, fixes in application or release version 17.1.3.1 are not guaranteed to be included in 17.2, as 17.2 might have been released before 17.1.3.1. Prereleases, also known as release candidates, will have the *-rcVsn* suffix, e.g., 17-rc1.

If you are not sure what OTP release you are using, you can find out by using the `erlang:system_info(otp_release)` BIF. In the *releases* directory for the release you are running, you will find the *OTP_VERSION* file that contains the OTP version number. You will find this file only in your development environment. If you look for it in your target installation, you will not find it unless you have put it there yourself.

Creating a Release

Having defined what is included in our release, the time has come to create it in a few simple steps, as shown in Figure 11-2:

1. Start by creating a binary boot file, which contains the commands required to load modules and start applications.

2. With your boot file in place, create a directory structure that includes all application directories, release directories, and, if required, the emulator. This package is target independent, but could be OS and hardware specific. Your directory structure must follow the directives described in "Release Directory Structure" on page 265, making it compatible with the boot file you created.

3. Create a start script defining your configurations, system limits, code search paths, and other system-specific environment variables, including a pointer to the boot file. Your script will be based on the *.src* files you saw in the *bin* directory of the emulator. The script will depend on the directory structure you have created and how you want your target system to behave.

4. With the start script in place, create a deployment package specific to your target environment. It could be a tar file, a Debian or Solaris package, a container, or any other instance that you can configure and deploy with tools of your choice or the hype of the moment.

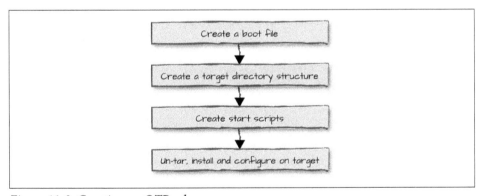

Figure 11-2. Creating an OTP release

In our example, we keep it simple by creating and deploying a tar file using the sys tools library that comes as part of the SASL application in the OTP distribution. The typical target directory structure includes all of the applications listed in the release file and, in the majority of cases, the Erlang runtime system. Once we've created our tar file, we will want to untar it and fix scripts, configuration files, and other target-specific environment variables before creating the final package. This step could be done manually or as part of your automated build process. It could be done locally on your computer or in your target environment. How you do it depends on the development and target environments as well as the tools you pick. There never has been, and never will be, a "one size fits all" approach.

Creating the Boot File

Let's start by creating our boot file. To do this, we need the `systools:make_script/2` library function. This function creates a binary boot file used by a start script to boot Erlang and your system. To get the `start_script/2` function to work, we need to copy the *bsc* application example, ensuring it follows the directory structure we covered in "The Application Structure" on page 206. The structure is available in this chapter's directory of the GitHub repository. If you download it and recreate the example on your computer, don't forget to compile the Erlang files and place them into the *ebin* directory.

The script starts off by looking for the application versions specified in the *basestation.rel* file. It does so using the code search path, and any other paths you might have included in your `{path, PathList}` environment variable. In our example, assuming we started Erlang in the same directory as the *bsc* directory, we would use the `[{path, ["bsc/ebin"]}]` option or start Erlang using `erl -pa bsc/ebin`. Remember, `PathList` is a list of lists, so even if you have only one directory, the directory must be defined in a list: `[Dir]`. Let's try it out:

```
$ erl -pa bsc/ebin/
Erlang/OTP 18 [erts-7.2] [smp:8:8] [async-threads:10] [kernel-poll:false]

Eshell V7.2  (abort with ^G)
1> systools:make_script("basestation", [{path, ["bsc/ebin"]}]).
Duplicated register names:
        overload registered in sasl and bsc
error
ok
```

Oops, `systools` detected a problem when building the script. Remember how, in your app file, you specified a list of registered processes? Apparently, there is another process defined in the *sasl* app file with the name `overload`. We actually introduced `freq_overload` in Chapter 7, and before changing it, had it registered with the name `overload` in Chapter 8. When creating the first app file, we ended up using the wrong name.

If you are running the script on your laptop, you might get errors informing you that the script was unable to find a certain version of the app file, an error that is easily reproducible if you change any of the versions in *basestation.rel*. This is where version control becomes important. You need to know exactly which module, application, and release versions you are running in production, because your system may be running for years on end and is likely to be managed by other people. Should you get called in to support someone else's mess, at least you'll know what version of the mess you have to deal with.

When creating your boot file, sanity checks are run to:

- Check the consistency and dependencies of all applications defined in the rel files. Do all the applications exist, and are there no circular dependencies? Ensure that the versions defined in the app files match those specified in the rel files.

- Ensure that the *kernel* and *stdlib* applications of type permanent are part of the release. Warnings will be raised if *sasl* is not part of the release, but the script and boot file generation will not fail. You can suppress these warnings by passing no_warn_sasl as one of the options when creating the boot file.

- Detect clashes in the registered process names defined in the application app files, ensuring that no two processes are registered with the same name.

- Ensure that all modules defined in the app files have corresponding beam files in the *ebin* directory. While doing so, the sanity check detects any module name clashes, where the same module (or module name) is included in more than one application. If you want to ensure that the beam files match the latest version of the source code, include src_tests in the options.

As we look at our release, we see that the registered process name clash arises as an error in our app file. Changing overload to freq_overload in the registered process names of the *bsc.app* file fixes the problem.

When viewing the resulting contents of the directory as shown in the following example, we discover two new files, *basestation.script* and *basestation.boot*. Before investigating them further, let's use the boot file to start the base station release:

```
1> systools:make_script("basestation", [{path, ["bsc/ebin"]}]).
ok
2> q().
ok
$ ls
basestation.boot        basestation.rel  basestation.script      bsc
$ erl -pa bsc/ebin -boot basestation
Erlang/OTP 18 [erts-7.2] [smp:8:8] [async-threads:10] [kernel-poll:false]


=PROGRESS REPORT==== 25-Dec-2015::20:37:46 ===
          supervisor: {local,sasl_safe_sup}
             started: [{pid,<0.35.0>},
                       {id,alarm_handler},
                       {mfargs,{alarm_handler,start_link,[]}},
                       {restart_type,permanent},
                       {shutdown,2000},
                       {child_type,worker}]
```

```
...<snip>...

=PROGRESS REPORT==== 25-Dec-2015::20:37:46 ===
          supervisor: {local,bsc}
             started: [{pid,<0.43.0>},
                       {id,freq_overload},
                       {mfargs,{freq_overload,start_link,[]}},
                       {restart_type,permanent},
                       {shutdown,2000},
                       {child_type,worker}]

=PROGRESS REPORT==== 25-Dec-2015::20:37:46 ===
          supervisor: {local,bsc}
             started: [{pid,<0.44.0>},
                       {id,frequency},
                       {mfargs,{frequency,start_link,[]}},
                       {restart_type,permanent},
                       {shutdown,2000},
                       {child_type,worker}]

=PROGRESS REPORT==== 25-Dec-2015::20:37:46 ===
          supervisor: {local,bsc}
             started: [{pid,<0.45.0>},
                       {id,simple_phone_sup},
                       {mfargs,{simple_phone_sup,start_link,[]}},
                       {restart_type,permanent},
                       {shutdown,2000},
                       {child_type,worker}]

=PROGRESS REPORT==== 25-Dec-2015::20:37:46 ===
          application: bsc
          started_at: nonode@nohost
Eshell V7.2  (abort with ^G)
1> observer:start().
ok
```

Because the *bsc* application was not placed in the *lib* directory, we have to provide the code search path to the *.app* and *.beam* files using the -pa directive to the erl command. Note all the progress reports that start appearing as soon as *sasl* is started (we've removed a few in our example). Just to be completely sure that the supervision tree has started, start the *observer* tool, select the Applications tab (Figure 11-3), and have a look at the *bsc* supervision tree.

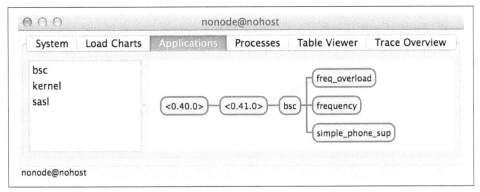

Figure 11-3. The observer Applications tab

This is how we start OTP-compliant simple target systems. Simple target systems are used by several popular open source projects, are more robust than basic target systems, and represent a step in the right direction. But we can (and will) do better! Before discovering how, let's review in more detail the contents of the files we've generated and the parameters we can pass to systools:make_script/2.

Script files

Figure 11-4 shows the basic relationships between files used to build a release. The *basestation.boot* file is a binary file containing all of the commands executed by the Erlang runtime system and needed to start the release. Unlike other files we look at, the boot file has to be a binary because it contains the commands that load the modules that allow the runtime system to parse and interpret text files. You can find the textual representation of the boot file's commands in *basestation.script*. And even better, for those of you who like to tinker, you can edit the file or write your own. (Do this while sparing a thought for those using OTP R1 back in 1996, when make_script/2 had not yet been written.)

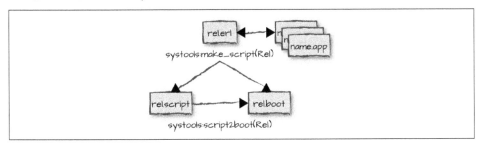

Figure 11-4. Creating boot and release files

Have a look at the contents of a script file. It is a file containing an Erlang term of the format {script, {ReleaseName, ReleaseVsn}, Actions}:

```
{script,
    {"basestation","1.0"},
    [{preLoaded,
        [erl_prim_loader,erlang,erts_internal,init,otp_ring0,prim_eval,
         prim_file,prim_inet,prim_zip,zlib]},
     {progress,preloaded},
     {path,["$ROOT/lib/kernel-4.1.1/ebin","$ROOT/lib/stdlib-2.7/ebin"]},
     {primLoad,[error_handler]},
     {kernel_load_completed},
     {progress,kernel_load_completed},
     {path,["$ROOT/lib/kernel-4.1.1/ebin"]},
     {primLoad, KernelModuleList},   %%
     {path,["$ROOT/lib/stdlib-2.7/ebin"]},
     {primLoad, StdLibModuleList},
     {path,["$ROOT/lib/sasl-2.6.1/ebin"]},
     {primLoad, SASLModuleList},
     {path,["$ROOT/lib/bsc-1.0/ebin"]},
     {primLoad, BscModuleList},
     {progress,modules_loaded},
     {path,
        ["$ROOT/lib/kernel-4.1.1/ebin","$ROOT/lib/stdlib-2.7/ebin",
         "$ROOT/lib/sasl-2.6.1/ebin","$ROOT/lib/bsc-1.0/ebin"]},
     {kernelProcess,heart,{heart,start,[]}},
     {kernelProcess,error_logger,{error_logger,start_link,[]}},
     {kernelProcess,application_controller,
        {application_controller,start, KernelAppFile}}
     {progress,init_kernel_started},
     {apply, {application,load, StdLibAppFile}},
     {apply, {application,load, SASLAppFile}},
     {apply, {application,load, BscAppFile}},
     {progress,applications_loaded},
     {apply,{application,start_boot,[kernel,permanent]}},
     {apply,{application,start_boot,[stdlib,permanent]}},
     {apply,{application,start_boot,[sasl,permanent]}},
     {apply,{application,start_boot,[bsc,permanent]}},
     {apply,{c,erlangrc,[]}},
     {progress,started}]}.
```

We replaced the *kernel, stdlib, sasl,* and *bsc* applications' module lists and app file contents with variables shown in italics to make the file more book-friendly and readable. The script file starts off by defining any modules that have to be preloaded before any processes are spawned. Let's step through these commands one at a time. Although you need not understand what they all mean if all you need to do is get a system up and running, having knowledge of the various steps helps when you have to dive into the internals of the kernel or need to troubleshoot why your system is not starting (or even more worrisome, not restarting):

preLoaded

Contains the list of Erlang modules that have to be loaded before any processes are allowed to start. You can find them in the *erts* application located in the *lib* directory. Of relevance to this section are the init module, which contains the code that interprets your boot file, and the erl_prim_loader module, which contains information on how to fetch and load the modules.

progress

Lets you report the progress state of your initialization program. The progress state can be retrieved at any time by calling the function init:get_status/0. The function returns a tuple of the format {InternalState, ProgressState}, where InternalState is starting, started, or stopping. ProgressState is set to the last value executed by the script. In our example, the only progress state that matters to the startup procedure is the last one, {progress, started}, which changes InternalState from starting to started. All other phases have no use other than for debugging purposes.

kernel_load_completed

Indicates a successful load of all the modules that are required before starting any processes. This variable is ignored in embedded mode, where loading of the modules happens before starting the system. We discuss the embedded and interactive modes in more detail later in this chapter.

path

A list of directories, represented as strings. They can be absolute paths or start with the $ROOT environment variable. These directories are added to the code search path (together with directories supplied as command-line arguments using -pa, -pz, and -path) and used to load modules defined in primLoad entries. Note how the generated paths—specifically, the one in the *bsc* application—assume that the beam files of the target environment are located in *$ROOT/lib/bsc-1.0/ebin* and not *bsc/ebin*. Note also how the application version numbers in the start scripts have been added to the path, assuming a standard OTP directory structure.

primLoad

Provides a list of modules loaded by calling the erl_prim_loader:get_file/1 function. If loading a module fails, the start script terminates and the node is not started. Modules may fail to be loaded when the beam files are missing, are corrupt, or were compiled by a wrong version of the compiler, or when the code search path is incorrect (e.g., if you forgot to add your application to the *lib* directory or have omitted the directory version number). In various places throughout this chapter we explain how to troubleshoot startup errors.

{kernelProcess, Name, {M, F, A}}

Starts a kernel process by calling apply(M, F, A). In our file, kernelProcess is used for three modules: heart, error_logger, and application_controller. You already know what the error logger and the application controller do. We look at heart in more detail in "Heart" on page 296. Once started, the kernel process is monitored, and if anything abnormal happens to it the node is shut down.

`{apply, {M, F, A}}`

Causes the process initializing the system to execute the apply(M, F, A) BIF, where the first argument is the module, the second is the function, and the third is a list of arguments for the function. If this function exits abnormally, the startup procedure is aborted and the system terminates. A function started in this manner may not hang and has to return, because starting the node is a synchronous procedure. If an apply does not return, the next command will not be executed.

Now that we are enlightened about each line of the script file, we can follow what is happening in our start script:

1. We start off by preloading all of the modules in the *erts* application, together with the error_handler in the *kernel* application. Once they load, we inform the script interpreter with {kernel_load_completed} and issue a progress report.

2. For all applications listed in the release file, we add the path to the end of the code search path and use primLoad to load all of the modules listed in the respective application app files. We then issue a modules_loaded progress report.

3. We start all of the kernel processes, starting with heart, the error_logger, and the application_controller (you already know about the latter two). We issue an init_kernel_started progress report.

4. We call application:load(AppFile) to load all the applications that are part of this release. This loads the four applications listed in our rel file: *kernel, stdlib, sasl*, and *bsc*. When complete, we issue an applications_loaded progress report.

5. Now that we've started the kernel processes and loaded all of the applications, it is time to start them. Note how, instead of calling application:start/1 in the {apply, {M, F, A}} tuple, we are calling application:start_boot/2. This is an undocumented function that, unlike application:start/2, assumes that the application has already been loaded and asks the application controller to start it.

6. Before issuing the final started progress report, we call c:erlangrc(). This function is not documented, but reads and executes the .*erlang* file in your home or Erlang root directory. This is a useful place to set code paths and execute other functions.

Be very careful of the code search paths in your target environment. The only reason our example can start the *bsc* application is that we provide the path to the beam files using -pa in the command-line prompt when starting Erlang. Our base station script expects them to be in *$ROOT/lib/bsc-1.0/ebin*. When generating the start script for the target environment, all applications are assumed to be in the directory *AppName-version* within the root directory *$ROOT/lib/*. This will become evident when we generate the target directory structure and files.

The make_script parameters

Let's look in more detail at all the options we can pass to the `make_script/2` call. We already know that `Name` is the name of the release file:

```
systools:make_script(Name, OptionsList).
```

Options include:

`src_tests`
By default, `systools` assumes that the beam files are up to date and represent the latest version of the source code. This flag causes it to instead verify that the beam files are newer than their corresponding source files and that no source files are missing, and issue warnings otherwise.

`{path,DirList}`
Adds paths listed in `DirList` to the code search path. This option can be used along with passing the `-pa` and `-pz` parameters when starting the Erlang VM that executes the `systools` functions. You can include wildcards in your path, so `"lib/*/ebin"` expands to contain all of the subdirectories in *lib* containing an *ebin* directory.

`local`
Places local paths instead of absolute paths in the start script. This flag is ideal for testing boot scripts using your code and the Erlang runtime system on your local machine.

`{variables,[{Prefix, Var}]}`
Replaces path prefixes with variables. This allows you to specify alternative target paths for some or all of your applications. Defining a prefix such as `{"$BSC", "/usr/basestation/"}` results in the path *$BSC/lib/bsc-1.0/ebin*, if the app and beam files are found in */usr/basestation/lib/bsc/ebin*. Similarly, it results in the path *$BSC/ernie/lib/bsc-1.0/ebin* if the local path is */usr/basestation/ernie/lib/bsc/ebin*.

`{outdir, Dir}`
Puts the boot and script files in `Dir`.

`exref` *and* `{exref, AppList}`
Tests the release with the *Xref* cross-reference tool, which looks for calls to undefined and deprecated functions.

silent
> Returns a tuple of the format {ok, ReleaseScript, Module, Warnings} or {error, Module, Error} instead of printing results to I/O. Use this option when calling systools functions from scripts or integrating the call in your build process where you need to handle errors.

no_dot_erlang
> Removes the instructions that load and execute the expressions in the *.erlang* file.

no_warn_sasl
> Can be used if you are not including *sasl* as one of your default applications and are not interested in the warnings that are generated.

warnings_as_errors
> Treats warnings as errors and refuses to generate the script and boot files if warnings occur.

Alternative Boot Files

If you look in the *releases* directory of the standard Erlang/OTP distribution you are currently running, you will find four boot files and three rel files. They start and load different applications. They include:

start_clean.boot
> Starts the *kernel* and *stdlib* applications as defined in the *start_clean.rel* file.

start_sasl.boot
> Starts the *kernel*, *stdlib*, and *sasl* applications as defined in the *start_sasl.rel* file.

no_dot_erlang.boot
> Starts the *kernel* and *stdlib* applications but does not execute commands in the *.erlang* file. This is useful when determinism is important, because it does not allow the code search paths to be manipulated and other user preferences to be modified.

The fourth file, *start.boot*, is a copy of whichever of the preceding files was selected as the default when installing Erlang. You can rename any of the three files in the list to *start.boot* yourself in the *releases* directory, should you wish to try them out.

You can write your own script files, generate them with `systools:make_script/2`, or change existing ones. If you need to generate a release boot file from a script file, use the `systools:script2boot(File)` function.

Changing script files was a necessity in the good old days when debugging startup issues. In order to pinpoint exactly where the problems occurred, we had to add progress reports after every operation. When working with projects with thousands of modules, if one of the beam files installed on the target machine got corrupted during the build or transfer process, the only way to find it was by adding progress reports after every primLoad command in the boot file. It told us in which application directory we had a problem, after which we loaded all of the modules individually, finding the culprit.

Today, you can turn on the startup trace functionality by passing the -init_debug flag to the erl command. It makes the startup phases much more visible. When users are unaware of this option, debugging startup errors can end up being worse than looking for a needle in a haystack. But there are still reasons for manipulating and writing your own release files: to reduce startup times by loading only specific modules and starting specific applications, or to change their start order.

Creating a Release Package

Now that we know the ins and outs of creating and starting a simple target system and have a boot file at hand, let's have a look at how the experts package, deploy, and start their releases. The most solid and flexible way of deploying an Erlang node is as an *embedded target system*. Unfortunately Erlang/OTP uses the term "embedded" in several contexts, which we explain in this chapter, so please don't assume it means the same thing each time we use it. Here, by *embedded* we mean our target system becomes part of a larger package running on the underlying operating system and hardware. It is capable of executing as a daemon job in the background, without the need to start an interactive shell or keep it open all the time, and it typically starts when the operating system is booted. To communicate without a shell, an embedded target system streams all I/O through pipes.

Because target environments differ based on design and operational choices, there is no "one size fits all" solution. The basic steps when creating a release package are as follows, but in practice you will often find the need to tweak them based on the details of what you are trying to achieve:

1. Create a target directory and release file.
2. Create the *lib* directory with the application versions specified in the rel file.
3. Create the release directory with the boot scripts and the application configuration file.
4. Copy the *erts* executable and binaries to the target directory.
5. Create a *bin* directory and copy the configuration files and the start scripts to it.

These steps are, at least in part, usually integrated in an automated build system and the install scripts executed on the target machine or run by one of the many available tools. Because OTP originally did not ship with tools to create target releases, and eventually included a complex tool focused on batch handling, the boundary for what is done by the build environment and what is done by the installation scripts on the target host varies among users. What also vary are the manual versus the automated steps. If you are doing your build on the same hardware and operating system as your target environment, you might be better off getting everything ready in one place. If you do not have this luxury, do not know where (or on what target machine) your deployment will be running, or need other target-specific configuration files created on the fly, parts of the procedure may have to be performed on the target environment.

Now we make our way through the steps required to manually create a target system, assuming that our development and target environments are the same. Based on how you are used to building, deploying, and configuring your target systems, it should be straightforward to understand where you should be drawing the boundary between what you do in your build process and what you do on the target host. We also cover some tools that can be used to automate this process.

We start off by creating the target directory, which we are going to call *ernie*,[1] and adding the *releases* and *lib* directories to it. Along with standard Unix commands, we use the `systools:make_tar/2` library function. We start in the same directory as the *bsc* application directory. The `make_tar` call also expects the system release and boot files to be located here, alongside a config file.

The configuration file is optional at this stage. You might want to generate target-specific values at install time, overriding those specified in the app files. If you choose to omit it at this stage, you must not forget to add it when installing the system, as otherwise your system will not start. The configuration file must be named *sys.config*, although you can change the name by tweaking the arguments you pass to the emulator when starting it.

We create our *ernie* target directory, rename the configuration file *sys.config*, and place it in the same directory as the *bsc* application and the rel and boot files. When done, we can create our tar file:

```
$ mkdir ernie
$ cp bsc.config sys.config
$ erl
Erlang/OTP 18 [erts-7.2] [smp:8:8] [async-threads:10] [kernel-poll:false]

Eshell V7.2  (abort with ^G)
1> systools:make_tar("basestation",
                     [{erts, "/usr/local/lib/erlang/"},
```

---

1 Ernie is the username of the account where the AXD301 ATM switch runs its Erlang nodes—a trip down memory lane for those who contributed to Erlang in some shape or form in the early days, including many of the reviewers of this book.

```
                          {path, ["bsc/ebin"]}, {outdir, "ernie"}]).
ok
2> q().
ok
3>
$ cd ernie
$ ls
basestation.tar.gz
$ tar xf basestation.tar.gz
$ ls
basestation.tar.gz      lib
erts-7.2                releases
$ ls lib/
bsc-1.0         kernel-4.1.1    sasl-2.6.1      stdlib-2.7
$ ls releases/
1.0             basestation.rel
$ ls releases/1.0/
basestation.rel start.boot      sys.config
$ ls erts-7.2/bin/
beam            dialyzer    erl.src     heart           start.src
beam.smp        dyn_erl     erlc        inet_gethost    start_erl.src
child_setup     epmd        erlexec     run_erl         to_erl
ct_run          erl         escript     start           typer
$ rm basestation.tar.gz
```

Our call to systools:make_tar(Name, OptionsList) generates the *basestation.tar.gz*
package. Name is the name of the release and OptionsList accepts all of the options
make_script takes, together with the {erts, Dir} directive. We give this directive if
we wish to include the runtime system binaries, resulting in the *erts-7.2* directory.
That is not always the case, because the runtime system binaries might already be
installed on the target machine, or a single version of Erlang might be used to run
multiple nodes. Also note that the *sys.config* file is included in the *releases/1.0* directory. If it is in a different directory from the rel file, you have to copy it in a later stage
of the installation.

You could deploy *basestation.tar.gz* to your target machine and run your local configuration scripts when you install the node, or do it in your build environment and create a single tar file for all deployments of this particular node. Keep in mind that your
node might run in tens of thousands of independent installations—one for every base
station controller your company sells—or, if hosted, in multiple occurrences of the
node, all in a single installation. Your configuration parameters will depend on your
needs and the type of installation; they might be the same across all tens of thousands
of deployments, or may have to be individually customized when installing the software on each target environment. Often, it is a combination of both. Configuration
scripts could be proprietary to your system and be included in the tar file, or be managed by third-party deployment and configuration tools such as Chef, Puppet, or
Capistrano.

In our example, we untar the *basestation.tar.gz* file manually. The remaining steps could run either on the target or in our build environment. When untarring the file, we find three new directories: the *lib* directory containing all of the application directories (including their version numbers), the *releases* directory, and the *erts* directory. The *erts* directory is there because we included the {erts, Dir} directive in the sys_tools:make_tar/2 call.

We already know that Name is the name of the release file:

```
systools:make_tar(Name, OptionsList).
```

OptionsList is a list that can be empty or can contain some combination of the following elements:

{dirs, IncDirList}
: Copies the specified directories (in addition to the defaults priv and ebin) to the application subdirectories. Thus, to add tests, src, and examples to the release, set the IncDirList to [tests, src, examples].

{path, DirList}
: Adds paths to the code search path. This option can be used along with the -pa and -pz parameters passed when starting the Erlang VM that runs the system. You can include wildcards in your path. For instance, ["lib/*/ebin"] will expand to contain all of the subdirectories in *lib* that contain an *ebin* directory.

{erts, Dir}
: Includes the binaries of the Erlang runtime system found in directory Dir in the target tar file. The version of the runtime system is extracted from the rel file. Make sure that the binaries have been compiled and tested on your target operating system and hardware platform.

{outdir, Dir}
: Puts the tar file in directory Dir. If omitted, the default directory is the same directory as that of the rel file.

exref *and* {exref, AppList}
: Tests the release with the *Xref* cross-reference tool, which looks for calls to undefined and deprecated functions. This is the same test executed by the systools:make_script/2 call when passing the same option.

src_tests
: Issues a warning if there are discrepancies between the source code and the beam files. This is the same test executed by the systools:make_script/2 call when passing the same option.

`silent`

> Returns a tuple of the format {ok, ReleaseScript, Module, Warnings} or {error, Module, Error} instead of printing the results to I/O. You can get formatted errors and warnings by calling Module:format_error(Error) and Module:format(Warning), respectively. Use this option if you are integrating sys tools in your build process; it works in the same way for this as for the sys tools:make_script/2 call.

Two additional options, {variables,[{Prefix, Var}]} and {var_tar,VarTar}, allow you to change and manipulate the way target libraries and packages are created. Use them when deviating from the standard Erlang way of doing things; for example, if you prefer to deploy your release as *deb*, *pkg*, *rpm*, or other packages or containers. They allow you to override the application installation directory (by default set to *lib*) and influence where and how the packages are stored. We do not cover these options in this chapter; for more information and some examples, read the systools reference manual page.

Start Scripts and Configuring on the Target

Now that we have our target files in place, we need to configure our start scripts. Here we go through these steps manually, later introducing tools that automate the process:

1. In the target directory (*ernie*, in our case), create a *bin* directory in which to place and edit the start scripts that will boot our system.

2. Create the *log* directory, to which all debug output from the start scripts is sent. It will be one of the first points of call when the system fails to start.

3. Create a file called *start_erl.data* in the *releases* directory containing the versions of the Erlang runtime system and its release.

4. If the original tar file did not contain a *sys.config* file, create one (possibly empty) and place it in the release version directory.

At this point, fingers crossed, everything will start. Let's go through these steps in more detail, adding and editing files as we go along. All of this is in the *ernie* directory:

```
$ mkdir bin
$ cp erts-7.2/bin/start.src bin/start
$ cp erts-7.2/bin/start_erl.src bin/start_erl
$ cp erts-7.2/bin/run_erl bin
$ cp erts-7.2/bin/to_erl bin
$ mkdir log
```

In our example, we create the *bin* directory and copy *start.src* and *start_erl.src* to it, renaming them *start* and *start_erl*, respectively. We also copy over *run_erl*, which the start scripts expect to be available locally, and *to_erl*, which we will use to connect to an embedded Erlang shell. The start script initializes the environment for the embedded system, after which it calls *start_erl*, which in turn starts Erlang via the *run_erl* script.

Think of *start_erl* as an embedded version of *erl* and *start* as a script you can use and customize as you please. Depending on your needs and requirements, you might also want your own version of the *erl* and *heart* scripts and, if running distributed Erlang, the *epmd* binary. All of these can be copied from the *bin* directory of the runtime system.

Now that the files and binaries are in place, we need to edit them accordingly. We modify the *start* file, replacing %FINAL_ROOTDIR% with the absolute path to the new Erlang root directory. In our case, this directory is *ernie*, and we change the file using perl with its -i in-place modification option, using the value of our shell's PWD variable for the replacement text. We then show you the before and after versions using the diff command:

```
$ pwd
/Users/francescoc/ernie
$ perl -i -pe "s#%FINAL_ROOTDIR%#$PWD#" bin/start
$ diff erts-7.2/bin/start.src bin/start
27c27
< ROOTDIR=%FINAL_ROOTDIR%
---
> ROOTDIR=/Users/francescoc/ernie
$ echo '7.2 1.0' > releases/start_erl.data
$ bin/start
$ bin/to_erl /tmp/
Attaching to /tmp/erlang.pipe.1 (^D to exit)

1> application:which_applications().
[{bsc,"Base Station Controller","1.0"},
 {sasl,"SASL  CXC 138 11","2.6.1"},
 {stdlib,"ERTS  CXC 138 10","2.7"},
 {kernel,"ERTS  CXC 138 10","4.1.1"}]
2> [Quit]
$ ls /tmp/erlang.*
/tmp/erlang.pipe.1.r /tmp/erlang.pipe.1.w
```

Having modified the *start* file, we create the *start_erl.data* file in the *releases* directory. It contains the version of the Erlang runtime system and the release directory containing all the boot scripts and configuration files for the release. These two items, in our example both numbers, are separated by a space.

We are now able to boot our system with the *start* command. Notice how, unlike when using the *erl* command, this release starts as a background job. To connect to the Erlang shell, we use the *to_erl* command, passing it the */tmp* directory where the read and write pipes reside.

 When running an embedded Erlang system, you might out of habit exit the shell using `Ctrl-c a`. `Ctrl-c` invokes the virtual machine break handler, after which you can execute one of the following commands:

```
BREAK: (a)bort (c)ontinue (p)roc info (i)nfo (l)oaded
       (v)ersion (k)ill (D)b-tables (d)istribution
```

As indicated, the a terminates the Erlang node.

To avoid termination, be careful to exit the shell using `Ctrl-d`. If you type `q()`, `halt()`, or `Ctrl-c a` out of habit, you will kill the whole background job. By using `Ctrl-d`, you exit the *to_erl* shell while keeping the Erlang VM alive running in the background.

If you are trying to connect to the pipes on your computer and get an error of the form *No running Erlang on pipe /tmp/erlang.pipe: No such file or directory*, look in the *log* directory to find out why your Erlang node failed to start. All start errors in your scripts will be recorded there. Problems might include wrong paths, missing *sys.config* files, a corrupt boot file, or an incorrectly named binary.

It is good practice to always include the *erl* command in the *bin* directory of your target system. This will come as a blessing when, after a failure of some sort, you are unable to restart your node. Your first point of call in these situations will be the SASL report logs, where crash and error reports will in most cases tell you what triggered the chain of errors that caused the node to fail. The last thing you want to do is to have to move the SASL logs to a remote computer every time you want to view them just because your Erlang nodes will not start. Be safe and always generate a second boot file similar to *start_sasl.boot* that contains the same application versions of *kernel*, *stdlib*, and *sasl* as your system.

In our example, we used the */tmp* directory for the read and write pipes, as it is the default directory used by our scripts. If you plan on running multiple embedded nodes on the same machine, though, this will cause a problem. A good practice is to redirect your pipes to a subdirectory of your Erlang root directory in your target structure. This allows multiple node instances to run on the same computer, a common practice in many systems. If you look at the last line of the start script, you will see where to replace `/tmp/` with the absolute path of your new pipes in the root directory. You can also redirect all of the logs elsewhere:

```
$ROOTDIR/bin/run_erl -daemon /tmp/ $ROOTDIR/log "exec ..."
```

Arguments and Flags

So far, so good. But what if we want to start a distributed Erlang node or add a *patches* directory to the code search path? Or maybe we have developed a dislike for the *sys.config* filename and want to retain the original *bsc.config* file. Or, even more importantly, are there flags we can pass to the emulator that will disable the ability to kill the node via Ctrl-c a?

When starting Erlang, we can pass three different types of arguments to the runtime system. They are *emulator flags*, *flags*, and *plain arguments*. You can recognize emulator flags by their initial + character. They control the behavior of the virtual machine, allowing you to configure system limits, memory management options, scheduler options, and other items specific to the emulator.

Flags start with - and are passed to the Erlang part of the runtime system. They include code search paths, configuration files, environment variables, distributed Erlang settings, and more.

Plain arguments are user-defined and not interpreted by the runtime system. You first came across them in "Environment Variables" on page 219 to override application environment variables in app and configuration files from the command line. You can use plain arguments in your application business logic.

The following sample command uses several different arguments:

```
erl -pa patches -boot basestation -config bsc -init_debug +Bc
```

This starts Erlang with the *patches* directory added to the beginning of the code search path. It also uses the *basestation.boot* and *bsc.config* files to start the system, and sets the init_debug flag, increasing the number of debug messages at startup. The +Bc emulator flag disables the shell break handler, so when you press the sequence Ctrl-c a, instead of terminating the virtual machine you terminate just the shell process and restart it.

Let's look at some of the emulator flags in more detail. We've picked high-level flags and system limit flags that do not deal with memory management, multicore architectures, ports and sockets, low-level tracing, or other internal optimizations. The internal optimizations are outside the scope of this book and should be used with care, only if you are sure of what you are doing. You can read more about the arguments we cover (and those we don't) in the manual pages for erl. The ones we list are those we have used ourselves in some shape or form before the need to optimize our target systems:

+Bc

It is dangerous to keep the break handler enabled in live systems, as your fingers are often faster than your mind (especially if this is a support call in the middle of the night when your mind is still fast asleep). If you are used to terminating the

---

shell that way, you will be inclined to do it on production systems as well. Using the +Bc flag makes Ctrl-c a terminate the current shell and start a new one without affecting your system. This is the option to enable for all your live systems.

+Bd

This allows you to terminate the Erlang node using simply Ctrl-c, bypassing the break handler altogether.

+Bi

This makes the emulator ignore Ctrl-c, in which case the only way to terminate your Erlang virtual machine is using the shell command q() or the halt() BIFs. This option is dangerous because it does not allow you to recover should an interactive call fail to return, thereby hanging the shell.

+e *Num*

This sets the maximum number of ETS tables, which defaults to 2,053. With Erlang/OTP R16B03 or newer, you can obtain the value of the maximum number of ETS tables at runtime by calling erlang:system_info(ets_limit).

+P *Num*

This changes the system limit on the maximum number of processes allowed to exist simultaneously. The limit by default is 262,144, but it can range from 1,024 to 134,217,727.

+Q *Num*

This changes the maximum number of ports allowed in the system, set by default to 65,536. The allowable range is 1,024 to 134,217,727.

+t *Num*

This allows you to change the maximum number of allowed atoms, set by default to 1,048,576. These limits are specific to Erlang 17 or newer and to Unix-based OSs. Default values might differ on other operating systems.

+R *Rel*

This allows your Erlang node to connect using distributed Erlang to other nodes running an older, potentially non–backward-compatible version of the distribution protocol.

Regular flags are defined at startup, retrieved in the Erlang side of the runtime system, and used by standard and user-defined OTP applications alike. Remember that large parts of the Erlang kernel and runtime system are written in Erlang, so how you define and retrieve flags in your application is identical to how Erlang defines and retrieves them in its runtime. Here are the main flags:

-Application Key Value

Sets *Application*'s environment variable *Key* to *Value*. We covered this option in "Environment Variables" on page 219.

`-args_file` *FileName*

Allows you to list all of the flags, emulator flags, and plain arguments in a separate configuration file named *FileName*, which is read at startup. The file can also contain comments that start with a # character and continue until the end of the line. Using an arguments file is the recommended approach, so as to avoid the need to mess with the start scripts to set or change arguments. This approach can also allow you keep the arguments file under version control with the rest of your code.

`-async_shell_start`

Allows the shell to start in parallel with other parts of the system, rather than the default of not processing what you type in the shell until the system has been completely booted. This is useful when you are trying to debug startup issues or figure out where timeouts are occurring.

`-boot` *filename*

Sets the name of the boot file to *filename.boot*. If you do not include an absolute path, the emulator assumes the boot file is in the *$ROOT/bin* directory.

`-config` *filename*

Sets the location and name of the configuration file to *filename.config*.

`-connect_all false`

Stops the `global` subsystem from maintaining a fully connected network of distributed Erlang nodes, in effect disabling the subsystem.

`-detached`

Starts the Erlang runtime system in a manner detached from the system console. You need this option when running daemons and background processes. The `-detached` option implies `-noinput`, which basically starts the Erlang node but not the shell process that runs the read-evaluate loop interpreting all the commands you type. The `-noinput` option in turn implies the `-noshell` command, which starts the Erlang runtime system without a shell, potentially making it a component in a series of Unix pipes.

`-emu_args`

Prints, at startup, all of the arguments passed to the emulator. Keep this on all the time in your production systems, as you never know when you will need access to the information.

`-init_debug`

Provides you with detailed debug information at startup, outlining every step executed in the boot script. The overheads of using `-init_debug` and `-emu_args` are negligible, but the information they provide is priceless when troubleshooting.

`-env` *Variable Value*

An alternate (and convenient) way to set host operating system environment variables. It is mainly used for testing, but is also useful when dealing with Erlang-specific values.

`-eval`

Parses and executes an Erlang expression as part of the node's initialization procedure. If the parsing or execution fails, the node shuts down.

`-hidden`

When using distributed Erlang, starts the Erlang runtime system as a hidden node, publishing neither its existence nor the existence of the nodes to which it is connected.

`-heart`

Starts the external monitoring of the Erlang runtime system. If the monitored virtual machine terminates, a script that can restart it is invoked. We cover *heart* in detail in "Heart" on page 296.

`-mode` *Mode*

Establishes how code is loaded in the system. If *Mode* is `interactive`, calls to modules that have not been loaded are automatically searched for in the code search path. Your target systems should run in `embedded` mode, where all modules should be loaded at startup by the boot file, and calls to nonexisting modules should result in a crash. You can still load modules in `embedded` mode using the `l(Module)` or `code:load_file(Module)` calls from the shell.

Running in `embedded` mode is recommended for all production systems. It ensures that in the middle of a critical call, you do not pause the process while traversing the code search path looking for a module that has not been loaded.

`-nostick`

Disables a feature that prevents loading and overriding modules located in sticky directories. By default, the *ebin* directories of the *kernel*, *compiler*, and *stdlib* applications are sticky, a measure intended to prevent key elements of the system from being accidentally corrupted.

-pa *and* -pz

Add directories containing beam files to the beginning and end of the code search path, respectively. One common use is to add -pa patches to point to a directory used to store temporary patches in between releases.

-remsh *node*

Starts a shell connected to a remote *node* using distributed Erlang. This is useful when running nodes with no shells or when you need to remotely connect to a node.

-shutdown_time *Time*

Specifies the number of milliseconds the system is allowed to spend shutting down the supervision trees. It is by default set to infinity. Use this option with care, though, because it overrides the shutdown values specified in the behavior child specifications.

-name *name and* -sname *name*

When working with distributed Erlang, these start distributed nodes with long or short names, respectively. If nodes are to communicate with each other, they must share a cookie, which can be set using the -setcookie directive, and all have either long or short names. Nodes with short and long names cannot communicate with each other.

-s *module*, -s *module function*, -s *module function args*

The first of these forms executes, at startup, *module*:start(). The second executes *module*:*function*(). The third is like the second but includes the argument list to the function. All args are passed as atoms. The -run option works similarly, except that if arguments are defined, they are passed as a list of strings to *module*:*function*/1. Functions executed by -run and -s must return, or the startup procedure will hang. If they terminate abnormally, they will cause the node to terminate as well, aborting the startup procedure.

When troubleshooting systems, you can connect to a remote node using distributed Erlang. For instance, assume you want to connect to node foo@ramone, which has cookie abc123. You would do so by starting an Erlang VM with the –remsh flag:

```
$ erl -sname bar -remsh foo@ramone -setcookie abc123
Erlang/OTP 18 [erts-7.2] [smp:8:8] [async-threads:10] [kernel-poll:false]

Eshell V7.2  (abort with ^G)
(foo@ramone)1> node().
foo@ramone
(foo@ramone)2> nodes().
[bar@ramone]
(foo@ramone)3>
BREAK: (a)bort (c)ontinue (p)roc info (i)nfo (l)oaded
       (v)ersion (k)ill (D)b-tables (d)istribution
```

```
a
$
```

All commands will be executed remotely in foo, with the results displayed locally. Be careful of how you exit the local shell. Using halt() and q() will terminate the remote node. Always use Ctrl-c a.

Let's now try using -s, -eval, and -run in the shell to get a feel for how they work:

```
$ erl -s observer
Erlang/OTP 18 [erts-7.2] [smp:8:8] [async-threads:10] [kernel-poll:false]

Eshell V7.2  (abort with ^G)
1> q().
ok
$ erl -noshell \
-eval 'Average = (1+2+3)/3, io:format("~p~n",[Average]), erlang:halt()'
2.0
$ erl -run io format 1 2 3
Erlang/OTP 18 [erts-7.2] [smp:8:8] [async-threads:10] [kernel-poll:false]

123Eshell V7.2  (abort with ^G)
1> q().
ok

$ erl -s io format 1 2 3
Erlang/OTP 18 [erts-7.2] [smp:8:8] [async-threads:10] [kernel-poll:false]

{"init terminating in do_boot",
 {badarg,[{io,format,[<0.24.0>,['1','2','3'],[]],[]},
          {init,start_it,1,[]},{init,start_em,1,[]}]}}

Crash dump is being written to: erl_crash.dump...done
init terminating in do_boot ()
```

We successfully use erl -s observer to call observer:start(). You do not see it in the shell output shown here, but it opens up an observer wxWidgets window. This is an efficient way to start debugging tools when starting the emulator. We then use the -eval flag to calculate the average of three integers, print out the result, and stop the emulator, all without starting the Erlang shell. In our third and fourth examples, we use -run io format 1 2 3 to call io:format(["1","2","3"]) and -s io format 1 2 3 to call io:format(['1','2','3']). The latter crashes because it attempts to call io:format/1 with a list of atoms, when it is expecting a string.

When using the -run and -s flags, beware of calling functions such as spawn_link and start_link that link themselves to the initialization process, because the process is there to initialize the system and not act as a parent. Although the process currently continues running after executing the initialization calls, you should not depend on that behavior because it is not documented and might change in a future release.

Applications can use the `init:get_arguments()` and `init:get_argument(Flag)` functions to retrieve flags. `Flag` can be one of the predefined flags `root`, `progname`, and `home`, together with all other command-line user-defined flags.

Plain arguments include all arguments specified before emulator flags and regular flags, after the `-extra` flag, and in between the `--` directive and the next flag. We can retrieve plain arguments using the `init:get_plain_arguments/0` call:

```
$ erl one -two three -pa bin/bsc -- four five -extra 6 7 eight
Erlang/OTP 18 [erts-7.2] [smp:8:8] [async-threads:10] [kernel-poll:false]

Eshell V7.2  (abort with ^G)
1> init:get_plain_arguments().
["one","four","five","6","7","eight"]
2> init:get_argument(two).
{ok,[["three"]]}
3> init:get_argument(pa).
{ok,[["bin/bsc"]]}
4> init:get_argument(progname).
{ok,[["erl"]]}
5> init:get_argument(root).
{ok,[["/usr/local/lib/erlang"]]}
6> init:get_argument(home).
{ok,[["/Users/francescoc"]]}
```

Heart

It is customary to run your embedded Erlang systems as daemon jobs, automatically starting them when the computer they are supposed to run on is booted. This means if there is a power outage or any other failure, or a maintenance procedure is performed that requires a reboot, your system will start automatically. But what happens if only the Erlang node itself crashes or stops responding? It could be an unexpected memory spike, a top-level supervisor terminating, a dodgy NIF causing a segmentation fault in the virtual machine, or even a rare bug in the virtual machine that causes the system to hang. This is why you need to enable *heart*. *Heart* can be seen as the supervisor of the node itself.

Heart is an external program that monitors the virtual machine, receiving regular heartbeats sent by an Erlang process through a port. If the external program fails to receive a heartbeat within a predefined interval, it attempts to terminate the virtual machine and invokes a user-defined command to restart the runtime system.

Let's write a very simple script, *bsc_heart*, that simply calls the *bin/start* command. We could just set *start* as the *heart* command, but real-world scenarios tend to be too complex for a blind restart and so a restart script is typically used. We could, after failed restart attempts, come to the conclusion that this is a cyclic restart from which we cannot recover, and opt to cease attempting to restart the node. Or, after a certain number of restart attempts, allowed only at variable (but increasing) time intervals, we could reboot the operating system. Or we could trigger other autodiagnostic scripts that would run sanity tests on the surrounding environment. The options are many, typically depending on your deployment environment and monitoring/alerting facilities, so restart scripts can be as simple or as complex as you want them to be. Let's use the following *bsc_heart* script, which we place in the *bin* directory of our target installation:

```
#!/bin/sh
#Basic Heart Script for the Base Station Controller

ROOTDIR=/Users/francescoc/ernie

$ROOTDIR/bin/start
```

We then set the HEART_COMMAND environment variable to call this script, edit the *start_erl* script to include -heart, and then start the base station controller. We then kill it in a variety of different ways. Despite killing the system, every time we connect to the I/O pipes, it's up and running:

```
$ $ cp bsc_heart ernie/bin/.
$ export HEART_COMMAND=/Users/francescoc/ernie/bin/bsc_heart
$ vim bin/start_erl
$ diff erts-7.2/bin/start_erl.src bin/start_erl
47c47
< exec $BINDIR/erlexec ... -config $RELDIR/$VSN/sys ${1+"$@"}
---
> exec $BINDIR/erlexec ... -config $RELDIR/$VSN/sys ${1+"$@"} -heart
$ bin/start
$ bin/to_erl /tmp/
Attaching to /tmp/erlang.pipe.5 (^D to exit)

1> halt().
heart: Sat Aug 23 12:49:47 2014: Erlang has closed.
[End]
$ bin/to_erl /tmp/
Attaching to /tmp/erlang.pipe.5 (^D to exit)

1>
BREAK: (a)bort (c)ontinue (p)roc info (i)nfo (l)oaded
       (v)ersion (k)ill (D)b-tables (d)istribution
a
[End]
$ bin/to_erl /tmp/
Attaching to /tmp/erlang.pipe.5 (^D to exit)

1>
```

We see that using halt() or Ctrl-c a kills the node, because every time we connect, the command prompt is 1 again. The *heart* system immediately restarts the process.

The following OS environment variables, all optional, can be set either in the start scripts, when booting your system using the -env flag, or wherever else you might choose to configure such variables:

HEART_COMMAND

> The name of the script triggered when the timeout occurs. If this variable is not set, a timeout will trigger a warning indicating the system would have been rebooted, and the system will not be restarted.

HEART_BEAT_TIMEOUT

> The number of seconds *heart* waits for a heartbeat before terminating the virtual machine and invoking the *heart* command. In Erlang 17 or newer, it can be a value greater than 10 and less than or equal to 65,535. Omitting this setting defaults the timeout to 60 seconds.

ERL_CRASH_DUMP_SECONDS

> How long the virtual machine is allowed to spend writing the crash dump file before being killed and restarted. Because crash dump files can be substantial, the virtual machine can take its time writing them to disk. The default setting when using *heart* and not setting this variable is 0, meaning that no crash dump file is written; the virtual machine is immediately killed and the *heart* command is immediately invoked. Setting the value to -1 (or any other negative number) allows the virtual machine to complete writing the crash dump file no matter how long it takes. Any other positive integer denotes the number of seconds allowed to the virtual machine to write the crash dump file before it terminates and is restarted.

In our example, we decided to set the environment variables in the Unix shell, but we could just as easily have edited the *start_erl* file or passed them as flags to erl using the -env *variable value* argument:

```
erl -heart -env HEART_BEAT_TIMEOUT 10
  -env HEART_COMMAND boot_bsc
```

Race conditions between *heart*, heartbeats, and restarts can occur. If you do not anticipate and check for these race conditions, they will leave you scratching your head when you are trying to figure out what went wrong. There have been cases where an Erlang virtual machine was chugging away under extreme heavy load, but the heartbeat never reached *heart* because of underlying OS issues, perhaps as a result of I/O starvation together with a low HEART_BEAT_TIMEOUT value. The lack of heartbeat caused *heart* to terminate the Erlang VM and restart it. No crash dump was generated because *heart*, at least on Unix-like systems, terminates its target with extreme prejudice via SIGKILL, which the target cannot catch. Killing the Erlang VM (and possibly rebooting the OS itself) might have been the solution to the problem, but it was not of any help to the poor developers who were looking for an Erlang-related VM crash, trying to figure out why there was no crash dump file.

Heart works on most operating systems. Discussing how it executes on Windows and other non-Unix-based OSs is beyond the scope of this book, as is exploring the ability to connect and configure it to work with the Solaris hardware watchdog timer. For more information, read the manual page for *heart* that comes with the standard Erlang distribution.

How Does Yaws Use Heart?

As an example of *heart* usage, let's consider the Yaws web server, originally developed by Claes "Klacke" Wikström and available from both the Yaws website (*http://yaws.hyber.org*) and GitHub (*https://github.com/klacke/yaws*). Yaws includes the ability to use *heart* in an interesting way: to get around *heart*'s stubborn habit of endlessly attempting to restart its target, the Yaws restart script keeps track of how many times it has been restarted within a specified time period, much like supervisor child restart counts in OTP. To accomplish this, Yaws sets HEART_COMMAND as shown here:

```
HEART_COMMAND="$ENV_PGM \
    HEART=true \
    YAWS_HEART_RESTARTS=$restarts \
    YAWS_HEART_START=$starttime \
    $program"
```

As you can see, the Yaws HEART_COMMAND value includes the setting of several other variables that its restart shell script examines when it executes due to a *heart* restart:

HEART *environment variable*
> Set to true so that Yaws knows *heart* is controlling it

YAWS_HEART_RESTARTS *environment variable*
> Tracks how many times Yaws has been restarted

YAWS_HEART_START *environment variable*
> Tracks the start time based on the Unix epoch (the number of seconds since January 1, 1970)

$restarts *and* $starttime *shell variables*
> Help Yaws calculate new settings for HEART_COMMAND based on the values of YAWS_HEART_RESTARTS and YAWS_HEART_START set for the previous restart

When you run Yaws, you specify via command-line arguments the maximum number of restarts allowed in a given period. If the Yaws shell script detects through these environment variables that it has restarted too many times in the specified period, it emits an error message and refuses to restart. For more details, see the source code for the Yaws start script (*http://bit.ly/yaws-start*).

The Erlang loader

You might sometimes run a release on embedded devices with little or no disk space and want to change the method the runtime system uses to load modules. Instead of reading them from a file, you might want to load them from a database or from another node across the network. The -loader argument specifies how the erl_prim_loader fetches the modules. The default loader, efile, retrieves the modules from the local filesystem. If you want to use the boot server on another machine, you must specify the inet loader. When using inet, you must include the name of the remote node where the boot server is running through the -id *name* argument, where *name* comes from the -name or -sname flags issued when starting the remote node. You must also include the IP address of that machine using the -hosts *address* flag, where *address* is a string IP address, such as one consisting of four integers separated by periods. An example is -id foo -hosts "127.0.0.1", which specifies that the boot server is running in the foo Erlang virtual machine on the local host.

To see loading in action, we first generate a *basestation.boot* file using the local option to systools:make_script/2. The local option is critical, as it ensures that our local copies of the *bsc* beam files can be found without us having to install them into the *lib* directory of the official release. It basically adds the local path to the *bsc* application into the boot server's load path so that generating the *basestation.boot* file succeeds:

```
$ erl -pa bsc/ebin
Erlang/OTP 18 [erts-7.2] [smp:8:8] [async-threads:10] [kernel-poll:false]

Eshell V7.2  (abort with ^G)
1> systools:make_script("basestation", [local]).
ok
```

Next, we start the boot server:

```
$ erl -name foo@127.0.0.1 -setcookie cookie
Erlang/OTP 18 [erts-7.2] [smp:8:8] [async-threads:10] [kernel-poll:false]

Eshell V7.2  (abort with ^G)
(foo@127.0.0.1)1> erl_boot_server:start([{127,0,0,1}]).
{ok,<0.42.0>}
```

With the boot server started and ready to serve requests, we can start our bar node:

```
$ erl -name bar@127.0.0.1 -id foo -hosts 127.0.0.1 \
    -loader inet -setcookie cookie \
    -init_debug -emu_args -boot basestation
Executing: /usr/local/lib/erlang/erts-7.2/bin/beam.smp
    /usr/local/lib/erlang/erts-7.2/bin/beam.smp --
    -root /usr/local/lib/erlang -progname erl --
    -home /Users/francescoc --
    -name bar@127.0.0.1 -id foo -hosts 127.0.0.1
    -loader inet -setcookie cookie
    -init_debug -boot basestation
{progress,preloaded}
{progress,kernel_load_completed}
{progress,modules_loaded}
{start,heart}
{start,error_logger}
{start,application_controller}
{progress,init_kernel_started}

...<snip>....

=PROGRESS REPORT==== 26-Dec-2015::12:59:05 ===
          supervisor: {local,bsc}
             started: [[{pid,<0.50.0>},
                        {id,simple_phone_sup},
                        {mfargs,{simple_phone_sup,start_link,[]}},
                        {restart_type,permanent},
                        {shutdown,2000},
                        {child_type,worker}]
{apply,{c,erlangrc,[]}}

=PROGRESS REPORT==== 26-Dec-2015::12:59:05 ===
         application: bsc
          started_at: 'bar@127.0.0.1'
{progress,started}
Eshell V7.2  (abort with ^G)
(bar@127.0.0.1)1> application:which_applications().
[{bsc,"Base Station Controller","1.0"},
 {sasl,"SASL  CXC 138 11","2.6.1"},
 {stdlib,"ERTS  CXC 138 10","2.7"},
 {kernel,"ERTS  CXC 138 10","4.1.1"}]
```

As the output shows, our node was able to boot by loading from the remote boot server. Although our example uses the local host (127.0.0.1), thus making one wonder whether loading is occurring over the network or from the local filesystem, you can try this on your own network on two different hosts and see for yourself that the necessary files are loaded from the remote boot server.

The init Module

The `init` module is preloaded in the Erlang runtime system. It manages arguments and the startup and shutdown procedures of your release. At startup, it executes all the commands in the boot file. Of interest to us is the ability the module gives us to restart the system, cleanly shut down all applications, and stop the node, as well as the ability to reboot the virtual machine. Here is a list of common uses for the module:

`init:restart/0`
> Restarts the system in the Erlang node without restarting the emulator. Applications are taken down smoothly, modules are unloaded, and ports are closed, after which the boot file is executed again, using the same boot arguments originally provided. You can use the `-shutdown_time` flag to limit the amount of time spent taking down the applications.

`init:reboot/0`
> Like `restart`, except that the emulator is also shut down and restarted. *Heart*, if used, will attempt to restart the system, causing a potential race condition that will resolve itself when it kills the emulator and restarts it. Timeout values set with the `-shutdown_time` flag will be followed.

`init:stop/0`
> Takes the system down smoothly and stops the emulator. If running, *heart* is also stopped before any attempts to restart the node are made. This is the correct way to stop running nodes, because it allows the applications to terminate and clean up after themselves and properly shut down. Calling `init:stop(Status)` has the same effect as calling `halt(Status)`. Timeout values set with the `-shutdown_time` flag will be followed.

`init:get_status()`
> Determines whether the system is being started, is stopped, or is currently running. It returns a tuple of the format `{InternalStatus, ProvidedStatus}`, where `InternalStatus` is one of `starting`, `started`, or `stopping`. When starting the system, `ProvidedStatus` indicates what part of the boot script `init` is currently running. It gets `Info` status from the last `{progress, Info}` term interpreted by the boot.

We have already covered other useful functions in the `init` module, including `get_arguments/0`, `get_argument/1`, and `get_plain_arguments/0`, in "Arguments and Flags" on page 290.

Rebar3

Many of the manual tasks we have gone through in this chapter are automated by various tools. Automation is required to generate templates, build the release, and generate the target structure. Because there have been no standards or comprehensive ways of shipping releases developed to date—just preferred or recommended approaches—tools that are now shipped with Erlang/OTP are complemented by tools developed by the community, and sometimes they overlap in functionality. In the remainder of this chapter, we cover *rebar3*, a general build tool that also manages releases and dependencies.

The *rebar3* tool is the second generation of *rebar*, one of the most widely used Erlang build tools and one that originated in the Erlang community. *Rebar3* is a comprehensive tool that addresses a number of project management needs, including dependency management, compilation, and release generation. You can also enhance or extend its functionality via plug-ins.

To obtain *rebar3*, you can either download a prebuilt version from its website:

```
$ curl -LO https://s3.amazonaws.com/rebar3/rebar3
```

or clone the *rebar3* Git repository and build it from source:

```
$ git clone https://github.com/erlang/rebar3.git
$ cd rebar3
$ ./bootstrap
===> Updating package registry...
...<snip>...
===> Compiling rebar
===> Building escript...
```

Some Erlang projects that have been around for a few years still include their own first-generation *rebar* executables in their source repositories. This was originally done to make it easier for users to build projects without forcing them to first build *rebar*, but given how widespread *rebar* became, following that outdated tradition and including your own copy of *rebar3* in your project is not necessary. A user need only place a copy of *rebar3* somewhere in the shell path, such as */usr/local/bin*, and use it from there.

Running *rebar3* with no arguments provides information about how to use it. Here is part of its output:

```
$ rebar3
Rebar3 is a tool for working with Erlang projects.


Usage: rebar [-h] [-v] [<task>]

  -h, --help      Print this help.
  -v, --version   Show version information.
  <task>          Task to run.


Several tasks are available:
...<snip>...

Run 'rebar3 help <TASK>' for details.
```

Elided from this output is the list of tasks that *rebar3* supports. That list is too long to show here in its entirety, but in general, *rebar3* tasks fall into the following categories:

Build commands
Support compilation of Erlang and non-Erlang sources and cleaning of build artifacts

Project creation commands
Generate skeleton projects based on templates

Dependency management commands
Support the retrieval, building, updating, cleaning, and removal of project dependencies

Release generation commands
Support the creation of releases and upgrades

Test commands
Support running unit tests, *common_test* suites, and property-based tests

Rebar3 also provides other miscellaneous commands that support project activities such as documentation, generating escript archives, and starting an Erlang shell with all project files and dependencies on the load path.

Generating a Rebar3 Release Project

You can use *rebar3* together with an appropriate project template to generate a project skeleton for a system like our base station controller example. Although our example uses only a single user-defined application, *bsc*, we use an approach that can accommodate multiple apps, since that is typical of most projects.

First, let's create a new directory, *ernie2*, and within it use *rebar3* to generate a new *bsc* release project:

```
$ mkdir ernie2
$ cd ernie2
$ rebar3 new release bsc desc="Base Station Controller"
===> Writing bsc/apps/bsc/src/bsc_app.erl
===> Writing bsc/apps/bsc/src/bsc_sup.erl
===> Writing bsc/apps/bsc/src/bsc.app.src
===> Writing bsc/rebar.config
===> Writing bsc/config/sys.config
===> Writing bsc/config/vm.args
===> Writing bsc/.gitignore
===> Writing bsc/LICENSE
===> Writing bsc/README.md
```

As the output shows, *rebar3* generates a number of directories and files for our release, including skeleton source files under the *apps/bsc/src* directory, a *sys.config* file under the *config* directory, and a *rebar.config* file. The latter provides directives that supply *rebar3* with project-specific details such as compiler flags, release information, and dependencies. Here's the basic *rebar.config* that *rebar3* generated for our *bsc* release project:

```
$ cd bsc
$ cat rebar.config
{erl_opts, [debug_info]}.
{deps, []}.

{relx, [{release, {'bsc', "0.1.0"},
         ['bsc',
          sasl]},

        {sys_config, "./config/sys.config"},
        {vm_args, "./config/vm.args"},

        {dev_mode, true},
        {include_erts, false},

        {extended_start_script, true}]
}.

{profiles, [{prod, [{relx, [{dev_mode, false},
                            {include_erts, true}]}]}
           }]
}.
```

This particular *rebar.config* file contains four tuples, each described in the following list. You can modify any of these settings or add others as required for your project:

- The `erl_opts` tuple provides compiler options for the *erlc* compiler.
- The `deps` tuple declares dependencies for the project. Fortunately, *bsc* depends on nothing outside of standard Erlang/OTP.

- The relx tuple provides settings for release generation. *Rebar3* uses the *relx* tool to generate releases. Because our goal in this section is to use *rebar3* to generate a *bsc* release, we investigate these settings in detail later.

- The profiles tuple provides a way of having different settings for different development tasks or roles. The prod profile generated here is, as its name implies, intended to provide settings for generating a production release.

Among the generated source file skeletons, take special note of the application resource file skeleton, *apps/bsc/src/bsc.app.src*. *Rebar3* generates this file rather than creating an actual application resource file because later, as part of its compilation process, it takes the *bsc.app.src* skeleton, automatically fills in its modules definition with the names of all the application source modules, and generates the *bsc.app* application resource file from that. We can see this by compiling our newly generated files, after first changing the "0.1.0" version numbers *rebar3* generated in the *bsc.app.src* file and *rebar.config* to the correct "1.0" *bsc* version (any text-filtering tool can be used for this purpose; we've entered a Perl one-liner here):

```
$ perl -i -pe 's/0\.1\.0/1.0/' ./apps/bsc/src/bsc.app.src ./rebar.config
$ rebar3 compile
===> Verifying dependencies...
===> Compiling bsc
```

and then looking at the *_build/default/lib/bsc/ebin/bsc.app* file generated by the compilation process:

```
$ cat _build/default/lib/bsc/ebin/bsc.app
{application,bsc,
            [{description,"Base Station Controller"},
             {vsn,"1.0"},
             {registered,[]},
             {mod,{bsc_app,[]}},
             {applications,[kernel,stdlib]},
             {env,[]},
             {modules,[bsc_app,bsc_sup]},
             {contributors,[]},
             {licenses,[]},
             {links,[]}]}.
```

As the file contents show, *rebar3* created the modules definition for us based on the Erlang modules present in the *src* directory. When we add more modules, *rebar3* automatically adds them to the application resource file for us during its compilation phase, which is much easier than manually editing the resource file ourselves. The only tricky part is that if you want to modify other fields of the application resource file, you have to remember to edit the *bsc.app.src* file rather than the generated *bsc.app* file.

To run the skeleton application, we can just start a *rebar3* shell, which ensures that all the appropriate project paths are on the Erlang load path. When the shell starts, it also starts our application:

```
$ rebar3 shell
===> Verifying dependencies...
===> Compiling bsc
Erlang/OTP 18 [erts-7.2] [smp:8:8] [async-threads:0] [kernel-poll:false]

===> Booted bsc
===> Booted sasl

...<snip>...

=PROGRESS REPORT==== 26-Dec-2015::21:58:36 ===
          application: sasl
          started_at: nonode@nohost
Eshell V7.2  (abort with ^G)
1> application:which_applications().
[{sasl,"SASL  CXC 138 11","2.6.1"},
 {bsc,"Base Station Controller","1.0"},
 {inets,"INETS  CXC 138 49","6.1"},
 {ssl,"Erlang/OTP SSL application","7.2"},
 {public_key,"Public key infrastructure","1.1"},
 {asn1,"The Erlang ASN1 compiler version 4.0.1","4.0.1"},
 {crypto,"CRYPTO","3.6.2"},
 {stdlib,"ERTS  CXC 138 10","2.7"},
 {kernel,"ERTS  CXC 138 10","4.1.1"}]
```

Our generated skeleton application contains no actual code, but still, it starts and runs correctly. Note that a *rebar3* shell starts some other applications *bsc* doesn't need, such as *inets* and *ssl*; if we were to start our application manually, these would not be present.

To fill out our project we can retrieve our original sources by copying our *bsc* example code, which is available in this chapter's directory of the book's GitHub repository:

```
$ cp -v <path-to-bsc-example-dir>/src/*.erl apps/bsc/src
<path-to-bsc-example-dir>/src/bsc.erl -> apps/bsc/src/bsc.erl
...
```

When that's complete, we can again use *rebar3* to clean and compile the project:

```
$ rebar3 do clean, compile
===> Cleaning out bsc...
===> Verifying dependencies...
===> Compiling bsc
```

If we again start a *rebar3* shell, we can see that our application runs as expected:

```
$ rebar3 shell
...<snip>...
```

```
1> application:which_applications().
[{sasl,"SASL   CXC 138 11","2.6.1"},
 {bsc,"Base Station Controller","1.0"},
 {inets,"INETS  CXC 138 49","6.1"},
 {ssl,"Erlang/OTP SSL application","7.2"},
 {public_key,"Public key infrastructure","1.1"},
 {asn1,"The Erlang ASN1 compiler version 4.0.1","4.0.1"},
 {crypto,"CRYPTO","3.6.2"},
 {stdlib,"ERTS   CXC 138 10","2.7"},
 {kernel,"ERTS   CXC 138 10","4.1.1"}]
```

Creating a Release with Rebar3

The *rebar3* tool uses *relx*, rather than the standard Erlang/OTP *reltool* facility, in an effort to make it easier for developers to create releases, due to *reltool* being widely viewed as being difficult to configure and use correctly.

Creating a release with *rebar3* is straightforward:

```
$ rebar3 release
===> Verifying dependencies...
===> Compiling bsc
===> Starting relx build process ...
===> Resolving OTP Applications from directories:
          /Users/francescoc/ernie2/bsc/_build/default/lib
          /Users/francescoc/ernie2/bsc/apps
          /usr/local/lib/erlang/lib
===> Resolved bsc-1.0
===> Dev mode enabled, release will be symlinked
===> release successfully created!
```

Once we've generated the release, we can verify that it works as expected:

```
$ _build/default/rel/bsc/bin/bsc console
Exec: /usr/local/lib/erlang/erts-7.2/bin/erlexec -boot ...
Root: /Users/francescoc/ernie2/bsc/_build/default/rel/bsc
/Users/francescoc/ernie2/bsc/_build/default/rel/bsc
Erlang/OTP 18 [erts-7.2] [smp:8:8] [async-threads:30] [kernel-poll:true]


=PROGRESS REPORT==== 27-Dec-2015::11:37:56 ===
          supervisor: {local,sasl_safe_sup}
             started: [{pid,<0.49.0>},
                       {id,alarm_handler},
                       {mfargs,{alarm_handler,start_link,[]}},
                       {restart_type,permanent},
                       {shutdown,2000},
                       {child_type,worker}]

...<snip>...

=PROGRESS REPORT==== 27-Dec-2015::11:37:56 ===
          application: sasl
```

```
            started_at: bsc@francescoc
Eshell V7.2  (abort with ^G)
(bsc@francescoc)1> application:which_applications().
[{sasl,"SASL  CXC 138 11","2.6.1"},
 {bsc,"Base Station Controller","1.0"},
 {stdlib,"ERTS  CXC 138 10","2.7"},
 {kernel,"ERTS  CXC 138 10","4.1.1"}]
```

Instead of the console argument to _build/default/rel/bsc/bin/bsc shown in this example, which starts the application and gives us an Erlang shell, you can instead specify **start** to start the release in the background, **attach** to get a shell attached to an already-started release, or **stop** to stop an already-started release. Run the command _build/default/rel/bsc/bin/bsc with no arguments to see a list of all its arguments and options.

Because of the default release settings in the relx tuple in *rebar.config*, this generated release is intended for development, not production. The default configuration sets dev_mode to true, which means application source files used to create the release are links to sources under the *apps/bsc/src* directory. The dev_mode setting also sets include_erts to false, which keeps the Erlang runtime from being included in the release. These settings are handy for development because they allow developers to edit their files under the *apps* area and have those changes instantly available for either building into a release or recompiling and reloading into an already-running release. The settings also allow developers to use the Erlang installation on the system rather than having to build one into each release, which enables quick testing of the release against multiple runtime versions.

Fortunately, though, building a production release is easy, even with these default settings in place, thanks to *rebar3* profiles. The profiles tuple in *rebar.config* includes a profile named prod that sets dev_mode to false and include_erts to true. To use the prod profile, we just specify it using the *rebar3* **as** directive on the command line:

```
$ rebar3 as prod release
===> Verifying dependencies...
===> Compiling bsc
===> Starting relx build process ...
===> Resolving OTP Applications from directories:
            /Users/francescoc/ernie2/bsc/_build/default/lib
            /Users/francescoc/ernie2/bsc/apps
            /usr/local/lib/erlang/lib
===> Resolved bsc-1.0
===> Including Erts from /usr/local/lib/erlang
===> release successfully created!
```

The **as** directive instructs *rebar3* to run the specified commands using the given profile. Pay particular attention to the text in bold near the bottom of this example; it shows that *relx* includes the Erlang runtime system this time, as directed by the prod profile. And because the prod profile sets dev_mode to false, if you look under *_build/prod/rel/bsc/lib/bsc-1.0/src* you'll see that the source files have been copied into the release, rather than linked back to the *apps* source area as with the default release.

The *rebar3* **tar** directive makes it trivial to create a tar file containing a release:

```
$ rebar3 as prod tar
===> Verifying dependencies...
===> Compiling bsc
===> Starting relx build process ...
===> Resolving OTP Applications from directories:
        /Users/francescoc/ernie2/bsc/_build/prod/lib
        /Users/francescoc/ernie2/bsc/apps
        /usr/local/lib/erlang/lib
        /Users/francescoc/ernie2/bsc/_build/prod/rel
===> Resolved bsc-1.0
===> Including Erts from /usr/local/lib/erlang
===> release successfully created!
===> Starting relx build process ...
===> Resolving OTP Applications from directories:
        /Users/francescoc/ernie2/bsc/_build/prod/lib
        /Users/francescoc/ernie2/bsc/apps
        /usr/local/lib/erlang/lib
        /Users/francescoc/ernie2/bsc/_build/prod/rel
===> Resolved bsc-1.0
===> tarball /Users/francescoc/ernie2/bsc/_build/prod/rel/bsc/bsc-1.0.tar.gz
        successfully created!
```

Rebar3 Releases with Project Dependencies

So far our *rebar3* example has been limited to including only a single application, *bsc*, which has no dependencies, but in practice Erlang applications often depend on other applications. Fortunately, *rebar3* is able to fetch such dependencies and compile them together with the application that depends on them.

Let's assume we decide to change *bsc* logging using the popular open source *lager* framework so that our logfiles can work with existing log rotation tools, and so that we can count on *lager* to protect our application from running out of memory should it attempt to emit a storm of log messages because of some unexpected persistent error condition. Adding a dependency on *lager* to the *bsc* application is easy—we just specify it in the deps tuple in the *rebar.config* file:

```
{deps, [{lager, {git, "git://github.com/basho/lager.git",
                 {tag, "3.0.2"}}}]}.
```

This directive tells *rebar3* that *lager* is a source dependency, with the git tuple telling *rebar3* the location from which it can fetch the *lager* source code and the tag tuple indicating the version of *lager* on which the *bsc* application depends.

With this directive in place, we can ask *rebar3* what our dependencies are:

```
$ rebar3 deps
lager* (git source)
```

Asking *rebar3* to compile causes it to fetch the source for the *lager* dependency as well as the sources for any dependencies *lager* itself has:

```
$ rebar3 compile
===> Verifying dependencies...
===> Fetching lager ({git,"git://github.com/basho/lager.git",
                           {tag,"3.0.2"}})
===> Fetching goldrush ({git,"git://github.com/DeadZen/goldrush.git",
                           {tag,"0.1.7"}})
===> Compiling goldrush
===> Compiling lager
===> Compiling bsc
```

This compilation occurs under the default profile, so if we look under *_build/ default/lib* after it completes, we see directories for *bsc*, for *lager*, and also for *goldrush*, a dependency of *lager*:

```
$ ls _build/default/lib
bsc  goldrush lager
```

To build a release including *lager*, we first need to modify *apps/bsc/src/bsc.app.src* to add lager into the applications list, following kernel and stdlib. With these changes in place, we can build a release under the default profile:

```
$ rebar3 release
===> Verifying dependencies...
===> Compiling bsc
===> Starting relx build process ...
===> Resolving OTP Applications from directories:
          /Users/francescoc/ernie2/bsc/_build/default/lib
          /Users/francescoc/ernie2/bsc/apps
          /usr/local/lib/erlang/lib
          /Users/francescoc/ernie2/bsc/_build/default/rel
===> Resolved bsc-1.0
===> Dev mode enabled, release will be symlinked
===> release successfully created!
```

If we look at the contents of the *_build/default/rel/bsc/lib* directory, we can see that *rebar3* built all the applications necessary to include in the release:

```
$ ls _build/default/rel/bsc/lib
bsc-1.0  goldrush-0.1.7 lager-3.0.2
```

We can then run our application and see that all the applications we expect to see are indeed running:

```
$ _build/default/rel/bsc/bin/bsc console
...<snip>....
(bsc@francescoc)1> application:which_applications().
[{sasl,"SASL  CXC 138 11","2.6.1"},
```

```
{bsc,"Base Station Controller","1.0"},
{lager,"Erlang logging framework","3.0.2"},
{goldrush,"Erlang event stream processor","0.1.7"},
{compiler,"ERTS  CXC 138 10","6.0.2"},
{syntax_tools,"Syntax tools","1.7"},
{stdlib,"ERTS  CXC 138 10","2.7"},
{kernel,"ERTS  CXC 138 10","4.1.1"}]
```

Not only are *bsc*, *lager*, and *goldrush* running, but the standard *compiler* and *syntax_tools* applications were started as well because *goldrush* uses them, which you can see by examining the `applications` list in the *_build/default/lib/goldrush/src/goldrush.app.src* file.

There is much more to *rebar3* than what our *bsc* application requires. It has a plug-in system that makes it extensible and customizable, ties into Erlang's *common-test*, *dialyzer*, and *eunit* facilities to support testing and code coverage and analysis, and supports publishing packages into the Erlang/Elixir *hex* package management system. And as we show next, in Chapter 12, *rebar3* also supports release upgrades.

Wrapping Up

You've got to agree that everything we presented here is a mouthful, and probably more detail than what you had originally bargained for when you started reading this chapter! Having said that, the steps involved in bundling up your OTP applications in a release and starting them as one unit are not many and are relatively straightforward. The reason we've gone into so much detail is that we want to explain not just how, but also why. You will thank us when you need to integrate Erlang/OTP releases in your build system or troubleshoot why a node that was running for years on end is refusing to start. You can't even begin to imagine how many systems we've reviewed that, despite being responsible for tens of thousands of transactions per day, hour, or minute (and in many cases even seconds!) are started using `erl -s Module`, are not OTP compliant, do not have *heart* configured, or are not set up as embedded target systems running as daemons. Start by creating a proper OTP release, integrating the process in your build system, and the rest will follow.

The preferred way to deploy your Erlang nodes that must run for years on end and be available 24/7 is as embedded target systems. You must be strict with revision control and be aware of the exact versions of your modules, applications, and configuration files. You will want to access the Erlang shell through I/O streams sent to a directory in your Erlang root directory (not */tmp*), allowing you to run multiple embedded nodes on that host.

Start your Erlang system as a daemon job, ensuring it is automatically started every time your computer or image is rebooted. Always ensure that you have the *erl* command at hand with a boot file that starts *kernel*, *stdlib*, and *sasl*, giving you access to the SASL logs on your local machine when your nodes have crashed and are refusing to start. And don't forget to set your emulator flags, normal flags, and plain arguments, adapting them to your internal operational requirements. Do you want to disable the break handler using +Bc but still allow the user to kill the shell? What about printing out the arguments passed to the emulator using -emu_args and printing startup trace reports using the -init_debug flag? And how do you want to implement and configure your *heart* script to handle emulator crashes? The combinations are many, and getting the right configuration in place that works for you and your organization can take years of operational experience and firefighting. You will eventually get there, but hopefully, taking into consideration all that we have covered in this chapter, the pager calls will be few and far apart, and never in the middle of the night.

Having said that, we know that not all systems are mission critical and require this level of supervision, complexity, and professionalism. Simple target systems can be both acceptable and respectable if they do their job and fulfill your requirements. If running many nodes on a single machine sharing the same Erlang installation works for you, there is no need to ship every release with its own Erlang virtual machine. You will not be able to individually upgrade applications and emulators, but then again, you might not care! The type of release that works for you, your organization, and the types of systems you are deploying is for you to judge. It can be as simple or as complicated as you need it to be. What is important is that you understand the tradeoffs involved in your choices, and do things without cutting corners, otherwise you will end up paying for it at a later date.

The process we have covered in this chapter, automated using libraries or tools, includes the following steps:

1. *Create a release resource file for your node, defining what will be included in your release.*

   The rel file will contain all of the applications and their respective versions, together with the version of the emulator to be used in the target deployment.

2. *Create a boot file containing all of the commands required to start your node.*

3. *Create the file structure you will deploy to your target system.*

   It will contain the *lib*, *releases*, and *bin* directories and, if you plan to ship it with its own emulator, the *erts* directory.

4. *Specific to your deployment (and possibly on the target host), configure your start scripts.*

   This will include your *start_erl.data* file and config files containing deployment-specific configurations, as well as any target-specific configuration scripts.

You can find an additional example of these steps in "Creating a Release Upgrade" on page 326, where we create a release of the coffee FSM example described in Chapter 6, preparing it for a software upgrade. But if you are too lazy to do these chores every time (we are) and do not need to integrate in existing build and release infrastructure, use existing tools and libraries for the bulk of the work and automate the rest. *Rebar3* simplifies all of this a great deal.

So far in this book, you have come across many different file types, all held together in a release. We've listed them in Table 11-1, as there is no better time than now to review them.

Table 11-1. Erlang/OTP file types

File type	File extension	Description
Erlang module	.erl	File containing the Erlang source code
Compiled module	.beam	Compiled Erlang source code file for the BEAM emulator
Application resource file	.app	File containing application resource and configuration data
Application upgrade file	appup	File containing application upgrade data
Release file	.rel	File containing release-specific application and emulator versions
Release upgrade file	relup	File containing release upgrade information
Start script	.script	Text-based version of the script used to boot the system
Binary start script	.boot	Binary version of the script used to boot the system
Configuration file	.config	File containing application-specific environment variables

We cover *.appup* and *relup* files in Chapter 12. They are used for live upgrades of the applications and regular upgrades of the emulator.

If you haven't had enough and want to read more about creating releases, head straight to the documentation that ships with Erlang/OTP. The OTP Design Principles User's Guide will tell you more about releases and release handling, going as far as creating the first release package ready for deployment in your target environment. The OTP System Principles User's Guide has sections that cover the starting, restarting, and stopping of systems, as well as describing in more detail the difference between the embedded versus interactive code-loading strategies. It overlaps with the OTP Design Principles User's Guide, which also covers the creation and configuration of target systems. In doing so, the user's guide introduces the *target_system.erl* module shipped in the *sasl* application's *examples* directory as well as in this chapter's directory in the book's GitHub repository. It is an example that automates many of the steps we covered manually when explaining how to build a release and target system, a necessity prior to the existence of *rebar* and *rebar3*, *relx*, and *reltool*. Have a look at it, as it has for many years been a good source of inspiration for those integrating Erlang into their existing build systems.

The user's guides are complemented by reference manual pages, of which the following are relevant to what we have just covered and so are worth mentioning:

- If you need more information on the rel file, look up the *rel* reference manual page. Given a rel file, `systools` describes the functions you need to create script, boot, and target tar files. The contents of the binary boot file and its script text counterpart are described in more detail in the *script* reference manual page. To find out more on how they are executed, review the `init` user manual pages.

- There might be times when you need to automate tasks on the target machine and integrate the release process with other tools you might be using (possibly for non-Erlang parts of your system). If that is the case, read the `release_han dler` manual page. It describes functions that allow you to unpack and install the tar file created by the `systools` calls. However, it does assume an installation of Erlang is already running on the target host, which might not always be the case. We cover this library in more detail in the next chapter when looking at live upgrades.

- If you need to load code remotely and the example in this chapter is not enough, the `erl_boot_server`, `erl_prim_loader`, and `init` user manual pages will help you.

- The `erl` and `init` manual pages describe most of the emulator flags and command-line flags, some of which we have not covered in this chapter. For plain arguments, you will have to refer to the user manual pages of the modules and applications using those arguments.

- The `heart` manual page is the place to look for more information on automated restarts, including configuration details and required environment variables when implementing your script. You will find the environment variables described in the `erl` manual page.

- If you are running on Windows, read the *start_erl* manual page. It is the equivalent of the *start* command we have been using in this chapter, allowing you to start your embedded system in Windows environments.

Reltool, which we did not cover, has both a user's guide and reference manual pages you will have to study in detail in the unlikely event your system requires the configuration complexity not handled by *rebar3*, which you can find at *https://www.rebar3.org*, or *relx*, which you can get either with *rebar3* or from GitHub (*https://github.com/erlware/relx*).

If all this seems intimidating, the best thing to do is to simply use *rebar3*. It can build and create releases for a wide variety of project types, can be extended for special cases through its plug-in system, and can download and help manage dependencies on other projects, and it works with the *hex* package management system for publishing your system so others in the Erlang community can use it. For more information about *rebar3* and *hex*, see the *rebar3* documentation (*https://www.rebar3.org/docs/hex-package-management*).

What's Next?

Erlang has been called the language of the system. It is not just a language suitable for solving a particular type of problem, but rather a language and a set of tools that allow you to develop, deploy, and monitor predictable and maintainable systems. While in this chapter we have covered how to package and deploy your first target systems, that is just the beginning of your adventure. What we cover next is how to manage bug fixes and deploy new functionality by doing live upgrades. We do so by introducing the upgrade tools and functionality that come as part of OTP and its behaviors. You've heard about Erlang achieving five-nines availability, software maintenance and upgrades included? Continue on to find out how we do it.

## CHAPTER 12

Release Upgrades

After your system goes live, it churns away in the background handling requests day in and day out. It self-heals when issues occur and restarts automatically after power outages or system reboots. But as with any piece of software, you are bound to continue optimizing it, fixing bugs as they are reported and adding new features. Irrespective of having thousands of instances of your coffee machine running on dedicated hardware monitored through a wireless link, or any other system whose requirements state that it must service its requests with 100% availability, upgrades included, then Erlang/OTP's software upgrade capabilities are something to study carefully. Imagine you not being able to have your morning coffee because of an ongoing firmware upgrade of your office coffee machine!

The built-in functionality in the Erlang VM that allows dynamic module loading might work for simple patches where the upgrade is backward-compatible. But have you thought of the cases where you've changed the functional API? Or where a process running a call to completion with an old version of the code cannot communicate with a process running a new version because of a change in the protocol? How do you handle state changes in your loop data between releases or database schema changes? And even more importantly, what if an upgrade fails and you need to downgrade?

Complex systems need to be upgraded in a coordinated and controlled manner. The built-in functionality used to dynamically load new modules, like everything else, of Erlang and OTP provides the foundations used to build the tools that coordinate and control these upgrades, greatly reducing and even hiding their complexity. Before introducing the tools themselves, let's review the semantics, terminology, and most commonly used functions relevant to our example to ensure we are all on the same page.

Software Upgrades

We cover module upgrades in "Upgrading Modules" on page 43. If you've already read it, you might recall that you can load a new module in the Erlang runtime environment by using the shell command l(Module), calling code:load_file(Module), or compiling the source code using c(Module) or make:files(ModuleList,[load]). At any one time, your runtime environment can have two versions of code for the same module loaded. We refer to them as the *old* and *current* versions. A process running the old module version will continue doing so until it issues a fully qualified function call; i.e., a call of the format *Module:Function(...)*, where the module name is used as a prefix to the function.

When a fully qualified function call occurs, the runtime checks to ensure that the process is running the current version of the code. If it is, the call continues using the current code. But if the process is still running the old version, the pointer to the code is switched to the current version before the call is made.

Calls to library modules have to be fully qualified because you are calling another module, so such a call will automatically use the current version. Recursive calls controlling process receive-evaluate loops, however, tend to recurse locally without a fully qualified call. We need to either change these local calls to be fully qualified, or add a new message that triggers a fully qualified function call in the receive-evaluate loop. Depending on the complexity of the upgrade, this function could either call the loop function in the new module or call a hook in the new module that handles any change of the process state, including loop data, ETS tables, and database schemas, before returning into the loop.

When not executing a fully qualified call, a process running the current version of a module will continue running it even after a new version is loaded in the system. If a process is already running the old version of a module—not the current version—when a version newer than the current one is loaded, that process will be unconditionally terminated. Processes will also be unconditionally terminated if they are running an old module version forcefully removed using the code:purge(Module) call.

Two-Module Limit

The two-module version limit is legacy debt from a design decision taken to simplify the JAM virtual machine (the most-used VM at the time) and to preserve memory in an architecture where memory was scarce. Today, the right design decision would be to allow an unlimited number of module versions in the runtime, and garbage collect them when they're no longer in use. In the JAM, in order to garbage collect code, you had to go through the stack of each process and look at the return addresses of each function call to work out which module version a process was using. This was a very

---

time-consuming activity the developers preferred to avoid, so they simplified it with the two-module limitation.

With two versions of the code allowed in the runtime system, we need a way to determine the current version of the module. The -vsn(Version). module attribute helps us achieve exactly that. Version can be any Erlang term, but it is most commonly a string, number, or atom. More often than not, it is set by a script triggered by the revision control system when committing the code to the repository (for example, if you use Git for source control, you could set Version to a string containing the output of git describe --long, which provides the most recent Git tag, the number of commits made since that tag, and the current commit hash). Placing the vsn attribute at the beginning of the module with the other attributes gives us the ability to determine the version of the code we are upgrading from, using it to control changes to the state, database schemas, protocols, and other non–backward-compatible internal data formats. You can find the version of the current module using the Mod:module_info/0,1 call.

The vsn attribute is not mandatory. If omitted, the compiler generates it at compile time using the beam_lib:md5/1 call to generate a 128-bit *md5 digest* of the module. The md5 digest is based on properties of the module, but excludes compile date and other attributes that are irrelevant to the code, since they may change without the code itself changing. This guarantees that a version will be tagged with the same 128-bit key regardless of compilation time, spaces, carriage returns, or comments in the code.

Remember the example FSM we looked at in "Coffee FSM" on page 119? Let's dust off the Erlang version and compile it to better understand how the vsn module attribute works. If you are using modules from the book's GitHub repository, the module we are using is under *ch12/erlang/coffee.erl.original*. Don't forget to change its filename to *coffee.erl*. You can then compile it as follows:

```
1> c(coffee).
{ok,coffee}
2> coffee:module_info(attributes).
[{vsn,[293551046745957884913825426256179654413]}]
3> {ok, {coffee, MD5Digest}} = beam_lib:md5(coffee).
{ok,{coffee,<<220,215,224,7,110,247,231,148,86,224,44,
             74,197,2,111,13>>}}
4> <<Int:128/integer>> = MD5Digest, Int.
293551046745957884913825426256179654413
```

In shell command 2, a call to coffee:module_info/1 returns the md5 digest in the vsn module attributes, something we confirm in shell commands 3 and 4 by getting the digest from the module and reversing the digest process. Let's now add the -vsn directive manually in our module and recompile:

```
-module(coffee).
-export(...).

-vsn(1.0).

...
```

This ensures the compiler will not override the version with the md5 digest and sets it instead to 1.0:

```
5> c(coffee).
{ok,coffee}
6> coffee:module_info(attributes).
[{vsn,[1.0]}]
```

Let's continue working with the Erlang version of the coffee machine FSM, adding a new upgrade message that triggers a fully qualified function call. This will allow us to upgrade the server in a controlled way, understanding the how and why of all the steps involved in the process. After that, we explore how it is done using OTP.

The First Version of the Coffee FSM

You might recall that the Erlang version of the coffee FSM consisted of three states, *selection*, *payment*, and *remove* (Figure 12-1). In our software upgrade example, we add a new state called *service*, which allows us to open the cabinet door and service the coffee maker. But before going there, let's add some generic code that executes the fully qualified call, giving us a baseline we can use to perform the upgrade itself. We can do this either by fully qualifying every call to the receive-evaluate loop, or by sending the process a message that triggers a fully qualified call.

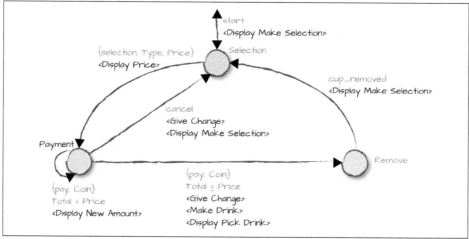

Figure 12-1. Coffee FSM

The recommended approach to upgrading your code is to separate the loading of the new module from each process's trigger of the upgrade. In our generic upgrade code, we load the module using `module:load_file/2`. We then inform the processes that have to trigger an upgrade through a fully qualified call by sending them the {upgrade, Data} message.

`Data` is an opaque data type containing upgrade-specific information used by the new module. It is there to act as a placeholder and to future-proof the code, allowing us to manipulate the process state in conjunction with the transition to the new module. As an example, pretend we are upgrading our frequency server and want to add more frequencies. We could use `Data` to pass the new frequencies to the server during the upgrade. A process that receives the upgrade message and its data then issues a fully qualified function call to `code_change/2`, where the first argument is the process state and the second is `Data`. In this function, we could append the new frequencies to the list of available ones, entering the receive-evaluate loop in the new module with the newly updated loop data.

Let's have a look at what the generic upgrade code for the coffee FSM looks like. Notice that we have added a version number to the module:

```erlang
-module(coffee).
-export(...).
-export([..., code_change/2]).
-vsn(1.0).

...

%% State: drink selection

selection() ->
    receive
        ...
        {upgrade, Data} ->
            ?MODULE:code_change(fun selection/0, Data);
        ...
    end.

%% State: payment
payment(Type, Price, Paid) ->
    receive
        ...
        {upgrade, Extra} ->
            ?MODULE:code_change({payment, Type,
                                 Price, Paid}, Extra);
        ...
    end.

%% State: remove cup
```

```
remove() ->
    receive
        ...
        {upgrade, Data} ->
            ?MODULE:code_change(fun remove/0, Data);
        ...
    end.

code_change({payment, Type, Price, Paid}, _) ->
    payment(Type, Price, Paid);
code_change(State, _) ->
    State().
```

Note how we need to handle the {upgrade, Extra} message in all states. Upon receiving it, we do a fully qualified function call to code_change/2, where the first argument is the FSM state and loop data and the second is Extra, which we transparently pass to the call. The code_change/2 function in the new module provides a place to change the old process state to one compatible with the new code base, possibly using Extra. Changes in the process state could include adaptations to the loop data format and contents, database schema changes, synchronization with other processes, changing process flags, or even going as far as manipulating messages in the mailbox.

Once done, code_change/2 yields control by calling the tail-recursive function returning the process to its new receive-evaluate loop. In our example, these functions are the FSM state functions selection/0, payment/3, and remove/0. This is the first version of the module, so we do not expect the code_change/2 clauses we've added to do anything; they simply return to the state from which the call originated. Adding these clauses avoids the undefined function runtime error that we explained will result if you attempt an upgrade and a process is running an old version of the coffee module.

This is our baseline code. If you are using the code in the book's repository, you will find it in the *erlang* directory for this chapter. Let's compile it, start the Erlang VM, and get our coffee FSM up and running, making sure it works before creating a new version of the module and doing a software upgrade:

```
$ cd erlang
$ cp coffee.erl.1.0 coffee.erl
$ erl -make
Recompile: coffee
Recompile: hw
$ erl -pa patches
Erlang/OTP 18 [erts-7.2] [smp:8:8] [async-threads:10] [kernel-poll:false]

Eshell V7.2  (abort with ^G)
1> coffee:start_link().
Machine:Rebooted Hardware
Display:Make Your Selection
```

```
{ok,<0.36.0>}
2> coffee:module_info(attributes).
[{vsn,[1.0]}]
3> coffee ! {upgrade, {}}.
{upgrade,{}}
4> coffee:module_info(attributes).
[{vsn,[1.0]}]
```

Note how in shell command 3 we trigger an upgrade without having loaded a new version of the FSM. This results in an execution of the code_change/2 call in the current version of the module.

Adding a State

Let's add a state for servicing the coffee FSM. It gets triggered when the coffee FSM is in the *selection* state and the cabinet door is opened. In any other state, the open door event is ignored. As we can see in Figure 12-2, closing the cabinet door triggers a reboot of the hardware and a transition back to the *selection* state. The closing door event is ignored in all other states.

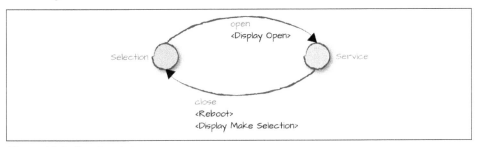

Figure 12-2. Service state

We've opted to keep the example simple, but could have easily inserted locks in the hardware by upgrading *hw.erl* to add the functions hw:lock() and hw:unlock(). These would represent safeguards that would ensure that the coffee machine door could be opened only in the *selection* state and would keep it locked when the machine is in other states.

Let's look at the new module, where we've highlighted the changes from version 1.0. The major differences are the addition of the *service* state, the open and close events, and actions executed in the code_change/2 function clauses.

First, we see the client functions open/0 and close/0, which respectively generate an event when the coffee machine door is opened and closed. In state *selection*, upon receiving the open event, we show *Open* in the display and transition to the *service* state.

The *service* state ignores all events except for users inserting coins and the closing of the coffee machine door. Upon closing the door, the hardware is rebooted and the display instructs the customer to make a selection. The open and close events are ignored in all other states:

```erlang
-module(coffee).
-export([tea/0, espresso/0, americano/0, cappuccino/0,
         pay/1, cup_removed/0, cancel/0, open/0, close/0]).
-export([start_link/0, init/0, code_change/2]).
-vsn(1.1).

start_link() ->
    ...

open() -> ?MODULE ! open.
close() -> ?MODULE ! close.


    ...

selection() ->
    receive
        {selection, Type, Price} ->
            hw:display("Please pay:~w",[Price]),
            payment(Type, Price, 0);
        {pay, Coin} ->
            hw:return_change(Coin),
            selection();
        {upgrade, Extra} ->
            ?MODULE:code_change(fun selection/0, Extra);
        open ->
            hw:display("Open", []),
            service();
        _Other ->    % cancel
            selection()
    end.

    ...

service() ->
    receive
        close ->
            hw:reboot(),
            hw:display("Make Your Selection", []),
            service();
        {pay, Coin} ->
            hw:return_change(Coin),
            service();
        _Other ->
            service()
    end.

    ...
```

```
code_change({payment, _Type, _Price, Paid},  _Extra) ->
    hw:return_change(Paid),
    hw:display("Make Your Selection", []),
    selection();
code_change(State, _) ->
    State().
```

In our code_change function, if a user has selected a drink and is in the process of paying for it, we return whatever amount has been paid and transition to the *selection* state. For all other states, we transition back to the state we were in prior to the upgrade. In our example, we don't need Extra, but as we are preparing the code for potential upgrades without knowing what these upgrades will be, the argument is worth including to future-proof our code and allow us to pass the variable and use it to change the process state in a later upgrade.

We place version 1.1 of the source code in the *patches* directory and compile it. Note how we started the Erlang runtime system with the -pa patches directive. When we first start the coffee FSM, this directory is empty. As we find and fix bugs, we place the new beam files here. Because this directory appears first in the code search path, beam files we put here will override beam files of the same module appearing later in the code search path. In another shell, type:

```
$ cd erlang/patches/
$ erl -make
Recompile: coffee
```

Using the same Erlang node where we started version 1.0 of the coffee FSM, we load the new version of the module by calling code:load_file/1. The code server looks for the first version of the coffee beam file in its code search path, and because the *patches* directory is at the top of list, the version we just compiled is chosen. The success of the operation is confirmed in shell command 6, showing us that the version attribute is now set to 1.1:

```
5> l(coffee).
{module,coffee}
6> coffee:module_info(attributes).
[{vsn,[1.1]}]
```

At this point, we have two versions of the coffee module loaded in the runtime system: the current one we just loaded and the old one used by the FSM process. When we order an espresso in shell command 7 and start paying for it in the subsequent command, the shell does a fully qualified call using the *current* version of the code—namely, the one we just loaded. The FSM process, however, is still using the *old* version of the coffee module.

If we were to load another version of the coffee module at this point, even 1.0, the coffee FSM process would be terminated because it is running the now deleted old version of the code. The current version would become the old version, while the newly loaded module would become the current one. We are not doing it in our example, but try it out yourself if you've compiled the code and are following along.

In shell command 9, we trigger an upgrade. This causes the coffee machine FSM, currently in state *payment*, to call `code_change/2` in the new module. It returns the change and, thanks to the new state *service*, now allows us to open and close the machine door so we can service it:

```
7> coffee:espresso().
Display:Please pay:150
{selection,espresso,150}
8> coffee:pay(100).
Display:Please pay:50
{pay,100}
9> coffee ! {upgrade, {}}.
Machine:Returned 100 in change
Display:Make Your Selection
{upgrade,{}}
10> coffee:open().
Display:Open
open
11> coffee:espresso().
{selection,espresso,150}
12> coffee:close().
Machine:Rebooted Hardware
Display:Make Your Selection
close
```

This is how basic Erlang can handle upgrades. The generic code is the handling of the `{upgrade, Extra}` message and the calling of `code_change/2`, which does a fully qualified call back to the receive-evaluate loop. This will be the same across all processes. What will differ among processes is what we do in `code_change/2` depending on the loop data, the process state, and the contents of `Extra` itself. Using these foundations, let's read on and see how we do it with OTP.

Creating a Release Upgrade

To upgrade releases using the tools and design principles provided by OTP, we have to start with a baseline consisting of a properly packaged and deployed OTP release following the principles covered in Chapter 11. We also need:

- One or more new versions of existing applications
- Zero or more new applications
- An application upgrade file for each application that has been changed
- Release resource and release upgrade files

The modules containing the bug fixes and new features are packaged into new or existing applications, where their version numbers are bumped up. Application upgrade files contain commands that tell us how to upgrade or downgrade from one application version to another. The release resource file, covered in "Release Resource Files" on page 269, is the file containing the emulator and application versions that make up the new release. Together with the application upgrade files and the release file of the baseline system we are upgrading from, the new release file is used to generate the release upgrade file. This file contains all the commands that have to be executed during the upgrade itself. After having installed the new code on the target machine, we run the instructions in the release upgrade file. If anything fails, the system is restarted using the old release. Through tests and observations, you have to determine if the system is stable. If so, it is made permanent. Restarting the system prior to it being made permanent will result in the old release being restarted. Let's do an upgrade and see how the different steps and components all work together.

In this chapter's section of the book's code repository, you will find the files used to create our first deployment. We've taken the *coffee_fsm.erl* example and created an OTP application out of it, supervisor and application behavior files included. We also created the *coffee.app* file and placed it in the *ebin* directory. Download it, compile it, and make sure you can get it up and running:

```
$ cd coffee-1.0/src ; erl -make ; mv *.beam ../ebin ; cd ../..
Recompile: coffee_app
Recompile: coffee_fsm
coffee_fsm.erl:2: Warning: undefined callback function
                          code_change/4 (behaviour 'gen_fsm')
coffee_fsm.erl:2: Warning: undefined callback function
                          handle_event/3 (behaviour 'gen_fsm')
coffee_fsm.erl:2: Warning: undefined callback function
                          handle_info/3 (behaviour 'gen_fsm')
coffee_fsm.erl:2: Warning: undefined callback function
                          handle_sync_event/4 (behaviour 'gen_fsm')
Recompile: coffee_sup
Recompile: hw
$ erl -pa coffee-1.0/ebin
Erlang/OTP 18 [erts-7.2] [smp:8:8] [async-threads:10] [kernel-poll:false]

Eshell V7.2  (abort with ^G)
1> application:start(sasl), application:start(coffee).

...<snip>...

=PROGRESS REPORT==== 10-Jan-2016::21:27:28 ===
          application: coffee
          started_at: nonode@nohost
ok
2> coffee_fsm:module_info(attributes).
[{behaviour,[gen_fsm]},{vsn,['1.0']}]
```

Even if the *coffee* application directory is not in the *lib* directory (yet), we've given it a version number for the sake of clarity. Note how, when compiling the code, we get the following warning:

```
Warning: undefined callback function
         code_change/4 (behaviour 'gen_fsm')
```

Up to now, we asked you to patiently bear with us and ignore this warning message, but no more. You should by now understand what it is for and have figured out how we are going to use it when we upgrade the coffee_fsm module. Note also how, when retrieving the module attributes in shell command 2, we get both the behavior type and the current module version number.

With our application running, let's create the boot file, a release file, and the target directory structure. We use the empty *sys.config* and *coffee-1.0.rel* files in the book's code repository. If you are typing along as you are reading this, getting your own version up and running, don't forget to update the standard OTP application and *erts* versions in the rel file to the Erlang release you are currently using. If you are not typing along, or do not have access to the code, we've included the contents of the *sys.config* and *coffee-1.0.rel* files for your convenience. If you are running the tests, based on the version of Erlang you are using, you might have to modify the standard OTP application version numbers:

```
$ cat sys.config
[].
$ cat coffee-1.0.rel
{release,
 {"coffee","1.0"},
 {erts, "7.2"},
 [{kernel, "4.1.1"},
  {stdlib, "2.7"},
  {sasl, "2.6.1"},
  {coffee, "1.0"}]]}.
$ mkdir ernie
$ erl
Erlang/OTP 18 [erts-7.2] [smp:8:8] [async-threads:10] [kernel-poll:false]

Eshell V7.2  (abort with ^G)
1> systools:make_script("coffee-1.0", [{path, ["coffee-1.0/ebin"]}]).
ok
2> systools:make_tar("coffee-1.0",[{erts, "/usr/local/lib/erlang/"},
                                    {path, ["coffee-1.0/ebin"]},
                                    {outdir, "ernie"}]).
ok
3> halt().

$ cd ernie; tar xf coffee-1.0.tar.gz; rm coffee-1.0.tar.gz
$ mkdir bin; mkdir log
$ cp erts-7.2/bin/run_erl bin/.; cp erts-7.2/bin/to_erl bin/.
$ cp erts-7.2/bin/start.src bin/start
```

```
$ cp erts-7.2/bin/start_erl.src bin/start_erl
$ perl -i -pe "s#%FINAL_ROOTDIR%#$PWD#" bin/start
$ diff erts-7.2/bin/start.src bin/start
27c27,28
< ROOTDIR=%FINAL_ROOTDIR%
---
> ROOTDIR=/Users/francescoc/ernie
$ echo '7.2 1.0' > releases/start_erl.data
```

Hello Joe, coffee machine working? Seems to be. We now need to create the *releases/RELEASES* file, required for upgrading and downgrading releases. We got away without it in the previous chapter, as it is only really required when downgrading to this release after a failed upgrade. When we do an upgrade and this file is not present, a new one is created, but it contains only information for the upgraded release. This is fine if the upgrade is successful, because when we upgrade a second time, we should be able to downgrade to the first upgraded version. The downside is that if the first upgrade fails, we are unable to downgrade to the original version once we've made the upgrade permanent, and we'll have to reinstall the node instead. Create the file as follows:

```
$ bin/start
$ bin/to_erl /tmp/
Attaching to /tmp/erlang.pipe.1 (^D to exit)

1> application:which_applications().
[{coffee,[],"1.0"},
 {sasl,"SASL  CXC 138 11","2.6.1"},
 {stdlib,"ERTS  CXC 138 10","2.7"},
 {kernel,"ERTS  CXC 138 10","4.1.1"}]
2> RootDir = code:root_dir().
"/Users/francescoc/ernie"
3> Releases = RootDir ++ "/releases".
"/Users/francescoc/ernie/releases"
4> RelFile = Releases ++ "/coffee-1.0.rel".
"/Users/francescoc/ernie/releases/coffee-1.0.rel"
5> release_handler:create_RELEASES(RootDir, Releases, RelFile, []).
ok
```

The *RELEASES* file contains a list with an entry for every release that has been installed. Every entry has information similar to that found in the rel file, including release and *erts* versions. Together with the application names and versions, however, an absolute path to the application directory is also included. While the first version of the *RELEASES* file will contain a single entry on the first release, subsequent upgrades will result in multiple entries:

```
%% File:releases/RELEASES
[{release,"coffee","1.0","7.2",
        [{kernel,"4.1.1",
                "/Users/francescoc/ernie/lib/kernel-4.1.1"},
         {stdlib,"2.7",
```

```
                        "/Users/francescoc/ernie/lib/stdlib-2.7"},
            {sasl,"2.6.1",
                    "/Users/francescoc/ernie/lib/sasl-2.6.1"},
            {coffee,"1.0",
                    "/Users/francescoc/ernie/lib/coffee-1.0"}],
        permanent}].
```

The Code to Upgrade

Now that we have our first OTP-compliant release up and running, let's create the new version of the coffee_fsm module, adding the new *service* state and its client functions. We start by bumping up the version attribute to 1.1. It might not mean much now, but if you have kept the discipline of bumping up the version (or doing it automatically through a script when tagging your code or building your release), payback time will come many upgrades later, in the early hours of the morning, when you are figuring out why the version of the code you think is running in production is actually not the one that should be running.[1]

We export the state functions service/2 and service/3 (you might recall that the gen_fsm callback State/2 handles asynchronous events and State/3 handles synchronous ones). We also export two client functions, open/0 and close/0, which asynchronously send the coffee machine door open and close events to the FSM. And finally, we export code_change/4, a behavior callback used to update the state of the behavior. All these should be familiar from reading "Adding a State" on page 323:

```
-module(coffee_fsm).
-behavior(gen_fsm).
-vsn('1.1').
-export([start_link/0, init/1]).
-export([selection/2, payment/2, remove/2, service/2]).
-export([americano/0, cappuccino/0, tea/0, espresso/0,
         pay/1, cancel/0, cup_removed/0, open/0, close/0]).
-export([stop/0, selection/3, payment/3, remove/3, service/3]).
-export([terminate/3, code_change/4]).

start_link() ->
    gen_fsm:start_link({local, ?MODULE}, ?MODULE, [], []).

...
cup_removed() -> gen_fsm:send_event(?MODULE,cup_removed).
open()         -> gen_fsm:send_event(?MODULE,open).
close()        -> gen_fsm:send_event(?MODULE,close).

...
```

---

1 Please don't ask us about this one!

In state *selection*, we handle the open event. This is the only state/event combination in which the transition to our new *service* state is allowed. In the *service* state, upon receiving the close event, we transition back to the *selection* state. In all other states, open and close events are ignored. The service/3 state callback function also handles the synchronous stop event, which stops the FSM and triggers a call to terminate/3:

```erlang
%% State: drink selection
selection({selection, Type, Price}, LoopData) ->
    hw:display("Please pay:~w",[Price]),
    {next_state, payment, {Type, Price, 0}};
selection({pay, Coin}, LoopData) ->
    hw:return_change(Coin),
    {next_state, selection, LoopData};
selection(open, LoopData) ->
    hw:display("Open", [ ]),
    {next_state, service, LoopData};
selection(_Other, LoopData) ->
    {next_state, selection, LoopData}.

%% State: service
service(close, LoopData) ->
    hw:reboot(),
    hw:display("Make Your Selection", []),
    {next_state, selection, LoopData};
service({pay, Coin}, LoopData) ->
    hw:return_change(Coin),
    {next_state, service, LoopData};
service(_Other, LoopData) ->
    {next_state, service, LoopData).

...

service(stop, _From, LoopData) ->
    {stop, normal, ok, LoopData}.

...
```

We now need to implement our new code_change/4 callback function. This callback takes three arguments when called within an event handler or a generic server, and four when called from within an FSM:

```erlang
Mod:code_change(Vsn, State, LoopData, Extra) ->
    {ok, NewState, NewLoopData} | %Finite State Machines
    {error, Reason}
Mod:code_change(Vsn, LoopData, Extra) ->
    {ok, NewLoopData} |    %Generic Servers
    {error, Reason}
Mod:code_change(Vsn, LoopData, Extra) ->
    {ok, NewLoopData} |    %Event Handler
    {error, Reason}
```

The first argument, Vsn, is the version of the old module you are upgrading from, or the version you're going to when downgrading back to the old module. In this example it is 1.0, and it could also be {down, 1.0} when downgrading to a previous version. When a module does not have a version directive, use the md5 module checksum, and when versions do not matter at all, use wildcards.

State is passed only to FSMs, and contains the state the FSM was in when the upgrade was triggered.

The final two arguments include the loop data and any extra arguments passed in the upgrade instructions specific for this module. In our example, we don't do anything with the _Extra arguments, nor do we manipulate the loop data.

The code_change/4 callback, when successful, has to return {ok, NewState, New LoopData}. Returning {error, Reason} will cause the upgrade to fail and the node to restart the previous version when dealing with generic servers or FSMs. In the case of event handlers, returning anything other than {ok, NewLoopData} or terminating abnormally will cause the handler to be removed from the event manager, but the node will not revert to its previous version and be restarted.

This is what our coffee FSM's code_change/4 OTP callback function looks like:

```
code_change('1.0', State, LoopData, _Extra) ->
    {ok, State, LoopData};
code_change({down, '1.0'}, service, LoopData, _Extra) ->
    hw:reboot(),
    hw:display("Make Your Selection", []),
    {ok, selection, LoopData};
code_change({down, '1.0'}, payment, {_Type, _Price, Paid}, _Extra) ->
    hw:return_change(Paid),
    hw:display("Make Your Selection", []),
    {ok, selection, {}};
code_change({down, '1.0'}, State, LoopData, _Extra) ->
    {ok, State, LoopData}.
```

We've changed the behavior slightly from the Erlang example. Regardless of the state we are in, *payment* included, we do not change the loop data and remain in the state we were originally in. This is normal in cases where we simply add functionality or a state. If we were to change the state or loop data as part of the upgrade, it would occur here.

If an upgrade failure triggers a downgrade and we are in the *service* state, we reboot the hardware and return to the *selection* state, because the *service* state does not exist in version 1.0. If the user is in the process of paying for a coffee, we return whatever amount the user has paid and move back to the *selection* state. Downgrades, as we will see, will cause the system to reboot and start the old version from scratch. So if your old version is dependent on some persistent values that were set at startup and later changed, make sure your code_change reverts to the correct values.

When we are done implementing the new modules, we package them in an application, bumping up the version. In our case, our new *coffee* application version is "1.1," whereas the versions of the hw, `coffee_app`, and `coffee_sup` modules are the same as in the application version. The version of the `coffee_fsm` module is now also 1.1.

Upgrading Records

The BEAM virtual machine does not have a data structure to specifically represent a record in a database sense. Instead, records are represented as tuples where the first element is an atom representing the record name and the other fields are tuple entries in the same order as they are defined. If your record format changes during a live software upgrade, the only way to update the format is using the tuple representation of records. This problem does not occur if you use maps instead of tuples. We'll show you how to change a record if you must represent it as a tuple.

Imagine a record for our frequency server of the format:

```
-record(freq, {free, allocated})
```

After initialization, in its tuple representation, it would look like this:

```
{freq, [5,6,7,8], []}
```

Assume that in our upgrade, we want to add a new field for frequencies that are blocked, making them unavailable while not being allocated. Our new record could look like this:

```
-record(freq, {free, allocated, blocked})
```

The `code_change/3` function in the new module would handle the upgrade and downgrade of the different record versions as follows:

```
code_change('1.0', {freq, Free, Alloc}, _Extra) ->
    {ok, {freq, Free, Alloc, []}};
code_change({down, '1.0'}, {freq, Free, Alloc, Blocked}, _Extra) ->
    {ok, {freq, Free++Blocked, Alloc}}.
```

When you need to change the record format in the Mnesia table, use the mnesia: `transform_table/3,4` functions. They will atomically apply a fun to all objects in the table that does the transformation, allowing you to also change the record name (not the table name) and update the attributes.

Application Upgrade Files

Now that we have the new version of our coffee machine FSM up and running, we need an application upgrade file containing a set of actions to be executed when upgrading or downgrading to other versions of the same application. Application upgrade files are similar in concept to app files, because they are used by systools to create the upgrade script. They have the name of the application with the *.appup* suffix and are placed in the *ebin* directory, alongside the app file.

Go into the Erlang root directory of your installation and type `ls lib/*/ebin/`
`*.appup`. The call will return all application upgrade files installed as part of your
Erlang release. Starting with Erlang/OTP version 17, *.appup* files are included in
every application. Prior to that, you could upgrade only some core applications, as
not all applications provided an *.appup* file. Let's have a look at the *sasl.appup* file for
its version 2.6.1:

```
{"2.6.1",
 %% Up from - max one major revision back
 [{<<"2\\.[5-6](\\.[0-9]+)*">>,[restart_new_emulator]}, % OTP-18.*
  {<<"2\\.4(\\.[0-9]+)*">>,[restart_new_emulator]}],    % OTP-17
 %% Down to - max one major revision back
 [{<<"2\\.[5-6](\\.[0-9]+)*">>,[restart_new_emulator]}, % OTP-18.*
  {<<"2\\.4(\\.[0-9]+)*">>,[restart_new_emulator]}]     % OTP-17
}.
```

Based on its contents, we should be able to figure out what happens when application
version 2.6.1 is upgrading or downgrading between OTP versions 17 and 18. When
upgrading from application version 2.4.X, 2.5.X, or 2.6, or downgrading to 2.6, 2.5.X,
or 2.4.X (where X is the patch release number), we need to restart the emulator.
Notice how regular expressions, placed in binaries, create a range of subreleases and
point to a list of upgrade and downgrade instructions. Instead of regular expressions,
you can also use strings defining specific versions, e.g., "2.4.5."

Inspect any other *.appup* files in the release you have installed and you will notice
they all follow this format:

```
{Vsn,
 [{UpFromV1, InstructionsU1}, ...,
 {UpFromVK, InstructionsUK}],
  [{DownToV1, InstructionsD1}, ...,
 {DownToVK, InstructionsDK}]}.
```

Vsn is the application version to which you are upgrading. *UpFromV<N>* are the application
versions from which you will be upgrading. In case something goes wrong,
DownToV<N> are the application versions to which you will be able to downgrade *Vsn*.
Vsn can be either a string with the exact version numbers, or a binary containing a
regular expression allowing you to describe multiple application versions on which to
execute upgrade and downgrade instructions. If you have installed OTP version 17 or
later, look at the various *.appup* files and you will notice that OTP standard applications
usually allow you to upgrade or downgrade by two revisions.

If you plan on using regular expressions, the following constructs will be more than
enough to denote ranges of versions:

- A period (.) matches any character, so the expression 1.3 will match any combination of characters starting with 1 and ending with 3.

- An asterisk (*) matches the preceding element zero or more times.

- A plus sign (+) matches the preceding element one or more times.

- A question mark (?) matches the preceding element zero or one times.

- The range [0-9] matches the elements between 0 and 9.

- The sequence \\. returns a period. You need to escape the backslash because Erlang itself uses the backslash to escape characters.

- A caret (^) at the beginning of the regular expression anchors the match to the beginning of the version string.

- A dollar sign ($) at the end of the regular expression anchors the match to the end of the version string.

As an example, <<"^1\\.[0-9]+$">> matches all versions of 1.X, <<"^1\\.0\\.[0-9]+$">> matches all versions of 1.0.X, and <<"^1\\.([0-9]+\\.)?\\.[0-9]+$">> will match versions 1.X or 1.X.X, where X is an integer.

If you are not sure of your regular expressions, test them using re:run(Vsn, RegExp), which returns nomatch if the match fails and {match, MatchData} otherwise. You can read more about the format of regular expressions in the manual pages for the re module.

Browsing the .appup files, you should have come across lists of actions associated with different versions. They include elements such as restart_new_emulator (used only when upgrading the erts, kernel, stdlib, and sasl applications), load_module, apply, restart_application, and update. In some cases, when no actions have to be taken, you will find a tuple {Vsn, [], []} with two empty lists. Actions are divided into high-level instructions and low-level ones. High-level instructions are translated to low-level ones when creating the release upgrade script.

Let's go back to our example, where we are going to upgrade the coffee FSM application from version 1.0 to 1.1. It will not be a complicated upgrade because no drivers or NIFs are involved, no new applications or modules are added to the release, and there are no interprocess and intermodule dependencies to worry about, let alone internal state or loop data changes. Behind the scenes, all we need to do is suspend all behavior processes with a dependency on the module coffee_fsm, load the new version of the module, purge the old one, call code_change, and resume the processes (Figure 12-3).

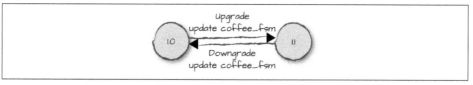

Figure 12-3. Coffee FSM version transitions

Our *coffee.appup* file contains a tuple containing the version we are upgrading to along with the high-level upgrade and downgrade instructions. In our case, update loads the new module and {advanced, {}} triggers the code_change/4 call, passing {} as the last argument:

```
%% File:coffee.appup
{"1.1",  % Current version
 [{"1.0", [{update, coffee_fsm, {advanced, {}}}]}], % Upgrade from
 [{"1.0", [{update, coffee_fsm, {advanced, {}}}]}]  % Downgrade to
 }.
```

During both an upgrade and a downgrade, the update high-level instruction will translate to the following set of low-level instructions:

1. Search for the object code for the module, load it from file, and cache it. This ensures that time-consuming file operations are done prior to suspending the processes.

2. Suspend any process that specified the module as a dependency in its child specification, using sys:suspend/1.

3. Purge any old version of the module being upgraded.

4. Load the new version of the module, making the current version the old one.

5. Purge any old version of the module, which prior to step 4 was the current version.

6. Call Mod:code_change/4.

7. Resume the suspended processes with sys:resume/1, allowing them to continue handling new requests.

So far, so good, but how do we associate a module dependency with a behavior process? Remember that in the supervisor child specification, you had to list the modules that implement the behavior:

```
{coffee_fsm, {coffee_fsm, start_link, []},
    permanent, 5000, worker, [coffee_fsm]}
```

We have to list them because this is where, during an upgrade or downgrade, sys tools tells the supervisors to suspend a particular process when upgrading one or more of its core modules. In behaviors such as event handlers and other special processes where the modules are not known at compile time, we would replace the module list with the term dynamic and query the process prior to an upgrade.

OTP needs to distinguish between dynamic and static module sets for scalability reasons. There is no point in asking millions of behaviors what modules they are running every time we do a software upgrade, only to discover they do not include the one being upgraded. Processes with dynamic modules are few and far apart, and rarely have an impact on performance when doing an upgrade. If you have dynamic children where you know millions of instances will coexist concurrently and the modules are not known at compile time, pick an upgrade strategy that scales or do not upgrade at all.

High-Level Instructions

Actions in our *.appup* file are grouped into high-level and low-level instructions, with high-level instructions being mapped to low-level ones when the upgrade scripts are generated. For the sake of simplicity (and your sanity), you are encouraged to use high-level instructions and avoid low-level ones where possible, even though they can be mixed together. Let's look at the high-level instructions in more detail:

{update, Mod}
> This instruction, and all of its variants, is used for *synchronized code replacements* where all processes dependent on Mod have to be suspended before loading the new version of the module. When it is loaded and its old version is purged, the suspended processes are resumed. This is the simplest variant of a module update command, as the code_change/3,4 behavior callbacks are not invoked. You will want to synchronize and suspend all processes with a dependency on Mod when you want all processes to consistently display the same properties toward other processes that interface with them. If you don't suspend them all prior to loading the new module, some processes might display the old behavior while others display the new one.

{update, Mod, supervisor}
> You will want to use this high-level instruction if Mod is a supervisor callback module and you are changing the supervisor specification returned by the init/1 callback function. Any change in the supervision tree needs to be handled using the supervisor:start_child/2 function if you are adding children. Use supervisor:terminate_child/2 and supervisor:delete_child/2 if you are removing children. We covered these functions in "Dynamic Children" on page 186. The update becomes even more complicated if you are changing the order in which you start the children because of rest_for_one dependencies. You will have to terminate children and restart them in the order specified in your init/1 callback function.

`{update, Mod, {advanced,Extra}}`, `{update, Mod, DepMods}`, `{update, Mod,`
`{advanced,Extra}, DepMods}`

> If we include the `{advanced,Extra}` tuple, the upgrade script invokes the
> `Mod:code_change/3,4` callback function, passing `Extra` as the last argument. You
> will need this option when the upgrade requires a change of your behavior state
> and loop data. For this and all other `update` instructions, you can omit
> `{advanced,Extra}` or replace it with `soft`, both of which result in `code_change`
> not being called. `DepMods` is a module list on which `Mod` depends. Behaviors using
> these modules will also be suspended.

`{update, Mod, {advanced,Extra}, PrePurge, PostPurge, DepMods}`

> `PrePurge` and `PostPurge` are by default set to `brutal_purge`. Use this option
> when you want processes running the old version of `Mod` to be unconditionally
> terminated before the updated module is loaded and after the module upgrade
> when the release is made permanent. You can override this behavior by setting
> `PrePurge` to `soft_purge`. If some processes are still running a version of the old
> code, `release_handler:install_release/1`, which triggers the execution of the
> *relup* file, returns `{error,{old_processes,Mod}}`. If `PostPurge` is set to
> `soft_purge`, the release handler will purge `Mod` only after the processes executing
> the old version have terminated their calls.

`{update, Mod, Timeout, {advanced,Extra}, PrePurge, PostPurge, DepMods}`

> Remember that behaviors are implemented as callback functions, so for a purge
> to fail, they must be executing in a callback for an unusually long amount of time
> or have an unusually long message queue. The default timeout value when trying
> to suspend a process is 5 seconds, but this can be overridden by setting the `Time`
> out field to an integer in milliseconds or the atom `infinity`. If a behavior does
> not respond to the `sys:suspend/1` call and the timeout is triggered, the process is
> ignored. It might later be terminated if the module it is executing is purged, or as
> the result of a runtime error when it starts running the new version of the mod-
> ule without properly going through the upgrade procedure. Use the `Timeout`
> option when, after testing your upgrades under heavy load, you see there is a
> need to increase the value.

`{update, Mod, ModType, Timeout, {advanced,Extra}, PrePurge, PostPurge,`
`DepMods}`

> By default, one of the `code_change/3,4` callback functions is executed after load-
> ing the new module. In the case of a downgrade, `code_change/3,4` is called
> before loading the module. You can override this by setting `ModType` to `static`,
> which loads the module and calls `code_change/3,4` before an upgrade or down-
> grade. If not specified, or if you want the default behavior, set `ModType` to
> `dynamic`.

`{load_module, Mod}, {load_module, Mod, DepMods}, {load_module, Mod, Pre`
`Purge, PostPurge, DepMods}`

> You want to use this low-level instruction for upgrades where you do not need to suspend the process. We refer to these upgrades as *simple code replacements*. The same applies to the instructions used for adding and deleting modules. DepMods lists all the modules that should be loaded before Mod. This argument is an empty list by default. PrePurge and PostPurge can be set to either soft_purge or brutal_purge (the default). They work the same way as they do with the update command. Use this instruction when dealing with library modules or extending functionality that does not affect running processes.

`{add_module, Mod}, {delete_module, Mod}`

> These commands translate to low-level instructions that add and delete modules between releases.

`{add_application, Application}, {add_application, Application, Type}`

> This instruction will add a new application to a release, including loading all of the modules defined in the app file and, where applicable, starting the supervision tree. The application types, covered in Chapter 9, defaults to permanent, but Type can also be set to transient, temporary, load, or none.

`{remove_application, Application}, {restart_application, Application}`

> You will want to use these commands when removing or restarting an application. Removing an application shuts down the supervision tree, deletes the modules from memory, and stops the application. If the upgrade or downgrade requires an application restart, this high-level command will translate to commands that stop and start the application and its supervision tree. You usually find application restarts in *.appup* files belonging to noncore OTP applications such as tools and libraries that can be restarted without affecting traffic in the live system.

You can mix high- and low-level instructions in the same *.appup* file, but for the vast majority of use cases, high-level instructions will be enough as most of your actions can be completed with them. We cover low-level instructions in the next section, as soon as we've done our first upgrade.

Release Upgrade Files

Now that we have our *coffee.appup* file and understand what the high-level instructions do, let's use this knowledge to generate an upgrade package. The first step is to create a new boot file using systools:make_script/2. It is not used for the upgrade itself, but is part of the package we deploy in case the upgraded node has to be rebooted (for whatever reason) after the upgrade. In the second shell command, we create a release upgrade file called *relup*, which is placed in the current working directory.

This file is generated using the emulator and application versions specified in the rel and *.appup* files, using them to retrieve and map high- and low-level instructions in the *.appup* files to a sequence of low-level ones. Compile all the code in your *coffee-1.1* application directory, and run the following commands:

```
1> systools:make_script("coffee-1.1", [{path, ["coffee-1.1/ebin"]}]).
ok
2> systools:make_relup("coffee-1.1", ["coffee-1.0"],["coffee-1.0"],
                        [{path, ["coffee*/ebin"]}]).
ok
3> systools:make_tar("coffee-1.1",
                      [{path, ["coffee-1.1/ebin"]},
                       {outdir, "ernie/releases"}]).
ok
```

In our third shell command, we create the tar file *coffee-1.1.tar.gz*. It contains the *lib* and *releases* directories specified in *coffee-1.1.rel*. Calling make_tar/2 picks up the *relup*, *start.boot*, and *sys.config* files automatically and creates a version 1.1 directory under *releases*. Note that, unlike in our first installation, we did not include the erts option. We are going to use the one already installed.

Let's look at the *relup* file more closely now that the low-level instructions have been generated. We explain them all in "Low-Level Instructions" on page 342, but even without having covered them, you should get a good idea of what is going on:

```
{"1.1",
 [{"1.0",[],
   [{load_object_code,{coffee,"1.1",[coffee_fsm]}},
    point_of_no_return,
    {suspend,[coffee_fsm]},
    {load,{coffee_fsm,brutal_purge,brutal_purge}},
    {code_change,up,[{coffee_fsm,{}}]},
    {resume,[coffee_fsm]}]}],
 [{"1.0",[],
   [{load_object_code,{coffee,"1.0",[coffee_fsm]}},
    point_of_no_return,
    {suspend,[coffee_fsm]},
    {code_change,down,[{coffee_fsm,{}}]},
    {load,{coffee_fsm,brutal_purge,brutal_purge}},
    {resume,[coffee_fsm]}]}]}.
```

Before covering the low-level commands in more detail, let's look at the systools:make_relup/3,4 call we used to generate the file itself:

```
systools:make_relup(RelName, UpFromList, DownToList, [Options]) ->
    ok | error | {ok,Relup,Module,Warnings} | {error,Module,Error}
```

The call takes RelName, the name of a release to which we are upgrading or downgrading. This points to the *RelName.rel* file, used to determine the version of the Erlang runtime system and the versions of the various applications. RelName can also be a tuple {RelName, Descr}, where Descr is a term that is included in the upgrade and downgrade instructions, returned by the function installing the release on the target machine.

The second and third arguments, UpFromList and DownToList, include the list of releases we want to upgrade from or downgrade to, respectively. They are all names that point to a specific version of a rel file used to determine which applications need to be added, removed, or upgraded. Using their respective *.app* and *.appup* files, the call also determines the sequence of commands that need to be executed. The fourth, optional, argument is a list of options that may include:

{path, DirList}
: Adds paths listed in DirList to the code search path. You can include wildcards in your path, so the asterisk in "lib/*/ebin" will expand to contain all of the subdirectories in *lib* containing an *ebin* directory. The code search path of the node creating the *relup* file must have paths to the old and the new versions of the *.rel* and *.app* files, as well as a path to the new *.appup* and *.beam* files.

{outdir, Dir}
: Puts the *relup* file in Dir instead of the current working directory.

restart_emulator
: Generates low-level instructions that reboot the node after an upgrade or downgrade.

silent
: Returns a tuple of the format {ok, Relup, Module, Warnings} or {error, Module, Error} instead of printing results to I/O. Use this option when calling systools functions from scripts or integrating the call in your build process where you need to handle errors.

noexec
: Returns the same values as the silent option, but without generating a *relup* file.

warnings_as_errors
: Treats warnings as errors and refuses to generate the *relup* script if warnings occur.

The format of the *relup* file itself is similar to the *.appup* file:

```
{Vsn,
  [{UpFromV1, Descr, InstructionsU1}, ...,
 {UpFromVK, Descr, InstructionsUK}],
  [{DownToV1, Descr, InstructionsD1}, ...,
 {DownToVK, Descr, InstructionsDK}]}.
```

The Descr term contains a term passed in the {RelName, Descr} tuple of the systools:make_relup/3,4 call. If Descr was omitted from the call, it defaults to an empty list. You will notice this in our example, as we left it out for the coffee machine *relup* example. `Descr` becomes relevant when automating the installation of the upgrade on the target machine, as its values can be used by the programs or scripts installing the upgrade.

Low-Level Instructions

Relup files consist of low-level instruction sets generated from the *.appup* files. For complex upgrades, you can write your files using low-level instructions or edit generated ones by hand. Low-level instructions consist of the following:

`{load_object_code, {Application, Vsn, ModuleList}}`
: Reads all the modules from the `Application` *ebin* directory, but does not load them into the runtime system. This instruction is executed prior to suspending the behaviors and special processes. This differs from the high-level instruction `load` that not only loads the module, but also makes it available to the runtime.

`point_of_no_return`
: This instruction should appear once in the *relup* script and should be placed where the system cannot recover after failing to execute one or more of the instructions in the *relup* file. Crashes occurring after this instruction will result in the old version of the system being restarted. It is usually placed after the `load_object_code` instruction.

`{load, {Module, PrePurge, PostPurge}}`
: Makes a module that has been loaded using `load_object_code` the current version. `PrePurge` and `PostPurge` can be set to `soft_purge` or `brutal_purge` (the default).

`{apply, {Mod, Func, ArgList}}`
: Calls `apply(Mod, Func, ArgList)`. If the `apply` is executed before the point of no return and fails or returns (or throws) `{error,Error}`, the call to `release_handler:install_release/1` returns `{error,{'EXIT',Reason}}` or `{error,Error}`, respectively. If it's executed after the point of no return and fails, the system is restarted with the old version of the release. This instruction could be used instead of the `code_change/3,4` callback function.

`{remove, {Module, PrePurge, PostPurge}}`
: Used together with `load` and `purge`. This instruction makes the current version of `Module` old.

`{purge, ModuleList}`
: Purges the old versions of all modules in `ModuleList`. Behaviors and special processes executing the old version of the code being purged are terminated.

`{suspend, [Module | {Module, Timeout}]}`
Suspends behaviors that depend on the `Module` list. `Timeout` is an integer in milliseconds or the atoms `default` (set to 5 seconds) or `infinity`. If the call to `sys:suspend/1` does not return within `Timeout`, the process is ignored but not terminated.

`{resume, ModuleList}`
Resumes suspended processes that depend on modules listed in `ModuleList`.

`{code_change, [{Module, Extra}]}, {code_change, Mode, [{Module, Extra}]}`
Triggers the `Module:code_change/3,4` call, passing `Extra` in all behavior processes running `Module`. `Mode` is up or down, defining the call as either an upgrade or a downgrade. If omitted, `Mode` defaults to up.

`{stop, ModuleList}`
This instruction results in the `supervisor:terminate_child/2` call for all behaviors with a dependency on one of the modules specified in `ModuleList`.

`{start, ModuleList}`
Starts all stopped processes with a dependency on a module in `ModuleList` by calling `supervisor:restart_child/2`.

`restart_new_emulator`
This instruction is used when upgrading the emulator or the *kernel, stdlib*, and *sasl* core applications. The emulator needs to be restarted right after upgrading these applications, but before executing the remainder of the *relup* file. All other applications will be restarted with their old versions running in the new emulator and upgraded when running the remainder of the *relup* file in the new emulator. When different processes end up running different application versions in this manner, non–backward-compatibility clashes between them can occur, so ensure all possible scenarios in your upgrade procedure have been properly tested before using this technique. If you are worried about the order of your low-level instructions, use high-level ones and let `systools:make_relup/3,4` generate the *relup* file. This instruction should be executed only once during the upgrade.

`restart_emulator`
This instruction is used when an emulator restart is required as part of an upgrade that does not involve the core applications or an emulator upgrade. It may appear only once in the *relup* file and has to be the last instruction.

Installing an Upgrade

Let's go back to the *coffee-1.1.tar.gz* file we generated and use it for our live upgrade. We assume that it has been placed in the *releases* directory of the target environment.

From the *ernie* root directory, we connect to the `coffee_fsm` node that we left running version 1.0. If it is not running, start it with `bin/start`. We unpack the new release using the `release_handler:unpack_release/1` call, uncompressing all the files, adding the *coffee-1.1* application to the *lib* directory, and creating the version 1.1 directory in the *releases* directory. We can see in shell commands 2 and 3 that after unpacking the new release it resides alongside 1.0, and that 1.0 is still running:

```
$ bin/to_erl /tmp/
Attaching to /tmp/erlang.pipe.1 (^D to exit)

1> release_handler:unpack_release("coffee-1.1").
{ok, "1.1"}
2> release_handler:which_releases().
[{"coffee","1.1",
  ["kernel-4.1.1","stdlib-2.7","sasl-2.6.1","coffee-1.1"],
  unpacked},
 {"coffee","1.0",
  ["kernel-4.1.1","stdlib-2.7","sasl-2.6.1","coffee-1.0"],
  permanent}]
3> application:which_applications().
[{coffee,"Coffee Machine Controller","1.0"},
 {sasl,"SASL  CXC 138 11","2.6.1"},
 {stdlib,"ERTS  CXC 138 10","2.7"},
 {kernel,"ERTS  CXC 138 10","4.1.1"}]
4> coffee_fsm:espresso().
Display:Please pay:150
ok
5> coffee_fsm:pay(100).
Display:Please pay:50
ok
6> release_handler:install_release("1.1").
{ok,"1.0",[]}
7> coffee_fsm:cancel().
Display:Make Your Selection
ok
Machine:Returned 100 in change
8> coffee_fsm:open().
ok
Display:Open
9> coffee_fsm:close().
Machine:Rebooted Hardware
Display:Make Your Selection
ok
10> application:which_applications().
[{coffee,"Coffee Machine Controller","1.1"},
 {sasl,"SASL  CXC 138 11","2.6.1"},
 {stdlib,"ERTS  CXC 138 10","2.7"},
 {kernel,"ERTS  CXC 138 10","4.1.1"}]
11> init:restart().
ok
12>
```

```
Erlang/OTP 18 [erts-7.2] [smp:8:8] [async-threads:10] [kernel-poll:false]

...<snip>...

Eshell V7.2  (abort with ^G)
1> application:which_applications().
[{coffee,"Coffee Machine Controller","1.0"},
 {sasl,"SASL  CXC 138 11","2.6.1"},
 {stdlib,"ERTS  CXC 138 10","2.7"},
 {kernel,"ERTS  CXC 138 10","4.1.1"}]
```

Next, we upgrade the release by executing the release_handler:install_release/1 call. If issues arise and a restart is triggered, the system will reboot and revert to the old version. If the system is stable, the current (new) version is made permanent by calling release_handler:make_permanent/1.

We then use the new client functions we've added to test the transition to and from state *service* before rebooting the node in shell command 11. Because we never made the release permanent, the node restarts version 1.0.

Next, in shell commands 2 and 3, we reinstall the release and make it permanent. At this point, we do not need files specific to 1.0 anymore. Unused releases can be removed from the system using the release_handler:remove_release/1 call. The call removes the applications that are only part of that release from the *lib* directory, removes the directory from *releases*, and updates the *RELEASES* file there. To revert back to the old version we have to reinstall it, covering all the steps we've just described, including creating an *.appup* file for version 1.0 of the coffee application, a *relup* file, and a tar file:

```
2> release_handler:install_release("1.1").
{ok,"1.0",[]}
3> release_handler:make_permanent("1.1").
ok
4> release_handler:remove_release("1.0").
ok
5> release_handler:which_releases().
[{"coffee","1.1",
  ["kernel-4.1.1","stdlib-2.7","sasl-2.6.1","coffee-1.1"],
  permanent}]
6> halt().
[End]
$ ls lib/
coffee-1.1 kernel-4.1.1 sasl-2.6.1 stdlib-2.7
```

That's it! A software upgrade during runtime, with the ability to fall back to old releases when issues occur or remove them when they are no longer needed.

The release handler is intended to work with embedded target systems. If you use it with simple target systems, you need to ensure the correct boot and config files are used in the case of a restart. How you do it is entirely up to you. You could replace existing files or have OS environment variables pointing to the correct ones.

The Release Handler

We introduced the SASL application in Chapter 9. It is one of the core OTP applications that has to be part of every release because it contains tools required to build, install, and upgrade the release itself. If you looked at SASL's supervision tree (Figure 12-4), you might have noticed the release handler process. It is responsible for unpacking, installing, and upgrading releases locally on each node. It also removes them and makes them permanent. We used the release handler and went through these phases in our example.

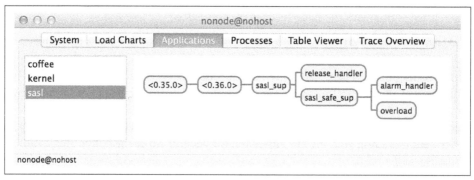

Figure 12-4. The release handler process

The release handler assumes a release tar file, created using `systools:make_tar/1,2` and placed in the *releases* directory. Each release version can be in one of the following states, as seen in Figure 12-5: *unpacked, current, permanent,* and *old*. State transitions occur when functions in the `release_handler` module are called or a release that has not been made permanent fails, triggering a system restart. At any one time, there is always a release that is either current or permanent. Let's look at the functions exported by the `release_handler` module, including those that trigger the transition more closely.

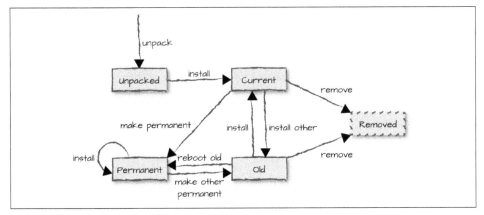

Figure 12-5. Managing a release

When dealing with your first target installation, the release handler becomes relevant only if Erlang is already installed on the target machine. As it wasn't when we created the first `coffee_fsm` release, everything had to be done manually. If you follow the steps, you will notice that the first call we did once version 1.0 of the system was up and running was to create the *RELEASES* file:

```
release_handler:create_RELEASES(Root, RelDir, RelFile, AppDirs) ->
    ok | {error, Reason}
```

This call creates the first version of the *RELEASES* file, stored in the *releases* directory. It contains the persistent state of the release handler, which includes the release applications, their versions, and their absolute paths. The Erlang VM executing this function must have permission to write to the *releases* directory. `Root` is the Erlang root directory, while `RelDir` is the path pointing to the *releases* directory. The *releases* directory is often located in the Erlang root directory, but you can override this by setting the OS or OTP environment variables described in "Release Directory Structure" on page 265. `RelFile` points to the release file located in the *releases* directory, while `AppDirs` is a list of {`App, Vsn, Dir`} tuples used to override the applications stored in *lib*. It is most commonly used when distributing Erlang in OS-specific packages and not OTP ones. This function unpacks the *Name.tar.gz* file located in the *releases* directory:

```
release_handler:unpack_release(Name) ->
    {ok, Vsn} | {error, Reason}
```

It checks that all mandatory files and directories are present, adding the applications in the *lib* and *release* directories under *releases*. It fails if the string `Name` is an existing release, or if there are issues unpacking or reading the mandatory files and directories. When we have unpacked the release, `install_release/1,2` triggers the software upgrade (or downgrade), executing the instructions specified in the *relup* file:

```
release_handler:install_release(Vsn)
release_handler:install_release(Vsn, OptList) ->
    {ok, OtherVsn, Descr} | {error, Reason} |
    {continue_after_restart, OtherVsn, Descr}
```

OptList is a list of options that allow us to override some of the default settings. They include:

- {error_action, restart | reboot} to specify if the runtime system is rebooted (init:reboot()) or restarted (init:restart()) as the result of an upgrade failure.

- {suspend_timeout, Timeout} to override the default (5-second) timeout for the sys:suspend/1 call, used to suspend a process prior to upgrading the code.

- {code_change_timeout, Timeout} to override the default (5-second) timeout for the sys:change_code/4 call, used to tell a suspended process to upgrade the code.

- {update_paths, Bool}, used when overriding the default *lib/App-Vsn* directory provided in the AppDirs argument in the create_RELEASES/4 call. Setting Bool to true will cause all code paths of the applications in AppDirs to be changed, including applications that are not being upgraded. Setting it to its default value of false will cause only the paths of the upgraded applications to be changed.

You might recall that the *relup* file contains tuples of the format {Vsn, Descr, Instructions}. Descr is part of the return value when the upgrade or downgrade was successful. If {continue_after_restart, OtherVsn, Descr} is returned, the runtime system and the core applications are being upgraded, requiring an emulator restart before the remainder of the script is executed.

If errors we can recover from have occurred, {error, Reason} is returned. Recoverable errors include Vsn already being the permanent release or the *relup* file missing, along with others that will result in the installation of the release failing, but not requiring a node restart. If the upgrade fails due to an unrecoverable error, the node is restarted or rebooted.

Installing releases and upgrading code can be a risky and time-consuming operation. This function mitigates risks of issues happening, checking if Vsn can be installed, ensuring that all mandatory files are available and accessible, as well as evaluating all low-level instructions in the *relup* file prior to the point_of_no_return:

```
release_handler:check_install_release(Vsn)
release_handler:check_install_release(Vsn,Options) ->
    ok | {error, Reason}
```

`Options` is a list containing `[purge]`, which soft purges the code when doing the checks. This will speed up the installation of the release itself, as all modules are soft purged prior to the upgrade itself.

When we have installed a new release and executed the instructions in the *relup* file, we keep the nodes under observation, possibly running diagnostic tests. If there are issues, restarting the node will use the old boot file and cause a restart of the old version. Calling `make_permanent/1`, makes the boot script that points to the upgraded release be the one used when rebooting or restarting the node. This call can fail for a variety of reasons, including `Vsn` not being the current version or not being a release at all:

```
release_handler:make_permanent(Vsn) -> ok | {error, Reason}
```

If a release has been made permanent, files specific to old releases can be removed. Calling `remove_release/1` will delete old applications no longer in use, with the `Vsn` directory containing the *.rel*, *.boot*, and *sys.config* files in the *releases/Vsn* directory. This call also upgrades the available releases in the *RELEASES* file. It fails if `Vsn` is a permanent or nonexisting release:

```
release_handler:remove_release(Vsn) -> ok | {error, Reason}
```

Houston, we have a problem. If your current release is not operating as expected and you need to revert to an old release (which you have not removed), this call reboots the runtime system with the old boot file, making it the new, permanent version:

```
release_handler:reboot_old_release(Vsn) -> ok | {error, Reason}
```

This call uses the *RELEASES* file and returns all the releases known to the release handler. `Status` is one of `unpacked`, `current`, `permanent`, or `old`:

```
release_handler:which_releases(Status)
release_handler:which_releases() -> [{Name, Vsn, Apps, Status}]
```

The `release_handler` module exports functions that make it possible to upgrade and downgrade single applications, creating a release upgrade script on the fly and evaluating it. These functions (which we are not covering in this book) are meant to facilitate and automate testing of application upgrades. They should not be used in production systems, as the changes are not persistent in the case of system restarts.

It is possible to install upgrades without the release handler while keeping its view consistent and up to date. This functionality comes in handy when dealing with OS-specific packages, when you do deployments and upgrades with other tools, or even when you write your own. There are functions that allow us to inform the release handler process of the addition and removal of releases and release-specific files. You can read about these functions as well as the ability to upgrade and downgrade single applications in the `release_handler` manual pages that come with the standard Erlang distribution.

Upgrading Environment Variables

When upgrading your release, the new package will include the new (and mandatory) *sys.config*. It will also contain a new app file for every new and upgraded application. These files might contain new or updated application environment variables, or if the files are no longer needed, they will have been omitted altogether. During the upgrade, the application controller will compare old environment variables with their current counterparts in the start scripts (set with the -*application key value* flag), config files, and app files, updating any differences accordingly. When done, the following callback function is called in the new application callback module, prior to resuming the processes:

```
Module:config_change(Updated, New, Deleted)
```

Updated, New, and Deleted are lists of {Key, Value} tuples, where each key is an environment variable and the value is what you want the variable set to. This is an optional callback that can be omitted, but is useful when process states depend on environment variables read at startup.

Making a release permanent will change the *sys.config* file pointed to by the start scripts to the new version. It is done only now because rebooting a node with a release that is not permanent reverts back to the previous release.

Upgrading Special Processes

Upgrading special processes is no different from upgrading behaviors. If you are doing a simple code replacement, load the new module through the add_module instruction. If the upgrade has to be a synchronized code replacement, use the same update high-level instruction you would use for OTP behaviors. Upon receiving a message of the format {system, From, Msg}, the special process invokes proc_lib:handle_system_msg/6, which suspends the process. (We covered system messages in "System Messages" on page 249.) If the update command had the {advanced,Extra} parameter in its Change field, the following callback function is called in the special process callback module:

```
Mod:system_code_change(LoopData, Module, Vsn, Extra) ->
    {ok, NewLoopData}
```

This call returns the tuple {ok, NewLoopData}. Module is the name of the callback module, and Vsn is either the version to which you are upgrading or, in the case of a downgrade, {downgrade, Vsn}. Vsn is a string in both cases.

One final note: remember the system message {get_modules, From} that special processes have to handle when they are not aware of their dependent modules? Those for which we use the dynamic atom in the supervisor specification, covered in "Dynamic Modules and Hibernating" on page 255? When upgrading, all processes whose child specifications in the supervisor have module dependencies set to dynamic reply to such a message with From!{modules, ModuleList}, containing the list of modules on which the special process currently depends. This will inform the release handler coordinating synchronized upgrades if this special process is part of a dependency chain and should be suspended during the upgrade of a particular module.

Upgrading in Distributed Environments

Synchronized software upgrades in distributed environments? Is that possible? Are we crazy enough to try it? If you have a small cluster, trust your network, and have dependencies connected to your upgrade across your nodes, then why not? Remember that distributed Erlang was originally intended for clusters that ran behind firewalls in the same data center, and more often than not, also in the same subrack. If you were upgrading a switch, distributed Erlang often ran on the same backplane the switch was controlling, so if you lost your network, there was nothing to control because you also lost your switch.

In a small cluster with a few nodes running in the same subrack, you have little to worry about. For larger clusters, clusters across data centers, or where networks are unreliable, devise a strategy to upgrade a node without the need to synchronize.

Enough warnings. Let's drink some Red Bull and get on with it. If you include the sync_nodes low-level instruction in your *.appup* file, the *relup* script that gets generated will synchronize with the other nodes also waiting to be upgraded and upgrade them too when they are also attempting to synchronize.

Synchronization is triggered by one of the following instructions:

```
{sync_nodes, Id, NodeList}
{sync_nodes, Id, {Mod,Func,ArgList}}
```

You can either hardcode NodeList in the *.appup* file, as in the first instruction, or use the second instruction to invoke apply(Mod, Func, ArgList) to get the list of nodes that recognize Id, which are the nodes to synchronize. Id can be any valid Erlang term. For the synchronization to be successful, remote nodes must be executing the same instruction with the same Id.

If you lose connectivity toward a remote node with which you are attempting to synchronize, either because of a network partition or because the remote node crashed, the node is restarted with the old release. There is no timeout, so if a remote node is not being upgraded or is out of sync, the local node attempting to upgrade will hang until all remote nodes have executed sync_nodes or connectivity toward one of the nodes is lost. This is why the technique in this section has some risks for nodes distributed across a wide-area network.

If you have not synchronized your upgrades properly, your cluster will hang waiting for all the other nodes. And if there are issues with your network connectivity or the upgrade in one of the other nodes fails, you will trigger a series of node restarts that will hopefully recover and continuing running the old release. But in the worst case, this technique might cause a cascading failure where you knock out one node after another when they fail to cope with the restart. You have been warned! Use synchronized distributed upgrades only when it is safe and the use case motivates it. If in doubt, perform rolling upgrades across your cluster instead, one node at a time, after making sure that nodes running the new release are interoperable with those still running the old.

Upgrading the Emulator and Core Applications

You upgrade the emulator and the core applications by providing their new versions in the new release file. The rest is taken care of for you when generating the *relup* file. Just remember to include the erts option in the systools:make_tar/2 call when upgrading the Erlang runtime system, as it will include the emulator in the new tar file. If you think it sounds simple, it is, but there are a few catches of which you need to be aware.

Upgrading the emulator and core applications (*erts*, *kernel*, *stdlib*, and *sasl*) requires a restart of the virtual machine, usually triggered by the restart_new_emulator instruction. Unlike with other upgrades, this will be the first instruction executed in the file, starting the new emulator and the new core applications, together with the old versions of the remaining applications. This two-phase approach allows the remaining behaviors and special processes being upgraded to call code_change as part of their upgrade, using new versions of the core applications while doing so.

If you are not happy with this approach, you can edit the *relup* file by hand. Replacing restart_new_emulator with the restart_emulator instruction will restart the emulator with the new versions for all applications. A restart of the emulator (which is not the new emulator) is the last instruction you should be executing in your *relup* file, as all it does is restart the system with the new boot file. This means that any instructions that follow restart_emulator are ignored, while any instructions before it are executed with the old emulator. A helpful instruction you have to add manually is apply, which you could use instead of code_change if opting to start the new versions of the applications directly.

Non–backward-Compatible Upgrades and Downgrades

There will be times when, as a result of the restart_new_emulator instruction, you restart old applications that you plan on subsequently upgrading with the new core applications. If the upgrade spans several releases, you might run the risk of your

---

noncore applications calling deprecated functions in the core applications that have since been removed. Deprecated functions are kept for two major releases, with warnings printed out when you compile the code that uses them, after which you can safely remove the functions. The solution is to replace any deprecated functions as soon as possible, and upgrade in several steps while testing the upgrades to ensure that all applications are forward-compatible.

If you are still running an emulator version older than R15 (and we know many of you are), you might run into problems when downgrading, as an attempt to load the new versions of the beam files will be made after restarting the old emulator. If you are affected, compile your new code with the old emulator and its corresponding version of the compiler.

In both of these edge cases, testing upgrades and downgrades is critical and will at a very early stage highlight any potential issues and incompatibilities.

Upgrades with Rebar3

Now that you understand all the details of upgrades, let's look at how to do them using the *rebar3* tool introduced in "Rebar3" on page 303. First, let's use *rebar3* to build a release, starting again with the code from *coffee-1.0*. The required commands are similar to those we used in "Rebar3" on page 303:

```
$ mkdir ernie
$ cd ernie2
$ rebar3 new release coffee desc="Coffee Machine Controller"
$ cd coffee
$ perl -i -pe 's/0\.1\.0/1.0/' ./apps/coffee/src/coffee.app.src ./rebar.config
$ cp <path-to-coffee-1.0>/coffee-1.0/src/*.erl apps/coffee/src
$ rebar3 as prod compile
===> Verifying dependencies...
===> Compiling coffee
_build/default/lib/coffee/src/coffee_fsm.erl:2:
  Warning: undefined callback function code_change/4 (behaviour 'gen_fsm')
_build/default/lib/coffee/src/coffee_fsm.erl:2:
  Warning: undefined callback function handle_event/3 (behaviour 'gen_fsm')
_build/default/lib/coffee/src/coffee_fsm.erl:2:
  Warning: undefined callback function handle_info/3 (behaviour 'gen_fsm')
_build/default/lib/coffee/src/coffee_fsm.erl:2:
  Warning: undefined callback function handle_sync_event/4 (behaviour 'gen_fsm')
$ rebar3 as prod release
===> Verifying dependencies...
===> Compiling coffee
...<snip>....
===> Starting relx build process ...
===> Resolving OTP Applications from directories:
          /Users/francescoc/ernie2/coffee/_build/prod/lib
          /Users/francescoc/ernie2/coffee/apps
          /usr/local/lib/erlang/lib
```

```
                    /Users/francescoc/ernie2/coffee/_build/prod/rel
===> Resolved coffee-1.0
===> Including Erts from /usr/local/lib/erlang
===> release successfully created!
```

We use the *rebar3* release template to set up an area for our *coffee* application, change
the version number to 1.0, copy our *coffee-1.0* sources into the new release area, run
`rebar3 compile` to verify that the code is valid (which, as we saw previously, results
in compilation warnings from compiling *coffee_fsm.erl* due to missing callback functions), and then build a release using the `prod` profile. We can now start our release to
make sure it runs correctly:

```
$ ./_build/prod/rel/coffee/bin/coffee console
...<snip>....
Machine:Rebooted Hardware
Display:Make Your Selection

=PROGRESS REPORT==== 24-Jan-2016::16:06:10 ===
          supervisor: {local,sasl_safe_sup}
             started: [{pid,<0.213.0>},
                       {id,alarm_handler},
                       {mfargs,{alarm_handler,start_link,[]}},
                       {restart_type,permanent},
                       {shutdown,2000},
                       {child_type,worker}]
...<snip>....
=PROGRESS REPORT==== 24-Jan-2016::16:06:10 ===
         application: sasl
          started_at: coffee@francescoc
Eshell V7.2  (abort with ^G)
(coffee@francescoc)1> application:which_applications().
[{sasl,"SASL  CXC 138 11","2.6.1"},
 {coffee,"Coffee Machine Controller","1.0"},
 {stdlib,"ERTS  CXC 138 10","2.7"},
 {kernel,"ERTS  CXC 138 10","4.1.1"}]
```

This gives us a release for *coffee* version 1.0. Next, we need a release for version 1.1, so
we copy that version of *coffee_fsm.erl* into our source directory, bump our version
numbers, and then generate a new release:

```
$ cp <path-to-coffee-1.1>/coffee-1.1/src/coffee_fsm.erl apps/coffee/src
$ perl -i -pe 's/1\.0/1.1/' ./apps/coffee/src/coffee.app.src ./rebar.config
$ rebar3 as prod release
===> Verifying dependencies...
===> Compiling coffee
...<snip>....
===> Resolved coffee-1.1
===> Including Erts from /usr/local/lib/erlang
===> release successfully created!
```

Before we can generate a *relup* file, we need our *coffee.appup* file. Because *rebar3* doesn't create an *ebin* directory in the usual place, we create one, copy the *coffee.appup* file there, and then use the rebar3 relup command:

```
$ mkdir apps/coffee/ebin
$ cp <path-to-coffee-1.1>/coffee-1.1/ebin/coffee.appup apps/coffee/ebin
$ rebar3 as prod relup
===> Verifying dependencies...
===> Compiling coffee
===> Starting relx build process ...
...<snip>....
===> Resolved coffee-1.1
===> Including Erts from /usr/local/lib/erlang
===> release successfully created!
===> Starting relx build process ...
...<snip>....
===> Resolved coffee-1.1
===> relup successfully created!
```

If we look at the contents of the generated *relup* file, we find that it's identical to that generated by systools:make_relup/4 in "Release Upgrade Files" on page 339:

```
$ cat ./_build/prod/rel/coffee/relup
{"1.1",
 [{"1.0",[],
   [{load_object_code,{coffee,"1.1",[coffee_fsm]}},
    point_of_no_return,
    {suspend,[coffee_fsm]},
    {load,{coffee_fsm,brutal_purge,brutal_purge}},
    {code_change,up,[{coffee_fsm,{}}]},
    {resume,[coffee_fsm]}]}],
 [{"1.0",[],
   [{load_object_code,{coffee,"1.0",[coffee_fsm]}},
    point_of_no_return,
    {suspend,[coffee_fsm]},
    {code_change,down,[{coffee_fsm,{}}]},
    {load,{coffee_fsm,brutal_purge,brutal_purge}},
    {resume,[coffee_fsm]}]}]}.
```

From here, you can create a tarball with rebar3 as prod tar and install and upgrade as shown in "Installing an Upgrade" on page 343.

Assuming you use *rebar3* as your build and release tool, it's worth your while to check out the *relflow* (*https://github.com/RJ/relflow*) tool, written by Richard Jones. It is purpose-built for systems that use Git for version control and *rebar3* to generate releases and upgrades, and it is designed to address all the tedious parts of upgrades, such as bumping version numbers and creating *.appup* files.

Summing Up

As with most things we've seen in this book, Erlang provides powerful basic language constructs that OTP uses to build libraries and frameworks that hide complexity, simplifying the development, deployment, and maintenance of Erlang-based systems. Starting with `code:load_file/1`, which handles the loading of a module in your runtime system, we looked at how to manage state changes in processes, database schema changes together with synchronization of processes and their dependencies, and dependencies in distributed environments.

In order to upgrade a target system, you need to start with a baseline installation. It will usually be the first release, the one you created manually. Unless you were using *rebar3*, it has to be a manual task, because most of the release-upgrade tools are written in Erlang and will not run without your baseline system. It's a classic chicken-and-egg problem.

With the baseline release in place, you need to follow these steps to successfully upgrade your system. Don't panic, as a lot of these steps are either automated, handled by existing tools, or both:

- Add the new functionality, package it into the respective modules and applications, and bump up the module and application versions.
- Create the new *rel* file containing new and upgraded applications while omitting the deleted ones.
- Generate your start scripts and new *sys.config* file, ensuring you can boot the new release on its own.
- If any of your behaviors or special processes require a state change or use a different data format (including database schema changes) as part of the upgrade, migrate your state and data format from the old version to the new one and back in your `code_change` functions.
- Write an *.appup* file for each application you are upgrading. Place these files in the *ebin* directory.
- Create a *relup* file containing all the low-level instructions executed during the upgrade.
- Create a package that you can deploy in the *releases* directory of the installation you are upgrading.
- Unpack the release and install it.
- If stable, make your new release permanent. If unstable, reboot the node, restarting the old release.

Once the release is unpacked, a number of transitions can take place on the node being upgraded. When you install a release and the upgrade is successful, the system starts running the new version. If the upgrade fails for any reason, the system is rebooted and reverts to the previous version. When running the new version, it can be made permanent. When this happens, any subsequent node restart will restart the latest version (Figure 12-6).

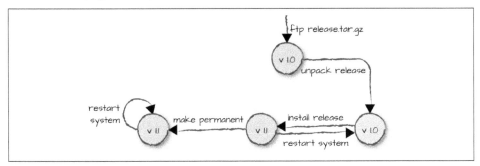

Figure 12-6. Upgrading a release

We also covered upgrades in distributed environments, which allow you to synchronize the nodes. This happens in the real world, but only for very small clusters where the network is reliable. If you are dealing with distributed data centers, cloud computing, virtualization, as well as lots of other layers of complexity and instability, you need to take a different approach to upgrades. Make sure that old and new nodes are backward-compatible and interoperable with each other, allowing them to coexist in the same cluster. Upgrade a few nodes, monitor them to ensure all is well, and keep on upgrading. If you lose a few machines or get a network partition or upgrade failures, keep on trying until all nodes have been successfully upgraded.

Let's take this argument a step further. For clusters where you have no single point of failure with multiple instances of the nodes running, do live upgrades really make sense? If you are able to do a rolling upgrade, cleanly shutting down nodes without losing any requests and stopping traffic, isn't it easier to shut down one node at a time, upgrade its code, then restart it to bring it back into the cluster? You would be able to upgrade your code without showing the embarrassing *Our system is down for maintenance, bear with us, we are doing this because your business is important and we value you as a customer* screen most online banks show us a little too frequently, and ensuring that you do not lose any requests as a result of the upgrade.

How you do your upgrades depends entirely on the size of your cluster, the infrastructure you have in place to control it, your redundant capacity, and the experience and size of your team. Software upgrades take time and money to implement, test, and deploy. And if things go wrong, most of the time, they will go wrong during an upgrade. If you are a startup that does not have to provide 99.999% availability, no one will care whether you bounce your nodes every now and then. If you are upgrading tens of thousands of switches, however, where each switch handles traffic for millions of subscribers with contractual penalties for downtime and outages, or an e-commerce site generating thousands of dollars in revenue every minute, users will care!

Software upgrades are a unique and powerful feature you can use in rare, but critical, moments. Use them where the extra effort makes sense, ensuring you test your upgrades and downgrades under heavy load, covering as many failure scenarios as possible.

If this chapter is not enough, the user guides and reference manuals, along with the module documentation that comes with the standard Erlang distribution, contain scattered but detailed information on release upgrades. You should start with the section on "Creating and Upgrading a Target System" in the OTP System Principles User's Guide. Tools are covered in the module documentation for systools and release_handler. Finally, *relup* and *.appup* files both have manual pages that describe the formats of the files, including all the instructions they may contain. Don't miss the "Appup Cookbook" chapter in the OTP Design Principles User's Guide. The same guide also contains descriptions of the code_change functions in the respective sections for every behavior and special process.

At the end of the day, though, our advice echoes what we recommended in the previous chapter: it's important to understand the underlying concepts, tools, and procedures, but unless your project requires extremely special considerations, you're best off using *rebar3*. It will handle many of the tedious tasks associated with releases and upgrades, can be extended if necessary, and has community support that you'll find helpful if you need advice or assistance.

What's Next?

With the knowledge provided in this chapter on how to package releases and perform live upgrades without affecting traffic, the time has come to look at how to architect a system. If you want a system with five-nines availability, what basic functionality should all of your production nodes have? What distributed architectural patterns should you be applying to get your nodes to scale? In the next chapter, we look at what it takes. So what are you waiting for? Turn the page and read on!

## CHAPTER 13

Distributed Architectures

Previous chapters have described the implementation of a single, simple node. A node is the smallest executable standalone unit consisting of a running instance of the Erlang runtime system. In this chapter we start to show how to expand from single nodes to distributed systems comprising multiple nodes. We try to help you figure out how to achieve availability, scalability, and consistency across these nodes. These qualities go hand in hand with reliability, which ensures that your system behaves correctly even under abnormal circumstances such as failure or extreme load.

Each node consists of a number of loosely coupled OTP applications, defined in its OTP release file. An OTP release determines the services the node provides and tasks it is capable of handling. Nodes that share a release file contain the same set of OTP applications and are considered to be nodes of the same type.

Nodes of one type can interact in a cluster with other node types to provide the system's end-to-end functionality. An Erlang system can comprise just one standalone node, but more typically consists of multiple nodes grouped in one or more clusters.

Clusters are needed for a variety of reasons. You might be implementing a microservices architecture, where each cluster of nodes provides a set of services. Or you might use clusters for scalability, sharding across identical clusters to increase computing power and availability. When dealing with distributed Erlang systems, which run on hybrid target environments in potentially geographically remote data centers, there is no single solution that fits all contexts. The lack of a single solution also means that tools and frameworks dealing with monitoring, management, and orchestration of Erlang nodes have to cater to different cluster patterns. Some tools might be ideal when dealing with deployments on Amazon or Rackspace, but they will not work on Parallela or Raspberry Pi clusters. Other tools will work best when deploying on bare metal, but not as well in virtual environments.

In this chapter and the next few, we cover the first steps involved in designing your distributed architecture. This chapter starts by looking at Erlang node types and describes how they are grouped together and interact with each other. This should help you determine how to split up your system into standalone nodes, each offering specific services. We describe the most common distributed architectural patterns used to provide these services and introduce some of the most popular distributed frameworks, such as "Riak Core" on page 367 and "Scalable Distributed Erlang" on page 372.

Although distributed Erlang will work out of the box, it is not always the right tool for the job. We cover other networking approaches you might need when connecting your Erlang and non-Erlang nodes to each other. We conclude by giving you a high-level approach on how to start defining the interfaces and data models of the individual node types.

Node Types and Families

Until recently, there were no common definitions covering distributed Erlang systems. OTP did a great job defining the individual components of a single node, but stopped short of describing how nodes are grouped together and how they interact in clusters. Although there was no ambiguity when developers in remote parts of the world spoke about generic servers, applications, or releases, confusion arose when trying to discuss clusters, the roles of nodes in clusters, or scalability patterns. These definitions were discussed and formalized[1] as part of the RELEASE project, EU-funded research addressing the scalability of the Erlang VM in distributed, many-core architectures. Before we start talking about distributed architectures, let's define our terminology.

Imagine a system consisting of three Erlang nodes. The first node runs web servers that keep pools of TCP connections open toward the clients. Clients could be mobile apps or web browsers. This receives HTTP requests, parses them into Erlang terms, and forwards them to a second node that handles the business logic of the system.

In handling the requests, the second node might interact with other nodes, each providing some form of service. For the sake of simplicity, let's assume it's a database node, possibly (but not necessarily) written in Erlang. To the end user, this all appears as a single system accessed as a black box. Erlang, the multiple nodes, and the distribution layer among the nodes are all hidden from the client users.

Figure 13-1 is an example of three *semantic node types* that classify the functionality and purpose of the nodes in the cluster. Multiple node instances of the same type

---

1 "Distributed Erlang Component Ontology," 30 June 2013 by Hoffmann, Cesarini, Fernandez, Thompson & Chechina.

could be running different versions of the same release. We run multiple instances of a single node for availability and scalability. We cover these topics in more detail in Chapter 14 and Chapter 15.

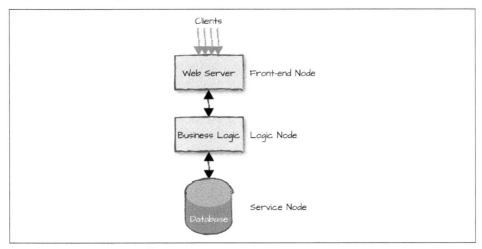

Figure 13-1. Semantic node types

The web server node is what we refer to as a *front-end node*. Front-end nodes are responsible for providing external connectivity to clients and handling all incoming requests. They act as gateways, keeping client connections open as needed, formatting inbound requests and outbound responses, and passing the requests onward to the nodes handling the business logic. They are part of the server-side software, serving, but not running, the presentation layer.

Logic nodes, also commonly referred to as *back-end nodes*, implement the system's business logic. They contain all of the code needed to handle client requests forwarded from the front-end nodes. They might also cache session data and access external services in other nodes when handling requests.

Finally, we have *service nodes*, which provide a service to the logic nodes. Such a service could be a database, an authentication server, or a payment gateway. Service nodes could themselves provide connectivity toward third-party services and APIs.

Node types are merely a way for us to describe the overall responsibility of each node. A single node, especially in small or simple systems, could have multiple responsibilities and act as both front-end and logic node, and even a service node, all in one. Think of a node that runs an Erlang web server (such as Yaws, Webmachine, or Cowboy), Erlang/OTP glue and business logic, and an Erlang database (such as Mnesia, CouchDB, or Riak) all in the same virtual machine. Combining all such applications into a single node like this reduces internode I/O and networking overhead by running everything in the same memory space, but it also produces a single point of failure and an architecture that might not scale. In contrast, in a multinode system, the responsibilities of the node types are spread across multiple nodes for maintainability, scalability, and availability.

When splitting your functionality into node types, try to keep memory-bound and CPU-bound functionality in separate nodes. That facilitates the fine-tuning of the VM and gives you flexibility in choosing the underlying hardware, optimizing for cost and performance. It also allows you to minimize the risk of a system failure, because not only are simple nodes easier to implement and test, but when they do fail, they will not affect the other nodes to the same extent as if all applications were running in the same node. A surge in simultaneous requests that causes a node to run out of memory should not affect the user database or the client connections. (We discuss how to handle surges in "Load Regulation and Backpressure" on page 419.)

We group node types running the same OTP release into a *node family*. This is a way of managing nodes as a single entity. You can have different node families with the same release, but grouped together based on criteria such as data center, cloud region, or even release version. Node families are then grouped into *clusters*, which together give you your *system*. Multiple clusters in systems are used to increase availability, reliability, and scalability, spreading services geographically across different data centers, possibly managed by different cloud or infrastructure providers.

To better understand the role of individual nodes, let's go into more detail using the example that we started looking at in Figure 13-1: an Erlang system that handles HTTP requests. We use it here and in the next two chapters to describe various concepts and tradeoffs we have to make when dealing with distributed systems.

Picture a system handling the back-end services of an e-commerce application. We focus on the login request originating from a client to the system. The client sends a login request using a RESTful API with data transmitted as JSON over HTTP. This request could originate from a mobile app or a web browser. The request is received by a web server running on the front-end nodes, which parses it into Erlang terms and forwards them to the logic node. The terms forwarded include the login request, the user ID, and the encrypted password.

The logic node checks the validity of the request and authenticates the user via an authentication server. If successful, a session ID and record are created and cached locally in the logic node. It returns the session ID back to the front-end server, which encodes it and returns it to the client with the acknowledgment that the login request was successful. The client uses the session ID in all subsequent communication for the duration of the session, and in each subsequent client request this ID is passed to the logic node and used to retrieve the record.

Regardless of whether you are using the three-layer architecture in Figure 13-1 or some other architectural pattern, the logic node is an important intermediary and checkpoint. Avoid having front-end nodes communicating directly with service nodes. Although it's not illegal, it often leads to poor system structure and confusion when trying to understand the system from an architectural view.

We add multiple instances of node types in our architecture to create distributed cluster patterns, also known as *system blueprints*. If you are happy with a static architecture that scales by adding independent instances of the system that do not interact with each other, the blueprint is easy. If your system scales to 1,000,000 simultaneously connected users executing 100,000 requests per second, roll out one per country and route user requests by pairing the inbound IP address to a geographical location. But if your app is a global online store that scales dynamically based on peaks and troughs, elastically adding computing capacity in the run-up to events such as payday, Black Friday, and Christmas and then releasing it again when not needed, extra thought needs to be put into the system from the start.

Both static and dynamic approaches to node (and hardware) management in your cluster go hand in hand with the strategies of how you distribute your data across nodes, node families, and ultimately clusters. How you connect your nodes and clusters together also becomes important, as does your data replication strategy across them. Users are logged on to the system and shopping away. Do you keep copies of their session data in all nodes or just some nodes? And every time a customer adds an item to a shopping basket, how are the changes propagated to other nodes? What happens if there is a network partition or failure? Or what about a software error or a node terminating? We cover these design choices in Chapter 14. They boil down to tradeoffs between availability, reliability, consistency, and scalability. What you need to do early on is understand the compromises that fit the needs of the system you are architecting and the end-user experience you want to provide.

Networking

So far, we've been talking about front-end nodes communicating with logic nodes, which in turn send requests to service nodes. We haven't mentioned distributed Erlang, because while it's ideal for smaller clusters within the same data center, it is not always the right solution when multidata center deployments, security, availability, and massive scalability come into the picture. In some cases, when lots of data needs to be transferred, a single socket becomes a bottleneck and you might want to use pools of connections found in libraries such as ranch or poolboy. RESTful APIs give you platform independence, as do other protocols such as AMQP, SNMP, MQTT, and XMPP. Distributed Erlang might still fit your needs, but rather than running it over TCP you might want to use alternative carriers such as 0MQ, UDP, SSL, or MPI.

In some systems, the network topology will go as far as providing different networks for different types of traffic. Traffic handling monitoring, billing, configuration, and maintenance would go through an *operations and maintenance* (*O&M network*), while traffic such as setting up of calls, instant messages, SMSs, or telemetry data would be routed through a *data network*. You would split them, as the data network would have higher bandwidth and availability requirements than the O&M one. You should avoid stopping or slowing down users playing a massively multiuser online game, but can get away with a delay in moving and processing billing records.

Demonstrating networking choices with our example will help clarify the choices you have to make. If you are concerned about security in your e-commerce site, you might want to place your front-end nodes in a demilitarized zone (DMZ), also known as a perimeter network (Figure 13-2). This is a physical or logical part of the network that exposes your nodes to an untrusted network (i.e., the Internet) used by the clients to access your services. DMZs were traditionally implemented in the hardware through the arrangement of managed network elements, and in the software using firewalls and other security measures. In cloud computing environments you do not get the hardware component, and have to instead mimic it through network connections and firewall rules. The end result, however, is still the same. By creating an additional layer of security around your back-end nodes, you reduce the risk of intrusion in your logical and service nodes by not exposing their interfaces.

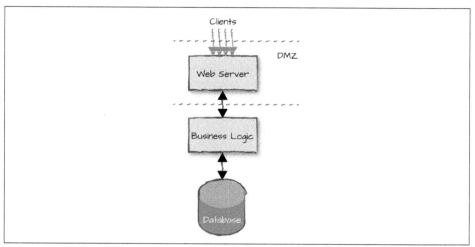

Figure 13-2. Demilitarized zones

If you were to use distributed Erlang, access to your front-end nodes would pretty much also mean access to your logic and service nodes as well. Gone are the days when no one knew about Erlang and when security through obscurity was enough to safeguard you. You must use sockets, possibly even encrypted sockets, between the web server and the nodes running the business logic, authenticating every request and checking its validity. Communication between the nodes running your business logic and your databases, however, takes place behind a firewall in what is considered to be a safe environment. The nodes can communicate transparently with each other using distributed Erlang.

Fallacies of Distributed Computing

If you think that your network is reliable and network partitions are rare, think again! Network issues occur when you least expect them, and if you are not handling all possible edge cases, the consequences and side effects can be disastrous. These are the "fallacies of distributed computing" described by Peter Deutsch and his associates decades ago, but just as relevant to the systems we design today.

If network connectivity to a remote node goes down or gets congested, how do you know it is a network issue, and not the remote node that has crashed or is slow at responding? Do you send back an error, or do you retry executing the call on a different node? And if you retry on a different node, how can you be sure the request you sent to the first node didn't already result in persistent side effects, with the network error or crash occurring before the node could send you back a reply? It is impossible to differentiate between a node crash and a slow node. Despite this, you need to make sure you have mapped all errors that can occur in every workflow associated with your requests.

Also keep in mind that operations across nodes result in higher CPU and I/O usage than operations executed locally as you have serialization costs, virtualized network interfaces, and the need to handle the protocols. Bandwidth is not unlimited and network latency affects the end-to-end performance of your requests. Keep all of this in mind when distributing your load, stress-testing your system, and fine-tuning it. It is not just about software; the behavior of your hardware and infrastructure is just as critical. Nodes and machines come and go during the lifetime of your system, something your program needs to handle effectively along with network topology changes.

Finally, remember your friendly system administrator, because there are administrators who sometimes do not follow procedures, make mistakes, or ignore warnings. The original fallacies paper makes the point that the network administrator might not even belong to the same organization. It is not just about the risk of an administrator tripping over the network cables, messing up configurations, or simply having different views on and strategies for how topologies should be managed. The basic issue is how your software handles these events and views of the world. Can your software manage twice the load on a particular node resulting from a load balancer or firewall misconfiguration?

Achieving resilience becomes even more difficult if you are using cloud infrastructure and do not control the network or know its topology, because partitions in those environments can be hard to understand and troubleshoot. Cloud computing typically has slower instances and busier networks, making the task even harder.

Distributed Erlang

There are two approaches to implementing your architecture using distributed Erlang. A static cluster has a fixed number of known parameters with fixed identities (hostnames, IPs, MAC addresses, etc.). It isn't provisioned to scale dynamically. In a dynamic cluster, the number of identities and nodes changes at runtime. In both cases, your system needs to be implemented with transitive connections in mind, because either network connectivity or the nodes themselves can fail (and restart). The only difference between a static and a dynamic system is that in the latter, alongside failing, nodes are started and stopped in a more controlled way. In a static system, they don't stop unless they fail.

Distributed Erlang clusters that are fully connected (Figure 13-3) are ideal for systems of certain size and requirements, but as we have said many times before, there is no "one size fits all" solution. Based on your node configuration and the size and frequency of messages sent across nodes, fully meshed Erlang clusters scale at the time of writing to about 70 to 100 nodes before performance degradation starts becoming evident. When a new node is added to the cluster, information on all visible (nonhidden) nodes that share the secret cookie gets propagated to it, connections are set up, and monitoring kicks in. So, with 100 connected nodes, you get 5,050 TCP connections (100+99+...+2+1) and heartbeats across them all, creating overhead in both the node and the network. Other single-process bottlenecks exist as well, such as *rex*, which handles Erlang remote procedure calls (RPCs), or the net kernel, which remotely spawns processes and deals with network monitoring.

How far you are able to scale your fully meshed distributed Erlang cluster depends on the characteristics of your system. Hidden nodes, covered in "Node Connections and Visibility" on page 49, act as gateways stopping the propagation of information across clusters of fully meshed nodes. They provide you with isolation and scalability, but you have to build frameworks that sit on top of them. You might be better off looking at alternative approaches or existing frameworks such as Riak Core and SD Erlang, which are covered in the following subsections.

Finally, you can create a special build that uses SSL as a bearer of Erlang distribution instead of plain TCP. You can read more about it in the "Using SSL for Erlang Distribution" (*http://bit.ly/erlang-ssl*) section of the Secure Socket Layer User's Guide.

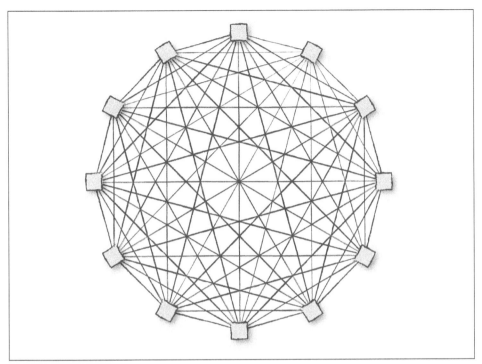

Figure 13-3. Distributed Erlang

Using Pids

If you are using process IDs instead of registered names across distributed Erlang clusters, keep in mind that if the remote node crashes and restarts, the pid on the restarted node might be reused. This could result in a process other than the intended one receiving your message. Always monitor remote nodes and processes, and take appropriate action if failure is detected. There is a counter for process IDs across nodes that gives you one or more generations of restarts with reused pids to avoid the problem, at least as long as the Erlang port mapper daemon (*epmd*) is alive.

Riak Core

Riak Core is a framework that provides an eventually consistent replicated data model on a system of masterless peer nodes providing high availability and helping guarantee no single point of failure. It is built on top of distributed Erlang and is the foundation of the distributed Riak key-value store, based on ideas from the 2007 Dynamo paper (*http://bit.ly/riak-dynamo*) from Amazon. It is an ideal framework for systems that require high availability and the need to self-heal after node or network failures. Fully explaining all the details of Riak Core would require a book of its own, so we cover just the highlights that make it a serious contender in the distributed frameworks space.

Riak Core runs on a cluster of physical nodes overlaid with a system of virtual nodes, also known as *vnodes*. The number of vnodes is configurable, but a typical Riak Core cluster includes 15–20 physical nodes that collectively host 256 vnodes. Each vnode claims a range of the 160-bit integer space of the SHA-1 hash function, which Riak Core uses as the basis of its *consistent hashing* system. Consistent hashing spreads key-value data evenly across the cluster while minimizing the amount of data relocation required as physical nodes are operationally added to or removed from the cluster.

To store data in a Riak Core cluster, a client sends a write request including both key and value. Riak Core hashes the key to obtain its hash value, then determines which vnode owns the range of 160-bit values that includes that hash value. Because Riak Core replicates each write, it first determines the replication factor for the request, which is called N and typically defaults to 3. It then stores N copies of the data, one in that primary vnode and the rest in the vnodes that respectively own the next N–1 hash ranges. Riak Core considers the write complete when the number of written copies equals the write factor, W. By default, W is N/2+1, which is 2 if N is 3.

To read data from a cluster, a client sends a request including the key. Riak Core first hashes the key to determine the primary vnode that should be holding the requested value. It then requests the value from that vnode and the N–1 next consecutive vnodes, and waits for the read factor, called R, to be fulfilled. Like W, by default R is N/2+1, which is 2 when N is 3. Once two copies of the value are successfully read, Riak Core returns the requested value to the client.

When a Riak Core cluster is first created, its physical nodes claim ownership of vnodes such that adjacent vnodes are not stored on the same physical node. Thus, by storing replicas in consecutive vnodes, and assuming the cluster comprises at least the minimum recommended five physical nodes, Riak Core tries its best to guarantee the replicas are stored on different nodes. Should any physical node crash or become unreachable, the other replicas can still respond to requests for reading or writing that data, thus providing availability even if the cluster is partitioned. The arrangement of vnodes on physical nodes is made clear in Figure 13-4, where, when looking up a value, the hash of the key points to the vnode, which in turn points to the primary Erlang node responsible for that value.

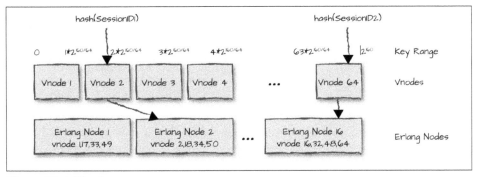

Figure 13-4. Vnodes

One advantage of using vnodes and consistent hashing pertains to the reshuffling that takes place when nodes get added or taken out of service. Assume that our cluster in Figure 13-4 has 16 nodes and we take node 1 permanently out of service. Riak Core redistributes vnodes 1, 17, 33, and 49 across existing nodes without needing to reshuffle all of the data across all nodes. The vnodes that are on the nodes still in service stay put. And if a new node is put into production, four vnodes will be moved to it from their current locations, affecting only the nodes where the vnodes are located.

Riak Core nodes are peers, and there is no master node. Nodes use a *gossip protocol* to communicate shared information such as cluster topology changes and the vnode claims to other randomly selected nodes. If updates to the cluster topology were missed on particular nodes for whatever reason, the gossip protocol forwards these changes, ensuring that the system heals itself.

Riak Core uses *hinted handoffs* to ensure that N copies of the data are stored, even if the primary vnode or some of the replica vnodes are down or unreachable because of a network partition. In such a case, Riak Core stores the data in an alternative vnode and gives that vnode a hint as to where the data really should be stored. When the unreachable vnodes again become available, the alternative vnodes hand the data off to them, thereby healing the system. Hinted handoffs are part of Riak Core's *sloppy quorums*. Writes require W acknowledgments to be considered successful, and similarly reads are considered successful with R results, but Riak doesn't care whether those quorums comprise primary or alternative vnodes (hence the term "sloppy"). If Riak were to instead use *strict quorums*, which consist only of primary vnodes, the result would be diminished system availability when primaries were down or unreachable.

As soon as we start distributing data and states across replicas, we introduce uncertainty. How do we know an operation was successfully replicated to all nodes? What if, because of partitions or node, network, hardware, or software failures, data becomes inconsistent?

In cases where nodes return different values without achieving a quorum, Riak Core tries to resolve the conflicting values using *dotted version vectors* (DVVs). DVVs provide a way for Riak Core to identify a partial ordering of write events for a given value that can help determine which of the values is the correct one. This ordering is based not on timestamps, which are too unreliable and too difficult to keep synchronized across a cluster of nodes, but rather on logical clocks based on monotonically increasing counters at each node that acts on the value. If the DVV information is not enough to resolve the conflict, all conflicting values of the state are returned to the client as sibling values, and the conflict must then be resolved by the client application, presumably using domain-specific knowledge to make its decision.

So, how does Riak Core help us implement our distributed architecture? Although you are still limited to a maximum of a hundred nodes in your core, you can use these nodes as hubs or gateways to other clusters, as shown in Figure 13-5. Logic nodes running Riak Core create a fully meshed ring used for messaging, job scheduling, and routing requests to service nodes, or to act as gateways to other clusters.

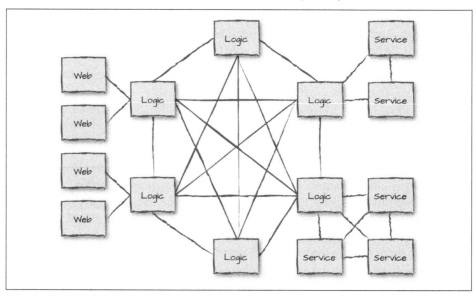

Figure 13-5. Riak Core patterns

Figure 13-6 uses another approach for massive scalability: a star architecture, where service nodes connected to each other can be used for storage and analytics purposes, increasing and decreasing in size dynamically based on load. Both patterns serve their purpose and overcome the scalability issues encountered with fully meshed networks. More complex patterns are available as well, as are simpler ones. Some include running multiple Riak Core clusters connected to each other via hidden nodes acting as gateways.

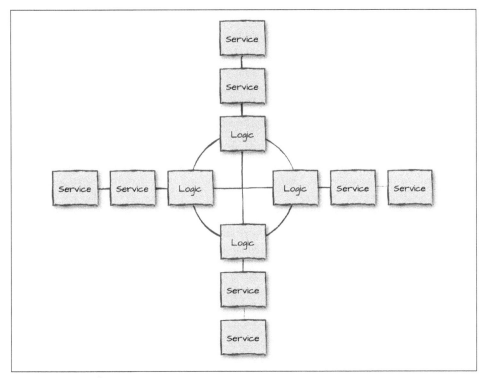

Figure 13-6. Riak Core star

If consistent hashing and Riak Core are the right approach for the problems you're solving, you may also want to look at the NkCLUSTER (*https://github.com/NetCom poser/nkclusterand*) application, a layer on top of Riak Core written to create and manage clusters of Erlang nodes and to distribute and schedule jobs on the cluster. NkDIST (*https://github.com/NetComposer/nkcluster*) is a library that evenly distributes processes, automatically moving them when the Riak Core cluster is rebalanced through the addition or removal of nodes. You can find NkDIST and NkCLUSTER documentation in their respective GitHub pages and repositories.

For further reading on Riak Core, we recommend Mariano Guerra's *Little Riak Core Book* on GitHub (*https://marianoguerra.github.io/little-riak-core-book/*). You can read the official documentation on Basho's website (*http://docs.basho.com/*) (Basho is the company that created and maintains Riak Core). A web search will also reveal many talks and tutorials. And finally, an excellent example of how to use Riak Core is Udon (*https://github.com/mrallen1/udon*), a distributed static file web server by Mark Allen.

Scalable Distributed Erlang

Scalable Distributed Erlang (SD Erlang) takes a different approach from that of Riak Core. SD Erlang emerged from the RELEASE research project at the University of Glasgow. Although at the time of writing it was not production-ready, the ideas behind it are interesting and have been shown to allow systems to scale to tens of thousands of nodes. The basic approach is to reduce network connectivity and the namespace through a small extension to the existing distributed Erlang.

SD Erlang defines a new layer called an *s_group*. Nodes can belong to zero, one, or more s_groups, and nodes that belong to the same s_group transitively share connections and a namespace. A *namespace* is a set of names registered using the `global:register_name/2` function in distributed Erlang or the `s_group:register_name/3` function in SD Erlang. Names registered in distributed Erlang are replicated on all connected normal (not hidden) nodes. In SD Erlang, the name is replicated on all nodes of the given s_group.

Figure 13-7 shows two s_groups named G1 and G2. Each contains three Erlang nodes. Because node C is shared by both s_groups, it can transmit messages between nodes in different s_groups. Node C is called a *gateway*.

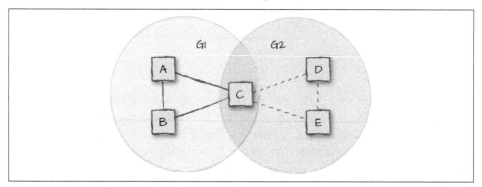

Figure 13-7. SD Erlang groups

Using the SD Erlang concept of node groups, a programmer can arrange nodes in different configurations, e.g., clustering nodes and connecting them via gateways.

To enable SD Erlang applications to be portable and scalable, a concept of *semi-explicit placement* is also introduced. This controls the placement of new nodes based on communication distances to other nodes and on node *attributes*. Node attributes are hardware-, software-, and programmer-defined characteristics of nodes that enable them to be aware of their unique characteristics and their neighboring nodes. Communication distances use the time it takes to transfer data from one node to another as a metric. Assuming connections with equal bandwidth, shorter transfer times correspond to smaller communication distances between nodes.

Documentation about SD Erlang is available on the University of Glasgow's site (*http://www.dcs.gla.ac.uk/research/sd-erlang/*). Lots of conference talks and articles about it are also available online.

Sockets and SSL

There will be times when distributed Erlang is not enough. On extremely high volume systems, bottlenecks can occur in the global name server, *rex*, or the net kernel—not to mention the distributed Erlang port itself, which, even if fast, is capable of handling only one request at a time, as it's designed for control messages rather than for data transfer. Or, as we saw in our DMZ example, you might want to avoid distributed Erlang for security reasons, limiting the openness the fully meshed network brings to the table. When distributed Erlang is not the right tool for the job, adding a thin layer above the `ssl` or `gen_tcp` libraries starts making sense. You open one or more sockets between the nodes, controlling the flow of information sent and received.

The System Monitor

How do you find out whether your distributed Erlang port is congested? Hidden deep in the documentation of Erlang/OTP is a BIF that allows you to trigger monitoring events associated with memory management and the scheduler. A call to `erlang:system_monitor(Pid, [busy_dist_port])` sets up monitoring. A trace message of the format {`monitor, SusPid, busy_dist_port, Port`} will be sent to `Pid` every time a process gets suspended because it is trying to send a message through an internode communication port already being used by another process. `SusPid` is the suspended process.

Other scheduler-related items that you can monitor include `busy_port` and `long_schedule`. Important memory-related monitors you can turn on include `long_gc` and `large_heap`, triggered if a process spends too long garbage collecting or allocates an unusually large heap.

Be careful how you handle system messages in live environments. We've seen millions of them being generated per hour in badly written systems under heavy load. You can read more about the `system_monitor` BIFs on the `erlang` manual page (*http://erlang.org/doc/man/erlang.html#system_monitor-0*). We will also cover monitoring in more detail in Chapter 16.

Bottlenecks can also occur when moving large volumes of data with sockets. As an example, we were once working with a system that managed instant messages. The instant messages tended to be short and bursty, so a single TCP connection from our DMZ coped well under extreme load. When we upgraded the same system to also manage email, queues quickly started building up in the front-end nodes when exposed to continuous heavy load. This had to do with the sizes of the messages being sent, which were much larger than the instant messages, causing the TCP socket processes to back up. The backup eventually caused the virtual machine to run out of memory. The network was far from saturated, so adding multiple connections between the front-end and logic nodes (Figure 13-8) got rid of the bottleneck.

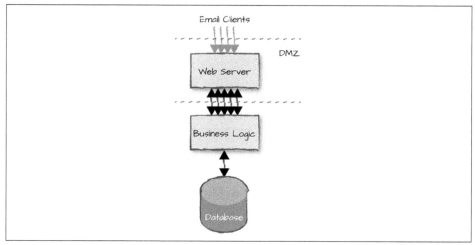

Figure 13-8. Communication bottlenecks

Typical use cases where we've had to use multiple connections across nodes include the transfer of images, logs, or emails and email attachments. The volumes of data have to be substantial for multiple connections to pay off, though, so avoid premature optimization. Start with a single connection and add more only when you have metrics showing you have a problem that multiple connections can fix.

This is a common approach for which there are a few open source libraries. The gen_rpc (*https://github.com/priestjim/gen_rpc*) application on GitHub has been benchmarked doing in excess of 60,000 RPC requests per second. If you need simple functionality, you can also write your own connection API. In its simplest guise, such an API would be a thin layer consisting of a few dozen lines of code that is highly optimized for the traffic and security requirements of your applications. That said, it might make sense to base your socket library on a process pool library such as Poolboy (*https://github.com/devinus/poolboy*).

The example in Figure 13-2 illustrates the security rationale for not always relying on Erlang to distribute processing. We would not want the front-end nodes communicating with the logic nodes using distributed Erlang, because an intruder who gained access to the stateless client nodes would also gain full access to all the connected nodes and be able to execute OS-level commands on the remote machines. Just imagine someone obsessed by tidiness executing rpc:multicall(nodes(), os, cmd, ["rm -rf *"]) in order to enjoy the peace and serenity a clean hard drive brings.

Even if you roll out your own TCP- or SSL-based communication library between the front-end and logic nodes, you can still use distributed Erlang to let the logic nodes communicate with each other and share data through Riak, Mnesia, or simple message passing. In turn, the logic nodes might use RESTful approaches to communicate with service nodes. When your system starts getting complicated, mixing communication methods for security, performance, and scalability purposes becomes common. The mix could be between nodes, node types, or node families.

Service Orientation and Microservices

Another pattern for creating systems that scale is microservices and service-oriented architectures (SOA). Although SOA is considered heavyweight and old-fashioned by some, it is widely used in enterprise systems and its ideas are fundamental to microservices. Both are similar in concept to the client-server paradigm where processes and nodes (or node families) provide services to other nodes and processes. These services, often standalone or loosely coupled, together provide the functionality required by your system. They are often expressed in terms of an API, where each service (or function) implements an action invoked by a node requesting the service. The services provided are the same as those we have looked at already in this book. They could include client front-end interfaces, authentication databases, logging, alarming, logic nodes, and other service nodes (Figure 13-9). Services should be packaged in a generic enough way to encourage reusability not just among other services, but also across systems.

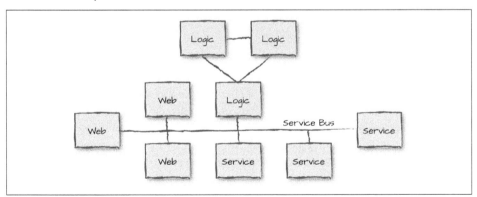

Figure 13-9. Service-oriented architectures

Services are connected together by a *service bus*. They use a protocol that describes how services exchange and interpret messages. This is done with *service metadata*, which describes what each service does and the data it requires. The metadata should be in a format that allows nodes to dynamically configure and publicize their services, which in turn allows other services to dynamically discover and use them. The messages themselves are often defined using JSON, XML, Protocol Buffers, Erlang terms, or even OMG IDL.

The service bus runs over a network and allows communication following a particular protocol. Requests can be sent using SOAP, HTTP, or AMQP. You could use web services, Java RMI, Thrift bindings, or even Erlang-based RPCs and message passing. Certain message buses have the added benefit of helping throttle requests and dealing with load regulation and backpressure. We cover these concepts in more detail in "Load Regulation and Backpressure" on page 419.

The advantage of standardized protocols is that they allow you to combine readymade components or standalone nodes, possibly implemented in multiple programming languages. At the same time, they force you to package your services in a way that encourages reusability across systems. This does, however, come at the cost of overhead in the size of the data shared across nodes as well as the encoding and parsing of the requests and replies.

Gproc

Gproc is an application by Ulf Wiger used for service discovery. It provides a registry where you can store metadata that describes process roles and characteristics. It allows you to use any Erlang term to register a process, and allows multiple aliases to a single process. Nonunique process properties can be stored and queried using match specifications and query list comprehensions. The registry is global, allowing the process metadata to be distributed and accessed across multiple nodes. You can find *gproc* and its documentation on GitHub (*https://github.com/uwiger/gproc*).

Peer to Peer

Peer-to-peer (p2p) architectures are probably the most scalable distributed architectural patterns of all, as they are completely decentralized and consist of nodes of the same type that set up ad hoc connections to other nodes. Every node has the same privileges, capabilities, and responsibilities, in contrast to client-server architectural patterns, where the purpose of some node types is to serve other node types.

In p2p architectures, every node is both a client and a server, allowing it to start a communication session in a decentralized way. Think of protocols such as BitTorrent, Gnutella, Gossip, and Kazaa. While to the masses, p2p is synonymous with file sharing, its use in the Erlang world is more associated with massively parallel computations, distributed file storage, and big data analytics. P2p nodes tend to form connections in unpredictable and rapidly changing ways, but with low overhead

---

(Figure 13-10). However, passing data through multiple nodes to get to its ultimate destination can result in extra overall load on the network.

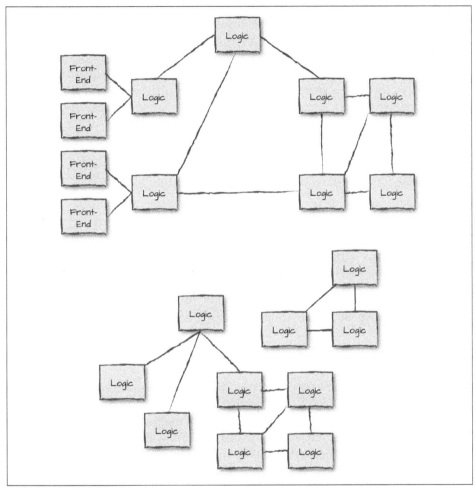

Figure 13-10. Peer-to-peer architectures

Having said this, there is nothing stopping you from using p2p nodes to act as communication hubs, with clients connecting to them in a way similar to the architectural patterns described with Riak Core. Although you do not come across them every day, these patterns are ideal for systems that need to continue executing in partitioned networks and do not require strong consistency.

Interfaces

Once you've split your node into node types and defined what services they will provide and how they will communicate with each other, the time comes to specify the interfaces the nodes export. Depending on the size and complexity of the system, this might be a daunting and discouraging task if you don't know where to start or how to break it down into smaller tasks. It's important, however, because interfaces are not only used by other nodes when sending requests; they will be used to implement the business logic, to test the nodes on a standalone basis, and to run end-to-end tests of the system.

Consider what you expect your system to do and break it down into stories and features. These could be client actions or actions triggered by external events. Walk through these actions and events, and in doing so, determine:

- The function to call when accessing the node
- The arguments you need to pass to the node in order to fulfill the request
- The data model of the tables and state each node must have or make available to fulfill this request
- Calls to other nodes, repeating this procedure for them
- Any destructive operations in the nodes, including table updates and state changes resulting from the call
- The return values of the call

The key to success is abstracting and simplifying everything without getting stuck in the details. At this stage of your architecture design, you do not need to determine every single item that can go wrong. You should not worry about complex algorithms or optimization strategies. Just think of positive use cases, and if you cover any errors, make sure they are only ones defined in the business logic of your system.

Let's walk through the example defined in "Node Types and Families" on page 360, where a client sends a login request to the front-end servers. Breaking down the story into smaller steps, this is what our line of thought would look like:

- The front-end server receives a REST-based *login* request with a UserId and an encrypted Password. It parses the request and corresponding JSON structure, converting the data to Erlang terms. It forwards the request to the logic node.
- The logic node receives the *login* request with the UserId and an encrypted Password.
  - It checks whether an ongoing session is already associated with the UserId, and if so, it reauthenticates the user and returns the existing SessionId.

- — If there is no session, the logic node forwards the request to the authentication server, authenticates the user, and returns the SessionId.
- The authentication server receives an *auth* request with a UserId and an encrypted Password.
  - — If the authentication is successful, the account is active, and the password has not expired, the server acknowledges the request and returns the UserData associated with the UserId.
  - — If the authentication fails, the authentication server returns the Reason for failure. Reasons could be unknown_user, bad_password, user_suspended, or password_expired.
- The logic node receives the result from the authentication server.
  - — If the authentication was successful and no session existed for this user, it creates a unique SessionId and stores it in a session table together with the User Data, the UserId, and a TimeStamp. It returns the SessionId to the front-end node.
  - — If the authentication was successful and a session existed for this user, it returns the existing SessionId to the front-end node.
  - — If the authentication failed, the logic node returns login_failed, user_suspended, or password_expired to the front-end node.
- The front-end node receives the responses from the logic nodes, creates a JSON structure, and replies to the original request.

We've kept everything at a high level, worrying only about function calls and parameters on a node level and discussing the return values and errors that can occur in the business logic of our system. Forget parse errors, processes, nodes crashing and being unavailable, or network connectivity issues for now. Note, however, that if there is a failed login, the logic node generalizes the error cases without exposing whether it is the UserId or Password that is incorrect; this is a security measure that makes it harder for attackers to determine whether a particular UserID exists.

Along with definitions of the interfaces, we make a first run of the data and state that are needed by these calls and expected to be stored in tables or behavior loop data. We also document how the calls change this data. Having gone through this exercise, Table 13-1 lists what we would expect to have extracted.

Table 13-1. Interfaces and tables

Web front-end node
login(UserId, Password) -> {ok, SessionId} | {error, login_failed}
No tables or state

Logic node
`login(UserId, Password) -> {ok, SessionId} | {error, login_failed | user_suspended | password_expired}`
SessionTable: SessionId, UserId, TimeStamp, UserData
UserTable: UserId, SessionId

Authentication server
`auth(UserId, Password) -> {ok, UserData} | {error, unknown_user | bad_password | user_suspended | password_expired}`
UserTable: UserId, Password, AccountState, TimeStamp, UserData

Doing this for all the use cases and stories will give you a solid foundation that you can use to design the individual nodes, as well as other stories and use cases you might have missed. If many users were involved in this project or will have to read the high-level design document, providing a short description of what the functions do will also help. You will go through many iterations of your interface as you design your system, rearranging your tables, moving functionality around, and reducing duplication of your data. Don't think you'll get it right on your first try.

Summing Up

In this chapter, we've covered the first steps in determining the distributed architecture of your system. You have to make choices at some point, being aware that these choices will be revisited during the implementation and verification phases. There is a lot to take into account, so be careful not to get lost in the details and overengineer your system. If you need to handle 10,000 requests per second dealing with small volumes of data, fully connected distributed Erlang will probably be enough, but if you are moving high volumes of data, distributed Erlang alone won't suffice. Do not fall into the trap of premature optimization, adding complexity that will slow down your system, decrease reliability, and increase maintenance costs without any added benefits. If unsure, start your project with a proof of concept ensuring your approach is the right one. It will validate your ideas and stop you from making mistakes in a production system.

These are the steps we've covered in this chapter:

1. *Split up your system's functionality into manageable, standalone nodes.*

   During this task, it will help to categorize the nodes as *front-end*, *logic*, or *service* nodes. Try to keep the services provided by your nodes simple, and remember that nodes are a way to isolate failure. Losing a node should have no impact on any requests that are not being routed through it.

2. *Choose a distributed architectural pattern.*

   When deciding on a pattern, take into account scalability, availability, and reliability. Will a static number of nodes be enough, or do you need dynamic scaling? Do you really need one of the distributed frameworks, or is a simple cluster running fully connected distributed Erlang enough for your needs? Although you need to design scalability and availability into your system from the start, do so without overengineering your system. Always start simple, and add complexity when you know you need it. Just because you can use Riak Core or SD Erlang does not mean you have to. Ask yourself whether the problem you are solving falls into the category of problems they solve.

3. *Choose the network protocols your nodes, node families, and clusters will use when communicating with each other.*

   Although most systems can get away with running as fully connected distributed Erlang clusters behind a firewall, there will be cases where you need to think out of the box to solve specific requirements your system might have. Do you need to optimize your network for bandwidth, speed, or both? What are your security requirements? And most importantly, how do you handle network unreliability? You need to choose different approaches for nodes running in the same subrack versus being located in geographically remote data centers. There are choices you might want to make up front, and others you will have to revisit when you have proper benchmark results to validate your choices.

4. *Define your node interfaces, state, and data model.*

   When specifying your interfaces, you will be validating the choices you made when you split the functionality of your system into manageable, standalone nodes. Getting your interfaces and data model right is also an iterative process that will require revisiting design choices. You will want to reduce duplication of data while minimizing the size and number of arguments you send in requests to other nodes. You will want to standardize your APIs across nodes while catering for external protocols and interfaces.

What's Next?

Now that we have covered node types, system blueprints, and node and node family connectivity, the time has come to look at failure scenarios and how to mitigate them. The next chapter covers retry strategies when requests fail because of software, hardware, or networking issues. These retry strategies go hand in hand with the partitioning and distribution of data and state across nodes and node families.

## CHAPTER 14

Systems That Never Stop

You need at least two computers to make a fault-tolerant system. Built-in Erlang distribution, no shared memory, and asynchronous message passing give you the foundations needed for replicating data across these computers, so if one computer crashes, the other can take over. The good news is that the error-handling techniques, fault isolation, and self-healing that apply to single-node systems also help immensely when multiple nodes are involved, allowing you to transparently distribute your processes across clusters and use the same failure detection techniques you use on a single node. This makes the creation of fault-tolerant systems much easier and more predictable than having to write your own libraries to handle semantic gaps, which is typically what's required with other languages. The catch is that Erlang on its own will not give you a fault-tolerant system out of the box—but its programming model will, and at a fraction of the effort required by other current technologies.

In this chapter, we continue explaining approaches to distributed programming commonly used in Erlang systems. We focus on data replication and retry strategies across nodes and computers, and the compromises and tradeoffs needed to build systems that never stop. These approaches affect how you distribute your data, and how you retry requests if they have failed for reasons out of your control.

Availability

Availability defines the uptime of a system over a certain period of time. *High availability* refers to systems with very low downtime, software maintenance and upgrades included. While some claim having achieved nine-nines availability,[1] these claims

---

[1] British Telecom issued a press release claiming nine-nines availability during a six-month trial of an AXD301 ATM switch network that carried all of its long-distance-traffic calls.

tend not to be long-lived. Nine nines of uptime means only 31.6 milliseconds of downtime per year! It will take you 10 times longer to blink, let alone figure out something has gone wrong. A realistic number often achieved with Erlang/OTP is 99.999% uptime, equating to just over 5 minutes of downtime each year, upgrades and maintenance included.

High availability is the result of your system having no single point of failure, and being fault-tolerant, resilient, and reliable. It can also be the result of having a system that even in the face of partial failure can still provide some degree of service, albeit reduced from normal levels. Let's look in detail at what these terms entail for the system you are trying to build.

Fault Tolerance

Fault tolerance refers to the ability of a system to act predictably under failure. Such failure could be due to a software fault, where a process crashes because of a bug or corrupt state. Or it could be due to a network or hardware fault, or the result of a node crashing. Acting predictably can mean looking for alternative nodes and ensuring that requests are fulfilled, or just returning errors back to the callers.

In the example in Figure 14-1, a client sends a request to the front-end node running the web servers. The request is parsed and forwarded to the logic node (Figure 14-1, part 1). At this point, the logic node, or a process in the logic node, crashes (Figure 14-1, part 2). If we are lucky, the front-end node detects this crash and receives an error. If we're unlucky, an internal timeout is triggered. When the error or timeout is received, an error is sent back to the client.

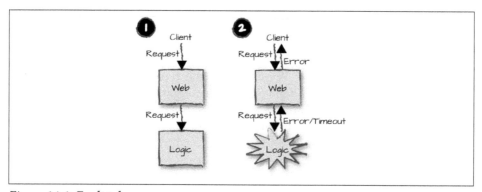

Figure 14-1. Fault tolerance

This system acts in a predictable way and is considered fault tolerant because a response has been sent back to the client. It allows the client to act in a predictable way, as long as the server, the type of request, and the protocol allow for it. The response might not be the one the client was hoping for, but it was a valid response. It is now up to the client to decide what to do next. It might retry sending the request, escalate the failure, or do nothing.

The hardest part in this use case is knowing whether the logic node actually failed, or if the failure is in the network between the nodes—or, even worse, if the logic node is just incredibly slow in responding, triggering a timeout in the front-end node while actually executing the request. There is no practical difference between a slow node and a dead node. Your front-end nodes need to be aware of all these conditions and handle the resulting uncertainty. This is done through unique identifiers, idempotence, and retry attempts, all of which we discuss later in this chapter. It might even require audit logs and human intervention. The last thing you want is for your purchase request to time out and for the client to keep on retrying until a request is actually acknowledged. You might wake to discover you purchased 50 copies of the same book.

Erlang has dedicated, asynchronous error channels that work across nodes. It does not matter if the node or process crashed, or if the crash was in a local or remote node. You can use the same proven error-handling techniques, such as monitors, links, and exit signals, within your node as well as within your distributed environment. The only difference will be latency if the exit signals are originating in remote nodes, something already taken care of through asynchronous message passing. Make sure that errors are propagated accordingly in your call chain, taking actions on every level that might address the issue. This includes the handling of false positives, as an action can be enacted, but crash or time out before its success is reported. Or it can time out due to network issues, but succeed asynchronously after the time out. This is one of the biggest challenges of asynchronous distributed systems.

Resilience

Resilience is the ability of a system to recover quickly from failure. In the example in Figure 14-2, the client sends a request to a web server node that crashes prior to handling the request (Figure 14-2, part 1). This might be caused by the client request, by a request from another client, or simply as the result of the Erlang runtime hitting a system limit such as running out of memory. The node could have failed even before the client sent its request. A heartbeat script detects the node failure and, depending on the number of restarts in the last hour, decides whether to restart the process or reboot the machine itself (as the error might be in one of the interfaces and could be eliminated through an OS restart). The client keeps on sending the same request, which repeatedly fails as the node is not available. But once the machine is rebooted or the node restarted, if it is safe to do so, the client request is accepted and successfully handled. The node failed, but quickly recovered on its own (Figure 14-2, part 2), minimizing downtime.

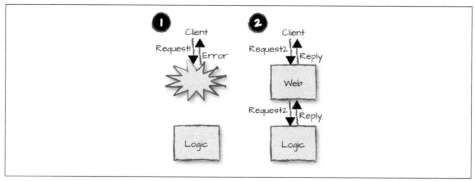

Figure 14-2. Resilience

As we've seen in many of the previous chapters in this book, the trick is to isolate failure, separating the business logic from the error handling. If a process crashes, its dependencies are terminated and quickly restarted. If a node goes down, a heartbeat script triggers an immediate restart. If a network or hardware outage occurs, the redundant network is used. By isolating functionality in manageable quantities in different node types, isolating failure becomes a straightforward and easy task. If you have a node that does too much, you increase the possible causes of a node crash through increased complexity, and you increase the recovery time.

Back-Off Algorithms in Clients

If you have a client that automatically tries to reconnect and send a request after a failure, make sure it uses a *back-off algorithm* to regulate the frequency of its retries. Picture your system with a few million connected devices handling a couple hundred thousand requests per second experiencing a 1-minute outage. The outage will result in all the devices trying to reconnect and send requests, creating a surge in traffic. This surge increases for every second of downtime, hitting the system with force as soon as it becomes operational again. If not handled properly, this will cause more front-end nodes to terminate, creating an even larger surge on the remaining ones and taking out the next batch until there are none left. This is what we call a *cascading failure*, something you need to guard against in both your client and server.

The easiest variant of a back-off algorithm in a client is based on Fibonacci, where the interval between retries increases from 1 second to 2, 3, 5, 8, and 13 seconds, respectively, capped at a large number such as 89, 144, or more seconds. An *exponential back-off algorithm* is one that increases the retry interval between failed requests exponentially, while the random delays created by a *random back-off algorithm* might be appropriate so that multiple nodes issue their retries at different times. The algorithm that best suits your needs will control the surge in failed retry attempts coming at the same time, allowing the system to recover and continue functioning even after a failure.

Reliability

The *reliability* of a system is its ability to function under particular predefined conditions. In software and distributed systems, these conditions often include failure and inconsistency. In other words, the system has to continue functioning even when components that comprise it fail themselves or when data becomes inconsistent because it fails to replicate across nodes. When looking at reliability, you need to start thinking of the redundancy of these components. When we mention components, we do not mean only hardware and software. We also mean data and state, which need to be replicated and consistent across nodes.

A *single point of failure* means that if a particular component in your system fails, your whole system fails. That component could be a process, a node, a computer, or even the network tying it all together. This means that in order for your system to have no single point of failure, you need to have at least two of everything. At least two computers with software distributed and running a failover strategy across them. At least two copies of your data and state. Two routers, gateways, and interfaces, so that if the primary one fails, the secondary takes over. Alternative power supplies (or battery backups) for the same reason. And if you have the luxury, place the two computers in separate, geographically remote data centers. You should also keep in mind that having only two of everything might itself be a problem waiting to happen, since if one of something goes down, the remaining instance automatically becomes a single point of failure. For this reason, using three or more instances instead of just two is normally a given when high reliability is a critical requirement. All of this comes at a higher bandwidth and latency cost.

Extraordinary Measures

One of the authors arrived at a customer site one morning to find a digger parked in the driveway and a bewildered builder holding two ends of a broken cable while doing the motion of trying to stick them back together. For a week, the site lost its Internet connection, landline phone service, and even mobile connectivity, because the antennas on the roof were using that very same cable. If you need to service requests after a natural disaster (or a clueless builder), make sure you have site redundancy.

US regulatory agencies' disaster recovery guidelines for financial institutions recommend a minimum distance of 200–300 miles between primary and secondary data centers. European telecommunication recommendations are not as extreme, but they do guarantee that if a site is hit by a nuclear bomb, or a bomb is dropped anywhere in between the two sites, one of the sites will be distant enough to be unaffected! That is the price you have to pay for high availability.

At the end of the day, availability becomes a question of costs, tradeoffs, and risks. The financial damage caused by a network outage might be less than the cost of installing a redundant network or having redundant hardware, turning it into a business decision. And this is a technical book about software, so let's leave the bean counters alone and get back on track.

What does having two or three of everything mean for your software? Your request hits one of the load balancers, which forwards it to one of the front-end nodes. The node used is chosen by the load balancer using a variety of strategies—random, round robin, hashing, or sending the request to the front-end node with the least CPU load or the one with the smallest number of open TCP connections. We prefer hashing algorithms, as they are fast and give you predictability and consistency with low overheads. When troubleshooting what is going (or what went) wrong with a request, having a deterministic route across nodes makes debugging much easier, especially if you have hundreds of nodes and decentralized logs.

Let's look at an example of how we avoid a single point of failure. The front-end node receives the request, parses it, and forwards it to a logic node (Figure 14-3, part 1). Soon after the request is forwarded, something goes wrong. The failure could have occurred anywhere, and we are unsure of the state of the request itself. We do not know whether the request ever reached the logic node, or whether the logic node started or even finished handling it. It could have been this very request that caused a process to crash, caused a synchronous call to time out, or caused the whole node to crash. Or perhaps the node might not have crashed at all; it might be extremely overloaded and slow in responding, or network connectivity might have failed. We should be able to distinguish between something crashing in the node itself and the node not responding. But beyond that, we just don't know.

What we do know, though, is that we have a client waiting for a reply. So, upon detecting the error, the front-end node forwards the request to a secondary logic node. This node handles the request (Figure 14-3, part 2) and returns the reply to the front-end node, which formats it and sends it back to the client (Figure 14-3, part 3). All along, the client has no idea of the drama happening behind the scenes. The resilience in the node where the error occurs ensures that it comes up again, reconnects to the front-end nodes, and starts handling new requests. So, despite part of our system failing, it still provided 100% uptime to the client thanks to our "no single point of failure" strategy.

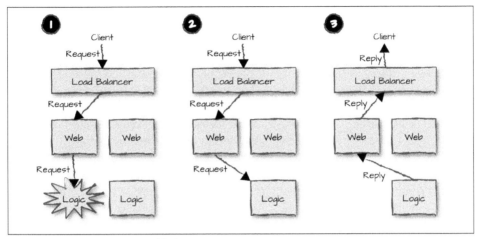

Figure 14-3. Single points of failure

At most once, exactly once, and at least once

When handling failure strategies, you need to start getting clever and make sure you have all edge cases covered. There are three approaches you can take for every request, because how you handle requests maps to message delivery semantics across nodes in distributed systems. In our example in Figure 14-3, the only guarantee you have is that your request has been executed *at least once*. If you are logging on to the system and the first logic node is so slow that the front-end node tries another one and succeeds with it, the worst-case scenario is that you log on twice and two sessions are created, one of which will eventually expire.

Similarly, if you are sending an SMS or an instant message, you might be happy with the *at most once* approach. If your system sends billions of messages a day, the loss of a few messages is acceptable relative to the load and the cost associated with guaranteed delivery. You send your request and forget about it. In our example with no single point of failure, when the front-end node sends the request to the logic node, it also immediately sends a reply back to the client.

But what if you were sending money or a premium rate SMS? Losing money, making the transfer more than once, or sending and charging for the same premium SMS multiple times because of an error will not make you popular. Under these circumstances, you need the *exactly once* approach. A request can succeed or fail. If failure is in your business logic, such as where a user is not allowed to receive premium rate SMSs, we actually consider the failed request to be successful, as it falls within the valid return values. Errors that should worry us are timeouts, software bugs, or corrupt state causing a process or node to terminate abnormally, leaving the system in a potentially unknown or undefined state. As long as you use the exactly once approach in a single node, abnormal process termination can be detected. As soon as you go distributed, however, the semantics of the request cannot be guaranteed.

The successful case is when you send a request and receive a response. But if you do not receive a response, is it because of the request never reaching the remote node, because of a bug in the remote node, or because the acknowledgment and reply of the successful execution got lost in transit? The system could be left in an inconsistent state and need cleaning up. In some systems, the cleanup is executed automatically by a script that tries to determine what went wrong and address the problem. In other cases, cleaning up might require human intervention because of the complexity of the code or seriousness of the failed transaction. If a request to send a premium rate SMS failed, a script could start by investigating if the mobile device received the remote SMS, if the user was charged for it, or if the request ever made it to the system. Having comprehensive logs, as we show in "Logs" on page 428, becomes critical.

A common pattern in achieving exactly once semantics with at most once calls is to use unique sequence numbers in the client requests. A client sends a request that gets processed correctly (Figure 14-4, part 1). If the response from the front-end node is lost or delayed, a timeout in the client is triggered. The client resends the request with the same identifier, and the logic node identifies it as a duplicate request and returns the original reply, possibly tagging it as a duplicate (Figure 14-4, part 2). You are still not guaranteed success, as the connectivity between the client and the server might not come up again. But it will work in the presence of transient errors.

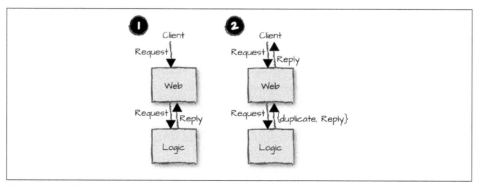

Figure 14-4. Duplicate requests

This approach relies on *idempotence*. The term describes an operation that the user can apply multiple times with the same effect as applying it once. For example, if a request changes a customer's shipping address, whether the system performs the request successfully once or multiple times has the same result, assuming the shipping address is the same in each request. Such a request can actually be executed multiple times because the side effects of any second or subsequent executions essentially have no observable effect. With our request identification scheme, though, the second and subsequent executions never occur.

Imagine a billing system for premium rate SMSs. You need to guarantee that if you charge the user, you will do so exactly once, and only after the SMS is received. An approach typically taken to guarantee this result is reserving the funds in the recipient account before sending the SMS. When reserving them, the billing system returns a unique identifier. The SMS is sent, possibly multiple times. The charge is made only when the first report notifying that it has been delivered is received by the billing system. The unique identifier is then used to execute the payment and charge the account. Subsequent attempts to use the same identifier, possibly when receiving multiple copies of the same delivery report, do not result in additional charges. And if the SMS never reaches its recipient, the reserved funds are eventually released after timing out. The timeout also invalidates the identifier.

At most once, at least once, and exactly once approaches all have advantages and tradeoffs. While deciding what strategy to use, keep in mind that requests and the messaging infrastructure that underpins them are unreliable. This unreliability needs to be managed in the business logic and semantics of every request. The easiest to implement and least memory- and CPU-intensive approach is the "at most once" approach, where you send off your request and forget about it. If something fails, you have lost the request, but without affecting the performance of all of the other requests that succeeded. The "at least once" approach is more expensive, because you need to store the state of the request, monitor it, and upon receiving timeouts or errors, forward it to a different node. Along with higher memory and CPU usage, it can generate additional network traffic. Theoreticians will argue that the at least once approach cannot be guaranteed to be successful, as all nodes receiving the request can be down. We'll leave them scratching their heads and figuring out what double and triple redundancy are all about. The hardest strategy is the "exactly once" approach, because you need to provide guarantees when executing what is in effect a transaction. The request can succeed or fail, but nothing in between.

These guarantees are impossible with distributed systems, since failure can also mean a request being successfully executed but its acknowledgment and reply being lost. You need algorithms that try to retrace the call through the logs and understand where a failure occurred to try to correct it or compensate for it. In some systems, this is so complex or the stakes are so high that human intervention is required.

Until now, we've said, "Let it crash." Yes, let it crash, and no matter which of the three strategies you pick, put your effort into the recovery, ensuring that after failure, your system returns to a consistent state. The beauty of error handling and recovery in Erlang is that your recovery strategy will be the same when dealing with all of your errors, software, hardware, and network faults included. If you do it right, there will be no need to duplicate code in a process recreating its state after a crash or recovering after a network partition or packet loss.

Sharing Data

When you are thinking about your strategies for avoiding a single point of failure and for recovery, you have to make a new set of decisions about whether and how you are going to replicate data across your nodes, node families, and clusters. Your decisions will affect your system's availability (which includes fault tolerance, resilience, and reliability) and, ultimately, also scalability. Luckily, you can defer some of these decisions to when you stress test and benchmark your system. You might want to make other decisions up front based on the requirements you already know and on past experiences in designing similar systems. But whatever your decision is, one of the hardest things when dealing with distributed systems is accessing and moving your data; it can be the cause of your worst bottlenecks. For every table and state, you have three approaches you can choose from: *share nothing*, *share something*, and *share everything*. Choose your data replication strategy wisely, and pick the one that most closely matches the level of scale or availability for which you are aiming.

Share nothing

The share-nothing architecture is where no data or state is shared. This could be specific to a node, a node family, or a cluster. Once you have addressed the underlying infrastructure, such as hardware, networks, and load balancing, share-nothing architectures can result in linearly scalable systems. Because each collection of nodes has an independent copy of its own data and state, it can operate on its own. When you need to scale, all you need to do is add more infrastructure and reconfigure your load balancers.

Figure 14-5, part 1 shows two front-end and two logic nodes. Using a login request, *Client1* and *Client2* send their credentials to initiate a session. This request is forwarded to one of the two front-end nodes using the load-balancing strategy configured in the load balancer. In our example, each node gets a request that it forwards to its primary logic node. These nodes each check the client credentials and create a session, storing the session state in a database.

Client1 now sends a new request right after the node storing its session data has crashed, losing everything (Figure 14-5, part 2). The front-end node forwards it to its standby logic node, which rejects the request because it is unaware of the session. The client, upon receiving an unknown session error, sends a new login request that is forwarded and handled by the second logic node. All future requests from this client should now be forwarded to the logic node containing the session. If they aren't and the node that crashed comes up again, the client will have to log on again

(Figure 14-5, part 3), and we just assume that the session in the standby node will eventually time out and be deleted.

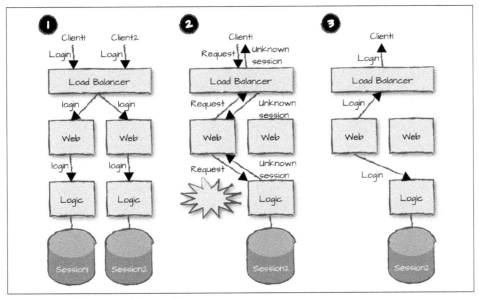

Figure 14-5. Share-nothing architecture

As we don't have to copy our session state across nodes, we get better scalability, because we can continue adding front-end and logic nodes as the number of simultaneously connected users increases. The downside of this strategy is that if you lose a node, you lose the state and all of the data associated with it. In our example, all sessions are lost, forcing users to log on again and establish a new session in another node. You also need to choose how to route your requests across nodes, ensuring that each request is routed to the logic node that stores its matching session data. This guarantees continuity after a node failure and recovery.

Share something

What do we do if we want to ensure that users are still logged on and have a valid session after a node failure? The share-something architecture, where you duplicate some but not all of your data, might address some of your concerns. In Figure 14-6, we copy the session state across all logic nodes. If a node terminates, is slow, or can't be reached, requests are forwarded to logic nodes that have copies of the session data. This approach ensures that the client does not have to go though a login procedure when switching logic nodes. But it trades off some scalability, because the session data needs to be copied across multiple nodes every time a client logs in and deleted when the session is terminated. Things get even more expensive whenever a node is added to the cluster or restarts, because sessions from the other nodes might have to be copied to it and kept consistent.

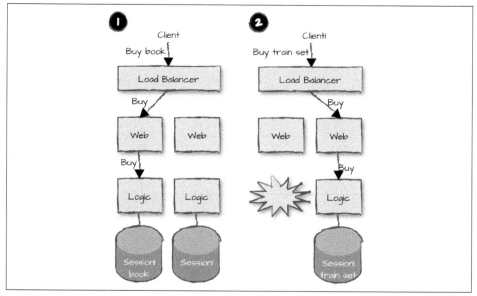

Figure 14-6. Share-something architecture

The strategy just described is called share something because it is a compromise: you copy some, but not all of the data and state associated with each session. The strategy reduces the overhead of copying while increasing the level of fault tolerance. Let's return to our e-commerce site. The session data is copied, so if a node is lost, the user does not have to log on again. However, the contents of the shopping cart are not copied, so upon losing a node, the users unexpectedly have their carts emptied. When a user is checking out and paying for the selected items, only those items in the active logic node's shopping cart will appear.

We have been assuming all along that if the logic node crashed, all of its data would be lost. What if the shopping cart were stored in a persistent key-value store which, upon restart, was reread? Or what if a network partition occurred, or the node was just slow in responding and, as such, presumed dead? When the node becomes available, you need to decide on your routing strategy—namely, which of the two logic nodes receives new requests. And because you have two shopping carts, they now need to be merged (Figure 14-7, part 1), or one of them has to be discarded.

How is this done? Do you join all of the items? What if we had added an item to the shopping cart in the second node? Will we end up with one or two copies of the item? Or what if we had sent a delete operation to the second node, but the operation failed because the item was not there? How you solve these problems depends on your business and your risks. Some distributed databases, such as Riak and Cassandra, provide you with options. In our example, the node that crashed becomes the primary again, and we move the contents of the second shopping cart to it (Figure 14-7, part 2).

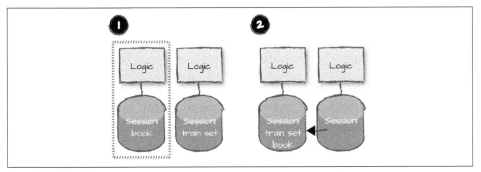

Figure 14-7. Network partitions with the share-something architecture

The Dynamo paper discussed in "Riak Core" on page 367 describes the Amazon way of merging its shopping cart when recovering from failures. If, during the merge, there is uncertainty over the deletion of an item, it gets included, leaving the responsibility to the shopper to either remove it when reviewing the final order or return it for a refund if it actually gets shipped. How many times, upon checkout, have you found an item in your Amazon shopping cart you were sure you had deleted? It has happened to us a few times.

The share-something architecture is ideal for use cases where you are allowed to lose an occasional odd request but need to retain state for more expensive operations. We used a shopping cart example. Think of an instant messaging server instead. The most expensive operation, and biggest bottleneck, is users logging in and starting a session. The session needs to access an authentication server, retrieve the user's contact list, and send everyone a status update. Imagine a server handling a million users. The last thing you want as the result of a network partition or a node crash is for a million users to be logging back on, especially when the system is still recovering from having sent 30 million offline status updates (assuming 60 contacts per user, of whom half are online).

One good solution is to distribute the session record across multiple nodes. What you do not share, however, are the status notifications and messages. You let them go through a single node with the "at most once" approach for sending messages in order to preserve speed. You assume that if the node crashes or is separated from the rest of the cluster through a network error, you either delay the delivery of the notifications and messages or lose some or all of them. How many times have you sent an SMS to someone close to you, only for them to receive it hours (or days) later, or never at all?

Consistency

When dealing with distributed systems, there are multiple forms of consistency that differ due to varying degrees of visibility, ordering, and replica coordination. In a perfect system, all nodes would see all updates at the same logical time and in the same order; no reads would ever return stale data; and there would be no latency anomalies, crashed nodes, network partitions, or lost messages. In our imperfect world, though, these guarantees do not hold and these problems actually do occur, and so systems must make tradeoffs between consistency, availability, and latency.

One weak form of consistency is *eventual consistency*, where updates at different replicas can occur in different orders, and reads can return stale values. While this consistency model sounds like it might do more harm than good, in practice it can be valuable for applications requiring read and write availability and predictable latency even when the system is operating under conditions of partial failure, as long as those applications can handle occasionally reading stale data.

Other forms of consistency, such as *monotonic read* and *monotonic write*, have to do with guarantees related to recency. When you read a value under a monotonic read model, you are guaranteed that you will never again see a value older than the one you just read. Similarly, with the monotonic write model you are guaranteed that any update you issue for a value will finish prior to any further updates you issue for the same value. These ordering guarantees come at a cost of increased coordination across the distributed system, and thus potentially increased latencies and lower availability.

Still stronger ordering guarantees are provided with the *read your own writes* consistency level, which is self-explanatory, and with a consistency model that's a combination of monotonic reads and writes where your update for a given value is guaranteed to never act on an instance older than your most recent read of the same value.

Even higher degrees of consistency can be achieved using *consensus protocols* such as Paxos, Zookeeper Atomic Broadcast (ZAB), and Raft, where a majority of replicas must vote and agree on updates for a given value. These protocols can deliver strong consistency guarantees, but to achieve them they require a high degree of coordination among replicas and so can have negative impacts on latency and availability. Even so, if your application requires this level of consistency guarantee, you are far better off using an implementation of a proven consensus protocol than trying to invent your own. For example, *Riak Ensemble* (*https://github.com/basho/riak_ensemble*) implements Multi-Paxos, an optimized version of basic Paxos.

One sometimes confusing point about these distributed system consistency levels is that they are different from the "C" in the Atomicity, Consistency, Isolation, and Durability (ACID) properties of transactional databases. In ACID, consistency means that effects of transactions become visible upon their completion and that no transactions violate database constraints.

Share everything

Share-nothing and share-something architectures might work for some systems and data sets, but what if you want to make your system as fault tolerant and resilient as possible? While it is not possible to have a distributed system where losing requests is not an option, you might be dealing with money, shares, or other operations where inconsistency or the risk of losing a request is unacceptable. Each transaction must execute exactly once, its data has to be strongly consistent, and operations on it must either succeed or fail in their entirety. Although you can get away with not receiving an SMS or instant message, finding an equity trade you thought had been executed missing in your portfolio or money missing from your bank account is indefensible. This is where the share-everything architecture comes into the picture. All your data is shared across all of the nodes, any of which might, upon hardware or software failure, take over the requests. If there is any uncertainty over the outcome of a request, an error is returned to the user. When things go wrong, they have to be reconciled after the fact. For example, if you try to withdraw from multiple ATMs more funds than you have in your account, you get the money, but then later the bank penalizes you for overdrawing your account. But with no single point of failure, using redundant hardware and software, the risk for this error should be reduced to a minimum.

In Figure 14-8, we duplicate the sessions and shopping cart contents in two logic nodes, each handling a subset of clients and duplicating the session state and shopping cart to the other nodes. If a node terminates, the other one takes over. Should the node recover, it will not accept any requests until all of the data from the active node has been copied over and is consistent with other nodes.

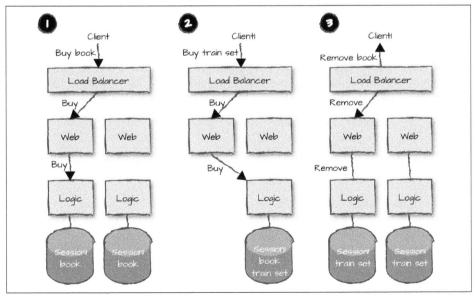

Figure 14-8. Share-everything architecture

We call this *primary-primary replication*. This contrasts with *primary-secondary replication*, where a single primary node is responsible for the data. The secondary nodes can access the data, but must coordinate any destructive operations such as inserts or deletes with the primary if they wish to modify the data. If the primary is lost, either the system stops working entirely, or it provides a degraded service level where writes and updates are not allowed, or one of the secondaries takes over as primary.

The share-everything architecture is the most reliable of all data-sharing strategies, but this reliability comes at the cost of scalability. It tolerates the loss of nodes without impacting consistency of data, but if some nodes go wrong, it also loses availability. This strategy is also the most expensive to run and maintain, because every operation results in computational overhead and multiple requests across the network to ensure that the data is kept replicated and consistent. Upon restarting, nodes must connect to a primary and retrieve a copy the data to bring them back in sync with the primary node, ensuring they have a correct and current view of the state and the data.

Although share-everything architectures do not necessarily require distributed transactions across nodes, you will need them when dealing with data such as money or shares you cannot afford to lose. This contrasts with the requirements we saw for messaging, where duplicating the messages through eventual consistency will greatly reduce the risk of them getting lost if you lose a node, but with no strong guarantee that you will never lose a message.

When you have decided on your data-sharing strategy, you need to go through each request in your API, trace the call, and try to map everything that can go wrong. Within the node itself, for synchronous calls, you need to consider behavior timeouts and abnormal process termination. If dealing with asynchronous messaging, ensure that message loss (when the receiving process has terminated) is handled correctly. Across nodes, you need to consider network errors, partitions, slow nodes, and node termination. When you're done, pick the recovery strategy that best suits the particular calls. This needs to be done for every external call, and will often result in a mixture of the three recovery strategies, depending on the importance of the state change.

CAP Confusion

The CAP theorem, a conjecture originally put forward in 2000 by Eric Brewer and formally proven in 2002 by Seth Gilbert and Nancy Lynch, states that in any distributed system it is impossible to fully provide *consistency*, *availability*, and *partition tolerance* at all times. For the purposes of CAP, these properties are defined as follows:

- Consistency guarantees that clients get correct responses to all requests.

- Availability guarantees that the system eventually services every request sent to it, for both reads and updates.
- Partition tolerance guarantees continued system operation even when the network or nodes fail and messages are delayed or lost.

The CAP theorem essentially states in a different way some issues we've already known about for decades, yet many view it as controversial and confusing. This stems from CAP having often been explained as requiring you to "pick two" of the three properties when designing a distributed system. Since one of the properties, partition tolerance, is inherent in the definition of distributed systems and is thus automatically chosen for you, the only realistic choice left was between consistency and availability. For example, some have claimed that Mnesia is a CA system, but clearly they've never attempted to use it during a network partition (conditions under which it is anything but available).

Real distributed systems tradeoffs are never as simple as the flawed "pick two" CAP dilemma. In 1977, decades before CAP, Leslie Lamport introduced the notions of safety and liveness for analyzing system properties, which Lamport, Bowen Alpern, Fred B. Schneider, and others explored and explained more deeply in the decades that followed. Simply put, *safety* means that as a distributed system operates, nothing bad happens, while *liveness* signifies that something good eventually happens. CAP consistency is a safety property because it implies correctness, whereas availability is a liveness property because it means clients always get valid replies.

The 1980s also gave us the Fischer-Lynch-Paterson (FLP) impossibility result, which proved that there is no distributed algorithm that can achieve consensus in an asynchronous system if even a single part of the system is failing. Both this theorem and the "P" in CAP indicate that delays and failure are inherent in distributed computing systems, both in hardware and software, and thus they can never be downplayed or ignored. In the face of failure, full consensus can't be achieved due to some nodes being unreachable, which in turn means agreement, consistency, and validity across the system suffer some degree of degradation. No matter how you analyze it, you run into these fundamental truths that all lead to the same conclusion: achieving full safety and liveness—or in CAP terms, full consistency and availability—is impossible in any practical distributed system.

In real-life systems, not only do the choices and tradeoffs between consistency and availability depend highly on the application, but different parts of the same application can require different tradeoffs. For example, a popular digital device at the time of writing is the fitness tracker. Such a device, worn by a user, collects health-related data, such as pulse rate, duration of fitness activities, or the number of steps taken while running or walking, and communicates the data to the device vendor. The vendor then makes the data available via the Web and mobile apps not only to the user, but perhaps also to the user's social network and designated health care providers as well. Even though all the data might be stored in a single database, the part of the overall application that handles user registration requires strong consistency to ensure two users don't register with the same username, whereas for the data delivery portions of the application, having a highly available data store is more important than providing fully consistent updates to all interested parties.

Applications such as these explain why some databases, such as Riak, can simultaneously support both strong consistency and eventual consistency, letting the application choose what it needs. And modern research, such as the work of Peter Bailis, has analyzed the consistency-availability spectrum in depth to show that applications can often operate correctly with less consistency and coordination than were previously considered necessary, and in some cases can even correctly accomplish tasks that were once thought to work only with full distributed transaction support.

CAP, safety and liveness, and other related approaches are all ways of explaining that distributed systems involve a broad spectrum of tradeoffs and choices. Due to their telephony backgrounds, the designers of Erlang/OTP were aware of these choices, but the growth of the Web and the scale of large websites has forced a much larger part of the industry to try to come to grips with all these distributed system issues because at scale, they all show up whether you like it or not, and typically at the worst possible time.

Tradeoffs Between Consistency and Availability

We were refactoring a system where the customer claimed they had never had an outage, servicing all requests with 100% availability, software upgrades included, for years on end. They were not using Erlang, and to add icing on the cake, were running everything on mainframes! When we began to scratch under the surface, we found out that their definition of availability meant that the front-end nodes were always up, accepting and acknowledging requests. In the case of errors and outages in their logic and service nodes, however, requests were logged and processed manually! We could argue that this system was indeed highly available, but unreliable, as it did not always function as defined. Getting it into a consistent state after failure required manual intervention. The choices you make in your recovery strategy are all about tradeoffs between consistency and availability, while your data-sharing strategy is about tradeoffs between latency and consistency.

On one side, you have the *exactly once* approach, ensuring that an operation executes to completion or fails. However, this is also the least available solution (Figure 14-9, part 1), as strong consistency requirements mean choosing consistency over availability. If things go wrong, the system might under certain circumstances become unavailable in order to ensure consistency. On the other end of the spectrum is weak consistency with high availability. By accepting the loss of occasional requests, you accept an inconsistent view of the state or data, handling this inconsistency in the semantics of your system. As a result, you can continue servicing your requests even under network partitions. The compromise is the *at least once* approach, which guarantees that a request has successfully executed on at least one node. It is then up to the semantics of the system, where necessary, to handle the propagation and merging of this state change to other nodes.

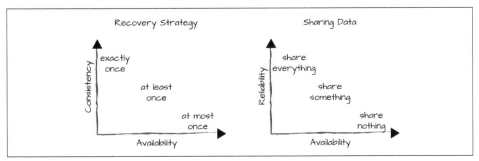

Figure 14-9. Tradeoffs between consistency, reliability, and availability

A similar argument can be made on the sharing of data approach (Figure 14-9, part 2), where the tradeoffs are between availability and reliability. Using the share-everything approach across nodes, you make your system more reliable, as any node with a copy of the data and state can take over the request correctly. While it is not always possible to guarantee that data is replicated, it is a safer approach than the share-something or share-nothing architectures, where some or all of the data and state are lost in the event of failure.

Nirvana would be reaching the top right of both graphs: a system that is consistent, reliable, and available. If you lose a node, the state is guaranteed to be replicated on at least one other node, and guaranteeing that your requests are either executed exactly once or fail and return an error message to the client will leave your system in a consistent state. Alas, having it all is not possible. If it were, everyone would just choose to do it this way, and distributed systems wouldn't be difficult at all!

Summing Up

In this chapter, we introduced the concept of *availability*, defined as the uptime of a system, errors and maintenance included. Availability is a term that encompasses the following additional concepts:

- *Fault tolerance*, allowing your system to act in a predictable way during failure. Failure could be loss of processes, nodes, network connectivity, or hardware.

- *Resilience*, allowing your system to quickly recover from failure. This could mean a node restarting after a crash or a redundant network kicking in after the primary one fails.

- *Reliability*, where under particular, predefined conditions, errors included, your system continues to function. If a node is unresponsive because it has terminated, is slow, or got separated from the rest of the system in a network partition, your business logic should be capable of redirecting the request to a responsive node.

Your levels of fault tolerance, resilience, and reliability, and ultimately availability, are the result of correctly applying the Erlang/OTP programming model and choices you make in your data-sharing and recovery strategies. This brings us to the next steps in determining our distributed architecture. The steps we covered in Chapter 13 included:

1. *Split up your system's functionality into manageable, standalone nodes.*
2. *Choose a distributed architectural pattern.*
3. *Choose the network protocols your nodes, node families, and clusters will use when communicating with each other.*
4. *Define your node interfaces, state, and data model.*

   You now need to pick your retry and data-sharing strategies:

5. *For every interface function in your nodes, you need to pick a retry strategy.*

   Different functions will require different retry strategies. When deciding if you want to use the *at most once*, *at least once*, or *exactly once* approach, you need to examine all possible failure scenarios in the call chain, software, hardware, and network included. Take particular care of your failure scenarios for the exactly once strategy.

6. *For all your data and state, pick your sharing strategy across node families, clusters, and types, taking into consideration the needs of your retry strategy.*

   In a data-sharing strategy, for both state and data, you need to decide if you want to *share nothing*, *share something*, or *share everything* across node families, clusters, and systems. You could also use consistent hashing to have multiple copies of the data, but not necessarily on all nodes.

In deciding on your sharing and retry strategies, you might need to review and change the design choices you made in steps 1–4. You mix and choose a variety of sharing and recovery alternatives specific to particular data, state, and requests. Not all requests have to be executed exactly once, and not all the data needs to be shared across all nodes. Guaranteed-delivery share-everything approaches are expensive, so use them only for the subset of data and requests that require them. And remember, things will fail. Try to isolate state, and share as little of it as possible among processes, nodes, and node families. Embrace failure and embed it in your architecture. Although it would be great to achieve the impossible and have systems that share everything and are strongly consistent, reliable, and available, in practice you have to choose your tradeoffs wisely based on system requirements, guarantees you want to provide to your customers, and the cost of operations.

What's Next?

Having covered distributed architectures and how we use replication of data and retry strategies to increase availability, the time has come to look at scalability. In the next chapter, we cover a new set of tradeoffs required for scale. We look at load-testing techniques, load regulation, and the detection of bottlenecks in your system.

## CHAPTER 15

Scaling Out

Distributing for scale and replicating for availability both rely on multiple instances of every node running on separate computers. But as computers can (and will) end up missing in action and connectivity among them will fail, scaling out is not only about adding computing capacity. Rather, scaling out must be carefully integrated and orchestrated with your consistency and availability models, where you have already chosen which tradeoffs to make. It's easy to say that you need to write a system that scales infinitely without losing a single request, but delivering it is never simple, and it's often the case that such an ideal implementation is unnecessary in practice to support your target applications. While Erlang/OTP systems do not scale magically, using OTP and making the right tradeoffs takes a large part of the pain out of the process.

In this chapter, we follow on from the distributed programming patterns and recovery and data-sharing patterns described in Chapter 13 and Chapter 14, focusing on the scalability tradeoffs you make when designing your architecture. We describe the tests needed to understand your system's limitations and ensure it can handle, without failing, the capacity for which it was designed. This allows you to put safeguards in place, ensuring users do not overflow the system with requests it can't handle. The last thing you want to deal with when under heavy load is a node crash, the degradation of throughput, or a service provider or third-party API not responding as a result of the wrath of Erlang being unleashed upon it.

Horizontal and Vertical Scaling

The *scalability* of a system is its ability to handle changes in demand and behave predictably, especially under spikes or sustained heavy loads. Scalability can be achieved *vertically*, by throwing more powerful computers at the problem, or *horizontally*, by adding more nodes and hardware.

Amdahl's Law

Amdahl's Law is used to predict the maximum speedup of your parallel program when adding cores. In simple terms, it tells us that a program will be as fast as its slowest component. When dealing with parallelism and concurrency, the slowest component is your sequential code. Amdahl's Law states that $S(N) = 1/((1–P) + P/N)$, where $S(N)$ is the speedup the system can achieve when executing with N cores, and P is the proportion of the program that can be made parallel. As N approaches infinity, the maximum speedup becomes $S(N) = 1/1–P$.

You can throw as many cores as you want at your parallel code, but if your sequential code takes 100 ms to run, no matter how fast your parallel code runs, you will not be able to run faster than 100 ms. Another way of looking at the principle is this: if 5% of your code base is sequential, your maximum speedup will be 20 times, and if 50% of your code is sequential, your maximum speedup will be 2 times. This is visible in Figure 15-1, which also shows the law of diminishing returns.

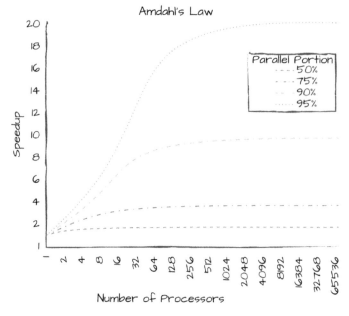

Figure 15-1. Amdahl's Law

When we reach a certain limit, adding more cores improves performance only marginally. This is where it makes sense to scale your system by partitioning your data set and operations into distributed nodes, running them in parallel.

Vertical scalability, also referred to as *scaling up*, might at first glance appear to be a quick win. You have a single server that guarantees strong consistency of your data. You just add larger chips, faster clock cycles, more cores and memory, a faster disk, and more network interfaces. Who does not like the feeling of opening a box containing the fastest, shiniest, highest capacity, yet slimmest computer on which to benchmark your software?

But alas, this approach is dated, because servers can only get so big, and the bigger they get, the more expensive they become. And you need at least two, because a super fast computer can still be a single point of failure.

Another argument for scaling horizontally is multicore. With machines supporting thousands of cores, no matter how parallel and free of bottlenecks your program might be, there are only so many cores a single VM will be able to optimally utilize. You need to also keep in mind that Amdahl's Law applies not only to your Erlang program, but to the sequential code in the Erlang VM. This likely means that in order to fully utilize the hardware, you have to run multiple distributed VMs on a single computer. If you need to deal with two computers or computers running multiple Erlang nodes, you might as well take the leap and scale horizontally.

Scaling horizontally, also known as *scaling out*, is achieved using cloud instances and commodity hardware. If you need more processing power, you can rent, buy, or build your own machines and deploy extra nodes on them. Distributed systems, whether you want them or not, are your only viable approach. They will scale better, are much more cost-effective, and help you achieve high availability. But as we have seen in the previous chapters, this will require rethinking how you architect your applications.

In small clusters running distributed Erlang, Erlang/OTP scales vertically or horizontally in essentially the same way. In both cases, scaling is achieved using the location transparency of processes, meaning they act the same way whether they run locally or remotely. Processes communicate with each other using asynchronous message passing, which in soft real-time systems absorbs at the cost of latency across nodes. And asynchronous error semantics also work across nodes. As a result, a system written to run on a single machine can easily be distributed across a cluster of nodes. This also facilitates *elasticity*, the ability to add and remove nodes (and computers) at runtime so you can cater not only for failure, but also for peak loads and systems with a growing user base.

Scaling with Native Code

A little-known fact about Erlang/OTP is its excellence as an integration platform. It supports a variety of standard networking protocols, allowing it to support applications that communicate with disparate components and bridge them together. It can also deal easily with proprietary protocols, through facilities such as its excellent networking socket APIs. Additionally, Erlang/OTP provides ports, which allow applications to call and exchange data with external programs. Developers have used these and other Erlang/OTP capabilities to successfully build database drivers, JSON parsers, special-purpose web clients and servers, and other integration-oriented components and applications.

Scalable systems often comprise multiple components written in different programming languages because different languages have complementary strengths and weaknesses. Sometimes, for example, the capabilities built into Erlang/OTP just aren't enough. Some applications require heavy mathematical calculations, and Erlang isn't well suited for performing those quickly. Other applications might need access to non-Erlang libraries that would be difficult or prohibitively expensive to rewrite in Erlang.

For these and other similar reasons, Erlang/OTP provides support for calling non-Erlang functions, termed *native implemented functions* (NIFs), directly from Erlang code. Some parts of Erlang/OTP itself are written as NIFs, such as portions of the lists, maps, ets, and crypto standard modules, among others. To other Erlang functions, NIFs look like regular Erlang functions. They accept regular Erlang terms as arguments and return regular terms as well, but under the covers these functions are implemented in a different language, typically C or C++. However, they execute directly within the Erlang runtime. When the runtime loads an Erlang module containing NIFs, it loads along with it a shared library containing the native function implementations, and then patches the module's BEAM code with instructions that invoke the native functions instead. The runtime provides a C API for NIFs allowing them to access and create Erlang terms, send messages to other processes, raise exceptions, and even schedule other NIFs for future execution. For a complete overview of the NIF API, see the erl_nif (*http://erlang.org/doc/man/erl_nif.html*) manual page that comes with the Erlang/OTP distribution.

Should you measure your application and find that parts of it are worth rewriting as NIFs for performance reasons, or if you must reuse an existing C/C++ library rather than reimplement it in Erlang, be very careful, because misbehaving NIFs can wreak havoc on the Erlang VM. Forget the "let it crash" philosophy if you're writing a NIF; they execute directly on the runtime's scheduler threads, so if a NIF crashes, it takes the entire VM down with it. You can also inflict a more insidious and slower death on the VM by making your NIFs run for more than 1–2 milliseconds at a time, as this causes the NIF to hog a VM scheduler thread and disrupt its carefully choreographed interactions with other scheduler threads. Over time, such disruptions can eventually lead to a phenomenon known as "scheduler collapse" where schedulers think they have no work to do and mistakenly go to sleep, leaving just one scheduler to handle the entire workload.

To avoid this, either make sure your NIFs execute quickly, or write them to break their work into short chunks that can be scheduled for future execution using the `enif_schedule_nif()` C API function. Another alternative is to use VM "dirty schedulers," which are pools of schedulers that do not have the same set of constraints as normal schedulers and are specifically designed for running only NIFs and native code. Dirty schedulers are marked experimental in Erlang 17 and 18, though, and so they are turned off by default. We hope that by Erlang 19, they will be a regular Erlang runtime feature available for any application that needs them.

Capacity Planning

Understanding what resources your node types use and how they interact with each other allows you to optimize the hardware and infrastructure in terms of both efficiency and cost. This work is called *capacity planning*. Its purpose is to try to guarantee that your system can withstand the load it was designed to handle, and, with time, scale to manage increased demand.

The only way to determine the load and resource utilization and balance the required number of different nodes working together is to simulate high loads, testing your system end to end. This ensures the nodes are able to work together under extended heavy load, handling the required capacity in a predictable manner without any bottlenecks. It also allows you to test your system's behavior in case of failure.

In Chapter 13, we suggest you divide your system functionality into node types and families and connect nodes in a cluster. Although one can argue that grouping the different applications of all your node types together—front-end, business logic, and service functionality in the same node—will run fast because everything is running in the same memory space, this solution is not recommended for anything other than simple systems. For complex systems, it is easier to divide and conquer, studying and optimizing throughput and resource utilization on nodes that are limited in functionality.

Balancing your system is also a cost optimization exercise, where you try to reduce the costs of hardware, operations, and maintenance. Imagine front-end nodes that parse relatively few simultaneous requests, but act as an interface to clients who keep millions of TCP connections open. These nodes will most likely be memory-bound and need a different type of hardware specification from a CPU-bound front-end node that has fewer, but more traffic-intensive, connections and spends most of its time parsing and generating JSON or XML. Logic nodes routing requests and running computationally intensive business logic will need more cores and memory, while a service node managing a database will probably be I/O-bound and need a fast hard disk.

An often overlooked item when dealing with capacity planning is ensuring you can handle the designated load even after a software, hardware, or network failure. If your system has two front-end nodes for every logic node and both run at 100% memory or CPU capacity, losing a front-end node means you will now be able to handle only half of your designated load. To ensure you have no single point of failure, you need at least three front-end nodes running at a maximum capacity of 66% CPU each and two back-end nodes averaging 50% CPU each. This way, losing any machine or node will still guarantee you can handle your peak load requirements. If you want triple redundancy, you will have to throw even more hardware at the problem.

When working with capacity planning, you will be measuring and optimizing your system in terms of throughput and latency. *Throughput* refers to the number of units going through the system. Units could be measured in number of requests per second when dealing with uniform requests, but when the CPU load and amount of memory needed to process the requests vary in size (think emails or email attachments), throughput is better measured in kilobytes, megabytes, or gigabytes per second.

Latency is the time it takes to serve a particular request. Latency might vary depending on the load of your system, and is often correlated to the number of simultaneous requests going through it at any point in time. More simultaneous requests often means higher latency.

The predictable behavior of the Erlang runtime system, where a balanced system under heavy load results in a constant throughput, addresses most use cases. But there might be instances where extreme usage spikes or third-party services that are slow in responding could result in a backlog of requests, an outage caused by the Erlang VM running out of system resources, or the need to apply load regulation so latency stays within predefined intervals.

In "Tradeoffs Between Consistency and Availability" on page 400, we discussed the tradeoffs between consistency and availability based on your recovery and data-sharing strategies and distributed architectural patterns. You might not have realized it, but you were also making tradeoffs with scalability (Figure 15-2).

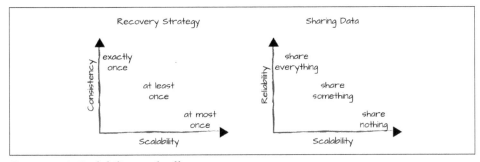

Figure 15-2. Scalability tradeoffs

The most scalable framework is SD Erlang. With it, you effectively share data within an s_group, but minimize what is shared across s_groups. Data and workflows shared among s_groups go through gateway nodes. By controlling the size of s_groups and the number of gateways, you can have strong consistency within an s_group and eventual consistency among s_groups.

Riak Core comes second, and despite being a fully meshed Erlang cluster, it can scale well by using consistent hashing to shard your data and load balancing jobs across the cluster. You can use it as a giant switch running your business logic, connecting service nodes that are part of the cluster, but not fully meshed to the core itself. With a hundred connected nodes in the core, where each node handles thousands of requests per second, most seriously scalable event-driven systems should fall under this category. Thanks to vnodes, you can start small and minimize disruption when nodes are added (or removed).

Lastly, a distributed Erlang cluster is limited in scale but does well enough to cater to the vast majority of Erlang systems. Even if you are aiming for tens of thousands of requests per second, you will often find it is more than enough. Be realistic in your capacity planning and add complexity only when you need it.

On one end of the scale are the exactly-once and share-everything approaches, which lean toward consistency and reliability, respectively. They are also the most expensive in terms of CPU power and network requirements, and as such, are also the least scalable. If you want a truly scalable system, you need to reduce the amount of shared data to a minimum and, if you have to share data, use eventual consistency wherever appropriate. Use asynchronous message passing across nodes, and in cases where you need strong consistency, minimize it in as few nodes as possible, placing them close to each other so as to reduce the risk of network failure.

Capacity Testing

Capacity testing is a must when working with any scalable and available system to help ensure its stability and understand its behavior under heavy load. This is true regardless of what programming language you use to code the system.

What is your system's maximum throughput before it breaks? How is the system affected by increased utilization or the loss of a computer resulting from a hardware or network malfunction? And is the latency of these requests under different loads acceptable? You need to ensure your system remains stable under extended heavy load, recovers from spikes, and stays within its allocated system limits. Too often, systems are deployed without any proper stress testing, and they underperform or crash under minimal load because of misconfiguration or bottlenecks. To reduce the risk of running into these issues when going live, you will have to apply the four testing strategies shown in Figure 15-3.

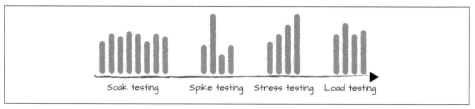

Figure 15-3. Capacity-testing strategies

They are:

Soak testing
> This generates a consistent load over time to ensure that your system can keep on running without any performance degradation. Soak tests can continue for months and are used to test not only your system, but the whole stack and infrastructure.

Spike testing
> This ensures you can handle peak loads and recover from them quickly and painlessly.

Stress testing
> This gradually increases the load you are generating until you hit bottlenecks and system limits. Bottlenecks are backlogs in your system whose symptom is usually long message queues. System limits include running out of ports, memory, or even hard disk space. When you have found a bottleneck and removed it, rerun the stress test again to tackle the next bottleneck or system limit.

Load testing

This pushes your system at a constant rate close to its limits, ensuring it is stable and balanced. Run your load test for at least 24 hours to ensure there is no degradation in throughput and latency.

Don't underestimate the time, budget, and resources it takes to remove bottlenecks and achieve high throughput with predictable latency. You need hardware to generate the load, hardware to run your simulators, and hardware to run multiple tests in parallel. With crashes that take days to generate, running parallel tests with full visibility of what is going on is a must. It will at times feel like you are looking for a needle in a haystack as you are troubleshooting and optimizing your software stack, hardware, and network settings.

Generating load

How you generate load varies across systems and organizations. You can use existing open source tools and frameworks such as Basho Bench, MZBench, and Tsung; commercial products; or SaaS load-testing services. Some tools allow you to record and replay live traffic. Or if you want to simulate complex business client logic or test simple scenarios, it might be easier to write your own tests. You will soon discover that to test an Erlang system, you will most likely need a load tool written in Erlang.

If you are connecting to third-party services or want to test node types on a standalone basis, you will need to write simulators, because your third parties will most likely not allow you to test against live systems. Simulators like the one shown in Figure 15-4 are often standalone Erlang nodes that expose the external API and, to some degree of intelligence, replicate their behavior. They are designed to handle the load of your external services, but often go far beyond that.

 Exercise extreme care when load testing the final instance of your system right before going live, and make sure you are connected to your simulators and have throttling in place toward your external service providers. We would advise against you discovering the hard way that your external service providers do not have any load control in place. We once ran load tests on an autodialer we were writing, forgetting to divert the requests to the simulators. The error caused a major outage of the IP telephony provider we were planning to use. They were not too happy. Nor were we, as we got kicked out and had to find and integrate with a new provider days before going live.

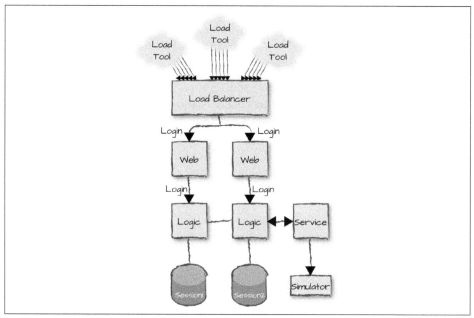

Figure 15-4. An Erlang system under load

Balancing Your System

In a properly balanced Erlang system running at maximum capacity, the throughput should remain constant while latency varies. If the work cost per request is constant and your system handles a peak throughput of 20,000 requests per second, when 20,000 requests are going through the system at any one time, the peak latency should be 1 second. If 40,000 requests are going through the system simultaneously, it will take the system 2 seconds to service a request. So, while throughput remains the same—20,000 requests per second—the latency doubles. The BEAM VM is one of the few virtual machines to display this property, providing predictability for your system even under sustained extreme loads.

In Figure 15-5 we show a graph where the y-axis represents the throughput of a typical Erlang system before being optimized. It could be the number of instant messages handled per second, the throughput in megabytes of data sent by a web server, or the number of log entries being formatted and stored to file. The x-axis shows the number of simultaneous requests going through the system at any one time. This degradation often manifests itself after hitting high CPU loads. At that point, the more requests there are going through the system, the lower the throughput and higher the latency. It is important that you understand this behavior of the BEAM virtual machine, as it is bound to affect you.

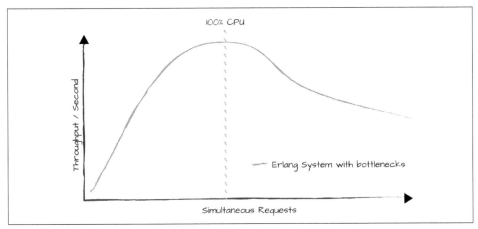

Figure 15-5. Degradation of an Erlang system under load

Line 2 in Figure 15-6 shows the result of removing bottlenecks in the system. You should get a constant throughput regardless of the number of simultaneous requests. The throughput at peak load might go down a little, but that is a small price to pay for a system that will behave in a predictable manner irrespective of the number of simultaneous requests going through it. Most other languages will experience degraded throughput because processes have high context-switching costs. Using the Erlang virtual machine, highly optimized for concurrency, greatly reduces the risk. The limit on how much a node can scale is now determined by system limits such as CPU load, available memory, or I/O. We refer to nodes hitting these limits as being *CPU-bound*, *memory-bound*, or *I/O-bound*. The shared area shows the performance degradation of a badly balanced system.

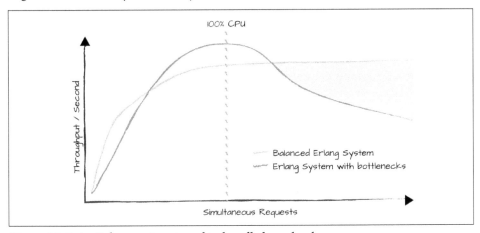

Figure 15-6. An Erlang system tuned to handle large loads

To find the bottlenecks in your system, start off testing a single node. Use simulators, but be wary of premature optimizations. Some node types might not need to be optimized, as they might never be subjected to heavy loads. And you might end up with nodes that are super fast, but continue to respond too slowly because service-level agreements with external APIs now become your bottleneck. The goals of your various capacity testing exercises are to measure and record how latency, throughput, and simultaneous requests going through the system affect one another.

In some cases, bottlenecks will throttle requests that surprisingly keep the service alive. The problem is that they tend to slow it down. For this reason, it sometimes makes sense to test your system on different hardware and VM configurations.

Consider your system stable only when all performance bottlenecks have been removed or optimized, leaving you to deal with issues arising from your external dependencies such as I/O, your filesystem, or network or external third-party services not being able to handle your load. These items are often out of your control, leaving it necessary to regulate your loads instead of continuing to scale up or out.

Finding Bottlenecks

When you are looking for bottlenecks on a process and node basis, most culprits are easily found by monitoring process memory usage and mailbox queues. Memory usage is best monitored using the `erlang:memory()` BIF, which returns a list of tuples with the dynamic memory allocations for processes, ETS tables, the binary heap, atoms, code, and other things.

You need to monitor the different categories of memory usage throughout your load testing, ensuring that there are no leaks and that resource usage is constant for long runs. If you see the atom table or binary heap increasing in size over time without stabilizing, you might run into problems days, weeks, or months down the line. At some point, you will also want to use the system monitor, described in "The System Monitor" on page 373, to ensure that process memory spikes and long garbage collections are optimized or removed. Message queues can be monitored using the `i()` or `regs()` shell commands.

If using the shell is not viable because you are working with millions of processes, the *percept* and *etop* tools will often work, as might the *observer* tool. Along with other monitoring tools, we discuss collecting system metrics in "Metrics" on page 433. If you are collecting system metrics and feeding them into your OAM infrastructure, you can use them to locate and gain visibility into bottlenecks.

Multicore Architectures and Memory Spikes

We were testing our first high-throughput system running on a multicore architecture. One of the acceptance tests was to show it could sustain the peak load it was designed to handle over a period of 24 hours. Despite all of the nodes running at 50% CPU with plenty of memory to spare, one of the nodes managing an API toward a third-party service provider crashed, on average, every 8 hours. We were throttling requests based on the service-level agreement, ensuring there were no more than a few hundred simultaneous requests. We polled the memory every 10 seconds, getting readings of hundreds of megabytes of free memory right before each crash. We rewrote the code and reduced memory consumption and CPU load by 50%, but that only delayed the problem, rather than eliminating it. The node now crashed every 16–20 hours.

Eventually we turned on the system monitor and noted that a few seconds before the crash, an unusually high number of long garbage collection and large heap trace events were generated. These were connected to the creation of a session, where an XML file sent back to us with session data caused a huge memory spike when parsed. We were seeing memory spikes when plotting our graphs, but did not think much about them because they were contained. What happened in the run-up to every crash was a surge in session initialization requests, causing these spikes to pool together and create a monster spike that caused the VM to run out of memory. We eventually discovered that using more cores increased the probability of this monster spike happening. In less than half a second, this memory surge used up all available memory and caused the node to crash.

The solution? We created a separate FIFO queue for session initialization, throttling the number of simultaneous requests that caused the memory usage to spike. Despite our controlling the problem by adding a bottleneck, the memory graphs became flat, throughput was not affected, and the system passed the stress tests.

The biggest challenge, however, is often not finding the bottlenecks, but creating enough load on your system to generate them. Multicore architectures have made this more difficult, as huge loads will often expose issues in other parts of the stack that are related not to Erlang, but to the underlying hardware, operating system, and infrastructure. One approach to detecting some of your bottlenecks is to run your Erlang virtual machine with fewer cores using the erl +S flag, or stress testing the node on less powerful hardware.

Synchronous versus asynchronous calls

Most commonly, bottlenecks manifest themselves through long message queues. Imagine a process whose task is to format and store logs to files. Assume that for every processed request we want to store dozens of log entries. We start sending our log requests asynchronously using gen_server:cast to a log server that can't cope with the load, because each request process is generating log entries at a rate faster than what the generic server process can handle. Multiply that by thousands of producers and slow file I/O, and you'll end up with a huge message queue in the consumer's mailbox. This queue is the manifestation of a bottleneck that negatively affects the behavior of your system. How does this happen?

Every operation in your program is assigned a number of reductions (covered in "Multicore, Schedulers, and Reductions" on page 32), each of which is roughly equivalent to one Erlang function call. When the scheduler dispatches a process, it is assigned a number of reductions it is allowed to execute, and for every operation, it reduces the reduction count. The process is suspended when it reaches a receive clause where none of the messages in the mailbox match, or the reduction count reaches zero. When process mailboxes grow in size, the Erlang virtual machine penalizes the sender process by increasing the number of reductions it costs to send the message. It does so in an attempt to control producers and allow the consumer to catch up. It is designed this way to give the consumer a chance to catch up after a peak, but under sustained heavy load, it will have an adverse effect on the overall throughput of the system. This scenario, however, assumes there are no bottlenecks. Penalizing senders with added reductions is not adequate to prevent overgrown message queues for overloaded processes.

A trick to regulate the load and control the flow, so as to get rid of these bottlenecks, is to use synchronous calls even if you do not require a response back from the server. When you use a synchronous call, a producer initiating a request will not send a new log request until the previous one has been received and acknowledged. Synchronous calls block the producer until the consumer has handled previous requests, preventing its mailbox from being flooded. It will have the same effect described in Figure 15-6, where, at the expense of throughput, you get a stable and predictable system. When using this approach, remember to fine-tune your timeout values, never taking the default 5-second value for granted, and never setting it to infinity.

Another strategy for reducing bottlenecks is to reduce the workload in the consumers, moving it where possible to the clients. In the case of log entries, for example, you could process them in batches, flushing a couple hundred of them at a time to disk. You could also offload work to the requesting process, making it format the entries instead of leaving that to the server. After all, formatting log entries can be done concurrently, whereas writing the log entries to disk must take place sequentially.

Now that you've optimized your code, learned your system's limits, and addressed its bottlenecks, you will need guarantees that your system will not fail over or degrade in performance if you hit those limits.

System Blueprints

If you have come this far, the time has come to formalize all your design choices into cluster and resource blueprints, combining them together into a system blueprint. Your *resource blueprint* specifies the available resources on which to run your cluster. It includes descriptions of hardware specifications or cloud instances, routers, load balancers, firewalls, and other network components.

Your *cluster blueprint* is derived from the lessons learned from your capacity planning. It is a logical description of your system, specifying node families and the connectivity within and among them. You also define the ratios of different node types you need to have a balanced system capable of functioning with no degradation of service. This blueprint can be used by your orchestration programs to ensure your cluster can be scaled in an orderly fashion, without creating imbalances among your nodes. It should also ensure your system can continue running after failure, with no degradation of service. Cluster blueprints are analogous to an Amazon autoscaling group on Amazon Web Services, but are more detailed. When you hit an upper limit in one of your clusters, deploy a new cluster.

Your cluster and resource blueprints are combined in what we call a *system blueprint*. With the system blueprint in hand, you can understand both how your distributed system is structured and how it can be deployed on hardware or cloud instances.

Load Regulation and Backpressure

A long, long time ago, on New Year's Eve, in a country far, far away, everyone picked up the phone and called to wish one another a happy and prosperous new year. Phone trunks were jammed. Calls were allowed through at the rate the various trunks were configured to handle, and the network kept on operating despite the surge. It behaved predictably for the maximum capacity it was designed to manage.

The system stayed afloat because it employed *backpressure* to limit the number of connected calls made through a trunk at any point in time. You always got the dial tone and were allowed to dial, but if you tried to access an international trunk with no available lines, your call was rejected with a busy tone. So you kept on trying until you got through. Backpressure is the approach of telling the sender to stop sending because there's no room for new messages.

From phone calls, the world moved to SMSs. As SMS became popular, the spike on New Year's Eve started getting larger, as did the delays in delivering the SMSs. And as soon as mobile phones allowed you to send SMSs in bulk to dozens of users, delays got even worse, with messages often arriving in the early hours of the morning when their senders (and recipients) had long since gone to bed. Rarely were SMSs rejected —they got through, but with major delays. The mobile operators were applying a technique called *load regulation*, where the flow of requests was diverted to a queue to ensure that no requests were lost. Messages were retrieved from the queue and sent to the SMS center (SMSC) as fast as it could handle them.

Calling each other or sending SMSs might be a thing of the past, but the techniques developed and used in the telecom space still remain relevant when dealing with massive scale. Together, load regulation and backpressure allow you to keep throughput and latency predictable while ensuring your system does not fail as a result of overload. The difference is that load regulation allows you to keep and remember requests by imposing limits on the number of simultaneous connections and throttling requests using queues, while backpressure rejects them. If you are using load regulation toward third-party APIs or service nodes, remember that all you are doing is smoothing out your peaks and troughs, ensuring you do not overflow the third party with requests. If you keep on receiving requests at a rate faster than they can handle, you will eventually have to stop queuing and start rejecting.

Little's Law

Little's Law is an equation $L = \lambda W$ stating that the *queue length*, L, is equal to the *arrival rate*, λ, multiplied by the *response time*, W. In most Internet-connected programs, the queue length is the number of client requests waiting to be (and currently being) serviced, the arrival rate is the number of client requests per time unit being accepted into and serviced by the system, and the response time is how long it takes to service one client request. Reorganizing the parameters in the equation, we get *response time = queue length / arrival rate*. This shows that if the queue length gets longer or the arrival rate—or perhaps more accurately, the throughput—decreases, the response time will go up.

In a live system, you cannot control the arrival rate, but it is hopefully constant, even under heavy load. What you can control, though, are the queue length, by applying backpressure, and the throughput, by removing bottlenecks from the request-processing path. By controlling the queue length and keeping the arrival rate constant throughout a balanced system, you control the response time. The key to getting the values right and applying backpressure at the right time is to have full visibility of what is going on in your system and to measure it.

Let's use our New Year's Eve SMS example. If the gateway is receiving more texts than can be handled by the SMSC (which forwards texts to your mobile terminal), it queues the texts in your load-regulation application, feeding them on a FIFO basis at the rate the SMSC can handle. This rate is called the *service-level agreement*. If the SMSs keep on coming in at this fast rate for a sustained period of time, the queue size is bound to hit its limit and overflow. When this happens, the gateway starts rejecting SMSs, either individually in the logic nodes or in bulk by triggering some form of backpressure in the front-end nodes, and not accepting them in the gateway nodes. This scenario is illustrated in Figure 15-7.

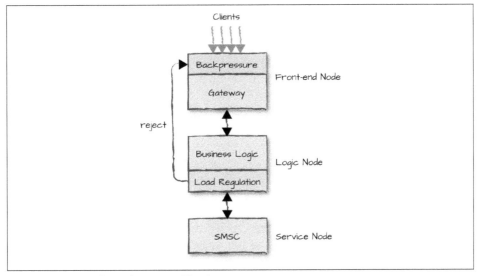

Figure 15-7. Load regulation and backpressure

In order to throttle requests and apply backpressure, you need to use load-regulation frameworks. These could be embedded into your Erlang nodes, or be found at the edges in the front-end and service nodes. Another common practice to control load is through load balancers. Software and hardware load balancers will, on top of balancing requests across front-end nodes, also throttle the number of simultaneously connected users and control the rate of inbound requests. Sadly, this will by default involve stress testing the load balancers themselves, opening a new can of worms.[1] Whoever said it was easy to develop scalable, resilient systems?

Keep in mind that load regulation comes at a cost, because you are using queues and a dispatcher can become a potential bottleneck that adds overhead. Start controlling load only if you have to. When deploying a website for your local flower shop, what is the risk of everyone in town flocking to buy flowers simultaneously? If, however, you are deploying a game back end that has to scale to millions of users, load regulation and backpressure are a must. They give you the ability to keep the latency or throughput of your system constant despite peak loads, and ensure your system does not degrade in performance or crash as a result of hitting system limits. There are two widely used load-regulation applications in Erlang: *Jobs* and *Safetyvalve*.

---

1 The sad part of this paragraph is that we've often caused load balancers to crash or behave abnormally and had to shut them down when load testing, because they weren't powerful enough to withstand the load we were generating.

Jobs and Safetyvalve

Jobs (*https://github.com/uwiger/jobs*), written by Ulf Wiger, is a scheduler for load regulation of Erlang-based systems. It provides a queuing framework where each queue can be configured for throughput rate, job type, and number of concurrent requests. You can add and modify queues at runtime. Queuing jobs delays their execution, and limits the number of simultaneous processes. The Jobs application also allows you to configure timeouts for jobs in the queue, provides strategies such as FIFO and LIFO to extract jobs from the queue, and provides queue limits. Once a queue's limit is reached, further jobs are rejected until spaces appear again on the queue.

The Jobs scheduler follows the Erlang way of submitting to load regulation by spawning a job process that asks for permission to execute. When permission is granted, it simply completes the task and terminates. Samples of the underlying memory usage and Mnesia load are taken to tell the scheduler to dampen (reduce) the job scheduling rate or number of concurrent requests when certain thresholds are exceeded. Sampling is done through a plug-in, so you can write your own plug-in and check other items, such as memory. Dampening effects are removed once the sampled values return to normal. In distributed systems, Jobs will propagate the load status across multiple nodes so they can also take appropriate action.

Another popular load-regulation framework is *Safetyvalve* (*https://github.com/jlouis/safetyvalve*). It was inspired by Jobs, but is much simpler in scope, focusing on queuing mechanisms to protect the system from overloads by controlling throughput and the number of simultaneous requests allowed to execute. Safetyvalve allows you to configure multiple queues. For every queue, you can set the queue type, queue polling frequency, and handling of bursts using the token bucket algorithm. You add tokens to a bucket every time you poll the system. The tokens allow you to execute requests in a burst when starting the system or after periods of inactivity. You can configure the rate at which tokens are added after every poll, as well as the maximum size of the token bucket, limiting the size of the burst. You can also configure the size of the queue as well as the maximum number of concurrent tasks allowed to execute.

Summing Up

In this chapter, we've covered the scalability aspects to take into consideration in Erlang/OTP-based systems. The key to the scalability of your system is ensuring you have loosely coupled nodes that can come and go. This provides elasticity to add computing power and scale on demand. You often want strong consistency within your nodes and node families and eventual consistency elsewhere. Communication should be asynchronous, minimizing guaranteed delivery to the subset of requests that really require it.

The steps to architecting your system covered in the previous two chapters included:

1. *Split up your system's functionality into manageable, standalone nodes.*
2. *Choose a distributed architectural pattern.*
3. *Choose the network protocols your nodes, node families, and clusters will use when communicating with each other.*
4. *Define your node interfaces, state, and data model.*
5. *For every interface function in your nodes, pick a retry strategy.*
6. *For all your data and state, pick your sharing strategy across node families, clusters, and types, taking into consideration the needs of your retry strategy.*

   Iterate through all these steps until you have the tradeoffs that best suit your specification. You will also have made decisions that directly impact scalability, resulting in tradeoffs between scalability, consistency, and availability. Now:

7. *Design your system blueprint, looking at node ratios for scaling up and down.*

   To define your cluster and resource blueprints, you should understand how you are going to balance your front-end, logic, and service nodes based on your choice of distributed architectural patterns and target hardware. You need to remember the goal of no single point of failure, ensuring you have enough capacity to handle the required latency and throughput, and can achieve resilience even if you lose one of each node type. When you're done, combine the two into a system blueprint.

   The only way to validate your system blueprint is through capacity testing on target hardware. Write your simulators and run soak, stress, spike, and load tests to remove bottlenecks and validate your assumptions.

8. *Identify where to apply backpressure and load regulation.*

   When capacity testing your system, you should strive to obtain a good idea of the system's limitations. Understand where to apply load regulation and backpressure, protecting your system from degrading in performance or crashing altogether. How many simultaneous requests can go through the system before latency becomes too high or some nodes run out of memory? Is your system capable of handling failure with no degradation of service? Also, make sure you do not crash your third-party APIs and services, maintaining the accepted service-level agreements.

Our last word of advice is not to overengineer your system. Premature optimizations are the root of all evil. Do not assume you need a distributed framework, let alone use one just because it is there or because you can. Even if you'll be writing the engine for the next generation of MMOGs or building the next WhatsApp, start small and ensure you get something that works end to end. Be prepared to use these frameworks, but hide them behind thin abstraction layers of software and APIs, allowing you to change your strategy at a later date. Then, when stress testing your system, recreate error scenarios. Kill nodes, shut down computers, pull out network cables, and learn how your system behaves and recovers from failure. During this stage you can decide what tradeoffs you will make between availability, consistency, and scalability. The difference in infrastructure cost between not losing any requests and losing the occasional one could mean an order of magnitude or more in hardware capacity. Do you really need 10 times more hardware, and the cost and complexity associated with it, for a service no one is paying for, and which very rarely fails anyhow?

What's Next?

Now that you have a system that you believe is scalable, available, and reliable, you need to ensure your DevOps team has full visibility into what is happening on the system after it has gone live. In the next chapter, we cover metrics, logs, and alarms, which allow personnel supporting and maintaining the system to monitor it and take actions before issues escalate and get out of hand.

## CHAPTER 16

Monitoring and Preemptive Support

If you have read this far, you must really be out to impress everyone with a system that is not only scalable and reliable, but also highly available. With the right tools and approach, the five nines once reserved for telecom systems are now easily attainable in whatever other vertical for which you might be developing software. But implementing everything described in the previous chapters is not enough. Just as important as resilient software, redundant hardware, networks, power supplies, and multiple data centers, your secret sauce to high availability is achieving a high level of visibility into what is going on in your system and the ability to act on the information you collect.

Your DevOps team will use all this information for two purposes: preemptive support and postmortem debugging. Monitoring the system will allow them to pick up early warning signs and address problems before they get out of control, either manually or through automation. Is your disk filling up? Trigger a script that does some housekeeping by deleting old logs. Has your load been increasing steadily over the past months as a result of an increase in registered users and concurrent sessions? Deploy more nodes to help manage the load before running out of capacity.

No matter how much of an optimist you might be, you will not be able to catch all problems and bugs before they manifest themselves. Sometimes things go wrong, making you rely on higher layers of fault tolerance to manage failure. When processes or nodes are restarted automatically, you need a snapshot of the state of the system prior to the crash. Together with your historical data, the state snapshot will allow you to quickly and effectively deal with postmortem debugging, figure out what caused the crash, and ensure it never happens again.

If you do not have snapshots of the system, debugging will be not be methodical and you will have to rely on guesswork. Finding a needle in a haystack would be easier. The last thing you want to count on is for errors to politely manifest themselves when you are sitting in front of the computer staring at the screen. They won't. The system will wait for your lunch or coffee break, or until you've gone home, before crashing. Ensuring you have the visibility and historical data will be time well spent prior to launch, paying for itself many times over when you are determining the causes of errors, fixing bugs, and putting in place preemptive measures to ensure the problems you experience do not happen again. In this chapter, we cover approaches to monitoring and preemptive support, introducing some of the most common support automation approaches.

Monitoring

Anyone can see, through a crash dump report, that a virtual machine ran out of memory. But what type of memory caused the crash? Was it the atom table, the memory taken up by the code, the process memory, the binary heap, or system memory? Maybe the system had a surge of login requests that in turn caused the memory spike. Or the latency of a request increased because of a slow third-party API, causing processes to live longer. Or a particular request type failed, triggering an I/O-intensive cleanup procedure, which in turn triggered a lot of other unexpected events or timeouts. Without proper visibility in place, you can only guess the current state of your system and are unable to spot trends and address issues before they escalate. After issues have escalated, lack of historical data makes troubleshooting both time-consuming and daunting. This is why systems need to be monitored, and information stored for later access.

Monitoring is done using a combination of the following facilities:

- *Logs* record state changes in your program. A state change could be part of your business logic, such as a user logging on and initiating a session, or a system state change such as a node joining the cluster.

- *Metrics* are obtained by polling a value at a particular point in time. You could be monitoring system metrics such as CPU utilization and memory usage, ETS table size, the number of open TCP connections, or business metrics such as latency, active sessions, or the number of login requests per hour.

- *Alarms* are a form of event associated with a state. They are raised when certain criteria are met, such as running out of disk space or hitting concurrent session threshold values. Similarly, they are cleared when these criteria are no longer valid: for example, after files are compressed or deleted, or after users log off.

Monitoring should be developed in conjunction with the configuration and management functionality of your system. We refer to this functionality as the operations, administration, and maintenance (OAM) part, or O&M if it does not allow you to configure and manage your business logic. In the remainder of the chapter, we focus on monitoring and use the term OAM to mean both.

In many Erlang systems, especially those designed by architects who have never had to support a live system, OAM support tends to be missing, incomplete, or bolted on as an afterthought. If you come across systems where the only way to find the number of active sessions is by manually adding the size of the ETS session tables across all nodes, or changing live configuration is achieved by calling `application:set_env`, they've done it wrong. All systems should let you inspect, manage, and do basic troubleshooting without any knowledge of Erlang or need to access the Erlang shell.

In the telecom world, this noncritical OAM functionality is put in its own node (or node pair for redundancy) for the same reasons discussed in "Node Types and Families" on page 360, namely reducing the overhead on the front-end, logic, and service nodes while increasing resilience. The OAM node should be designed to ensure that in case of failure, your system is still capable of servicing requests. This means that only critical OAM functionality is put in non-OAM nodes, usually reduced to a few critical alarms and the ability to check the liveness of the node.

OAM nodes can be used to handle both Erlang and non-Erlang components of your software. They act as a hub toward the wider operations and maintenance infrastructure of the organization where you deploy your software (Figure 16-1). This wider OAM infrastructure would also monitor and manage your network, switches, load balancers, firewalls, hardware, OS, and stack. It could include open source tools such as Graphite, Cacti, Nagios, Chef, or Capistrano; proprietary tools; or the use of SaaS providers such as Splunk, Loggly, or NewRelic. Connectivity could be one of many standards and protocols, including SNMP and standard management information bases (MIBs), YANG/NETCONF, REST, web sockets, or whatever the flavor of the month might be (as long as it is not CORBA).

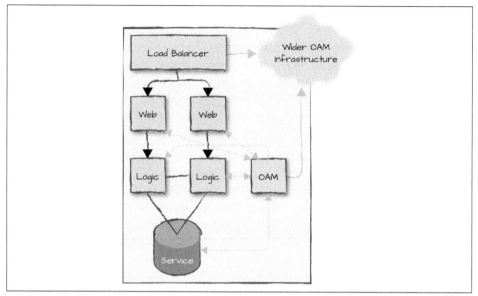

Figure 16-1. Operations and maintenance nodes

Logs

A log is an entry in a file or database that records an event that can be used as part of an audit trail. The entry could reflect a system event in the Erlang VM or operating system, or an event that triggers a state change in your business logic. Logs are used for a variety of purposes, including tracing, debugging, auditing, compliance monitoring, and billing. Different log entries are usually tagged, allowing you to decide the level of granularity of what is stored at runtime. Common tags include *debug, info, notice, warning,* and *error.*

The different ways logs are used by different people with varying technical skills and tool sets makes it hard to suggest a "one size fits all" approach. What is important, however, is to have logs that allow those using them to uniquely follow the flow of requests across nodes in order to locate issues or gather required data.

Picture our e-commerce example, where millions of requests run through the system daily. How do you handle a complaint from a customer who claims they never received their package, despite their credit card being charged? How do you narrow down your search and link the missing message to process crash reports or networking issues? You need to quickly find where in your code the request disappeared and admit guilt, or prove your innocence using a solid audit trail as evidence, thereby shifting the focus for finding the problem to your warehouse team or the courier.

Can you then use the same logs to create a customer profile based on the items purchased? Or look at the durations of user sessions to understand their shopping behavior? Understand how many users fill customers' shopping carts but never check out? Or add up the total number of sales and, for revenue assurance purposes, compare it with the figures provided by the bank handling the credit card transactions? That is the level of granularity to aim for.

We saw the SASL logs that you get for free when using OTP in "The SASL Application" on page 231. If configured correctly, you get binary logs with supervisor, progress, error, and crash reports. You can also add your own handlers, forwarding crash and error logs to a central location. But saving the information is just the start to finding all the help it can provide when mined properly. Imagine a system with hundreds (or even thousands) of nodes, elastically scaling up and down. If you did not forward them to a central log repository, you would have to SSH onto a machine, connect to the Erlang shell, start the report browser, and search for crash reports, hoping they had not been rotated. If that were the case, how would you ever find out if something went wrong?

At one site we ran systems where processes were crashing daily. Since they were being automatically restarted, we were not aware of the issues, and the system was perceived as running normally, when in fact, a very small fraction of the requests were failing. Failure had been isolated so well, we had no idea our system was riddled with bugs. That's not cool. If you want high availability, you need to automate the discovery of the SASL crash and error reports, and then ensure any faults get addressed. Although they may appear to be small in number, a user out there is experiencing each fault. And if many of these issues happen in quick succession, they could cause the supervisor to reach its maximum number of restarts, terminate, and escalate the issue, possibly taking the node down. Increasing the number of allowed restarts in your supervisor specification is not the solution. You need to solve the root problem that causes the crashes.

Users have often added their own log entries to the SASL logs, but this isn't recommended because it mixes logs of different types and purposes in the same file. It might work for smaller systems with little traffic, but as soon as you have to handle tens of thousands of requests per second or more, where each request results in multiple log entries, you will quickly outgrow the capabilities of the SASL logs and will definitely want separate files (and possibly formats) for every log type.

Lager

Lager (*https://github.com/basho/lager*) is one of the most popular open source logging frameworks for Erlang. It provides highly optimized logging capabilities in Erlang systems that integrate with traditional Unix logging tools like *logrotate* and *syslog*. Log levels such as *debug, info, notice, warning, error, critical, alert,* and *emergency* can be assigned different handlers, allowing you to decide how to manage the information provided. Default handlers format your logs for offline viewing, for terminal output, and for forwarding to SMS, pagers, and other service providers. Most of the OTP error messages are reformatted into more readable ones. *Lager* also has overload protection and throttling, allowing logs being sent to it to toggle between asynchronous and synchronous calls depending on the mailbox size. It also introduces the notion of a sink, allowing you to forward only the most critical log entries.

To understand what business-specific items you should be logging, trace the functional information flow of each request, identifying where the request will change the state of the system, and then log items that will get the user to select different branches. Think about what will give the maintainers, support engineers, DevOps team, accountants, auditors, marketing, and customer service representatives a good overview of what is happening or has happened. Every time a notable change in state occurs, log useful information that was not previously stored.

Ensure that you can, through unique identifiers, link together the various log entries, recreating the functional information flow. You cannot rely on timestamps alone, because the quantities of data will be huge. Nor can you rely on the session ID, user ID, or phone number, as they will not be unique across multiple requests. Assign a unique ID every time a unique request is received by an external client. As external requests might consist of several independent requests within your system or other external systems, unique identifiers might vary from one log to another. To link them together, you must ensure they are available in the function call where you invoke the log and store them together. While log entries can be added later, you must think through your logging strategy before you start coding, as the logs might be the only reason for using unique IDs in your business logic. You do not want to refactor all your code because you've realized that right before a call to an external API, you do not have the request ID generated elsewhere. You should also be prepared to change what you log based on feedback from maintainers, the DevOps team, and other log consumers.

Try to reduce repetition across logs. Store information only once and link it together with other logs using your identifiers. Using a single log to store everything might work during development, but when tens of thousands of sustained transactions take place per second, it will be hard to efficiently extract useful data out of the file and it could become a potential bottleneck. Ideally, your logs should create a relational model, where depending on the flow, a log entry in a file with a unique ID is linked to an entry in another file. This unique ID could be a session ID, which links items browsed by a user, items placed in and removed from a shopping cart, and items paid for on checkout. One log file could contain all the items browsed by a user, including the time spent viewing an item, another file items added to and deleted from the shopping cart, and a third log file items that were paid for. Items that were paid for on checkout might have another unique ID generated by the payment gateway, linking the session to one or more payments. All payment logs, in turn, would not have to store the session ID, as the link between the two would be made from the checkout log.

Another way to view the logs is as FSMs, where every entry is a state, and transitions to new states take place based on a set of conditional evaluations in your business logic. Replaying the state transitions in the FSM would allow DevOps engineers to retrace the steps taken by users adding items to their shopping baskets and paying for them.

Identify the different levels of logging, and especially what is useful only in debug mode, so as to not overload the system with useless logs. As a minimum requirement, always log the incoming and outgoing requests and results where appropriate so you are later able to identify the problematic system or component. As an example, if you are calling an external API, create a log entry with the request, the latency, and any unique request ID the external API has provided you. If the API request to your external service times out, just replace the result with a timeout tag. You can later analyze the log and see whether you need to increase the timeout values.

You will have to log system-specific items in your business-specific logs irrespective of what the node or system does. We have already discussed SASL logs, which you get as part of OTP. Always log all Erlang shell commands and interactions. You will be surprised to learn how many outages are caused by operations staff who are not used to working in the shell. Knowing what they have done can be just as important for proving that your code was working correctly as it is for restoring the service. How you log shell commands will depend on your target architecture. You could redirect your I/O, use bash commands, or add a hook to log the entries in the Erlang VM itself.

Other items to log could include network connectivity and memory issues, which are notifications arising from the `system_monitor` BIF described in "The System Monitor" on page 373. Be careful with the latter, as we have caused nodes to crash after they ran out of disk space as a result of logging millions of distributed Erlang port busy notifications in a 24-hour period. The same applies to badly written code that caused memory spikes, triggering long gc and large heap messages. In these cases, an incremental counter that bumped up every time such a message was generated would be better than logging the messages themselves. You can build in the ability to toggle the logging of the messages, so that you can switch to retrieving details when you need to debug the situation.

It is often also worth logging times when code is loaded or purged, node restarts, and the successful saving (and renaming) of crash dumps. Log whatever you believe will make your life easier and help you understand and correlate abnormal behavior or corrupt system state to a series of events.

If you store logs locally, use append-only files, and make sure your data is organized properly. It is common for log files to be stored offline, in databases, or with SaaS providers. Disk space is cheap. Logs could be stored as CSV files in plain text and fed into a variety of systems used for troubleshooting, billing, compliance, and revenue assurance. Logs could follow a standard such as *syslog*, or have a proprietary format. Make sure the data is accessible in a friendly format for those who need it. To slightly misuse Pat Helland's wise words, "a database is a cache of your event logs," if your database (or state) gets corrupted, the logs should tell you why. If it is not corrupt, they will tell you why not.

Where Is My Text Message?

We once received a support call where a very angry user complained he had received SMS goal notifications hours after the soccer (football for our European chums) match had ended. Equipped with his number, we found the front-end node where the request to send SMSs to this number reached our system. In our logs, we found that three SMSs had been sent to that number that day. Each SMS had been assigned a unique identifier when it entered the system.

Based on the timestamps in the logs, we figured out that two SMSs were sent during the match in conjunction with the team scoring, and the third, which we guessed contained the final score, was sent after the match had ended. When an SMS reached our system, we created a log entry with its identifier, along with information such as the SMS type and the cost code stating how much the operator should charge the user to deliver it. In our case, we used the identifier and the fact that the SMS was a premium-rated message to locate the next log entry. Checks in this part of the business logic were made there to ensure that the account was active, that it was allowed to receive premium-rated SMSs, and in the case of prepay subscriptions, that there were enough funds in the account to pay for the message. We found that entry in seconds, and were able to see from the log entry that all checks were affirmative. The user was a postpay subscriber (billed monthly based on use), his account was not suspended, and he was allowed to receive premium rate SMSs. Using the unique identifier, we checked the logs in the service node that sent the SMSs to the SMSC for delivery to the mobile terminal. The SMSC returned its own unique identifier, which was logged together with the timestamp at which the request was acknowledged. According to the logs, it took a few milliseconds from the moment the system

---

received the request in the front-end nodes for the message to work its way through all of the checks and on to the SMSC via the service node.

We then used the unique identifier from the SMSC to search the delivery report log sent to our system from the SMSC. Indeed, at 30-minute intervals in the hours that followed, we got terminal detached messages, followed by a final delivery report that the SMS had been successfully delivered. As per the complaint, it was a few hours after the match had ended. Looking at the unique identifiers for the other two SMSs, we got a similar story, with a delivery receipt with a timestamp similar to the first one.

Why weren't the messages delivered, since our system handled them so promptly? The answer was in the terminal detached messages, telling us that the user either was out of coverage or had his handset switch off. It took us a couple of minutes to respond to this request and prove our innocence. We could not have done it without precise timestamps, unique identifiers, and detailed information allowing us to link the different logs together. With this in mind, think of systems where requests disappear, with no clue about what went wrong. Good luck proving your innocence there.

Metrics

Metrics are sets of numeric data collected at regular intervals and organized in chronological order. Metrics are retrieved from all levels of your application stack. You need to retrieve data on the OS and network layers, on the middleware layer (which includes the Erlang virtual machine and many of the libraries described in this book), and in your business layer. Metrics can be used in many parts of a business and are needed for many reasons, all similar to the reasons you need alarms and logs:

- Developers use metrics to improve the performance and reliability of the system and troubleshoot issues after they have occurred.
- DevOps engineers monitor the system to detect abnormal behavior and prevent failures.
- Operations staff use metrics to predict trends and usage spikes, using the results to optimize hardware costs.
- Marketing uses them to study long-term user trends and user experience.

To visualize metrics, imagine an incremental counter called *login* that is bumped up every time someone tries to log on to the system. If they are successful, *login_success* could be bumped up, or upon failure, *login_failure* incremented instead. We could take this further, and create counters for different failure types such as *bad_password*, *unknown_user*, *user_suspended*, and *userdb_error*. Such metrics could help identify attempts to hack into the system, help monitor fraud attempts, or maybe just prove a poor user experience. If you are getting hundreds of unknown user or bad password errors from the same source, you might want to ask those responsible for security to review the logs and determine what is going on. Marketing might want to determine how many users who fail to log on actually retry and eventually succeed. This would also be determined by examining the logs, but metrics would provide the first hint that something is wrong.

The operations team might want to make sure the system load doesn't exceed available resources, requesting metrics on the memory usage of the Erlang VM. You can poll not only the total memory usage, but also how much memory is used by processes, the system, the atom table, ETS tables, binaries, and to store the code. You could even take it a step further and differentiate between the space allocated to store process and atom memory versus the memory actually used.

As a developer, you might not think much about these issues as you rush to deliver the system, but once you have gone live and someone who does not speak Erlang has to figure out why it is running low on memory, imagine the power of being able to correlate spikes in process memory usage or large portions of time spent on garbage collecting data with particular user operations such as logging in.

Figure 16-2 plots the different types of memory usage in the Erlang VM, alongside total memory consumption. We can clearly see that the 50% increase in memory is due to an increase in the used process memory, which probably correlates either to increased system usage or to a buildup of processes that aren't being properly terminated.

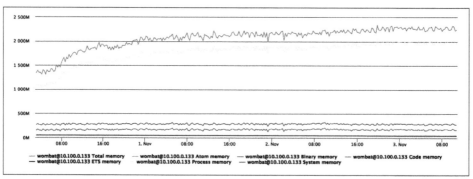

Figure 16-2. Memory usage

Metrics collected take on different values and formats depending on their purpose. One typical value is an *amount*, a discrete or continuous value with incremental and decremental capabilities. A common form of amount is *counters*, as we have seen.

Gauges are a form of counter that provide a value at a particular point in time. Although the number of login attempts since we started the system might not help someone in operations, the number of ongoing sessions will. Other typical examples of gauges are to measure memory or hard disk usage.

Time is another common measurement, mainly used to measure latency in all levels of the stack. Data collectors tend to group time readings into *histograms*, collections of values (not necessarily only time-related) that have had some form of statistical analysis applied to them. Histograms may show averages, minimum and maximum values, or percentiles. As examples, what was the latency of the fastest 1% of the requests? And the slowest 1%?

The third type of metric is a value in a particular *unit of time*. These are commonly called *meters*, which provide an increment-only counter whose values are evened out with mean rates and exponentially weighted moving averages. The adjustments ensure you do not see spikes and troughs that might occur.

A *spiral* is a form of meter with a sliding window count, showing the increment of a counter in a particular time frame. If you are showing a value relative to the last minute, the sliding count could drop readings older than 1 minute and replace them with new ones, each second. Values you could show include the bit rate per second and operations per second, such as the number of initiated sessions.

Metrics have a timestamp associated with them. They are retrieved and stored in a time series database at regular intervals. A time series database is optimized to handle data indexed by timestamps, allowing you to access data in chronological order. Metrics are often aggregated and consolidated over time to provide overviews on a system level. You might want to collect all counters from a particular node type or see the total number of requests for all nodes in the last 15 minutes, hour, day, or month.

Look at the counter in Figure 16-3, which shows the total length of all the process message queues over a 12-hour period. It was plotted based on data collected when investigating a node crash that occurred at 3:34 AM. The node crashed after running out of memory. The metrics not only allowed us to identify what caused the crash, but provided an operational insight: had someone been monitoring the process message queue length, there was a 3-hour window where the issue could have been noticed and addressed.

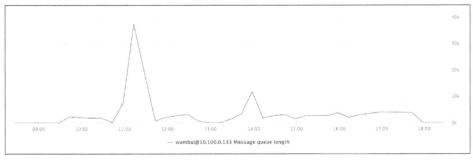

Figure 16-3. Message queue length

In Erlang, ETS tables have the atomic operation `ets:update_counter` that allows you to increment and decrement counters. They can be used for speed, but beware of global locks and bottlenecks when scaling on multicore architectures. Recommended open source applications that focus on metrics include *folsom* and *exometer*. They offer some of the basic system metrics you expect out of your Erlang VM, and let you create your own metrics on a per node-basis.

Exometer

Exometer consists of a group of applications providing a package to gather and export metrics in individual nodes. It provides predefined data points and metric types that can be sampled, as well as APIs and callback functions to add user-defined metric types. When a state needs to persist between sampling, it is possible to implement probes that run in their own process space, storing state and using it to gather the metrics. Metrics and data points can be exported to third-party tools and APIs, including Graphite, OpenTSDB (via Telnet), AMQP, StatsD, and SNMP. You can also choose to develop and add your own custom reporters. *Exometer* operates with very low impact on memory, CPU, and network usage so as to minimize its effects on resources required by the applications it's measuring and monitoring.

Alarms

Alarms are a subset of events associated with a state. While an event will tell you that something happened, an alarm will indicate that something is ongoing. For instance, an event tells you that a socket was closed abnormally, but an alarm warns of your inability to create any socket connections toward an external database.

An alarm is *raised* when the issue you are monitoring manifests itself. This could represent, for instance, losing the last socket connection toward the database or failing to create a connection at startup. The alarm is said to remain *active* until the issue is resolved—maybe on its own accord, or through automatic or manual intervention—and the state reverts back to normal. This could happen when connectivity toward the database is restored. When this happens, the alarm is said to be *cleared*.

Alarms can also be associated with a severity. Severities include *cleared*, *indeterminate*, *critical*, *major*, *minor*, and *warning*. Each alarm severity is configured individually in the OAM node on a system-by-system basis, allowing the DevOps teams (and automated scripts) to react differently to them. For example:

- An alarm about a disk that's 80% full might be associated with a minor severity. You can get notified about it during office hours and deal with it after the coffee break.

- However, if the disk continues filling up and becomes 90% full, the severity might rise to major. You can get called about that during office hours, out of office hours, and on weekends, but not between 11 PM and 7 AM.

- If the disk becomes 95% full, the severity might then go to critical; regardless of when this occurs, a pager call alerts someone, perhaps getting them out of bed, to investigate and address the cause before the node runs out of space and crashes.

In other systems, however, where nodes can crash without affecting availability and reliability, a node that crashed because its disk is full could be handled when convenient during office hours, assuming there is enough redundancy to guarantee the system can still handle the load. There is no one size fits all solution; each system is unique and must be managed differently.

Alarms can originate from the affected node or in the OAM node itself. They can be based on thresholds or state changes, or a mixture of the two.

In *threshold-based* alarms, metrics are monitored and the alarm is raised if a limit is exceeded in one of the metrics. Depending on the exceeded value, such as a disk full alarm, you could configure and apply different severities based on the requirements of your system. Other examples of threshold-based metrics include system limits such as memory, number of sockets, ports, open files, or ETS tables. If you are monitoring the number of requests that went through your system using an incremental counter, and this counter has not changed in the last minute, there is probably an issue and you will want to have someone investigate.

Most threshold-based alarms can be managed in the OAM node, but there are exceptions created by the frequency at which you transfer the data and the volumes you are willing to move. As an example, processes with very long message queues are usually a symptom of issues about to happen. They are easy to monitor, but the monitoring and raising of alarms has to happen on the managed nodes, as it is not feasible to send the message queue lengths of all processes to the OAM node. There will also be times where you want to detect these issues and raise an alarm immediately, without having to wait for the OAM node to receive the metrics and raise a threshold-based alarm.

State-based alarms are triggered when a potentially harmful state change occurs. They include alarms highlighting hardware issues such as a cabinet door being opened or a cooling fan failing. Other examples include the connectivity toward an external API or database being unresponsive or a node going down.

It's up to you to decide how many alarms to send and the levels of detail to include in these alarms. You might want to do sanity checks in your system. What happens if a *.beam*, *.boot*, *.app*, or *sys.config* file gets corrupted? You will not notice until the node is restarted. Although a node can take a few seconds to restart, marginally affecting your uptime, identifying the corrupt file is enough to kiss your five nines goodbye. Isolating the corrupt file and fixing it is not easy and will take time, drastically increasing your downtime. If you think it will not happen to you, think again, because it has happened to many others, us included!

SASL has a basic alarm handler, which we cover in "The SASL Alarm Handler" on page 165. It allows you to raise and clear alarms, but does not handle severities and dependencies. The idea behind the SASL alarm handler is to manage alarms on the affected nodes. These can be forwarded to more complex alarm applications in your OAM node or external tools. But if you do write your own OAM node, you will need something more complex and configurable, handling alarm duplication, severities, and operator interaction.

Elarm

The *elarm* (*https://github.com/esl/elarm*) application is the de facto Erlang-based alarm manager used in production systems to manage alarms. It allows you to configure severities and actions, as well as implement handlers that forward requests via email or SMS, or to external systems such as Nagios or pager duty. Users (or the system) can acknowledge and clear alarms as well as add notes for other members of the DevOps team. You can configure alarms to provide users with default information such as severity, probable cause, and repair actions. All alarm events are logged, and the current state of alarms can be queried and filtered. While the SASL alarm handler is ideal for basic alarm handling, *elarm* is what you should be running in your OAM nodes, making it the focal point where all of the alarms are collected, aggregated, and consolidated. This information is then used to make decisions on actions and escalation, be it automated or manual.

No two systems are alike. Based on their functionality, traffic load, and user behavioral patterns, they will need to be managed and configured differently. A critical alarm in one system might be a nonissue or a warning in another. Once you've gone live, you will need to configure and fine-tune your alarms. This is commonly done when you handle false positives and false negatives. A *false positive* is an alarm generated because of a nonissue. It could be caused by an overly sensitive threshold or even paranoid management asking you to monitor too much. In cases where disks fill up slowly, a 70% disk full alarm could be active for months without any need for intervention. But in systems where disks fill up quickly, such an alarm might warrant waking someone up in the middle of the night, as it might be a warning that the node is going to crash within the hour. It is important to fine-tune your system and eliminate false positives, as too many of them will result in serious alarms being ignored.

It is also important to do the opposite: namely, manage false negatives. A *false negative* is when alarms should have been raised, but are not. This could be because of threshold configuration or lack of coverage in particular parts of the system. After every failure or degradation of service, review which alarms could have been raised (if any) and start monitoring events that might indicate that failure or service degradation is imminent.

We see alarms in systems too rarely, and when they do exist, they have often been added as an afterthought. The majority are threshold-based, with the only state-based alarms being based on external probes sending requests to the system. Alarms play a critical role in detecting and addressing anomalies before they escalate and have been a must in the telecoms space for decades. It is time for other verticals to adopt these practices widely and apply the lessons learned about them. It will greatly facilitate support automation (covered in the following section) and be one of the pillars you can count on when trying to achieve five-nines availability.

Preemptive Support

Support automation is the building of a knowledge base that is used to reduce service disruption by reacting to external stimuli and resolving problems before they escalate. If you are allowed only minutes of downtime per year, downtime is something you need to plan for when designing your system. It is no good detecting something has gone wrong and expecting a human to intervene and manually run a script. Being allowed a few minutes of downtime per year means running that script through automation. Automation is achieved through the collection and analysis of metrics, events, alarms, and configuration data. If certain patterns are detected in the metrics and sequence of events, a set of predefined actions are taken, preemptively trying to resolve the problem before it occurs. It could be something as simple as deleting files, configuring a load balancer, or deploying a new node to increase throughput while decreasing latency.

You need to keep three main areas of support automation in mind when designing your Erlang system:

- *Proactive support automation* is focused on reducing downtime using end-to-end health checks and diagnostic procedures. It could be implemented through an external system that sends requests to test availability, latency, and functionality.

- *Preemptive support automation* gathers data in the form of metrics, events, alarms, and logs for a particular application; analyzes the data; and uses the results to predict service disruptions before they occur. An example is noticing an increase in memory usage, which predicts that the system might run out of memory in the near future unless appropriate corrective actions are taken. These actions could include enabling load regulation and backpressure, request throttling, starting or stopping nodes, and migration of services using capability-based deployment.

- *Self-support automation* describes the tools and libraries that can be used to troubleshoot solutions and to diagnose and resolve problems. They are invoked as the result of proactive and preemptive support automation.

An example of proactive support automation is external probes that simulate users sending HTTP requests, monitoring the well-being of the system by sending requests to different parts of it. In our e-commerce example, probes could include tests to ensure that the product database is returning search results, that users can log on and start a session, and that checkout and payment procedures are successful. There is, after all, no point in having a shop where customers can browse the items, but not buy them!

You want to know about issues with your system long before your customers find out, and already be working on a resolution before the moaning on social media starts. Make sure that the probes run outside of your network. We've been caught out as a result of a defective switch, where probes within the firewalls were not detecting anomalies but customers outside the perimeter network were not able to access the system.

In the case of preemptive support, if you know what needs to be done when an alarm is raised or the thresholds of certain metrics are met, you should automate actions. In the disk full example we gave in "Alarms" on page 436, upon receiving the 80% disk space alarm, you could start compressing logs. If compressing logs doesn't help and the alarm severity is raised with a 90% disk full alarm, you could change the wraparound time of your logs and shut down those that will not affect service. If you are unfortunate enough to get a 100% disk full alarm, start deleting anything not required and not critical to the correct functioning of the system.

Other examples of automated preemptive support include deploying of new nodes when existing system capacity is not enough, reconfiguring load balancers, and changing thresholds used to trigger load regulation and backpressure. As an example, clients using *lager* send log entries asynchronously for speed, but as soon as the *lager* mailbox hits a certain size, the asynchronous calls are replaced by synchronous ones in an attempt to slow down the producers and allow *lager* to catch up.

Preemptive support does not have to be completely automated. Do not underestimate the value of having your DevOps team analyze logs, alarms, and metrics, especially under peak or extended heavy load, to predict and avoid outages that you might not have thought of.

A Needle in a Haystack

We had nodes crashing and restarting for months at a customer site without noticing. Refactoring of the code we never soak tested resulted in us not handling the EXIT signal from the ports we were using to parse inbound XML. Yaws recycles processes by default, so every process ended up having thousands of EXIT messages from previous requests that had to be traversed every time a new request was received. The nodes regularly ran out of memory and crashed. When restarted, the mailboxes were cleared, and the buildup to the next crash would commence.

Customers complained that at times, the system was slow. We blamed the speed problems on their Windows servers. From external probe testing, we occasionally saw system availability drop from 100% to 99.999%. We rarely caught this issue because the external probes sent one request per minute and took a few hundred milliseconds to process it, while the node took 3 seconds to restart. So, we blamed this drop in availability on the operations team messing with firewall configurations.

Even with triple redundancy, the system was failing, but we did not notice. It was only when we happened to be logged on to one of the front-end nodes and realized that it was running at 100% CPU while handling only 10 requests per second that we realized we had a problem and started investigating.

Had we monitored the message queues, we would have picked up this issue immediately and prevented it from escalating. Had operations viewed CPU utilization and request latency graphed over time, they would have noticed something was wrong. And had someone looked at the logs, they would have seen that the nodes were crashing and restarting regularly. Armed with this information, even if we had not been able to fix the EXIT signal problem immediately we could have at least reconfigured Yaws to limit its process recycling to temporarily work around the problem.

We learned our lesson, so after having solved this issue, we started monitoring the latency of the requests. It paid off, as we noticed that every hour, exactly on the hour, latency spiked from a few hundred milliseconds to a few seconds! Investigation traced the issue to synchronous calls taking place when the log files were being rotated. Flushing the file to disk stopped all other requests because of the synchronous nature of the calls to the log process. We ended up spawning a process that opened the new file and took care of all new log entries, allowing the old file to be flushed in the background.

Summing Up

Monitoring systems is never dull. If you want five-nines availability, do not take anything for granted; monitor everything, and spend the time necessary to regularly review alarms, logs, and metrics. The reviews should be both manual and automated. You never know what you or one of your tools is going to find. The only thing you can be sure of is that these issues will manifest themselves, and will do so when you least expect it.

Just because you've isolated failure on a function, process, application, and node level does not mean allowing processes to crash is acceptable. The "let it crash" approach gives you the programming model you need to reduce crashes through simplicity. Make sure you are aware failure is occurring, and fix the issues as soon as you detect them. You need to be aware something is about to happen with enough margin to allow you to react to it before your users notice.

And finally, don't waste time looking for needles in a haystack. Have all the data at hand so that you can prove your innocence (or admit guilt) when anomalies do manifest themselves.

That's it! Who ever said designing systems that are scalable and highly available was hard? All you need to do is follow our 10 easy steps:

1. *Split up your system's functionality into manageable, standalone nodes.*

2. *Choose a distributed architectural pattern.*

3. *Choose the network protocols your nodes, node families, and clusters will use when communicating with each other.*

4. *Define your node interfaces, state, and data model.*

5. *For every interface function in your nodes, pick a retry strategy.*

6. *For all your data and state, pick your sharing strategy across node families, clusters, and types, taking into consideration the needs of your retry strategy.*

7. *Design your system blueprint, looking at node ratios for scaling up and down.*

8. *Identify where to apply backpressure and load regulation.*

9. *Define your OAM approach, defining system and business alarms, logs, and metrics.*

10. *Identify where to apply support automation.*

And finally, when all of these pieces are in place and running, keep on revisiting your tradeoffs and assumptions as your requirements evolve. Add more resilience and visibility as and when you need it. Identify the reason for every outage and put in place the early warning signals in your monitoring system, along with resilience in your software and infrastructure, to ensure it never happens again.

For further reading, we suggest you look at the documentation that comes with *lager*, *elarm*, *exometer*, and *folsom*. You can find it in their respective repositories on GitHub. *Stuff Goes Bad, Erlang in Anger* (*https://www.erlang-in-anger.com*) is an ebook by Fred Hébert we warmly recommend. The Erlang/OTP system documentation also has a user's guide on OAM principles, mainly focusing on SNMP. It should be read alongside the documentation for the operations and maintenance applications *os_mon*, *otp_mibs*, and *snmp*.

What's Next?

This is the last chapter we are planning on writing—at least for a while. You will be the one writing the next chapter when applying the knowledge from this book in designing your scalable and highly available systems using Erlang/OTP and its programming model. In doing so, keep in mind the words spoken by Håkan Millroth at one of the very first Erlang User Conferences: to run a successful project, you need good tools, good people, and a little bit of cleverness. You've discovered the good tools, and you have the cleverness, and hopefully good people. We are now looking forward to hearing all about your success stories! Thank you for reading so far, and good luck!

Index

About the Authors

Francesco Cesarini is the founder and technical director of Erlang Solutions (*http://www.erlang-solutions.com*). He has used Erlang on a daily basis since 1995, starting his career as an intern at Ericsson's Computer Science Laboratory, the birthplace of Erlang. He then moved on to Ericsson's Erlang Training and Consulting arm, where he worked on the R1 release of OTP, applying it to turnkey solutions and flagship telecom applications. In 1999, soon after Erlang was released as open source, he founded what has today become Erlang Solutions. With offices in seven countries and on three continents, they have become the go-to partners for scalable, highly available end-to-end solutions. As technical director, Francesco is leading the development and consulting teams at Erlang Solutions and is responsible for the product and research strategies of the company. He is also the coauthor of *Erlang Programming*, a book published by O'Reilly. He lectured at the IT University of Gothenburg for over a decade, and since 2010 has taught the concurrency-oriented programming course at Oxford University. You can find him rambling on Twitter using the handle *@FrancescoC*.

Steve Vinoski is a software developer at Arista Networks. He has spent most of his software development career, spanning more than 30 years, working in the areas of middleware and distributed computing systems. He discovered Erlang in 2006 after nearly 20 years of developing middleware systems primarily in C++ and Java, and he's used Erlang as his primary development language ever since. Steve has contributed to a variety of Erlang projects, including the Riak database and the Yaws web server. He's also contributed dozens of bug-fix and feature patches to the Erlang/OTP code base.

Steve is also a long-time author, having written or coauthored over 100 published articles and papers covering middleware, distributed systems, and web development, as well as a couple of books. He wrote "The Functional Web" column for *IEEE Internet Computing (IC)* magazine from 2008–2012, and prior to that, from 2002–2008, wrote the "Toward Integration" column for *IC* as well. He also serves on the magazine's editorial board. From 1995–2005, Steve coauthored the popular "Object Interconnections" column on distributed object computing for the *C++ Report* and later the *C/C++ Users Journal*. Over the years Steve has also given hundreds of conference and workshop presentations and tutorials on middleware, distributed systems, web development, and programming languages, and has served as chair or program committee member for many dozens of conferences and workshops.

Colophon

The animal on the cover of *Designing for Scalability with Erlang/OTP* is the European plaice (*pleuronectes platessa*), a common flatfish. The European plaice lives off the coast of Europe, as far north as the Barents Sea and as far south as the Mediterranean. They are found at depths between 10 and 50 meters, where they burrow in the sandy or muddy bottom.

The European plaice has dark green or brown colored scales and are covered with orange spots. Adults can grow as large as one meter in length, but most grow to about half that size. They feed on marine worms, bivalves, and crustaceans.

The European plaice is a common staple of North German and Danish cooking, and is commonly caught by fishermen throughout Europe. It is especially popular in Denmark when fried and paired with french fries and remoulade sauce. The European paice was overfished in the 1970s and 1980s, but thanks to conservation efforts, its population is increasing, and in 2012 the population was measured at its highest level since 1957.

Many of the animals on O'Reilly covers are endangered; all of them are important to the world. To learn more about how you can help, go to *animals.oreilly.com*.

The cover fonts are URW Typewriter and Guardian Sans. The text font is Adobe Minion Pro; the heading font is Adobe Myriad Condensed; and the code font is Dalton Maag's Ubuntu Mono.

Get even more for your money.

Join the O'Reilly Community, and register the O'Reilly books you own. It's free, and you'll get:

- $4.99 ebook upgrade offer
- 40% upgrade offer on O'Reilly print books
- Membership discounts on books and events
- Free lifetime updates to ebooks and videos
- Multiple ebook formats, DRM FREE
- Participation in the O'Reilly community
- Newsletters
- Account management
- 100% Satisfaction Guarantee

Signing up is easy:

1. Go to: oreilly.com/go/register
2. Create an O'Reilly login.
3. Provide your address.
4. Register your books.

Note: English-language books only

To order books online:
oreilly.com/store

For questions about products or an order:
orders@oreilly.com

To sign up to get topic-specific email announcements and/or news about upcoming books, conferences, special offers, and new technologies:
elists@oreilly.com

For technical questions about book content:
booktech@oreilly.com

To submit new book proposals to our editors:
proposals@oreilly.com

O'Reilly books are available in multiple DRM-free ebook formats. For more information:
oreilly.com/ebooks